**Digital and
Analog Systems,
Circuits,
and Devices:**
AN INTRODUCTION

McGRAW-HILL ELECTRICAL AND ELECTRONIC ENGINEERING SERIES

FREDERICK EMMONS TERMAN, Consulting Editor
W. W. HARMAN, J. G. TRUXAL, and R. A. ROHRER, Associate Consulting Editors

McGraw-Hill Book Company
New York
St. Louis
San Francisco
Düsseldorf
Johannesburg
Kuala Lumpur
London
Mexico
Montreal
New Dehli
Panama
Rio de Janeiro
Singapore
Sydney
Toronto

CHARLES BELOVE
Professor of Electrical Engineering and Computer Technology
New York Institute of Technology

HARRY SCHACHTER
Associate Professor of Electrical Engineering
Polytechnic Institute of Brooklyn

DONALD L. SCHILLING
Professor of Electrical Engineering
The City College of the City University of New York

Digital and Analog Systems, Circuits, and Devices:

AN INTRODUCTION

This book was set in Times New Roman.
The designer was Barbara Ellwood;
the drawings were done by Oxford Illustrated Limited.
The editors were Charles R. Wade and Michael Gardner.
Matt Martino supervised production.

Library of Congress Cataloging in Publication Data

Belove, Charles,
    Digital and analog systems, circuits, and devices.

    (Electronics & electrical engineering series)

    1. Electric engineering.   I. Schachter, Harry, 1922–   joint author,
II. Schilling, Donald L., joint author.   III. Title.

TK146.B34   621.3   72–39043

ISBN 0-07-004420-1

Digital and Analog Systems, Circuits, and Devices: An Introduction

23456789 MAMM 76543

To our wives:
Golda, Rosie, and Annette

CONTENTS

PREFACE

The field of electrical engineering has undergone several remarkable changes over the past two decades. The advent of radar, the digital computer, and more recently the transistor are examples of changes which were sparked by the tremendous technological developments during World War II. Within the last few years we have witnessed the development of the integrated circuit (IC) in which many transistors and other components are fabricated at the same time on one tiny chip of silicon. The use of ICs has resulted in the construction of systems such as minicomputers, which are inexpensive and occupy little space. This in turn has increased the use of these systems.

In a revolution such as this, there is an immediate need for new teaching philosophies and methods using updated textbooks. This text is intended for a first course in electrical engineering for beginning electrical engineering and electrical technology students. It can also be used as a service course for other engineering disciplines and for physics and math students desiring some knowledge of the principles of electrical engineering.

The primary objective of this text is to introduce the student to the major areas of electrical engineering. These include digital computers, digital and analog circuits, electronics, communications, control, electromagnetic theory, material science, and energy conversion. Each topic is treated in a separate chapter in sufficient detail so that a student subsequently taking a full course in any of the topics will not have to repeat the material in this text. Because of the large number of important subareas of electrical engineering, many universities require that a student begin to specialize in certain areas relatively early in his college career. Where this is the case, those chapters covering areas not to be part of the students' specialty constitute an adequate treatment of the topic.

It is assumed that the student using this text has had at least one semester of calculus and elementary physics and is concurrently taking more advanced courses in calculus and physics.

The organization of the text is as follows:

Chapter 2 discusses the *digital computer*. In today's engineering world, this is the single most important tool of an engineer. Switching algebra is developed by means of illustrative examples, in which combinatorial as well as sequential circuits are considered. The first-order differential equation is presented and solved using digital computer techniques. Finally, elementary machine-language programming is presented in such a way that the student understands the organization of a typical computer.

Chapters 3 and 4 deal with *circuit analysis*. However, unlike present-day texts which cover only analog *RLC* circuits, these two chapters also cover digital circuits, which are supplanting analog circuits in many applications. The authors consider this necessary in a modern engineering curriculum. Furthermore, the digital-system response to a series of pulses, or a single pulse, is easily calculated by the student. This gives him a "physical feel" for the analog counterparts of the digital signals: the step, impulse, and exponential waveforms.

Chapter 5 presents *basic transistor circuits* in a manner consistent with the philosophy of emphasizing the digital aspects of modern electrical engineering. Although both digital and analog circuits are considered, digital circuits such as DTL and ECL gates and flip-flops are emphasized. This is also a first in a text of this type.

Chapter 6 is an introduction to *communications systems*. The operation of conventional AM and FM systems is described. In addition, the modern techniques of pulse-code modulation and error-correcting codes are included. The trade-off between signal-to-noise ratio and bandwidth is carefully explained.

Chapter 7, on *automatic control*, considers such standard control topics as sensitivity and stability. However, examples are chosen from everyday life. These include the operation of the human eye as an automatic control system and a thermostatically controlled home heating system.

Chapter 8, on *electromagnetic theory*, presents a subject which is typically one of the most difficult in electrical engineering, in a clear, concise manner. Taking into account the prerequisite physics course that the student has had, Maxwell's equations are introduced and applied to examples such as radar ranging and antennas.

A new major area, *material science*, is discussed in Chapter 9. Emphasis in this chapter is on the fabrication of integrated circuits. This material can supplant the three to four weeks of lectures on this topic that have beome a part of most junior electronics courses.

Chapter 10, on *energy conversion*, discusses the conventional motor-generator and the modern laser. The increasing use of this modern energy-conversion device is an indication of its future importance.

Considerable thought and effort has been devoted to the pedagogy and clarity of presentation. Consistent with the level of presentation, every effort has been made to include material which projects future developments. Great care has been exercised in the development of approximately 250 homework problems and 70 illustrative examples.

The authors are pleased to acknowledge the encouragement and constructive criticism of Professors J. G. Truxal and R. A. Rohrer. Thanks must also go to Mrs. Joy Rubin, Mrs. Ada Schilling, Miss Jeannie Belove, and others, who with great patience and perseverence did a fine job of typing clean copy from hardly legible penciled notes. We also thank Mr. J. F. Greco who did an excellent job of preparing the solutions manual and answer book.

Charles Belove
Harry Schachter
Donald L. Schilling

LIST OF ABBREVIATIONS

UNIT	ABBREVIATION
ampere	A
angstrom	Å
centimeter	cm
coulomb	C
cubic meter	m^3
cycle per second (hertz)	Hz
farad	F
gram	g
henry	H
joule	J
kilogram	kg
meter	m
mho	℧
microampere	μA
micron	μm
microsecond	μs
newton	N
newton-meter	N·m
ohm	Ω
radian	rad
root mean square	rms
second (time)	s
volt	V
watt	W
weber	Wb

RECOMMENDED DECIMAL PREFIXES

PREFIX	SYMBOL	MULTIPLE
tera	T	10^{12}
giga	G	10^9
mega	M	10^6
kilo	k	10^3
milli	m	10^{-3}
micro	μ	10^{-6}
nano	n	10^{-9}
pico	p	10^{-12}

EXAMPLES

MHz (megahertz) $= 10^6$ Hz
kΩ (kilohm) $= 10^3$ Ω
mA (milliampere) $= 10^{-3}$A
pF (picofarad) $= 10^{-12}$F

NOTATION USED FOR dc AND TIME-VARYING QUANTITIES

Lowercase symbols with uppercase subscripts (i_B, v_{BE}, etc.) = total instantaneous value
Lowercase symbols with lowercase subscripts (i_b, v_{be}) = instantaneous value of time-varying component
Uppercase symbols with uppercase subscripts (I_E, V_{CE}) = dc values
Uppercase symbols with subscript m (I_{bm}, I_{cm}) = peak value of sinusoidal quantity
Uppercase symbols with lowercase subscripts (I_b, I_c) = rms value of sinusoidal quantity

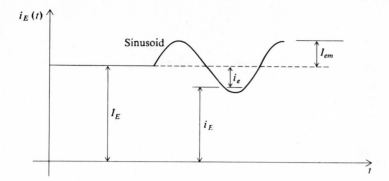

$i_E(t) = I_E + i_e(t) = I_E + I_{em} \sin \omega t$

$i_e(t) = I_{em} \sin \omega t$

Graphical illustration of notation.

1
INTRODUCTION

This text is intended to provide the student with an idea of basic electrical engineering principles and to indicate to him where this field is headed. Broadly speaking, electrical engineering encompasses any area which uses electricity. Thus, in addition to devices and systems such as motors and generators, television, FM and AM radio, and computers, electrical engineers also work in such diverse areas as biomedical electronics, transportation, ecology, and law enforcement. In this text we introduce some of the ideas which form the foundations of electrical engineering and show the reader applications in some of the newer areas.

As an example of a modern application of electrical engineering, consider providing classroom lectures to those areas in the world with so few people that it is impractical to provide each area with its own teacher. Today, such lectures are *televised* and transmitted via *communications satellites* to such areas. Each family in the receiving area is provided with a television set, and by watching the teacher on their receiver, the children learn their lessons. It is interesting to note that the same scheme is currently being used to show operations being performed by surgeons in different parts of the world to medical students.

Let us describe the system in Fig. 1-1 in detail. The figure shows a pictorial representation of the complete system with only the most important parts included. Actually,

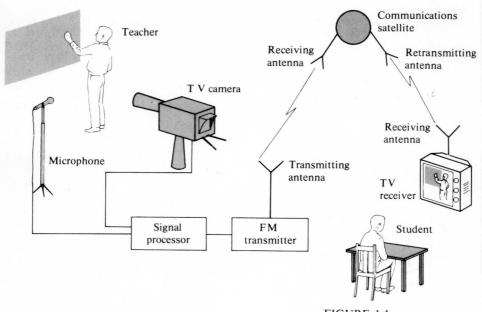

FIGURE 1-1
An electrical engineering system.

the system is tremendously complex, and for purposes of discussion, is broken down into *subsystems*. We will discuss these subsystems in the sections to follow.

1.1   THE TELEVISION TRANSMITTER

The first part of our system is the TV camera. Its basic operation is somewhat similar to a motion-picture camera in which the incoming light exposes a film. The color and intensity characteristics of the light result in different levels of exposure on the film. In a TV camera, the light from the scene impinges on a light-sensitive element which converts the light into a *voltage* that is proportional to the color and intensity of the light. The camera is designed so that each area of the scene is recorded as a separate voltage. Thus the entire scene can be recreated on the TV screen. Simultaneously, the speech is recorded using a microphone, a device which converts sound to voltage. Note that the picture and the sound are handled separately. The picture system is called the *video*, and the sound system is called the *audio*. In a TV system, the voltage produced by the sound (the audio) is then *frequency-modulated* (Chap. 6) and combined with the voltage obtained from the camera (the video). The process by which they are combined

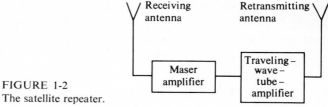

FIGURE 1-2
The satellite repeater.

is called *frequency-division-multiplexing* (Chap. 6). The combined voltage is then frequency-modulated and transmitted to the satellite. This is accomplished by an *antenna* (Chap. 8) which converts the FM voltage into electromagnetic waves. The antenna is usually directional to ensure that the signal is transmitted only to the satellite and is not widely dispersed. The electromagnetic waves propagate with the speed of light at *microwave frequencies*. However, in the not too distant future, the electromagnetic waves will be generated by a *laser* (Chap. 10) and will propagate at much higher optical frequencies. This greatly increases the maximum usable transmitting distance and allows a much larger number of messages to be transmitted simultaneously.

1.2   THE COMMUNICATIONS SATELLITE

The *communications satellite* is a small sphere, approximately 3 ft in diameter, filled with electronic equipment. Its purpose is to receive and retransmit the signals from the transmitter.

It is launched into an appropriate orbit by a rocket and is kept in the desired position by a sophisticated *automatic control system* (Chap. 7). The satellite can be followed (tracked) by radar, and if it should stray off course, a digital computer programmed with the correct course can send correction signals to the satellite. These signals trigger automatically controlled positioning systems which bring the satellite back on course.

The satellite contains two highly directional antennae, one to receive the transmitted signal and correction signals and the other to retransmit the TV signal to its appropriate destination. After the signal is captured by the receiving antenna, it is amplified by very sensitive, low-noise amplifiers, and the amplified signal is then retransmitted via the transmitting antenna to the desired destination. A block diagram of the principal parts of the receive/transmit system of the satellite is shown in Fig. 1-2. Note that the sole function of the satellite is to amplify and retransmit the incoming signal. Thus the satellite is called a *repeater*. In Fig. 1-2 we see that the incoming signal is first amplified by a *maser* amplifier. This is a special type of amplifier which generates very little internal noise (Chap. 6). The output of the maser goes to a transmitting amplifier called a *traveling-wave tube*. This is a power amplifier that feeds the transmitting antenna from which the signal is transmitted.

1.3   THE HOME RECEIVER

The signal transmitted from the satellite is received at the student's home, or at the medical school, just like any other TV program. The electric signal received by the TV receiver is processed and converted by the picture tube into an image identical with that viewed by the camera at almost the same instant. The time difference between the viewing by the camera and the viewing at the receiver is very small, typically several thousandths of a second. This delay is principally due to the time it takes for the signal to be transmitted from the ground to the satellite and back, a topic discussed in Chap. 8.

Although it is not always feasible because of the distances involved, it is desirable to have some means by which the student can question the teacher. When it is possible, the overall system acquires a *feedback* path over which the teacher can correct an error in the response of the student. Various aspects of feedback systems are discussed in Chap. 7.

1.4   SUPPORTING SUBSYSTEMS

In addition to the main components we have discussed, there are many subsystems and components which perform supporting functions. A few of these are:

> *Power supplies* (Chap. 10) required to activate the motors, transistors, and other components throughout the system
> *Motors* (Chap. 10) needed to move the TV camera and other components
> *Transistors* and other solid-state devices whose fabrication is discussed in Chap. 9
> *Circuits* (Chaps. 3 and 4) which enable transistors and other components to operate properly and perform their required functions
> *Computers* (Chap. 2) to monitor the position of the satellite and perform other required calculations

1.5   CONCLUSION

Undergraduate engineering students can usually take a certain amount of electives during their course of study and can thus specialize in a particular area of interest. Some specialize in *systems engineering*. A systems engineer is responsible for the overall design and fabrication of sophisticated systems. Other students will tend to specialize in only one narrow area, for example, circuit design, motor design, transistor fabrication, etc. It is our hope that this text will provide the student with an introduction to many of these areas so that he can make his decision on a course of study.

2

DIGITAL COMPUTERS

INTRODUCTION

The digital computer is one of the greatest inventions of the century. It has affected every aspect of our lives. In addition to its impact on the business world, it has provided the engineering profession with a tool of limitless scope. Thus it is proper that we begin this text with an explanation of how the computer operates.

The digital computer employs transistors to perform many of its operations. These transistors operate like switches, being either ON or OFF. Thus the complicated functions performed by the computer can be thought of as being accomplished by interconnecting large numbers of switches. These interconnections are designed to implement the laws of logic and are manipulated so that the desired calculations are performed. For a computer to use logic, a means must be provided by which verbal logic statements can be translated into symbolic statements. The mathematical technique used for logical analysis of systems containing large numbers of ON-OFF elements is called *Boolean algebra*. This algebra is characterized by a set of rules similar to those of our common algebra, but are based on only two possible states: ON-OFF (or TRUE-FALSE), called logic states.

In this chapter we will show how the computer is organized using basic rules of logic, to perform arithmetic operations such as adding, subtracting, multiplying, and

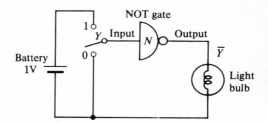

FIGURE 2.1-1
The NOT function.

dividing, and how it solves simple equations. It is not possible in an introductory text to do more than scratch the surface of this vast topic. However, we hope it will whet the student's appetite for later courses in computer science, which are now part of many engineering curricula.

2.1 LOGIC FUNCTIONS

There are three logic functions that are performed by the components of a digital computer, the NOT, AND, and OR functions. The first function we shall consider is the NOT function. To illustrate this, consider a light bulb controlled by a switch. If the light bulb is lit, we call the event L. Then, if the light bulb is NOT lit, the event is NOT L, or symbolically $\bar{L}$.

We note that the light bulb must be in only one of two states, lit or NOT lit. Thus L and $\bar{L}$ are said to be *complementary*. Since the events described have only two possibilities, we represent them with the binary symbols 1 and 0, corresponding to true and false; i.e.,

$$L = 1 \text{ if the light bulb is lit (true)}$$

and $$L = 0 \text{ if the light bulb is NOT lit (false)}$$ (2.1-1)

Observe that in the binary system, where there are only two symbols, 1 and 0, a state which is NOT represented by the symbol 1 is represented by the symbol 0.

The symbol we use to represent a device which implements the NOT function is shown in Fig. 2.1-1. Thus, if $Y = 1$ (the input is connected to the + side of a battery), the output is $\bar{Y} = 0$ (the bulb does not light), and if $Y = 0$ (the input is connected to ground), the output is $\bar{Y} = 1$ (the bulb lights). The physical implementation of the NOT and the other functions considered in this chapter is discussed in Chap. 5. There we shall show that by properly designing a *transistor amplifier* we can obtain a voltage output of 0 volts when the input voltage is 1 volt (V), and an output voltage of 1 V when the input voltage is 0 volts.

The second logic function to be considered is the AND function. To illustrate this function consider the statement

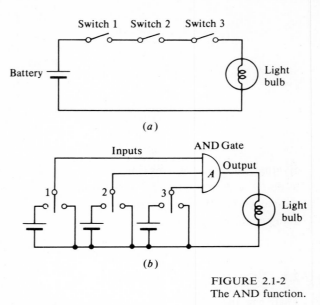

(a)

(b)

FIGURE 2.1-2
The AND function.

If events *A* AND *B* occur (are true), then event *Y* will occur (be true).

The logic AND function can relate two or more input events. For example, we might require that if events *A* AND *B* AND *C* occur, then *Y* occurs. It is convenient to write this symbolically as $A \cdot B \cdot C = Y$, where the dot ($\cdot$) is read as the word AND.

Let us illustrate the use of the AND and NOT functions with the aid of Figs. 2.1-2 and 2.1-3. Figure 2.1-2*a* shows a circuit where the lamp will light only if the mechanical switches, switch 1 AND switch 2 AND switch 3, are closed. The device which performs the AND function is called an AND *gate*, and its electrical schematic symbol is shown in Fig. 2.1-2*b*. The AND gate is designed so that when switches 1 AND 2 AND 3 are connected to their respective batteries, the lamp will light.

Now consider a slightly different problem, such as the one shown in Fig. 2.1-3*a*. Here we see that the lamp will be lit if mechanical switch 1 is closed AND switch 2 is NOT closed. (The student may notice that if switches 1 AND 2 are closed, the battery is short-circuited. This will destroy the battery. If the student intends to build this circuit, he should place a resistor in series with the battery to limit its current.) Figure 2.1-3*b* shows the electrical schematic representation of this problem. Switch 1 is connected to one of two inputs of an AND gate, and switch 2 to the input of a NOT gate. Thus the second input to the AND gate is NOT switch 2. If switch 1 is connected

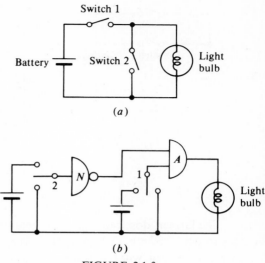

FIGURE 2.1-3
The use of an AND and a NOT gate.

to the battery AND switch 2 is connected to ground, the light will light. This can be written symbolically

$$L = S_1 \cdot \bar{S}_2 \qquad (2.1\text{-}2)$$

where L represents the "light on" condition and the bar over S_2 represents NOT S_2.

Our third and last logic function is the OR function. This function is easily illustrated by the sentence

If events A OR B occur (are true, either separately or together), then event Y will occur (be true).

For example, consider the system shown in Fig. 2.1-4a. Here we see that the lamp will light if mechanical switch 1 OR mechanical switch 2 is closed (or if both switches 1 AND 2 are closed). The symbol for an OR gate is shown in Fig. 2.1-4b. Symbolically, we represent the OR function by a plus (+) sign. Thus the OR statement is written

$$L = S_1 + S_2 \qquad (2.1\text{-}3)$$

Let us now illustrate the use of the logic functions NOT, AND, and OR to solve a well-known brain teaser.

EXAMPLE 2.1-1 A farmer has a large dog which is part wolf, a goat, and several heads of cabbage. In addition, the farmer owns two barns, a north barn and a south

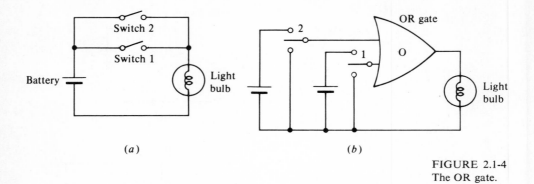

(a)   (b)

FIGURE 2.1-4
The OR gate.

barn. The farmer, dog, cabbages, and goat are all in the south barn. The farmer has chores to perform in both barns. However, if the dog is left with the goat when the farmer is absent, he will bite the goat, and if the goat is left alone with the cabbages, he will eat the cabbages. To avoid either disaster, the farmer asks us to build a small portable computer having four switches, representing the farmer, dog, goat, and cabbage. If a switch is connected to a battery, the character represented by the switch is in the south barn; if the switch is connected to ground, the character is in the north barn. The output of the computer goes to a lamp, which lights if any combination of switches will result in a disaster. Thus the farmer can go about his chores, using the computer to tell him what he must take with him from one barn to another in order to avoid a disaster.

How do we build this computer?

SOLUTION   To design the computer we must state very precisely what it is we wish to do. We want the lamp to light if:

1   The farmer is in the north barn AND the dog AND the goat are in the south barn, OR if
2   The farmer is in the north barn AND the goat AND the cabbages are in the south barn, OR if
3   The farmer is in the south barn AND the dog AND the goat are in the north barn, OR if
4   The farmer is in the south barn AND the goat AND the cabbages are in the north barn.

We now represent symbolically the farmer being in the south barn by the letter F. Hence, if the farmer is NOT in the south barn, i.e., if he is in the north barn, he is represented by $\bar{F}$. Similarly, we have

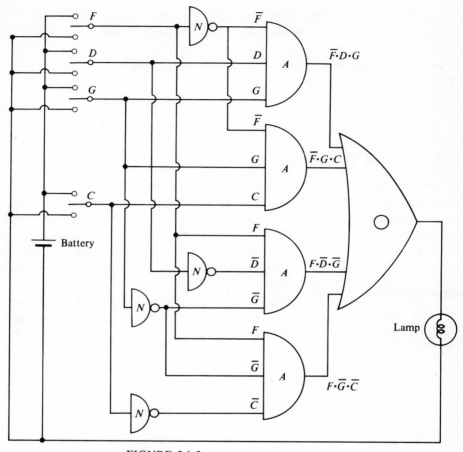

FIGURE 2.1-5
A special-purpose computer to solve the dog-goat-cabbage problem.

D = dog in the south barn
$\bar{D}$ = dog in the north barn

G = goat in the south barn
$\bar{G}$ = goat in the north barn

C = cabbages in the south barn
$\bar{C}$ = cabbages in the north barn

We can now write the symbolic logic statement which combines all the possibilities leading to a disaster:

$$L = \bar{F} \cdot D \cdot G + \bar{F} \cdot G \cdot C + F \cdot \bar{D} \cdot \bar{G} + F \cdot \bar{G} \cdot \bar{C} \qquad (2.1\text{-}4)$$

where L indicates that the light is ON.

To construct our special-purpose computer we need four switches (one for each of the characters F, D, G, and C), one lamp, one battery, and NOT, AND, and OR gates. The completed computer which represents Eq. (2.1-4) is shown in Fig. 2.1-5. The reader should trace the circuit and verify that the lamp will light only if any of the four terms in (2.1-4) are TRUE.

////////

2.2   TRUTH TABLE

Every problem, if it has a unique solution, can be phrased in terms of the three logic functions NOT, AND, and OR. The more sophisticated the problem, the larger the number of variables and gates becomes, until we have difficulty in stating the problem precisely in words, i.e., taking into account all the possibilities. Fortunately, mechanical procedures have been developed which we can employ to tabulate all the different possibilities that can arise. Using these procedures, we can easily obtain the correct symbolic statement of the problem in a systematic way.

The most basic procedure employed, and also one of the best, is the *truth table*. A truth table makes use of the fact that if we have N two-state variables (switches), there are 2^N different ways of combining them. For example, let $N = 2$. Then we have the following possibilities:

1 S_1 open and S_2 open
2 S_1 open and S_2 closed
3 S_1 closed and S_2 open
4 S_1 closed and S_2 closed

This can be written in tabular form as

S_1	S_2
Open	Open
Open	Closed
Closed	Open
Closed	Closed

If we represent the word *open* by a 0 and the word *closed* by a 1, we have a truth table:

S_1	S_2
0	0
0	1
1	0
1	1

We note that in modulo-2 arithmetic, 00 is 0, 01 is 1, 10 is 2, and 11 is 3. Thus, to write the four possibilities, we merely write the numbers 0 to 3 in modulo-2 (binary) arithmetic. If there are three variables, there are eight possibilities, ranging from $000 = 0$ to $111 = 7$. If there are four variables, as in Example 2.1-1, there are sixteen possibilities, ranging from $0000 = 0$ to $1111 = 15$.

The following examples illustrate the use of the truth table.

EXAMPLE 2.2-1

(a) Write the truth table to find $C = A \cdot B$.
(b) Write the truth table to find $C = A + B$.
(c) Write the truth table to find $C = A \cdot \bar{B}$.

SOLUTION   (a) Since we are discussing the use of two switches A and B, we have four possibilities:

$$A \cdot B = C$$

$$0 \cdot 0 = 0$$
$$0 \cdot 1 = 0$$
$$1 \cdot 0 = 0$$
$$1 \cdot 1 = 1$$

because C is equal to 1 only when A AND B are 1. Thus the truth table for $C = A \cdot B$ is

A	B	C
0	0	0
0	1	0
1	0	0
1	1	1

(b) The truth table for $C = A + B$ is

A	B	C	$A + B = C$
0	0	0	$0 + 0 = 0$
0	1	1	$0 + 1 = 1$
1	0	1	$1 + 0 = 1$
1	1	1	$1 + 1 = 1$

since $C = 1$ if either A or B or both A and B are 1.

(c) The truth table for $C = A \cdot \bar{B}$ is

A	B	$\bar{B}$	C	$A \cdot \bar{B} = C$
0	0	1	0	$0 \cdot 1 = 0$
0	1	0	0	$0 \cdot 0 = 0$
1	0	1	1	$1 \cdot 1 = 1$
1	1	0	0	$1 \cdot 0 = 0$

In part c we are concerned with the variables A AND $\bar{B}$. To avoid errors we wrote a column for B and next to it a column for $\bar{B}$. We refer to B when writing $\bar{B}$ since $\bar{B} = 1$ if $B = 0$, and $\bar{B} = 0$ if $B = 1$. The B column can, of course, be omitted here; it is included because it helps to reduce the possibility of making an error.

EXAMPLE 2.2-2   A light located in the center of a hall is to be operated by separate electronic switches located at both ends of the hall. Either switch should be able to turn the light ON or OFF. Design the light switching system.

SOLUTION   There are two switches S_1 and S_2. Thus there are $2^2 = 4$ possibilities: $0 \cdot 0$, $0 \cdot 1$, $1 \cdot 0$, $1 \cdot 1$. Let us assume that when S_1 AND S_2 are both open ($S_1 = 0$, $S_2 = 0$), the light L is off ($L = 0$). Thus the first entry in the truth table is

S_1	S_2	L
0	0	0

Now if either S_1 or S_2 is closed ($0 \cdot 1$ or $1 \cdot 0$), the light L goes on ($L = 1$). Hence the first, second, and third entries are

S_1	S_2	L
0	0	0
0	1	1
1	0	1

Finally, if we have the condition $S_1 S_2 = 0 \cdot 1$ and S_1 is closed ($S_1 S_2 = 1 \cdot 1$), the light must go off. Also, if we have the condition $S_1 S_2 = 1 \cdot 0$ and S_2 is closed ($S_1 S_2 = 1 \cdot 1$), the light must go off. Hence, when $S_1 S_2 = 1 \cdot 1$, $L = 0$. This completes the truth table, which contains all possible combinations of the variables:

S_1	S_2	L
0	0	0
0	1	1
1	0	1
1	1	0

The utility of the truth table lies in the fact that we can derive the required *logic equation* by inspection from the table. For example, consider the second row of the table. In words, this row states that if S_1 is open (connected to ground) AND if S_2 is closed (connected to a battery), the light is on ($L = 1$). Proceeding to the third row, we have another combination which leads to $L = 1$, that is, S_1 closed AND S_2 NOT closed. Thus either the second OR third row leads to $L = 1$. This is much more

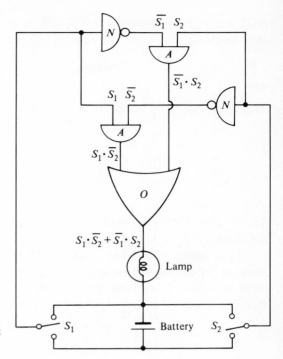

FIGURE 2.2-1
A special-purpose computer to light a
lamp using two switches at two different
locations.

succinctly expressed by the logic equation

$$\bar{S}_1 \cdot S_2 + S_1 \cdot \bar{S}_2 = L \qquad (2.2\text{-}1)$$

Note that the variables within each row are connected by the AND function,
since both conditions must be met in order to light the lamp. In addition, the statements obtained for each row are connected by the OR function since either row having
$L = 1$ will light the lamp. We again take note of the fact that any variable having the
value 0 in the truth table must be given the NOT symbol when used in an equation.
Thus $\bar{S}_1 \cdot S_2 = L$ means that $L = 1$ when $S_1 = 0$ AND $S_2 = 1$.

The electronic light switching system representing Eq. (2.2-1) is shown in Fig.
2.2-1. The student should trace the circuit to show that it correctly represents
Eq. (2.2-1). This particular circuit is called an EXCLUSIVE-OR, since the bulb will
light when one of the switches S_1 or S_2 is closed, but not when both are closed.
////////

The solution given by Eq. (2.2-1) is not unique, and equivalent statements are
possible. The reason for this is illustrated by the following example.

Let $Y = \bar{S}_1 \cdot \bar{S}_2$. Then, since Y results if S_1 does NOT occur AND if S_2 does

NOT occur, Y will NOT occur if S_1 OR S_2 do occur. Translating these words into a logic equation,

$$\bar{Y} = S_1 + S_2 \qquad (2.2\text{-}2)$$

and
$$Y = \overline{(\bar{Y})} = \overline{S_1 + S_2} = \bar{S}_1 \cdot \bar{S}_2 \qquad (2.2\text{-}3)$$

This result can easily be proved from the truth table.

S_1	S_2	$\bar{S}_1$	$\bar{S}_2$	$\bar{S}_1 \cdot \bar{S}_2$	$S_1 + S_2$	$\overline{S_1 + S_2}$
0	0	1	1	1	0	1
0	1	1	0	0	1	0
1	0	0	1	0	1	0
1	1	0	0	0	1	0

The fifth and the last columns are identical for *all possible* combinations of S_1 and S_2; therefore $\bar{S}_1 \cdot \bar{S}_2 = \overline{S_1 + S_2}$.

The above result, known as De Morgan's first theorem, is one of the basic theorems of the algebra of logic. Using the basic properties of the AND, OR, and NOT functions, other logic theorems can be derived. The more important of these theorems are listed below. The student should verify these results using a truth table.

IF	THEN	
$Y = A + \bar{A}$	$Y = 1$	$(2.2\text{-}4a)$
$Y = A \cdot \bar{A}$	$Y = 0$	$(2.2\text{-}4b)$
$Y = A + A$	$Y = A$	$(2.2\text{-}4c)$
$Y = A \cdot A$	$Y = A$	$(2.2.4d)$
	An identity $A = \bar{\bar{A}}$	$(2.2\text{-}4e)$
$Y = A \cdot B$	$\bar{Y} = \overline{(A \cdot B)} = \bar{A} + \bar{B}$	$(2.2\text{-}4f)$
$Y = A + B$	$\bar{Y} = \overline{(A + B)} = \bar{A} \cdot \bar{B}$	$(2.2\text{-}4g)$
$Y = A + \bar{A} \cdot B$	$Y = A + B$	$(2.2\text{-}4h)$
$Y = A \cdot B + A \cdot C$	$Y = A \cdot (B + C)$	$(2.2\text{-}4i)$

As an example of the use of these theorems consider that

$$Y = (A \cdot B) + C$$

Then

$$\bar{Y} = \overline{(A \cdot B) + C}$$

and using (2.2-4g),

$$\bar{Y} = \overline{(A \cdot B)} \cdot \bar{C}$$

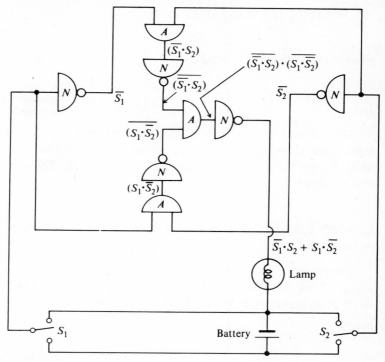

FIGURE 2.2-2
An alternative form for the two-switch circuit which uses only NOT and AND gates.

Thus from (2.2-4*f*)

$$\overline{Y} = (\overline{A} + \overline{B}) \cdot \overline{C}$$

Manipulation of the logic equation, as above, often results in an alternative form which requires a smaller number of gates in a circuit realization. This becomes extremely important in the design of computers, where many thousands of gates are required and reliability and economy are often improved when fewer elements are involved.

EXAMPLE 2.2-3 *The two-switch problem revisited* Equation (2.2-1) is not unique. Find an equivalent expression for *L* involving only AND and NOT functions. Synthesize a circuit which will implement the logic equation.

SOLUTION   From (2.2-1)

$$L = \bar{S}_1 \cdot S_2 + S_1 \cdot \bar{S}_2$$

Hence from (2.2-4g)

$$\bar{L} = \overline{(\bar{S}_1 \cdot S_2)} \cdot \overline{(S_1 \cdot \bar{S}_2)}$$

and
$$L = \bar{\bar{L}} = \overline{\overline{(\bar{S}_1 \cdot S_2)} \cdot \overline{(S_1 \cdot \bar{S}_2)}} \qquad (2.2\text{-}5)$$

The system which implements (2.2-5) is shown in Fig. 2.2-2. This system requires three more elements than the original solution shown in Fig. 2.2-1. However, it requires only two types of elements, rather than three. Thus, for some applications, it is preferable.

EXAMPLE 2.2-4   Use a truth table to show that Eq. (2.1-4) is the correct solution of Example 2.1-1.

SOLUTION   We begin by forming a truth table for the four variables F, D, G, and C. Then we select all the possibilities that result in a disaster, and hence in the lamp being lighted ($L = 1$). We have for the truth table:

F	D	G	C	L
0	0	0	0	0
0	0	0	1	0
0	0	1	0	0
0	0	1	1	1
0	1	0	0	0
0	1	0	1	0
0	1	1	0	1
0	1	1	1	1
1	0	0	0	1
1	0	0	1	1
1	0	1	0	0
1	0	1	1	0
1	1	0	0	1
1	1	0	1	0
1	1	1	0	0
1	1	1	1	0

NOTE: $F,D,G,C \begin{cases} 0 = \text{north barn} \\ 1 = \text{south barn} \end{cases}$

$L \begin{cases} 0 = \text{lamp not lit} \\ 1 = \text{lamp lit} \end{cases}$

Note that there are six conditions which can result in the lamp being lit yet we only have four terms in (2.1-4). To find the discrepancy, we write the expression for L obtained from the truth table:

$$L = \bar{F} \cdot \bar{D} \cdot G \cdot C + \bar{F} \cdot D \cdot G \cdot C + \bar{F} \cdot D \cdot G \cdot \bar{C}$$

This states that the light will go on if F is open AND G is closed AND C is closed AND if D is open OR closed. Thus D is not needed in the expression.

$$+ F \cdot \bar{D} \cdot \bar{G} \cdot \bar{C} + F \cdot \bar{D} \cdot \bar{G} \cdot C + F \cdot D \cdot \bar{G} \cdot \bar{C} \qquad (2.2\text{-}6)$$

This states that the light will go on if F is closed AND D is open AND G is open AND C is open OR closed. Thus C is not needed in this expression.

The expression for L can be simplified either by precise statements as above or, in difficult problems, by simplifying the problem mathematically, using the logic relations of Eq. (2.2-4). Thus we can write, for the first two terms of (2.2-6),

$$\bar{F} \cdot \bar{D} \cdot G \cdot C + \bar{F} \cdot D \cdot G \cdot C = \bar{F} \cdot G \cdot C \cdot \underbrace{(D + \bar{D})}_{1 \ [\text{Eq.}(2.2\text{-}4a)]} = \bar{F} \cdot G \cdot C \qquad (2.2\text{-}7a)$$

and adding the third term,

$$\bar{F} \cdot G \cdot C + \bar{F} \cdot D \cdot G \cdot \bar{C} = \bar{F} \cdot G \cdot \underbrace{(C + D \cdot \bar{C})}_{C + D \ [\text{Eq.}(2.2\text{-}4h)]} = \bar{F} \cdot G \cdot C + \bar{F} \cdot G \cdot D \qquad (2.2\text{-}7b)$$

Similarly, we have for the last three terms

$$F \cdot \bar{D} \cdot \bar{G} \cdot \bar{C} + F \cdot \bar{D} \cdot \bar{G} \cdot C + F \cdot D \cdot \bar{G} \cdot \bar{C} = F \cdot \bar{D} \cdot \bar{G} + F \cdot \bar{G} \cdot \bar{C} \qquad (2.2\text{-}8)$$

Hence

$$L = \bar{F} \cdot G \cdot C + \bar{F} \cdot G \cdot D + F \cdot \bar{D} \cdot \bar{G} + F \cdot \bar{G} \cdot \bar{C} \qquad (2.2\text{-}9)$$

which is identical with (2.1-4).

////////

2.3 NUMBER SYSTEMS AND COUNTING CIRCUITS

The discussion up to this point has been concerned with the basic concepts of logic and logic circuits, and the symbols 0 and 1 have been used to signify ON-OFF or TRUE-FALSE. We are now ready to make the transition from the rules of logic to the arithmetic operations which the computer must perform, where the symbols 0 and 1 have numerical significance. Since most computers operate in the binary system, we shall confine the discussion to this system.

Let us begin by considering a number in the decimal system, the system with which we are most familiar. For illustration, our number is $N = 673$. If we dissect

N, we find that by $N = 673$ we really mean $N = 600 + 70 + 3$, or

$$N = 6 \times 10^2 + 7 \times 10^1 + 3 \times 10^0 \qquad (2.3\text{-}1)$$

In this representation the number 10 is called the *base* of the number system, and is given the symbol b. Thus N can be written in a more general form as

$$N = a_2 b^2 + a_1 b^1 + a_0 b^0 \qquad (2.3\text{-}2)$$

where $b = 10$, $a_2 = 6$, $a_1 = 7$, and $a_0 = 3$.

The a's in this representation can have values from 0 to 9, that is, from 0 to $b - 1$. Thus a total of b digits or symbols is required for a system with base b. In computer work, various systems are used, such as binary $b = 2$, octal $b = 8$, and hexadecimal $b = 16$. The most important is the binary system, for which $b = 2$. As noted above, two digits, 0 and 1, called *bits*, are required. The word bit is a contraction of the words *binary digit*. Thus the binary number 10110 is a shorthand representation for

$$
\begin{aligned}
N &= a_4 b^4 \;+\; a_3 b^3 \;+\; a_2 b^2 \;+\; a_1 b^1 \;+\; a_0 b^0 \\
&= 1 \times 2^4 + 0 \times 2^3 + 1 \times 2^2 + 1 \times 2^1 + 0 \times 2^0 \\
&= 16 \qquad + \quad 0 \quad + \quad 4 \quad + \quad 2 \quad + \quad 0 \\
&= 22
\end{aligned}
\qquad (2.3\text{-}3)
$$

where the a's can now take on the values 0 or 1.

In Secs. 2.4 to 2.9 we discuss how the logic circuits of the preceding sections are connected to perform arithmetic operations using binary numbers. In addition to AND, OR, and NOT gates, we require some device which is capable of storing bits for use in various stages of the calculation. This device, called a *memory*, will be explained next.

2.3-1 The Flip-Flop

Consider entering an elevator in a building having seven floors and pressing the button for the second floor. Assume that another passenger enters just after you do and presses the button for the third floor. The elevator control system *remembers* that you pressed the button for the second floor. The device that remembers which buttons have been pushed is a memory.

Many different types of memories are used in digital computers. One type, familiar to all of us, is a magnetic tape. A signal recorded on the tape remains there, and may be replayed at any time, until the recording is erased. Thus the magnetic tape is a semipermanent memory.

In this section we shall discuss a device called a *flip-flop*, which has a temporary memory. A flip-flop can be used to store a single bit. However, the flip-flop is con-

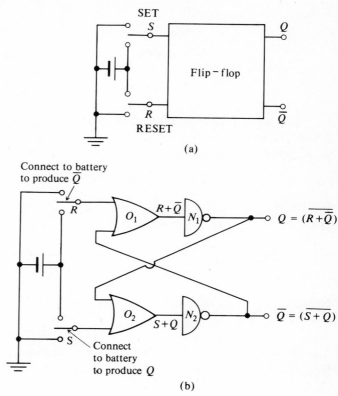

FIGURE 2.3-1
A flip-flop. (*a*) Block diagram; (*b*) construction using OR and NOT gates.

structed using transistors which require an external source of power (such as a battery) to operate (Chap. 5). When the power is removed, the bit stored in the flip-flop is automatically erased.

A block diagram of a flip-flop is shown in Fig. 2.3-1*a*. The device has two inputs, called the SET (S) input and the RESET (R) input, and two complementary outputs, called Q and $\bar{Q}$. The flip-flop is designed so that if the S input is connected momentarily to a battery, the Q output becomes 1 ($\bar{Q}$ output becomes 0) until the R input is connected momentarily to the battery. At that time the Q output becomes 0 and the $\bar{Q}$ output becomes 1. Note that the Q (and hence the $\bar{Q}$) output remembers which input was applied last. The operation of the S-R flip-flop is not defined for the case of S AND R simultaneously being connected to the battery. A truth table describing these logic operations is

S	R	Q
0	1	0
1	0	1
0	0	Retains its previous value.
1	1	Not defined. If this happens in a flip-flop circuit, Q can take on either value; i.e., the practical outcome is ambiguous.

The flip-flop can be constructed using OR and NOT gates, as shown in Fig. 2.3-1b. To show that this interconnection of gates results in the desired truth table, we write the logic equations describing the circuit. Thus, for Q,

$$Q = \overline{R + \overline{Q}} \qquad (2.3\text{-}1)$$

and for $\overline{Q}$,

$$\overline{Q} = \overline{S + Q} \qquad (2.3\text{-}2)$$

Let us assume that $S = 1$ and $R = 0$. Then (2.3-2) states that

$$\overline{Q} = \overline{1 + Q} = \overline{1} = 0 \qquad (2.3\text{-}3a)$$

Hence $Q = 1$. Now from (2.3-1) we have

$$Q = \overline{0 + \overline{Q}} = \overline{0 + 0} = 1 \qquad (2.3\text{-}3b)$$

This of course checks (2.3-3a). Similarly, we can show that if $R = 1$ and $S = 0$, then from (2.3-1)

$$Q = \overline{1} = 0$$

and hence $\overline{Q} = 1$. Equation (2.3-2) is used to verify this result. The third entry in the truth table can be illustrated as follows: Assume $S = 1$ and $R = 0$, so that $Q = 1$. Now set $S = 0$; then (2.3-1) states that, since $R = 0$,

$$Q = \overline{(\overline{Q})} = Q \qquad (2.3\text{-}4a)$$

and (2.3-2) states that

$$\overline{Q} = \overline{Q} \qquad (2.3\text{-}4b)$$

Hence Q does not change when the input is removed.

The flip-flop memory can be interconnected to other flip-flops to form many interesting devices. Some of these are discussed in the following examples.

EXAMPLE 2.3-1   The four flip-flops shown in Fig. 2.3-2a form a circuit called a four-stage *register* which may be used to store any decimal number from 0 to $2^4 - 1 = 15$

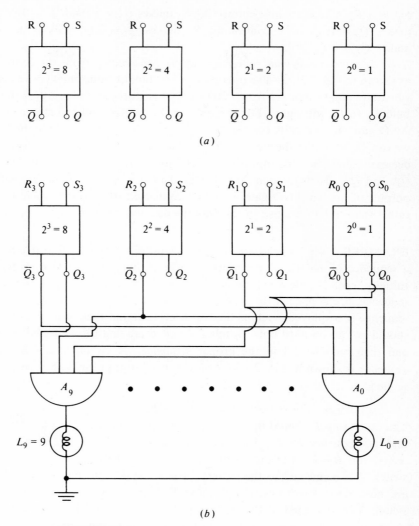

(a)

(b)

FIGURE 2.3-2
The register. (a) A four-stage register; (b) a binary-to-decimal converter.

in binary form. If the number 9 is to be stored in the register, which terminals should be connected momentarily to a battery? What is the output of each register?

SOLUTION   Since $9 = 1 \cdot 2^3 + 0 \cdot 2^2 + 0 \cdot 2^1 + 1 \cdot 2^0$, the Q output of the 2^3 flip-flop should be 1, the Q output of the 2^2 flip-flop 0 (the $\bar{Q}$ output is 1), the Q output of the 2^1 flip-flop 0 (the $\bar{Q}$ output is 1), and the Q output of the 2^0 flip-flop 1. The inputs which must be momentarily connected to a battery to obtain these outputs are

S_3, R_2, R_1, and S_0. Thus, connecting S_3 makes $Q_3 = 1$ (and $\bar{Q}_3 = 0$), connecting R_2 makes $\bar{Q}_2 = 1(Q_2 = 0)$, connecting R_1 makes $\bar{Q}_1 = 1(Q_1 = 0)$, and connecting S_0 makes $Q_0 = 1(\bar{Q}_0 = 0)$.

A *binary-to-decimal converter* can be constructed from the four-stage register as shown in Fig. 2.3-2b. The operation of the binary-to-decimal converter is such that when any binary number from 0000 to 1001 is stored in the register, the appropriate bulb L_0 to L_9 will light. For example, if the number 1001 is stored in the register, AND gate A_9, which is connected to Q_3, $\bar{Q}_2$, $\bar{Q}_1$, and Q_0, will light L_9. Similarly, we can show that if the number 0 is to be converted from binary form (0000) to its decimal equivalent, the inputs of AND gate 0, A_0, would be connected to $\bar{Q}_3$, $\bar{Q}_2$, $\bar{Q}_1$, and $\bar{Q}_0$. Hence, when 0000 is stored in the register, lamp L_0 will light. The outputs of the ten AND gates could be connected to a *printer*, such as a typewriter, rather than to light bulbs. In this way the decimal number can be recorded on paper.

EXAMPLE 2.3-2   *A sequential circuit*   Flip-flops are often used in circuits involving a sequence of events. For example, consider that there are two switches A and B. Initially, both A and B are connected to ground. However, if A and then B, in this sequence, are connected to a battery, we want a light bulb to go on. If a different sequence is employed, such as first connecting B and then A to the battery, the bulb should not go on until both switches A and B are first disconnected from the battery and then reconnected in the proper sequence. A circuit which accomplishes this sequence is shown in Fig. 2.3-3. Analyze its operation for both correct and incorrect sequences.

SOLUTION   If a switch is connected to the battery, it shall be represented by a 1. Thus the lamp L should light ($L = 1$) after the sequence $AB = 00, 10, 11$. Consider that this sequence occurs. First, both A and B are not connected to the battery. Thus $A = 0$ and $B = 0$. The output of A_1 is then 1, and the $\bar{Q}$ output becomes 1. Next, switch A is connected to the battery, $A = 1$ and $B = 0$. Both inputs to the flip-flop are now zero: $S = 0$ and $R = 0$. The flip-flop maintains its state $\bar{Q} = 1$. Finally, switch B is connected to the battery, yielding $A = 1$ and $B = 1$. The output of gate A_3 is 1 ($\bar{Q}$ is still 1) hence the output of A_4 is 1 and the bulb lights.

Now consider the operation of the system if an alternative sequence occurs. For example, consider the sequence $AB = 00, 01, \ldots$. Then, as before, $\bar{Q}$ is initially 1. However, when $AB = 01$, the set S input to the flip-flop becomes 1 and $Q = 1(\bar{Q} = 0)$. As long as $\bar{Q}$ remains equal to 0, the AND gate A_4 output remains 0 and the bulb will not light. To make $\bar{Q}$ return to 1, we must make the R input 1. This can be accomplished only by disconnecting A and B from the battery, i.e., making $AB = 00$.

This example illustrates the use of the flip-flop in circuits in which time sequence is a factor. Examples of other sequential circuits are given below.

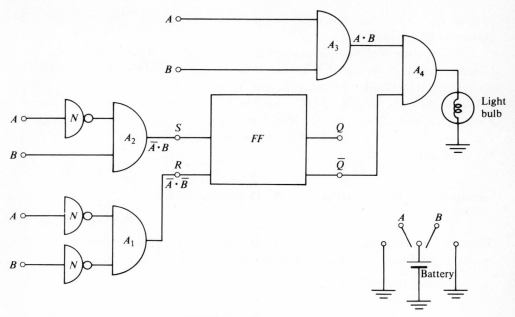

FIGURE 2.3-3
A device which lights a bulb after the sequence $AB = 00, 10, 11$.

EXAMPLE 2.3-3 *A 2-bit shift register—A delay circuit* A signal consisting of a serial transmission of pulses is shown in Fig. 2.3-4a. These pulses of voltage are generated by connecting switch P to the positive terminal of the battery for T seconds (s). The normal position of switch P is position N which yields zero volts.

It is desired to compare the pulse occurring at any time t with the pulse occurring T seconds earlier.

Design a circuit which will yield an output when the two pulses are the same, i.e., when either both pulses are 1 or both are 0.

SOLUTION The required circuit can be designed using NOT, AND, and OR gates and flip-flops interconnected to form a shift register. A one-stage register, as shown in Fig. 2.3-4b, is a cascade of flip-flops interconnected so that, whatever the Q output of the first flip-flop is at time t, this output becomes the output of the second flip-flop at the next unit of time, $t + T$. Thus, if $Q_1(t)$ is the output of flip-flop 1 at time t, and $Q_2(t + T)$ is the output of flip-flop 2 at time $t + T$, then

$$Q_2(t + T) = Q_1(t)$$

The progression of the output Q_1 to Q_2 is controlled by a *clock*. The clock is a switch, as shown in Fig. 2.3-4c, which is either connected to 1 V for $T/2$ or connected to terminal N for $T/2$, thereby producing a periodic pulse train. The clock pulse occurs every T seconds.

The operation of the shift register shown in Fig. 2.3-4b can now be explained. Consider first that the signal at the input terminal I is 1, then gate A_1 receives a positive input; while if the input is 0, gate A_2 receives a positive input. Thus, when $I = 1$ and the clock pulse occurs ($C = 1$), then $S_1 = 1$ and Q_1 becomes 1. If, however, $I = 0$, then when $C = 1$, R_1 becomes 1 and $\bar{Q}_1 = 1$. This is illustrated using the *timing diagram* shown in Fig. 2.3-4d. Here we see that S_1 is 1 when the clock C AND the input I are both 1:

$$S_1 = C \cdot I \qquad (2.3\text{-}5)$$

and that $R_1 = 1$ when the clock C is 1 AND the input I is NOT 1:

$$R_1 = C \cdot \bar{I} \qquad (2.3\text{-}6)$$

Since $Q_1 = 1$ when S_1 becomes 1 and $\bar{Q}_1$ becomes 1 ($Q_1 = 0$) when $R_1 = 1$, the resulting waveform for Q_1 is easily found to be that shown in the figure.

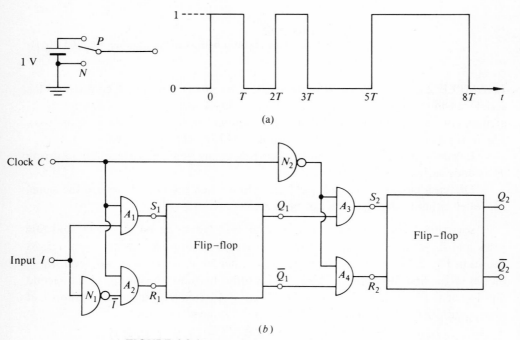

(a)

(b)

FIGURE 2.3-4

(a) A *serial* transmission of binary pulses. (b) A one-stage shift register. (c) The clock C and its waveform. (d) Timing diagram. (e) Final implementation of circuit to solve Example 2.3-3.

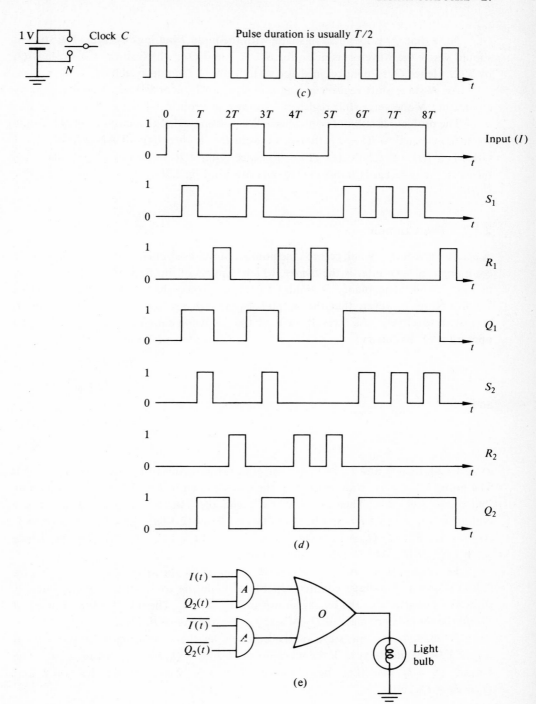

Pulse duration is usually $T/2$

(c)

Input (I)

S_1

R_1

Q_1

S_2

R_2

Q_2

(d)

(e)

Note that Q_1 is identical in shape with the input I but lags by $T/2$. The student should verify the waveforms given for S_2, R_2, and Q_2, which show that Q_2 lags Q_1 by $T/2$. Hence Q_2 is identical in shape with the input I but delayed by T.

An N-stage shift register giving a delay of NT seconds can be constructed by connecting N one-stage shift registers, as shown in Prob. 2.3-4.

The problem is still not completed. We must now design a circuit to light a bulb when $I(t)$ is equal to $I(t - T)$; that is, we want $L = 1$ when $I(t) = 1$ AND $I(t - T) = 1$ OR when $I(t) = 0$ AND $I(t - T) = 0$. Since $Q_2(t) = I(t - T)$ and $\overline{Q_2(t)} = \overline{I(t - T)}$, the circuit may be easily implemented, as shown in Fig. 2.3-4e.

////////

2.3-2   The Counter

A *counter* is a device which records the number of pulses applied to its input. The basic component of a counter is the *binary*, which consists of flip-flops connected as shown in Fig. 2.3-5a. The binary is similar to the one-stage shift register shown in Fig. 2.3-4b. Note, however, that the outputs Q_0 and $\overline{Q}_0$ are connected to the inputs R_i and S_i, respectively. As a result we have the following equations which describe the operation of the binary:

$$S_i = I \cdot \overline{Q}_0 \qquad (2.3\text{-}7a)$$

$$R_i = I \cdot Q_0 \qquad (2.3\text{-}7b)$$

and

$$S_0 = \bar{I} \cdot Q_i \qquad (2.3\text{-}8a)$$

$$R_0 = \bar{I} \cdot \overline{Q}_i \qquad (2.3\text{-}8b)$$

Using (2.3-7) and (2.3-8), we can obtain the waveforms shown in Fig. 2.3-5b. The input I is a pulse train similar to the clock shown in Fig. 2.3-4c. Let us assume that initially $Q_0 = 0$. Then at $t = 0$, $I = 1$ and $Q_0 = 0$; thus, using (2.3-7a), $S_i = 1$ and hence $Q_i = 1$. At $t = \frac{1}{2}$, I becomes 0, and from (2.3-8a), $S_0 = 1$; hence $Q_0 = 1$. At $t = 1$, $R_i = I \cdot Q_0 = 1$; hence $\overline{Q}_i = 1$. At $t = 1.5$, $R_0 = \bar{I} \cdot \overline{Q}_i = 1$; hence $\overline{Q}_0 = 1$ ($Q_0 = 0$). At $t = 2$ the sequence repeats.

To construct a counter we *cascade* binaries as shown in Fig. 2.3-6. Figure 2.3-6a shows a four-stage counter capable of counting to 15. Each of the binaries shown is identical with the binary shown in Fig. 2.3-5a. The inputs are each marked I_j and the outputs are marked Q_j, where j is the number of the binary.

To explain the operation of the counter, let the waveforms of I and Q_0, in Fig. 2.3-5b, be identical with the waveforms of I_0 and Q_0 ($= I_1$), in Fig. 2.3-6. The output $Q_1 = I_2$ can then be obtained from Fig. 2.3-5b by letting $I_1 = I$ and $Q_1 = I_2 \equiv Q_0$, etc.

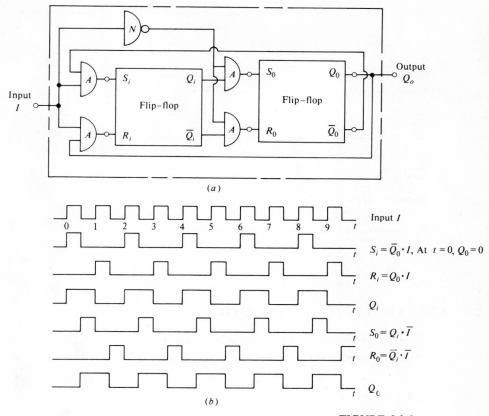

(a)

(b)

FIGURE 2.3-5
(a) A binary. (b) Waveforms.

The outputs are Q_3, Q_2, Q_1, and Q_0. The number of pulses N applied to the input (from 0 to 15) are found from the outputs using the equation

$$N = Q_3 2^3 + Q_2 2^2 + Q_1 2^1 + Q_0 2^0 \qquad (2.3\text{-}9)$$

For example, refer to count $N = 1$, $Q_3 = Q_2 = Q_1 = 0$, and $Q_0 = 1$. As another example, consider the count $N = 9$. Now $Q_3 = 1$, $Q_2 = 0$, $Q_1 = 0$, and $Q_0 = 1$. When $Q_3 = Q_2 = Q_1 = Q_0 = 1$, $N = 15$. If another count is added ($N = 16$), the student can verify (Prob. 2.3-5) that $Q_3 = Q_2 = Q_1 = Q_0 = 0$; i.e., the counter starts a new count beginning at 0.

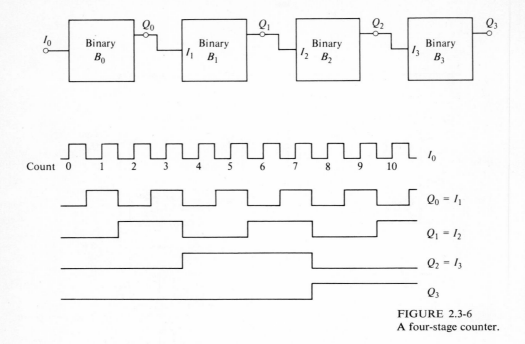

FIGURE 2.3-6
A four-stage counter.

2.4 ADDITION AND SUBTRACTION

We now turn our attention to the operations of addition and subtraction as performed by a digital computer.

2.4-1 The Half-adder

The rules for *addition* of two binary digits are relatively simple:

$$0 \oplus 0 = 0$$
$$0 \oplus 1 = 1$$
$$1 \oplus 0 = 1 \qquad (2.4\text{-}1)$$
$$1 \oplus 1 = 10$$

Here the $\oplus$ sign stands for "plus," using modulo-2 arithmetic, and does not mean OR as in a logic equation. To construct an adder, we must take the rules for addition as given by (2.4-1) and transform them into logic equations. The required logic operations are then implemented using AND, OR, and NOT gates. As we will see, this is relatively easy, except for the fact that we have to account for the *carry* term.

To illustrate the problems which arise in addition, we obtain the sum of the numbers 25 and 18 both in the decimal and binary systems. Note how the carry terms are treated in each system.

Decimal   We first add 5 and 8. The *sum* is 3 and a 1 is *carried*:

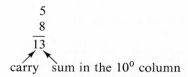

We next add the 2 (from the 25) and 1 (from the 18). The result is 3. To this we add the carry term 1. The sum in the 10^1 column is then 4:

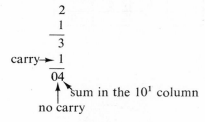

The sum is therefore $S = 4 \times 10^1 + 3 \times 10^0 = 43$.

Binary   In binary notation 25 is equivalent to 011001 and 18 is equivalent to 010010. To add these terms we use the rules of (2.4-1):

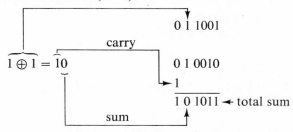

Note that we first add $1 \oplus 0 = 01$, a sum of 1 and a carry of 0. We next add $0 \oplus 1 = 01$. Then $0 \oplus 0 = 00$ and $1 \oplus 0 = 01$. The fifth terms are $1 \oplus 1 = 10$. Here the sum is 0 and the carry is 1. The last terms are $0 \oplus 0 = 00$, to which we add the carry. The result is a sum of 1. The final result is 101011. Observe that the carry term is normally added *after* the addition is performed.

We normally add in the manner indicated above. However, we do it mentally, rarely considering the steps needed to perform the addition. A computer is a combination of electronic circuits, and in order for the computer to add, we must arrange the circuits to perform each step in sequence.

$S = A \cdot \bar{B} + \bar{A} \cdot B$, Exclusive – OR
$C = A \cdot B$

Two numbers to be added		Carry	Sum
A	B	C	S
0	0	0	0
0	1	0	1
1	0	0	1
1	1	1	0

(a)

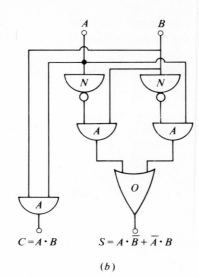

$C = A \cdot B$ $S = A \cdot \bar{B} + \bar{A} \cdot B$

(b)

FIGURE 2.4-1
(a) Truth table for binary addition. (b) A half-adder.

The truth table for the addition of two numbers is shown in Fig. 2.4-1a. The two binary numbers to be added are A and B. Each number can have the value 0 or 1. Each row of the table corresponds to one of the rules given by (2.4-1). The sum and carry terms are analogous to the sum and carry that we use intuitively when adding numbers in the decimal system.

From the table we obtain two logic equations, one for the sum and one for the carry:

$$S = A \cdot \bar{B} + \bar{A} \cdot B \qquad (2.4\text{-}2a)$$

[Note that this is the EXCLUSIVE-OR, A OR B but NOT (A AND B)]
and
$$C = A \cdot B \qquad (2.4\text{-}2b)$$

We see that this addition generates a sum and carry but does *not accept* a carry from a previous addition. For this reason, a circuit which implements (2.4-2) is called a *half-adder*. A realization of a half-adder is shown in Fig. 2.4-1b. The student should note that other circuits that implement (2.4-2) can be found by manipulating (2.4-2) using the rules given in (2.2-4). (See Prob. 2.4-3.)

2.4-2   The Full Adder

In order to add 2-digit binary numbers, for example, x_1x_0 and y_1y_0, we first add x_0 and y_0. The result is given by (2.4-2):

$$S_0 = x_0 \cdot \bar{y}_0 + \bar{x}_0 \cdot y_0$$
$$C_0 = x_0 \cdot y_0 \qquad (2.4\text{-}3)$$

C_0	x_1	y_1	C_1	S_1
0	0	0	0	0
0	0	1	0	1
0	1	0	0	1
0	1	1	1	0
1	0	0	0	1
1	0	1	1	0
1	1	0	1	0
1	1	1	1	1

FIGURE 2.4-2
Truth table for addition of the second
digits of two binary numbers.

We then must add x_1 and y_1, and to their sum the carry C_0. A truth table illustrating the various possibilities is shown in Fig. 2.4-2. From the table we find that the sum term S_1 is given by the logic equation

$$S_1 = \bar{C}_0 \cdot (\bar{x}_1 \cdot y_1 + x_1 \cdot \bar{y}_1) + C_0 \cdot \overline{(\bar{x}_1 \cdot y_1 + x_1 \cdot \bar{y}_1)} \qquad (2.4\text{-}4a)$$

and the carry can be shown to be

$$C_1 = x_1 \cdot y_1 + C_0 \cdot (\bar{x}_1 \cdot y_1 + x_1 \cdot \bar{y}_1) \qquad (2.4\text{-}4b)$$

Note that there are many possible expressions for S_1 and C_1. The logic expressions in (2.4-4) were selected to simplify the system design.

If we compare S_1, given by (2.4-4a), with (2.4-2a), using the definitions

$$A \equiv \bar{x}_1 \cdot y_1 + x_1 \cdot \bar{y}_1$$

and

$$B \equiv C_0$$

we see that S_1 is the sum of A and B, where A is the sum of x_1 and y_1. This is implemented using two half-adders, as shown in Fig. 2.4-3a. The complete adder, called a *full adder*, is shown in Fig. 2.4-3b. The carry signal C_1 is 1 if x_1-y_1 are both 1 (this combination results in a carry output C from the x_1-y_1 half-adder) OR if C_0 AND $A(=\bar{x}_1 y_1 = x_1 \bar{y}_1)$ are both 1 (this is the carry output C_{AB} of the AB half-adder). Thus

$$C_1 = C + C_{AB}$$

Since the full adder can accept a carry from a previous addition and generate a carry to the next addition, the system shown in Fig. 2.4-3b can be used to sum the third and each subsequent pair of digits. A complete adder to add two signals, each having 5 digits, is shown in Fig. 2.4-4. The student should verify that the system of Fig. 2.4-4 yields the correct sum of x and y.

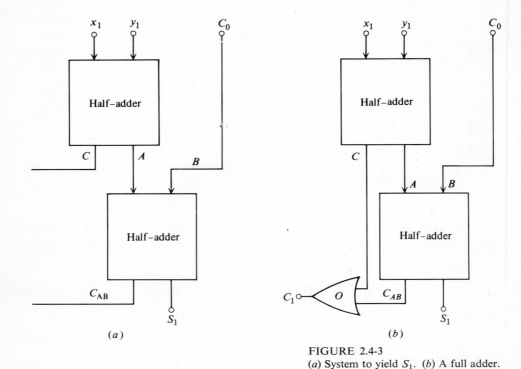

FIGURE 2.4-3
(a) System to yield S_1. (b) A full adder.

2.4-3 Subtraction

Subtraction is very similar to addition and is very easy to perform in the binary number system. To illustrate the method used, consider subtracting $A = 239$ from $B = 423$ in the decimal system. We note that 239 is equal to $1{,}000 - 761$. Thus the subtraction can be performed by adding 761 to 423 and then subtracting 1,000; that is, in equation form,

$$B - A = 423 - 239 = 423 + (1{,}000 - 239) - 1{,}000$$
$$= 423 + 761 - 1{,}000$$
$$= 1{,}184 - 1{,}000 = 184$$

This is known as the method of *subtracting by complements*, and the number $1{,}000 - 239 = 761$ is called the *10s complement* of the number 239. On the surface this technique appears to be a roundabout approach to the problem. However, a major advantage is that it can be implemented to employ only addition. Note that the final answer 184 can be obtained from the previous operation (1,184) by *erasing* the most significant digit.

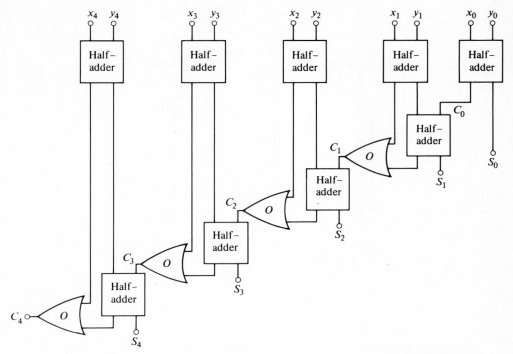

FIGURE 2.4-4
A 5-digit parallel adder.

To illustrate this further, consider subtracting the binary number $B = 00110$ from $A = 11000$. We take the 1s complement of $B = 00110$, which is simply 11001. This complement is obtained by passing each digit through a NOT gate. (Note that the sum of the number and its complement is 11111.) However, by analogy with our example in the decimal system, we want the sum to be 100000, not 011111. Hence, after taking the 1s complement, we must add the number 00001. The result can then be added to the first number, which in this example is $A = 11000$. The result is

$$1s \text{ complement of } B \oplus A \qquad \oplus 00001 = \bar{B} \oplus A \oplus 00001$$

$$11001 \oplus 11000 \oplus 00001 = 110010$$

Now we subtract from this number, the number 100000. This is done by neglecting the leading bit. The answer is therefore 10010.

In general, to subtract the binary number $y_4 y_3 y_2 y_1 y_0$ from the number $x_4 x_3 x_2 x_1 x_0$ we add the three numbers $x_4 x_3 x_2 x_1 x_0$, $\bar{y}_4 \bar{y}_3 \bar{y}_2 \bar{y}_1 \bar{y}_0$, and 00001. The answer then contains only 5 digits, $z_4 z_3 z_2 z_1 z_0$. The sixth bit z_5 is neglected.

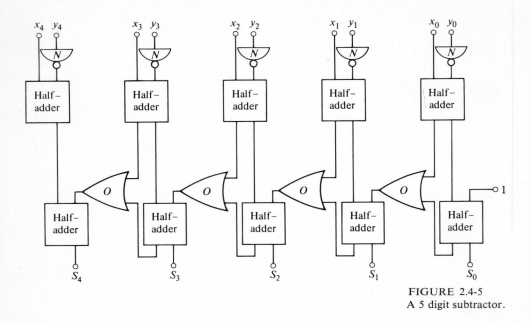

FIGURE 2.4-5
A 5 digit subtractor.

A system which can perform 5-digit subtraction is shown in Fig. 2.4-5. Note the similarity between the *adder* and the *subtractor* shown in Figs. 2.4-4 and 2.4-5. Because of the slight changes required to convert an adder to a subtractor, the computer employs only adders.

2.4-4 Minus Signs and Magnitudes

Very often we are interested in subtracting two numbers whose difference is a negative number. We are then faced with two problems; the first is how to indicate the $(-)$ sign, and the second is how to determine which of the two numbers to be subtracted is the larger.

Often the highest-order bit in a binary system is used to indicate the sign, 0 for plus and 1 for minus. Thus, in a 6-bit system, the number

$$000101 = 5$$
$$\underset{\text{sign bit}}{\uparrow}$$

while the number

$$100101 = -5$$
$$\underset{\text{sign bit}}{\uparrow}$$

To find the larger of two numbers (magnitude only), we compare the bits of each number, starting with the extreme-left-hand bit, excluding the sign bit. When a pair of corresponding bits of each number differ, the number with the 1 bit is the larger.

EXAMPLE 2.4-1   Subtract 7 from 5, using the method of 1s complements.

SOLUTION

$$X = x_3 x_2 x_1 x_0 = 0111 = 7$$
$$Y = y_3 y_2 y_1 y_0 = 0101 = 5$$

where x_3 and y_3 are used as the sign bits.

We first determine which number, X or Y, has the greater magnitude by comparing x_2 and y_2. They are the same; so we next compare x_1 and y_1. Since $x_1 = 1$ and $y_1 = 0$, X is the larger number, and the final answer must be given a sign bit indicating a negative result.

Next, Y is complemented, omitting the sign bit, to get $\overline{Y} = 010$. The next step is to add $X \oplus \overline{Y} \oplus 001$.

$$
\begin{aligned}
X &= 0111 \\
\oplus \overline{Y} &= 010 \\
\hline
X + \overline{Y} &= \overline{1001} \\
+ 001 & 001 \\
\hline
X + \overline{Y} + 001 &= \overline{1010}
\end{aligned}
$$

The result obtained neglecting the sign bit is 1010. The left-hand 1 is neglected, and the magnitude of the answer is 010.

The complete answer is 1010, where the sign bit 1 has been inserted because $|X| > |Y|$.

////////

2.5   MULTIPLICATION

Multiplication using binary numbers is far simpler than multiplication in the decimal system. To illustrate this, let us multiply 27 by 25.

$$
\begin{array}{r}
27 \\
\times\ 25 \\
\hline
135 \\
+\ 540 \\
\hline
675
\end{array}
$$

135   Represents the sum $27 + 27 + 27 + 27 + 27$.
+ 540   Represents the sum $27 + 27$. We insert a 0
675   for the space resulting from a shift.

The individual steps are as follows: Add 27 five times and *store* the result. Then add 27 two times, and store this result. *Shift* the second sum to the left by 1 digit and then add the two sums.

This procedure is greatly simplified using binary digits since we multiply by 1 and 0 only, where

$$0 \cdot 0 = 0$$
$$1 \cdot 0 = 0$$
$$0 \cdot 1 = 0$$
$$1 \cdot 1 = 1$$

Using these basic rules of multiplication, let us illustrate the procedure by again multiplying 27 by 25.

Using binary notation,

$$
\begin{array}{r}
11011 = 27 \\
\times\ 11001 = 25 \\
\hline
11011 \\
+\ 000000 \\
+\ 0000000 \\
+\ 11011000 \\
+\ 110110000 \\
\end{array}
$$ A zero is inserted in place of the shift

$$\overline{1010100011} = 1 \times 2^9 + 1 \times 2^7 + 1 \times 2^5 + 1 \times 2^1 + 1 \times 2^0 = 675$$

The procedure followed by a computer is somewhat different from the procedure shown above, and is illustrated by the following example.

EXAMPLE 2.5-1   Multiply the binary numbers 11011 and 11001 in such a way as to ensure that only two binary numbers are added simultaneously.

SOLUTION

$$
\begin{array}{r}
11011 \\
\times\ 11001 \\
\hline
11011 \\
000000 \\
\end{array}
$$ two multiplications

$$
\begin{array}{r}
\hline
011011\ \text{sum} \\
0000000 \\
\hline
0011011\ \text{sum} \\
11011000 \\
\hline
11110011\ \text{sum} \\
110110000 \\
\hline
1010100011\ \text{final sum}
\end{array}
$$

Note that we began by performing two multiplications. We then shifted the second result by 1 bit and added the two results. We next multiplied by the third bit, shifted

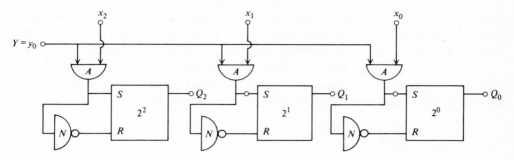

If $Y = 1$, flip-flops are in state $Q_i = x_i$

FIGURE 2.5-1
Multiplication of the binary number $x_2\ x_1\ x_0$ by Y, where Y is either a 1 or a 0.

the result by 2 bits, and then summed again. This procedure is continued through the final sum.

A system capable of multiplying 3 binary digits by a 1 or a 0 is shown in Fig. 2.5-1. The system contains a three-stage register (three flip-flops) and NOT and AND gates. The 3-bit number is $X = x_2 x_1 x_0$, and the number multiplying it is $Y = y_0$, where y_0 is either a 1 or a 0.

The logic statement defining the multiplication is

$$Q_i = y_0 \cdot x_i \qquad (2.5\text{-}1)$$

that is, $Q_i = 1$ if $y_0 = 1$ AND $x_i = 1$; otherwise $Q_i = 0$.

Referring to Fig. 2.5-1, we see that a flip-flop is set (S), so that $Q_i = 1$, if y_0 AND x_i are each 1. In addition, we see that if $y_0 \cdot x_i$ is NOT 1, then that flip-flop is reset (R) so that $Q_i = 0$.

EXAMPLE 2.5-2 *Multiplication by a multiple of 2* Prove that multiplying the number $X = a_3 2^3 + a_2 2^2 + a_1 2^1 + a_0 2^0$ by the number $Y = 1 \cdot 2^k$ yields

$$Z = a_3 2^{3+k} + a_2 2^{2+k} + a_1 2^{1+k} + a_0 2^k$$

SOLUTION The product Z of X and Y is simply

$$Z = (a_3 2^3 + a_2 2^2 + a_1 2^1 + a_0 2^0)2^k = a_3 2^{3+k} + a_2 2^{2+k} + a_1 2^{1+k} + a_0 2^k$$

This simple result is extremely important, since it illustrates that multiplication by the kth multiple of 2 simply requires that the bits representing X be shifted to the *left* by k. This is called *scaling*.

////////

2.6   INTEGER AND DECIMAL NUMBERS

Until now we have considered adding, subtracting, and multiplying integer numbers. The results have, of course, also been integers. In the next section we consider division. When we divide one integer by another, the result is not always an integer.

When writing a number that requires the insertion of a *decimal point* in its decimal representation, we must correspondingly insert a *binary point* in the binary representation. Thus a noninteger number N is written in binary as (Sec. 2.3-2)

$$N = \cdots + a_2 2^2 + a_1 2^1 + a_0 2^0 + a_{-1} 2^{-1} + a_{-2} 2^{-2} + \cdots \qquad (2.6\text{-}1)$$

and in binary notation,

$$N = \ldots a_2 a_1 a_0 \underset{\text{binary point}}{,} a_{-1} a_{-2} \ldots \qquad (2.6\text{-}2)$$

where each a_i is either a 1 or a 0; for example, the decimal number 14.625 is written in binary form as 1110.101.

The introduction of the binary point has served to complicate the writing of the binary number and to complicate the logical operations required to perform arithmetic operations. In many cases the decimal, and hence binary, points can be *remembered*, and the problems solved as though the numbers were integers. As an illustration of this operation, consider dividing 7 by 3. If we decide to obtain accuracy to four places beyond the decimal point, we can calculate 70,000/3, and remember where the decimal point belongs. The trouble that arises when using this technique is that an inordinately large number having 17 binary digits must be used to write the number 70,000.

The following examples illustrate the use of the binary point.

EXAMPLE 2.6-1   Add the numbers 14.30 and 7.90. The desired accuracy is to the nearest *tenth*.

SOLUTION   The number 14.30 cannot be written exactly in binary form. We approximate the number by

$$N_1 = 1110.01001 = 1 \times 2^3 + 1 \times 2^2 + 1 \times 2^1 + 0 \times 2^0 + 0 \times 2^{-1}$$
$$+ 1 \times 2^{-2} + 0 \times 2^{-3} + 0 \times 2^{-4} + 1 \times 2^{-5} = 14.28125$$

Note that in this example greater accuracy can be obtained if $N_1 = 1110.01010 = 14.3125$. However, computers usually select the binary representation which yields a number less than or equal to the given number. Similarly, we write the number 7.90 as

$$N_2 = 0111.11100 = 1 \times 2^2 + 1 \times 2^1 + 1 \times 2^0 + 1 \times 2^{-1} + 1 \times 2^{-2} + 1 \times 2^{-3} = 7.875$$

The sum is

$$1110.01001$$
$$0111.11100$$
$$\overline{10110.00101} = 22.1575 \approx 22.2 \text{ rounded to the nearest tenth}$$

Note that the rounded answer is correct to the nearest tenth. However, the hundredths place in 22.1575 is in error. The accuracy can of course be increased by increasing the number of binary digits (to the right of the binary point) used to approximate the decimal part of each number.

EXAMPLE 2.6-2   Subtract 7.90 from 14.30.

SOLUTION   The difference is found by subtracting the binary numbers:

$$1110.01001 = N_1$$
$$-0111.11100 = N_2$$

To do this we take the complement of N_2, add it to N_1, and then add the binary number 0000.00001. (Why?) The procedure is

$$\begin{aligned} N_1 &= &1110.01001 \\ N_{2\text{complement}} &= &1000.00011 \\ \text{Partial sum} &= &\overline{10110.01100} \\ \text{Add} & &00000.00001 \\ \text{Answer} &= &\overline{10110.01101} = 6.40625 \approx 6.4 \text{ rounded to the nearest tenth} \end{aligned}$$

EXAMPLE 2.6-3   Multiply 7.90 by 14.30.

SOLUTION

$$
\begin{array}{r}
1110.01001 \\
\times \; 0111.11100 \\
\hline
0000\;00000 \\
00000\;00000 \\
111001\;00100 \\
1110010\;01000 \\
11100100\;10000 \\
111001001\;00000 \\
1110010010\;00000 \\
11100100100\;00000 \\
000000000000\;00000 \\
\hline
1110000.0111011100 = 112.46434375 \\
= 112.5 \text{ rounded to the nearest tenth}
\end{array}
$$

The correct answer is $112.97 \approx 113$ rounded to the nearest tenth. The reason for the error is that we have approximated the numbers 7.9 and 14.3 by numbers which are less than the original numbers. The error is increased by the multiplication process.

For example, in the present problem, to ensure an error of less than 0.1 when the number 14.3 is approximated by $14.3 - u$ and the number 7.9 by $7.9 - v$, we must select u and v so that the magnitude of the difference between the correct answer found by multiplying 7.9 by 14.3, and the approximate answer found by multiplying $(7.9 - v)$ by $(14.3 - u)$, is less than 0.1. Thus

$$|7.9 \times 14.3 - (7.9 - v)(14.3 - u)| < 0.1 \qquad (2.6\text{-}3)$$

Simplifying yields

$$7.9u + 14.3v - uv < 0.1 \qquad (2.6\text{-}4)$$

If we represent 7.9 by the binary number

$$N_2' = 0111.1110011 = 7.8984375 \qquad (v = 0.00015625)$$

and if we represent 14.3 by the binary number

$$N_1' = 1110.0100110 = 14.296875 \qquad (u = 0.003125)$$

the error is approximately 0.045. We see that to maintain a low error in this problem we must include 7 bits to the right of the binary point. If only 6 bits are included, the error becomes 0.159, which is larger than the specified error of 0.1. The error introduced due to an insufficient number of binary bits is called *roundoff error*.
////////

The above examples show that the introduction of a binary point requires the use of additional logic circuits. To further illustrate this point, let us consider the multiplication process, with and without the binary point.

Consider first that we multiply the binary number $X = x_2 x_1 x_0$ by the binary number $Y = y_1 y_0$. A *flow diagram* presenting the sequence of events which must occur to obtain the product is shown in Fig. 2.6-1a. The flow diagram should be compared with the sequence of operations employed in Example 2.5-1.

Now consider multiplying the binary numbers $P = p_1 p_0 \cdot p_{-1}$ and $Z = z_0 \cdot z_{-1}$. The flow diagram for this multiplication is shown in Fig. 2.6-1b. The use of a binary-point addition system which is required for noninteger multiplication adds considerable complication to the logic circuitry.

2.7   DIVISION

2.7-1   Repeated Subtraction

Just as multiplication is performed by repeated additions, *division* can be performed by repeated subtractions. Using this technique, the result is always an integer, with the remainder neglected.

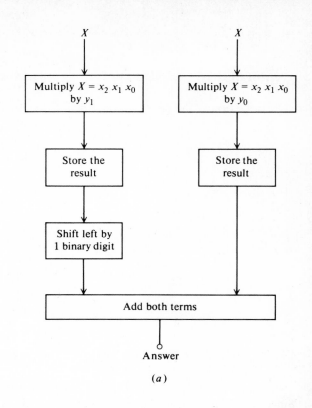

(a)

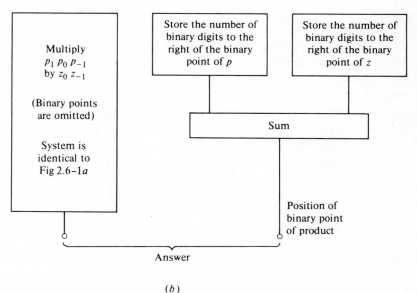

(b)

FIGURE 2.6-1
(a) Flow diagram for the multiplication of integers. *(b)* Multiplication of two noninteger numbers.

EXAMPLE 2.7-1   Divide 14 by 2, using repeated subtractions.

SOLUTION   The operations are detailed as follows:

	Number of subtractions
14	
$\underline{-2}$	1
12	
$\underline{-2}$	2
10	
$\underline{-2}$	3
8	
$\underline{-2}$	4
6	
$\underline{-2}$	5
4	
$\underline{-2}$	6
2	
$\underline{-2}$	7
0	

Since seven subtractions have occurred, the result is $14/2 = 7$.
////////

The problem associated with this technique can be illustrated by dividing 15 by 2. In this case we find seven subtractions and a remainder of 1. The subtractions now cease since 1 is less than 2. Thus the technique of repeated subtraction can be used whenever we require an answer accurate to the nearest integer.

It is useful to indicate graphically each step required in our division technique. To do this we again employ the flow chart and use as components in our flow chart, blocks representing circuits which we have previously discussed. A flow chart for division by *repeated* subtraction is shown in Fig. 2.7-1. Note that we must initially store in registers the two numbers to be divided. They are then subtracted in block 4. Since we do not use $X = x_2 x_1 x_0$ again, its register can be *emptied* by application of a RESET pulse.

The difference $D_1 = X - Y$ is then stored in register 6 and compared with Y in block 7. If $Y > D_1$, the process stops, while if $Y \leq D_1$, we form a second difference, $D_2 = D_1 - Y$, and continue as before.

Eventually, a difference D_N results which is less than Y. Subtraction is no longer possible, and the procedure ends. Since N differences have taken place, the answer obtained using repeated subtraction is simply N.

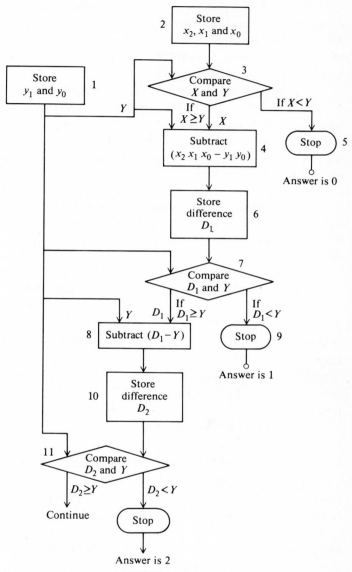

FIGURE 2.7-1
Flow chart for division by repeated subtraction.

The student has perhaps noticed the redundancy in this system. This redundancy arises because each step consists of storing either X, D_1, D_2, ... or D_N, comparing Y and the appropriate difference, then stopping the sequence or repeating the operation. Hence blocks 2, 6, and 10 serve the same function, as do blocks 3, 7, and 11, 4 and 8, and 5, 9, and 12.

A flow chart which eliminates redundancy by reusing blocks 2 to 5 is shown in Fig. 2.7-2. It is this system which would be constructed as a special-purpose digital computer for division. To see how this system operates, consider that we have manually inserted the binary numbers X and Y into the registers 1 and 2. Now we close a switch (not shown) which starts a clock (also not shown) which synchronizes all the operations so that they occur in the correct sequence.

Thus, at $t = 0$, we compare X and Y in 3. If $D(t = 0) = X \geq Y$, we subtract $X - Y$. This output is then inserted into the register (unit 2) at $t = 1$. Since a subtraction has occurred, the counter reads 1. This process then repeats until $D < Y$, when the clock stops. We *read* the counter by connecting the counter output to some type of display unit.

The student should verify that the system shown in Fig. 2.7-2 operates properly to divide two numbers, using the technique of repeated differences.

2.7-2 Long Division

When dividing noninteger numbers or when requiring a noninteger answer, we employ *long division*. Long division using binary numbers is much easier to perform mathematically than long division using the decimal system, since we multiply by only a 1 or a 0. However, to synthesize the long-division operation is far more complicated than to synthesize the repeated-subtraction operation.

We first illustrate long division by the following example.

EXAMPLE 2.7-2   Divide 7 by 3. Obtain an answer correct to the nearest tenth.

SOLUTION   Using binary digits, we divide 111($=7$) by 011($=3$). To obtain an answer correct to the nearest tenth, we must obtain an answer correct to four places to the right of the binary point. The reason for requiring four-place binary accuracy is that this represents 2^{-4}, which is equal to 0.0625, which is less than 0.1. Three-place binary accuracy represents 2^{-3}, which is 0.125, a number greater than 0.1. The procedure is as follows:

STEP 1

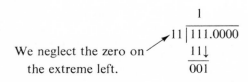

We neglect the zero on
the extreme left.

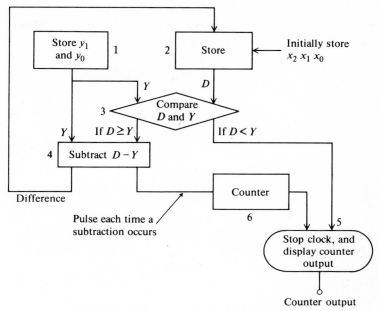

FIGURE 2.7-2
A flow chart for a practical subtractor.

Note that, in this first step, we divided 11 into 11. The difference is 00. We bring down a 1. We must now divide 11 into 01. Since 01 is less than 11, we put a 0 on top and bring down the zero. We now divide 11 into 10. Since 11 is greater than 10, we again record a 0 on top and bring down another 0. Since 11 is less than 100, we record a 1 on top. Subtraction yields a 1. The process continues as shown:

$$
\begin{array}{r}
10.0101 = 2.3125 \approx 2.3 \\
11\,\overline{\smash{)}\,111.0000} \\
11 \\
\overline{001\,0} \\
-00 \\
\overline{100} \\
-11 \\
\overline{0010} \\
-00 \\
\overline{100}
\end{array}
$$

/////////

As a preliminary to drawing a flow chart, let us state precisely what it is that we must do to divide $X = x_2 x_1 x_0$ by $Y = y_1 y_0$. We first compare X and Y; if $X \geq Y$, we subtract $X - Y \equiv D_{10}$, using repeated subtractions.

STEP 1   By repeated subtractions we divide 111 by 011.

$$
\begin{array}{r}
111 \\
-011 \\
\hline
100 \\
-011 \\
\hline
001
\end{array}
$$

Two subtractions are needed. Our partial answer is therefore 10.

STEP 2   We next increase the remainder R by 2 by *shifting* the 1 to the left by 1 digit This is identical with bringing down a 0. We then compare Y with $R_1 = 10$. Since in our example $Y > R_1 = 10$, we enter a partial answer of 10.0 and shift R_1 again to the left, yielding $R_2 = 100$. Since $Y < R_2 = 100$, we divide using repeated subtractions.

$$
\begin{array}{r}
100 \\
-011 \\
\hline
R_3 = 001
\end{array}
$$

One subtraction is needed. The partial answer is therefore 10.01. The procedure is now continued.

Note that, after the initial repeated subtraction, we can have either one subtraction or no subtraction.

We see from the outline of the long-division procedure that it includes an initial repeated subtraction followed by shifting-comparison-subtraction operations. These additional operations result in an increase in complexity in the long-division system.

A flow chart for this system is shown in Fig. 2.7-3. The flow chart shows that the long-division procedure is begun by repeated subtractions. The final counter output yields the integer value of the output. The final value of D which is the initial remainder is inserted in the shift register. Y and R are compared. If $Y > R$, the registered digits are shifted to the left, increasing their value. If $Y \leq R$, they are subtracted. This remainder is then inserted in the shift register, replacing the "old" values.

The output shift register is increased by 1 whenever a subtraction occurs. Shifting to the left occurs whenever $Y > R$. Thus the output shift register records the digits occurring to the *right* of the binary point.

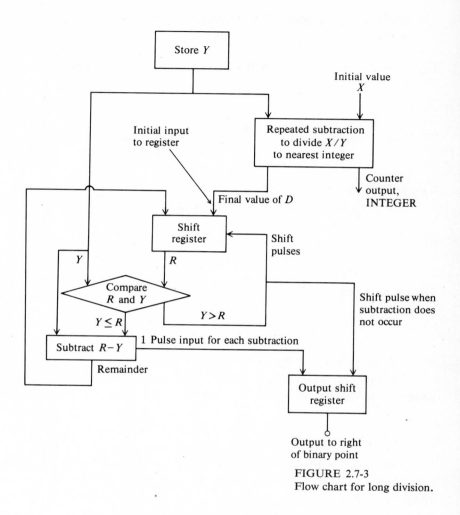

FIGURE 2.7-3
Flow chart for long division.

2.8 OTHER MATHEMATICAL OPERATIONS

Using the basic operations of addition, subtraction, multiplication, and division, we are able to compute logarithms, square roots, and transcendental functions, to evaluate integrals, and to solve differential equations. Examples are left for the problems. In the next section we shall show how the computer can be used to solve a differential equation.

2.9   COMPUTER SOLUTION OF A DIFFERENTIAL EQUATION

Let us consider the first-order differential equation

$$\frac{dx(t)}{dt} + \frac{1}{T} x(t) = 0 \qquad x(0) = X_0, \; T = \text{constant} \qquad (2.9\text{-}1)$$

The solution of this equation can be shown, by direct substitution, to be

$$x(t) = X_0 e^{-t/T} \qquad t \geq 0 \qquad (2.9\text{-}2a)$$

This result is shown in Fig. 2.9-1a.

To prove that (2.9-2a) actually is the solution to (2.9-1), we first differentiate $x(t)$.

$$\frac{dx(t)}{dt} = \frac{-X_0}{T} e^{-t/T} \qquad (2.9\text{-}2b)$$

Then substituting (2.9-2a) and (2.9-2b) into (2.9-1) yields

$$-\frac{X_0}{T} e^{-t/T} + \frac{1}{T} X_0 e^{-t/T} = 0$$

This verifies the solution given in (2.9-2a).

To find the solution numerically, using digital computer techniques, we first approximate the derivative by its definition as a *difference*.

$$\frac{dx(t)}{dt} \approx \frac{x(t + \Delta t) - x(t)}{\Delta t} \qquad (2.9\text{-}3)$$

The approximation approaches the exact derivative [the slope of $x(t)$] as Δt approaches zero. When solving problems digitally, we must be ready to accept the error which results from Δt not being zero. Figure 2.9-1b illustrates the error that can arise if Δt is chosen to be too large. In this figure $\Delta t = T$. The result is that the difference $[x(t + \Delta t) - x(t)]/\Delta t$ is not a good approximation to the derivative dx/dt. Although we are at liberty to choose Δt to be as small as we desire, we shall see that decreasing Δt increases the number of calculations needed to solve (2.9-1), thereby increasing the time and the cost required to perform the computations. Thus we make a compromise between accuracy, time, and cost. Such a compromise can best be made by an experienced programmer. Here, for simplicity, we select $\Delta t = 0.01\,T$.

Substituting (2.9-3) into (2.9-1), we have

$$x(t + \Delta t) = x(t) \left(1 - \frac{\Delta t}{T} \right) \qquad (2.9\text{-}4)$$

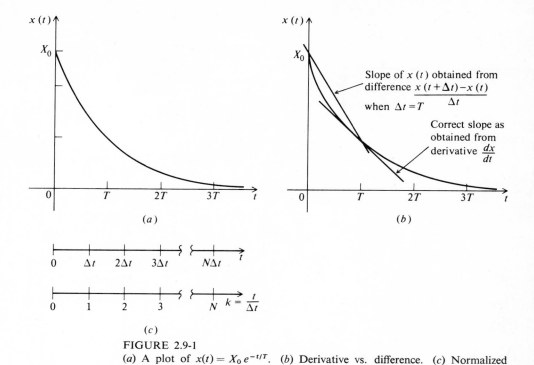

FIGURE 2.9-1
(a) A plot of $x(t) = X_0\, e^{-t/T}$. (b) Derivative vs. difference. (c) Normalized representation of the abscissa.

Letting $\Delta t = 0.01\,T$ yields

$$x(t + 0.01\,T) = 0.99x(t) \qquad (2.9\text{-}5)$$

To put (2.9-5) in a form which is amenable to computer solution, we choose $t = k\,\Delta t = 0.01kT$. Then

$$x(t + \Delta t) = x[(k + 1)\Delta t] = 0.99x(k\,\Delta t) \qquad X(0) = X_0 \qquad (2.9\text{-}6a)$$

The solution to this equation $x(t)$ can be determined as a function of $t = k\,\Delta t$ or as a function of k as shown in Fig. 2.9-1c. It is often simpler to solve in terms of k. Using this normalized representation yields

$$x(k + 1) = 0.99x(k) \qquad X(0) = X_0 \qquad (2.9\text{-}6b)$$

The solution begins by multiplying 0.99 by $X(k = 0) = X_0$. Then $X(1) = 0.99X_0$. $X(2)$ is found by multiplying $X(1)$ by 0.99, etc.

A flow chart showing the sequence of steps required to solve (2.9-6b) is given in Fig. 2.9-2a. The output of the multiplier is usually converted to a decimal number and then *printed out*, or *displayed*, as a voltage on an oscilloscope, as a function of k.

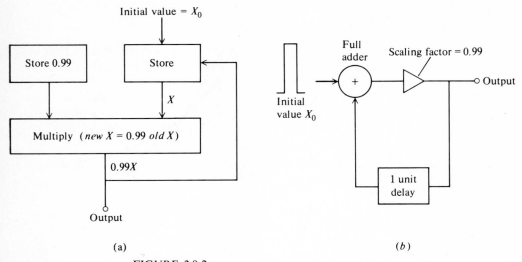

FIGURE 2.9-2
(a) System capable of solving a first-order linear differential equation. (b) Circuit to perform functions indicated in flow chart.

To convert our answer from $x(k)$ to $x(t)$ we merely multiply each value of k by the value of Δt.

Figure 2.9-2b shows the circuit, employing logic elements, needed to solve (2.9-6b). Note that the circuit is a synthesis of the flow chart. The initial value is inserted into an adder. Multiplication by 0.99 is obtained by *scaling* (Example 2.5-2). The result is delayed by a sufficient amount of time so that the electronic circuits can operate properly.

2.10 PROGRAMMING

The original digital computers consisted of many logic gates whose inputs and outputs were made available to the programmer. The programmer then interconnected these gates with wires in accordance with a flow diagram. As computers became larger, certain programs were *built into* the computer. For example, shift registers, adders, subtracters, multipliers, and dividers were made available. Thus, to multiply two numbers, one selected a *multiplier* which had two inputs and one output. The two numbers were inserted (this is called *read-in*), and the output was printed out by a typewriter, electrically connected to the computer.

As computers became still larger, it became feasible for more than one problem to be solved simultaneously. The problems being solved became very complicated, and manual interconnection of logic gates and even preconnected *packages* became unwieldy. It then became necessary to interconnect electronically the various arithmetic operations that can be performed by the computer. These electronic connections are made and changed internally as the calculation progresses. The programmer must indicate the connections to be made and their sequence. The sequence of instructions which the computer must execute to solve the problem is called a *program*. The symbolism used to write this program is called a *language*.

Ideally, we would like to be able to insert the flow diagram into the computer and have the computer translate our picture into electronic signals which would properly connect the appropriate gates. Unfortunately, the languages used today are not quite so easy to employ. All the instructions given to the computer must be in binary form. Since we are more familiar with standard alphabetic notation and the decimal system, we *type* all the required instructions, using alphabetical and decimal notation. These instructions are either punched on computer cards, with which you may be familiar, or typed on a typewriter connected electronically to the computer. In either case, the punch or typewriter converts the information into binary form for feeding into the computer, where the instructions are stored. When the START button is pushed, the computer follows the instructions in the order in which they are presented.

To illustrate how the computer is able to receive and carry out basic instructions, we consider the elementary computer shown in Fig. 2.10-1.

The basic unit in every computer is the *memory*. It is in this memory that all input data and instructions are stored. Typically, small general-purpose computers can store 4,000 different data entries and instructions. Each of the 4,000 *storage areas* is called a *bin*, and each bin has an *address*, from 1 to 4,000.

Various commonly employed functions such as sin x may also be stored, so that when x is provided, sin x is immediately available. Furthermore, we shall see that intermediate results in our calculations are stored in the memory while awaiting further instructions.

We have previously discussed a specific type of memory unit, called a register. Most computers today use ferrite-core memories, magnetic devices capable of storing large amounts of binary information in very little space.

The instructions (program) and all the data required to solve a specified problem are punched on cards and placed in the *input unit*. The control unit has in it a *clock* which, when started, presents the first card in the input unit to a *card reader*. The card reader converts the binary digits punched on the card to the electric signals. As an example, consider that the first three cards contain data. Then the control unit transfers these data to the area of the memory where data is stored.

After the data are stored, the next input card read is usually some arithmetic operation. These operations are performed as indicated in the preceding sections.

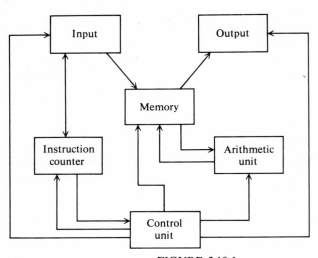

FIGURE 2.10-1
An elementary digital computer.

All the systems required to perform an arithmetic calculation are located in the *arithmetic unit* which connects to the memory by means of logic gates. Thus an input instruction might be to "connect the memory to a particular arithmetic function," etc. The output unit prints out, using magnetic tape, punched cards, or a printer, the results requested by the input cards.

We see then that the instructions are provided by the input unit and are carried out by a sophisticated interconnection of logic gates using the memory and arithmetic units. The results are then available from the *output* device selected.

To see how this is accomplished, let us assume that our computer is designed to operate by writing each instruction, or data entry, on a separate computer card. To record the binary symbol 1, we punch a hole in the card, and to record the binary symbol 0, we do not punch a hole. The entry made on each card will contain 13 binary digits: 4 to locate the memory bin in which the instruction or data are to be stored, 4 to describe the instruction or data recorded, and 5 to define the sequence in which the computer cards are to be read. Note that using 4 binary digits gives us 15 different possibilities (we exclude 0000 from consideration since a blank card would indicate this number), and 5 digits give us 31 cards.

A computer card indicating the third instruction, having an instruction code 0010, which is to be stored in memory storage bin 14, is sketched in Fig. 2.10-2. The memory storage bin is commonly called an *address*.

The possible instructions which our computer is capable of following are as follows:

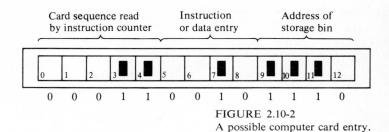

FIGURE 2.10-2
A possible computer card entry.

POSSIBLE COMPUTER INSTRUCTIONS

Instruction code (in binary form)	Address (memory storage bin)	Operation
0000	Address	Get a data value from the input device and place it in the specified storage location.
0001	Address	Place the contents of the storage device at the given address in the arithmetic unit (called an *accumulator*).
0010	Address	Add the contents of the memory location (at the given address) to the contents of the accumulator, and leave the sum in the accumulator.
0011	Address	Subtract the contents of the memory location (at the given address) from the contents of the accumulator, and leave the difference in the accumulator.
0100	Address	Multiply the contents of the memory location (at the given address) and the contents of the accumulator, and leave the product in the accumulator.
0101	Address	If the number in the accumulator is positive, set the instruction counter so that the indicated address is the next instruction to be performed. If the number is not positive, continue the program.
0110	Address	Place the contents of the accumulator into the memory location given by the address.
0111	Address	Place the contents of the memory location (at the given address) into the output device.
1000	Address	STOP the computer.

Note that the address is a binary number representing the memory location of interest. Thus, if our computer memory can store 4,096 *words* (pieces of information), then we need $\log_2 (4,096) = 12$ binary digits to locate a specified memory bin. In the examples to follow we shall assume a storage capacity of 16 bins. We therefore need only 4 binary digits to locate a specified bin. Note that each instruction has 13 binary digits: 5 for the instruction sequence, 4 for the instruction code, and 4 for the memory address.

EXAMPLE 2.10-1 Solve the equation $y = ax + b$ when $a = 2$, $x = 3$, and $b = 4$, using the hypothetical computer described above.

SOLUTION We begin by punching the data on three data cards. On the first card we punch $a = 2$, on the second $x = 3$, and on the third $b = 4$.

We must now instruct the computer as to what should be done with the data. This is called the *program*.

Instruction number (card sequence)	Instruction code	Address (storage bin)	Instruction
00001	0000	1000	Place the number $a = 2$ in storage bin 8 (1000).
00010	0000	1001	Place the number $x = 3$ in storage bin 9 (1001).
00011	0000	1010	Place the number $b = 4$ in storage bin 10 (1010).
00100	0001	1000	Place $a = 2$ in the accumulator.
00101	0100	1001	Multiply $x = 3$ by $a = 2$ and leave the product in the accumulator.
00110	0010	1010	Add $b = 4$ to the product $ax = 2(3)$ and leave the sum in accumulator.
00111	0110	1100	Place the accumulator result $ax + b = 10$ into memory bin 12.
01000	0111	1100	Place the number stored in memory bin 12 into the output device.
01001	1000	0000	STOP the computer.

Note that nine steps had to be performed to solve this simple problem. Each instruction is typed onto a different card. The data cards and the instruction cards are separately stacked in the input device of the computer. The computer, when started, *reads* each instruction card, and the binary instructions then connect the appropriate logic gates so that the information on the data cards goes to the correct memory location, the number in the correct memory location goes to the accumulator, the correct arithmetic operation is performed, etc.
////////

Our next example illustrates the use of instruction 0101. This is called a *transfer* instruction.

EXAMPLE 2.10-2 Obtain and print out the solution to the differential equation

$$\frac{dx}{dt} + \frac{1}{T}x = 0 \qquad x(0) = X_0$$

Follow the procedure indicated in Sec 2.9, and let $\Delta t = 0.01T$ and $X_0 = 1$.

The equation to be programmed on the computer is [Eq. (2.9-6b)],

$$x(k + 1) = 0.99x(k) \qquad x(k = 0) = 1 \qquad (2.10\text{-}1)$$

The values of $x(k)$ for $k = 0, 1, 2, \ldots, 10$ are to be printed out. The computer is to STOP after computing the value of $x(k = 10)$.

SOLUTION   The underlying philosophy in the solution of (2.10-1) is that since $x(0) = 1$, $x(1) = 0.99$. Then $x(2) = 0.99x(1)$, etc. We want the computer to first store the value $x(k)$, then multiply $x(k)$ by 0.99 and store this result. We now call this new value $x(k)$ and continue this process until $k = 10$. When $k = 10$, we stop the computer.

We employ instruction code 0101 to solve this problem. This instruction allows us to break our sequence, and thereby reread an earlier instruction card. Note that $k = 10$ is our largest value of k. Thus, when $k + 1 = K = 11$, we want to stop the program.

We employ five data cards $K = 11$, $a = 0.99$, $b = 1$, $k = 0$, and $x(0) = 1$. The instructions required to solve (2.10-1) are as follows:

Instruction no.	Code	Address	Operation
(1) 00001	0000	1000	Store K in bin 8 (1000).
(2) 00010	0000	1001	Store a in bin 9 (1001).
(3) 00011	0000	1010	Store b in bin 10 (1010).
(4) 00100	0000	1011	Store k in bin 11 (1011).
(5) 00101	0000	1100	Store X in bin 12 (1100).
(6) 00110	0111	1011	Print k (the value in bin 11) (1011).
(7) 00111	0111	1100	Print X (the value in bin 12) (1100).
(8) 01000	0001	1001	Place a in the accumulator.
(9) 01001	0100	1100	Multiply X by a.
(10) 01010	0110	1100	Place the product aX in bin 12 (1100).
			Note that this instruction first *erases* the number stored in bin 12, and then inserts the *new* product aX in bin 12.
(11) 01011	0001	1011	Place k in the accumulator.
(12) 01100	0010	1010	Add 1 to the value of k.
(13) 01101	0110	1011	Place the sum $1 + k$ in bin 11 (1011).
			NOTE: $1 + k$ is our new value of k.
(14) 01110	0001	1000	Place K in the accumulator.
(15) 01111	0011	1011	Subtract contents of bin 11 (1011) from K.
(16) 10000	0101	0110	If accumulator contains a positive number, return to INSTRUCTION NUMBER 6: 0110; otherwise continue (that is, if $k < K = 11$, return to instruction 6. If $k = K = 11$, continue program to instruction 17).
(17) 10001	1000	0000	STOP the computer.

We see from this example that the TRANSFER instruction allows us to repeat our operations without typing redundant instructions. This is equivalent to the "loop" in the flow diagram shown in Fig. 2.9-2.

////////

The reader has by this time convinced himself that an easier way of writing programs can be found. This is indeed true. For example, using FORTRAN IV, the instruction

$$Y = A * X + B$$

is the only instruction necessary to find Y in Example 2.10-1, after A, X, and B are stored. However, a complicated machine, called a *compiler*, must be employed to convert our simplified symbolic language into machine-language instructions.

In the remaining chapters we shall show how logical gates are formed, and how the digital computer can be used to solve complicated problems.

PROBLEMS

2.1-1   John has decided to go to the movies if Alice will go with him and if he can use the family car. However, Alice has decided to go to the beach if it is not raining and if the temperature is above 80°F. John's father has made plans to use the car to visit friends if it rains or if the temperature is above 80°.

Under what conditions will John go to the movies? Construct a special-purpose computer using NOT, AND, and OR gates, switches, battery, and a light bulb to help you solve the problem. The bulb should light if John goes to the movies.

2.1-2   Buses leave the terminal every hour on the hour unless there are less than 10 passengers or if the driver is late. If there are less than 10 passengers, the bus will wait 10 min or until the number of passengers increases to 10. If the bus leaves on time, it can travel at 60 mi/h. If the bus leaves late, or if it rains, it can travel at only 30 mi/h.

Under what conditions can the bus travel at 60 mi/h?

2.1-3   Seven switches operate a lamp in the following way: If switches 1, 3, 5, and 7 are closed and switch 2 is open, or if switches 2, 4, and 6 are closed and switch 3 is open, or if all seven switches are closed, the lamp will light.

Show, using NOT, AND, and OR gates, how the switches must be connected.

2.2-1   Prove, using a truth table, that the theorems given by (2.2-4*a*) to (2.2-4*i*) are valid.

2.2-2   The circuit shown in Fig. P2.2-2 does not make efficient use of the logic gates. Find, using Eqs. (2.2-4), a different circuit using fewer gates but having the same characteristics.

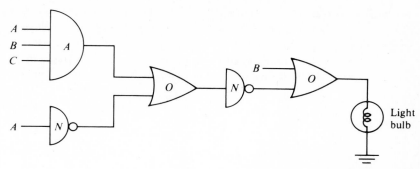

2.2-3   An economist proposed the following technique to make money in the stock market:

1   If the dividends paid on a stock exceed those paid on a bond, buy the stock.
2   If the dividends paid on a bond exceed those paid on a stock, buy the bond unless the growth rate of the stock is at least 25 percent per year for the past 5 years, in which case the stock should be purchased.

   The economist designed a special-purpose computer to tell him what to buy. The computer requires three switches, for higher dividend in stock, higher dividend in bond, and 25 percent growth rate, and two lamps, one to light if a stock is selected and the other to light if a bond is selected. In addition, AND and NOT gates (do not use OR gates) and a battery are required.

   Design the computer which uses the smallest number of these gates and which will provide the correct answer to the economist.

2.3-1   Write the number $N = 673$ in the octal ($b = 8$) system.

2.3-2   Design a sequential circuit to light a lamp if switches A, B, and C are closed in the sequence

$$ABC = 000, 100, 110, 111$$

2.3-3   Design a sequential circuit to operate a coffee machine. After the exact change is inserted (which turns on the machine) the customer pushes one of three buttons: sugar; cream; sugar and cream. If sugar and cream is desired, sugar must be added first.

2.3-4   (a) Show how to connect flip-flops to obtain a two-stage shift register.
   (b) Discuss how your results can be extended to N stages.

2.3-5   Show that the counter in Fig. 2.3-6 recycles to 0 following a count of 15.

2.3-6   Design a counter to operate in base-3 arithmetic.

2.4-1   Add the binary numbers:
   (a) 0111, 0101   (b) 0101, 1011

2.4-2   Using mod-4 arithmetic, add $123 + 201$.

2.4-3   Obtain a circuit for a half-adder using NOT and OR gates but not AND gates.

2.4-4   Subtract $1011 - 0111$. Use 1s complement arithmetic.

2.4-5 In base-4 arithmetic, subtract $201 - 123$. Use 3s complement arithmetic.

2.4-6 Subtraction using the 1s complement technique can be employed even when the answer is negative. To subtract B from A, we first add A and $\bar{B}$. If the most significant bit is a 1, we add the 1 to the sum $A + \bar{B}$. The answer $D = A + \bar{B} + 1$ is positive. If, however, the most significant bit is a zero, we complement the sum, $A + \bar{B}$; the answer $D = \overline{A + \bar{B}}$ is negative.

Verify that this technique works by subtracting $Y = 111$ from $X = 101$.

2.5-1 Multiply the binary numbers 110 and 010.

2.6-1 Write the number 8.31 in binary notation.

2.6-2 Add 1.48 and 2.59 using binary notation. Carry your answer to 4 bits to the right of the binary point.

2.6-3 Subtract 0.25 from 0.5 using binary notation and 1s complement arithmetic.

2.7-1 Verify that the system shown in Fig. 2.7-2 operates properly to divide two numbers, using the technique of repeated differences, by obtaining the quotient of 7/2.

2.7-2 Divide 111.01 by 0.001.

2.7-3 Divide 01.0 by 10.01.

2.8-1 Using the series

$$\log x = 2\left(u + \frac{u^3}{3} + \frac{u^5}{5} + \cdots\right) \qquad u = \frac{x-1}{x+1}, \; x > 0$$

show how a computer might evaluate log 3 using a flow diagram.

2.8-2 Show, using a flow diagram, how a computer might evaluate the integral $I = \displaystyle\int_0^{10} x \, dx$.

2.9-1 Show how to solve numerically the differential equation

$$\frac{dx}{dt} + \frac{1}{2} x(t) = 0 \qquad x(0) = 2$$

(*a*) Assume $\Delta t = 1$.

(*b*) Assume $\Delta t = 0.2$.

(*c*) Plot (*a*) and (*b*) on the same graph as the exact solution $x(t) = 2e^{-t/2}$ and compare your answer.

2.9-2 Show how to solve numerically the differential equation

$$\frac{d^2x}{dt^2} + 2\frac{dx}{dt} + x = 0 \qquad x(0) = 4, \quad \frac{dx}{dt}\bigg|_{t=0} = 0$$

Assume $\Delta t = 0.01$. Let $\quad \dfrac{d^2x}{dt^2} = \dfrac{x(t + \Delta t) - 2x(t) + x(t - \Delta t)}{(\Delta t)^2}$

2.9-3 The differential equation

$$\frac{d^2y}{dx^2} + \left(1 + \frac{1}{4x^2}\right)y = 0 \qquad y(0) = 1, \frac{dy}{dx}\bigg|_{x=0} = 0$$

is called *Bessel's differential equation of order zero*. Its solution $J_0(x)$ is called the *Bessel function of order zero of the first kind.*

Show how $J_0(x)$ can be obtained by numerical integration. Represent d^2y/dx^2 as

$$\frac{d^2y}{dx^2} = \frac{y(x + \Delta x) - 2y(x) + y(x - \Delta x)}{(\Delta x)^2}$$

(*a*) Let $\Delta x = 1$.

(*b*) Let $\Delta x = 0.1$.

2.10-1 Write a computer program, using the computer instructions given in Sec. 2.10, to determine log 3, where

$$\log x = 2\left(u + \frac{u^3}{3} + \frac{u^5}{5} + \cdots\right) \qquad u = \frac{x - 1}{x + 1}, x > 0$$

2.10-2 Write a computer program, using the computer instructions given in Sec. 2.10, to determine the integral

$$I = \int_0^{10} x \, dx$$

Let $\Delta x = 1$.

2.10-3 Write a computer program, using the computer instructions given in Sec. 2.10, to print out the solution to the differential equation

$$\frac{d^2y}{dx^2} + \left(1 + \frac{1}{4x^2}\right)y = 0 \qquad y(0) = 1, \left.\frac{dy}{dx}\right|_{x=0} = 0$$

for $\Delta x = 0.1$, $0 \le x \le 9$.

REFERENCE

MARCUS, M. P.: "Switching Circuits for Engineers," Prentice-Hall, Inc., Englewood Cliffs, N.J., 1967.

3

SIGNALS AND CIRCUIT ELEMENTS

INTRODUCTION

Electrical systems today are either digital or analog or some combination of both. About a decade ago, basic courses in electrical engineering were concerned only with analog systems. The advent of the transistor and the integrated circuit has made digital circuits economical and readily available. Because digital networks have significant advantages for many applications, they are being used more and more in place of their analog counterparts. For this reason this chapter and the next include both analog and digital elements and networks. Some of the basic characteristics of both of these types of systems will be presented. We first describe and define the basic signals and then consider how the basic components respond when these signals are applied.

3.1 TERMINOLOGY, CONVENTIONS, DEFINITIONS, AND SYMBOLS

To establish a common language and elementary ground rules, we introduce some important definitions and conventions. These definitions will be presented here in the language of electric circuits and elements, although similar definitions and terminology apply to all types of systems, such as mechanical, hydraulic, and acoustical systems.

The electric circuit   An electric *circuit* consists of an interconnection of actual physical devices such as batteries, resistors, transistors, and motors. The purpose of any electric circuit is to either transfer or transform *energy*, with *information* an important form of energy. Within the circuit, this information is carried in the form of analog or digital *signals* (time functions) which take on an infinite variety of forms. The central problem of circuit analysis is to determine how a given circuit will react to a given signal. In this chapter and the next we shall begin to examine this problem.

   An example of a complex circuit is shown in Fig. 3.1-1. In the example, information is transferred from the brain waves, processed by the computer, and transformed into mechanical energy which produces motion of the artificial arm. Within the system, both analog and digital signals are used.

3.1-1   Electric Current

In a circuit, the transfer of energy is accomplished by transferring electric *charge* from one device to another. The mks unit of charge is the coulomb (abbreviated C). The smallest known unit of charge is carried by one electron, and is -1.602×10^{-19} C.

   Charge motion is most conveniently measured in terms of *current*, which has both magnitude and direction. The magnitude is equal to the rate at which charge passes through a cross-section area of the circuit, as shown in Fig. 3.1-2a. The positive direction for the current is defined as the direction of the flow of positive charge. Thus, if we consider the flow of negative charges such as electrons, the negative charges or

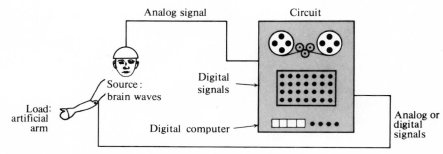

FIGURE 3.1-1
Example of an electric circuit; the control of an artificial limb by a digital computer.

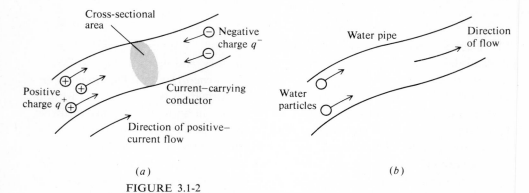

Cross-sectional area

Negative charge q^-

Positive charge q^+

Current–carrying conductor

Direction of positive–current flow

Water pipe

Direction of flow

Water particles

(a)

(b)

FIGURE 3.1-2

Electric current. (a) Pictorial representation of current flow. Note that the effect of the negative charge flowing from right to left is the same as that of the positive charge flowing from left to right. (b) Water-flow analogy.

electrons flow in a direction opposite to the current direction. If both positive charges q^+ and negative charges q^- are in motion in the same circuit, it can be shown that these charges move in opposite directions (Fig. 3.1-2a). The total current in this case is

$$i(t) = \frac{dq}{dt} = \frac{dq^+}{dt} - \frac{dq^-}{dt} \qquad (3.1-1)$$

where $i(t)$ = total current, coulombs per second (C/s) or amperes (A)

$q(t)$ = equivalent positive charge, C

q^+ = positive charge, C

q^- = negative charge, C

t = time, s

Current is often referred to as a *through* variable because it is the amount of charge passing through a cross section in unit time. The idea of charge flow can be compared to a system of pipes in which water is flowing. Current in the electric circuit is analogous to the flow rate, in gallons per second, of water flowing past a cross-section boundary of one of the pipes, as shown in Fig. 3.1-2b.

EXAMPLE 3.1-1 In semiconductor devices, the current is composed of *electron* current and *hole* current. A "hole" carries the same amount of charge as an electron, but the charge is positive. In a certain device, the current crossing a given area consists of 5×10^{18} electrons per second in one direction and 2×10^{18} holes per second in the opposite direction. Find the current.

SOLUTION   For the electrons,

$$\frac{dq^-}{dt} = 5 \times 10^{18} \text{ electrons/s} \times -1.602 \times 10^{-19} \text{ C/electron} = -0.80 \text{ C/s} = -0.80 \text{ A}$$

For the holes,

$$\frac{dq^+}{dt} = 2 \times 10^{18} \text{ holes/s} \times 1.602 \times 10^{-19} \text{ C/hole} = 0.32 \text{ C/s} = 0.32 \text{ A}$$

Then, from Eq. (3.1-1), $i = dq^+/dt - dq^-/dt = 0.32 - (-0.80) = 1.12$ A.
////////

3.1-2 Voltage

To obtain current flow, we must apply forces to set the charges in motion. The moving charges have work done on them by an external force so that they gain kinetic energy, or the charges do work and lose kinetic energy. The capability of a current to transfer energy can be expressed in terms of the potential difference through which the current moves in going from one point to another. Potential difference or *voltage*, as it is usually called, is measured in volts (V) and is defined as the change in energy of a unit charge as it is transferred from point *a* to point *b*. Thus a 1-V potential difference is required to add 1 joule (J) of energy to 1 C of charge. Mathematically, this is written

$$v_{ab} = \frac{dw}{dq} \qquad (3.1\text{-}2)$$

where v_{ab} = voltage between points *a* and *b*

dw = energy, J, gained or lost by charge dq while passing from *a* to *b*

Because voltage must be specified between two points, it is classified as an *across* variable. If point *a* is at a higher potential than point *b*, we say that there exists a voltage *drop* from *a* to *b* and we understand the notation v_{ab} to mean "the voltage drop from *a* to *b*." As in the case of current, we specify voltage in terms of its *magnitude* and *polarity*. Figure 3.1-3 illustrates the sign convention commonly used for voltage polarity, a + sign at the assumed higher potential point, and a − sign at the lower potential point. Note that a voltage drop of 5 V from *a* to *b* would be written $v_{ab} = 5$ V. Then the voltage from *b* to *a* would be a *rise*, and we write $v_{ba} = -5$ V. When using double-subscript notation, the polarity signs may be omitted on the figure, since they are implied by the subscripts. Often single-subscript notation is used for voltage. For example, if the voltage v_{ab} in Fig. 3.1-3a is to be written in single-subscript notation as v_1, then the polarity must be indicated on the diagram, as shown.

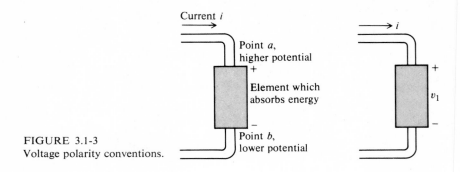

FIGURE 3.1-3
Voltage polarity conventions.

Sources of voltage are obtained by transforming chemical, mechanical, or atomic energy to electric energy. Some examples with which we are all familiar include batteries, generators, and solar cells.

3.1-3 Energy and Power

Instantaneous *electric power* is defined as the rate at which energy is gained or lost. Mathematically,

$$p = \frac{dw}{dt} \qquad (3.1\text{-}3)$$

where p is measured in watts (W).

We can relate power to current and voltage by noting that

$$p = \frac{dw}{dt} = \frac{dw}{dq}\frac{dq}{dt} = v_{ab}i \qquad (3.1\text{-}4)$$

where the current i is positive if it flows in at terminal a. Thus instantaneous power is simply the product of instantaneous voltage and instantaneous current.

If the sign of the power p is positive, power is being absorbed and transformed into other forms of energy (e.g., heat). If p is negative, we have a source of electric power.

The total energy change from time t_1 to t_2 is found by integrating the power

$$w_{12} = \int_{t_1}^{t_2} p \, dt = \int_{t_1}^{t_2} v_{ab}i \, dt \qquad (3.1\text{-}5)$$

EXAMPLE 3.1-2   In a plating bath used to plate automobile bumpers, a steady current of 1,000 A must be maintained for 30 s to achieve a specified plating thickness. The voltage between plating anodes is 6 V. Find the power dissipated during the plating cycle and the total energy required.

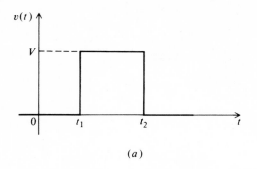

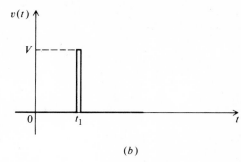

FIGURE 3.2-1
Digital signals. (*a*) Single pulse; (*b*) narrow pulse.

SOLUTION   Applying Eq. (3.1-4),

$$P = VI = 6 \text{ V} \times 1,000 \text{ A} = 6,000 \text{ W} = 6 \text{ kW*}$$

To find the total energy, we apply (3.1-5) as follows:

$$w_{\text{total}} = \int_0^{30} P \, dt = [6,000t]_0^{30} = 180,000 \text{ W} \cdot \text{s} = 180,000 \text{ J}$$

////////

3.2   DIGITAL SIGNALS

In digital systems, information is transmitted throughout the system by *pulses*. A typical pulse signal was discussed in connection with shift registers in Sec. 2.3-1 and is shown in Fig. 2.3-4.

Some other common types of pulse signals will be discussed in this section.

3.2-1   The Single Pulse

The basic component of any digital signal is the single pulse shown in Fig. 3.2-1*a*. It is represented, for convenience, as a voltage and is characterized by its amplitude (or height) V, starting time t_1, and duration, or width, $t_2 - t_1$. Any (or more than one) of these properties can be varied from pulse to pulse to convey information.

* The prefix k (kilo) stands for 1,000. Thus 6 kW (kilowatts) = 6,000 W. Other common prefixes which will be used throughout this text are M (mega) = 10^6, m (milli) = 10^{-3}, μ (micro) = 10^{-6}, p (pico) = 10^{-12}.

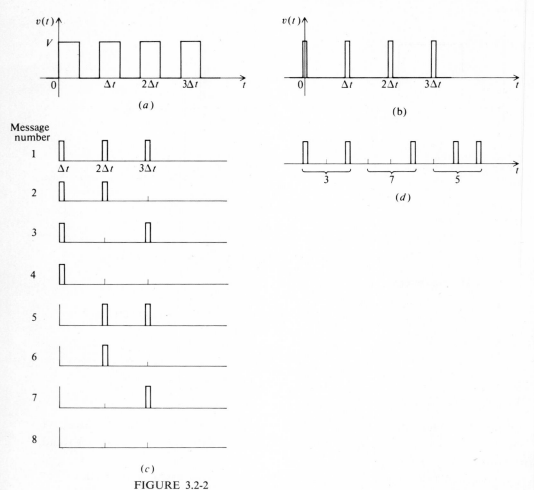

FIGURE 3.2-2
Digital signals. (*a*) Constant-amplitude pulse train; (*b*) narrow-width pulse train;
(*c*) message code; (*d*) signal transmitting messages 3-7-5.

Often the pulse width is a constant. When this is the case, only the amplitude and starting time of the pulse are important, and we represent the pulse as shown in Fig. 3.2-1*b*. In most digital communications systems only one amplitude is used, corresponding to the binary number 1. The binary number 0 is indicated by the *absence* of a pulse.

3.2-2 Pulse Trains

Constant-amplitude pulse trains To vary the information in a signal, a train of pulses is used. The simplest type of pulse train has a constant amplitude, uniform width, and uniform spacing, as shown in Fig. 3.2-2*a*. The time from the beginning of one pulse to the beginning of the next is called the *period* of the pulse train. If the pulse width is much less than the period, we use the representation of Fig. 3.2-2*b*. In both cases the information content is very small since no characteristic of either signal is varied. To convey information using this pulse train we need only agree on a "code" which is implemented by omitting certain pulses. For example, a pulse train of either positive or zero amplitude pulses and time duration $3\Delta t$ can represent eight different messages. This is illustrated in Fig. 3.2-2*c*. A typical message is shown in Fig. 3.2-2*d*.

Variable-amplitude pulse train Often the desired information is contained in the amplitude of the signal. Such signals are called *pulse-amplitude modulated* (PAM) signals and are used in some types of communications systems. An example is shown in Fig. 3.2-3. In this example, the pulse width is very narrow compared with the period of the pulse train, and the pulse amplitudes vary according to the function $V_m \sin \omega t_n$. The sine function is very important in engineering, and we shall discuss it in more detail in a later section.

3.3 ANALOG SIGNALS

In contrast to digital signals, analog signals are continuous functions of time, as shown in Fig. 3.3-1. This signal might represent a speech wave converted to a voltage by means of a microphone and displayed on an oscilloscope. In such a signal, the information is contained in the time variation of the signal *amplitude*.

Analog signals fall into two classes, periodic and nonperiodic. In the following sections we consider the mathematical description and characteristics of the most important signals of each type, the step and the sine wave. These are particularly important because it turns out that many more complicated signals can be *decomposed* into *sums* of these basic signals. As we shall see later, this often greatly simplifies circuit analysis.

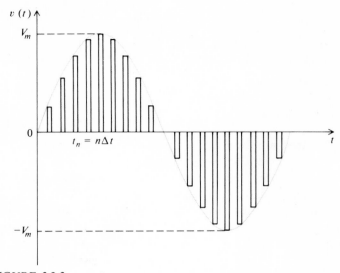

FIGURE 3.2-3
Pulse-amplitude-modulated signal. The modulating signal is $V_m \sin \omega t$.

3.3-1   The Step Function

We are often interested in the response of a network to a suddenly applied excitation. The elementary function which describes this is the step function. Figure 3.3-2a shows a circuit which applies 1 V to the network by means of a switch. The arrow indicates that the switch contact moves from a to b at time $t = t_0$. If the switch motion is assumed to take place instantaneously, the *waveform* of $v_i(t)$ will be as shown in Fig. 3.3-2b. This is the *unit step function*, which is given the symbol $u(t - t_0)$. We then write

$$u(t - t_0) = \begin{cases} 0 & t < t_0 \\ 1 & t > t_0 \end{cases} \qquad (3.3\text{-}1)$$

The step is left undefined precisely at $t = t_0$, where the jump takes place.

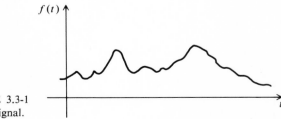

FIGURE 3.3-1
Analog signal.

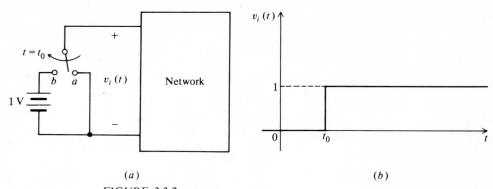

(a)   (b)

FIGURE 3.3-2
The step function. (a) A circuit which applies a step function; (b) plot of the unit step function.

From the point of view of information-carrying capacity, the step function is relatively uninformative, since it contains only two pieces of information, its amplitude and its starting time. However, it becomes much more interesting when combined with other steps to form pulses, as shown in the following example.

EXAMPLE 3.3-1   Express the pulse waveform shown in Fig. 3.3-3a as a sum of step functions.

SOLUTION   The first jump can be written $3u(t)$. At $t = 2$ s, the waveform returns to zero. This can be accounted for by adding a *negative* step that starts at $t = 2$. From definition (3.3-1) we see that the step starts when its *argument* is zero; thus $u(t - 2)$ starts when $t = 2$. Similar remarks can be made about steps at $t = 3$ and $t = 6$. We can then write

$$v(t) = 3u(t) - 3u(t - 2) + 3u(t - 3) - 3u(t - 6)$$

The individual terms are sketched in Fig. 3.3-3b.

////////

Using the technique illustrated by Example 3.3-1, pulse waveforms can be expressed mathematically as sums of step functions. Pulse waveforms are extremely important, because any analog signal can be transmitted using pulses with no loss of information by a process called *sampling*, which we shall discuss in Sec. 6.5.

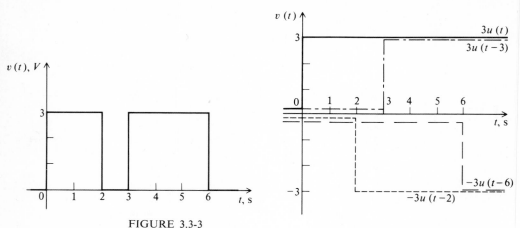

FIGURE 3.3-3
Waveforms for Example 3.3-1. (*a*) Pulse waveform; (*b*) individual steps which add up to the original waveform.

3.3-2 Sinusoidal Signals

In this section we consider the sine wave. The importance of this waveform is the fact that most electric energy is generated and utilized in the form of sinusoidal alternating current (ac), and many communications systems (broadcast-band AM and FM, for example) utilize sinusoidal waveforms. The sine wave shown in Fig. 3.3-4 is also the basic building block for more complex periodic waveforms. The property that all such waveforms share is that they repeat themselves every T seconds, where T is called the period. In mathematical terms, this is expressed simply as

$$v(t) = v(t + T) \qquad (3.3\text{-}2)$$

The expression for the alternating voltage of Fig. 3.3-4 can be written in terms of sines or cosines. Since the cosine is the base of a shorthand method we are going to introduce later, we use it to write

$$v(t) = V_m \cos(\omega t + \theta) \qquad (3.3\text{-}3)$$

The three parameters which completely define $v(t)$ are:

1 The *maximum*, or *peak*, value V_m.
2 The *angular frequency* $\omega = 2\pi/T$ radians per second (rad/s) . More often, we speak of the *cyclic* frequency f. This is the reciprocal of the period ($f = 1/T$) in cycles per second; the unit for cycles per second is the hertz (Hz). The angular and cyclic frequencies are related by $\omega = 2\pi f$.

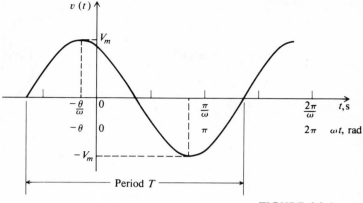

FIGURE 3.3-4
Sinusoidal waveform.

3 The *phase angle θ*. This depends on the time origin, and for the cosine is the angle between the first positive maximum and $\omega t = 0$.

In ac circuit analysis we are interested in the *steady-state* response to sources such as the sinusoidal voltage of Eq. (3.3-3). A shorthand method for performing the required calculations involves the use of *phasors*, which are manipulated using the algebra of *complex numbers*. Before we present the method, a short review of complex algebra is in order.

The algebra of complex numbers   The complex plane is shown in Fig. 3.3-5a. Along the horizontal x axis we plot the real numbers. The vertical axis contains the imaginary numbers jy. The letter j should be thought of as an *operator* of unit length which rotates the real number $+1$ through $90°$ in a counterclockwise direction. If we operate on $j1$ with j, we achieve a rotation of $180°$, which takes us around to -1. Symbolically,

$$j(j) = j^2 = -1$$

or
$$j = \sqrt{-1} \qquad (3.3\text{-}4)$$

Thus j can be treated as if it were $\sqrt{-1}$ in algebraic computations.

A point in the complex plane defines a complex number. For example, z_1 in Fig. 3.3-5a has a real part 2 units in length and an imaginary part 2 units long. We then write the number as

$$z_1 = x_1 + jy_1$$
$$= 2 + j2 \qquad (3.3\text{-}5)$$

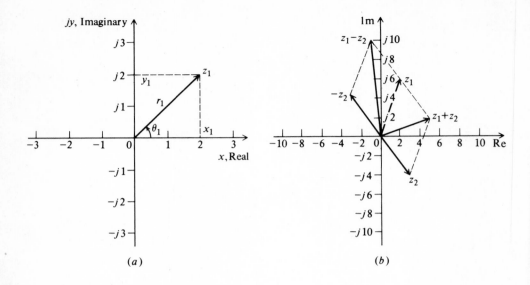

FIGURE 3.3-5
(*a*) The complex plane. (*b*) Addition and subtraction of complex numbers.

Here, the notation we shall use is

$$x_1 = \text{Re } z_1 \qquad (3.3\text{-}6)$$

which is read "x_1 is the real part of z_1," and

$$y_1 = \text{Im } z_1 \qquad (3.3\text{-}7)$$

that is, "y_1 is the imaginary part of z_1."

Equation (3.3-5) is the *rectangular*, or *cartesian*, form of the complex number. Note that we can also locate z_1 in the plane by specifying its magnitude (distance from the origin) r_1 and angle with the real axis θ_1, as shown in the figure. This leads to the *polar* form. From the geometry,

$$
\begin{aligned}
z_1 &= x_1 + jy_1 \\
&= r_1 \cos \theta_1 + jr_1 \sin \theta_1 \\
&= r_1(\cos \theta_1 + j \sin \theta_1) \qquad (3.3\text{-}8)
\end{aligned}
$$

Now, a key relation in complex-number arithmetic is Euler's identity (proved in Prob. 3.3-6), which states that

$$e^{j\theta} = \cos \theta + j \sin \theta \qquad (3.3\text{-}9)$$

Thus $e^{j\theta}$ is an operator which rotates a vector of unit length through an angle of θ deg (or radians, depending on the units being used). Using this in (3.3-8), we have the polar form

$$z_1 = r_1 e^{j\theta_1} \qquad (3.3\text{-}10a)$$

This is often written in abbreviated notation as

$$z_1 = r_1 \angle \theta_1 \qquad (3.3\text{-}10b)$$

To convert from polar to rectangular form, we use (3.3-8). For rectangular to polar conversion, we obtain, from the geometry of Fig. 3.3-5a,

$$r_1 = \sqrt{x_1{}^2 + y_1{}^2} \qquad (3.3\text{-}11a)$$

$$\theta_1 = \arctan \frac{y_1}{x_1} \qquad (3.3\text{-}11b)$$

Arithmetic operations ADDITION AND SUBTRACTION These operations are best carried out using the rectangular form, or graphically. Consider finding $z_1 + z_2$, where $z_1 = 2 + j6$ and $z_2 = 3 - j4$. Then

$$\begin{array}{r} 2 + j6 \\ +3 - j4 \\ \hline 5 + j2 \end{array}$$

i.e., the real and imaginary parts are added separately.

To find $z_1 - z_2$, we simply change the signs of x_2 and y_2 and add. Then

$$\begin{array}{r} 2 + j6 \\ +(-3 + j4) \\ \hline -1 + j10 \end{array}$$

The graphical solution of these examples is shown in Fig. 3.3-5b. It is always a good idea to sketch, roughly to scale, the complex numbers involved in such calculations. From such sketches we can estimate the magnitude and angle of the resultant vector and thus have a rough check on our arithmetic.

MULTIPLICATION AND DIVISION These operations are best carried out using the polar form.

$$z_1 z_2 = r_1 e^{j\theta_1} r_2 e^{j\theta_2} = r_1 r_2 e^{j(\theta_1 + \theta_2)} = r_1 r_2 \angle (\theta_1 + \theta_2)$$

$$\frac{z_1}{z_2} = \frac{r_1 e^{j\theta_1}}{r_2 e^{j\theta_2}} = \frac{r_1}{r_2} e^{j(\theta_1 - \theta_2)} = \frac{r_1}{r_2} \angle (\theta_1 - \theta_2)$$

Using the numbers from the preceding example,

$$z_1 = 2 + j6 = 6.3 \angle 71.5° \qquad z_2 = 3 - j4 = 5 \angle -53°$$

$$z_1 z_2 = (6.3)(5) \angle (71.5° - 53°) = 31.5 \angle 18.5°$$

$$\frac{z_1}{z_2} = \frac{6.3}{5} \angle (71.5° + 53°) = 1.26 \angle 124.5°$$

Both of these operations can be carried out in rectangular form. This is left as an exercise (Prob. 3.3-7).

Rotating vectors   Now refer to Fig. 3.3-6 and consider the "complex" voltage $V_m \angle \theta$. Suppose we let this vector rotate counterclockwise with constant angular velocity ω. Then the angle it makes with the real axis will be a function of time, i.e., if we denote the angle at time t by $\psi(t)$, then

$$\psi(t) = \omega t + \theta$$

Consider the projection of this rotating vector on the positive real axis. This is

$$v(t) = V_m \cos \psi(t) = V_m \cos (\omega t + \theta) \qquad (3.3\text{-}12)$$

which is exactly the same as (3.3-3), the equation for the general sinusoid. The exponential form for the rotating vector is $V_m e^{j(\omega t + \theta)}$, and the projection on the real axis can be interpreted as

$$v(t) = \text{Re } V_m e^{j(\omega t + \theta)} \qquad (3.3\text{-}13a)$$

$$= \text{Re } V_m e^{j\theta} e^{j\omega t} \qquad (3.3\text{-}13b)$$

$$= \text{Re } \overline{V}_m e^{j\omega t} \qquad (3.3\text{-}13c)$$

where

$$\overline{V}_m = V_m e^{j\theta} = V_m \angle \theta \qquad (3.3\text{-}14)$$

The complex number $\overline{V}_m$ is called a *phasor* and should be thought of as the amplitude and phase shift of the rotating vector $e^{j\omega t}$. The key to the phasor method of ac circuit analysis is that the phasor of (3.3-14) contains all the information in (3.3-12), except for ω, in a shorthand form. Since, in a linear circuit driven by a sinusoidal source of angular frequency ω, all currents and voltages are of the same frequency, the information in the phasor voltages and currents is all that is required.

EXAMPLE 3.3-2   Given the two voltages

$$v_1(t) = 10 \cos (\omega t + 30°)$$

$$v_2(t) = 15 \cos (\omega t + 45°)$$

Find $v(t) = v_1(t) + v_2(t)$ using (a) trigonometric identities and (b) phasors.

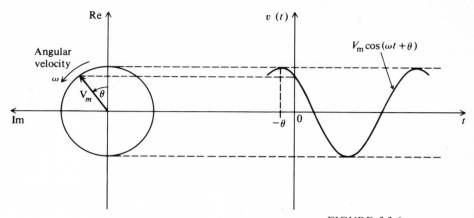

FIGURE 3.3-6
Projection of rotating vector.

SOLUTION   (a) Since $\cos (x + y) = \cos x \cos y - \sin x \sin y$,

$$
\begin{aligned}
v_1(t) &= 8.7 \cos \omega t - 5 \sin \omega t \\
v_2(t) &= 10.6 \cos \omega t - 10.6 \sin \omega t \\
\hline
v(t) &= 19.3 \cos \omega t - 15.6 \sin \omega t
\end{aligned}
$$

To combine these terms we use the identity

$$
a \cos \omega t + b \sin \omega t = \sqrt{a^2 + b^2} \cos\left(\omega t - \arctan \frac{b}{a}\right)
$$

Thus

$$
v(t) = \sqrt{(19.3)^2 + (15.6)^2} \cos\left(\omega t - \arctan \frac{-15.6}{19.3}\right)
$$

$$
= 24.8 \cos(\omega t + 39°)
$$

(b) Using phasors, we write

$$
\begin{aligned}
\overline{V} = \overline{V}_1 + \overline{V}_2 &= 10 \angle 30° + 15 \angle 45° \\
&= 8.7 + j5 + 10.6 + j10.6 \\
&= 19.3 + j15.6 \\
&= 24.8 \angle 39°
\end{aligned}
$$

Then, converting back to the time domain,

$$
v(t) = 24.8 \cos(\omega t + 39°)
$$

////////

The phasor method is clearly easier to apply analytically. Note also that the phasor addition can be carried out graphically, as was done in Fig. 3.3-5b.

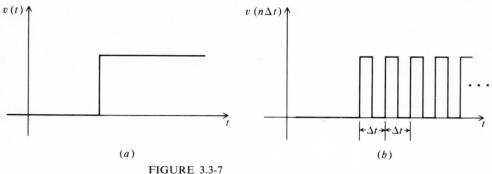

FIGURE 3.3-7
Sampler waveforms. (*a*) Analog input signal; (*b*) digital output signal.

3.3-3 Similarity between Digital and Analog Signals

The student will have noticed that the constant-amplitude pulse train appears to be the digital counterpart of the analog step function, and the PAM sine-wave signal is the digital counterpart of the continuous sine wave. This is indeed true, and it is possible to obtain either signal from the other by the use of electronic circuits.

To obtain the digital signal from the analog signal a *sampling* circuit is used. Typical waveforms are shown in Fig. 3.3-7. The sampling circuit generates a sequence of narrow pulses spaced Δt apart. The height of each pulse is equal to the corresponding amplitude of the analog signal, and we see that the resulting digital signal is *pulse-amplitude modulated* by the analog input signal.

To reconstruct the analog signal, given the digital signal, a "clamp-and-hold" circuit is used, for which typical waveforms are shown in Fig. 3.3-8. The circuit gives an output voltage equal to the height of the corresponding input pulse. This voltage is maintained until the next pulse appears and we get a stepwise signal v_1 as shown in Fig. 3.3-8*c*. To remove the "steps" in the waveform of v_1, the clamp-and-hold circuit is followed by a "filter" circuit which yields the continuous analog signal $v(t)$ shown in Fig. 3.3-8*d*. It is shown in Sec. 6.5 that under certain conditions the analog signal can be reproduced without error.

3.3-4 Fourier Series

Up to this point we have discussed *aperiodic* signals such as the step function and *periodic* signals consisting of single-frequency sinusoids. Many signals encountered in practice are periodic but nonsinusoidal; for example, the square or rectangular wave and the triangular wave. In this section we present the basic theory of the *Fourier series*, which is used to represent such signals as sums of sinusoids.

Any physical, periodic function $f(t)$ may be expressed as a Fourier series, i.e.,

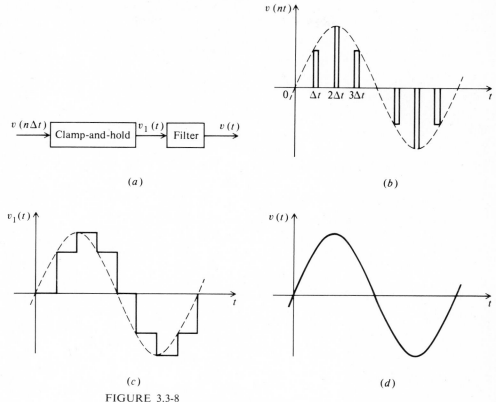

FIGURE 3.3-8
Reconstruction of analog signal from PAM signal. (*a*) Circuit; (*b*) PAM wave-form; (*c*) output of clamp-and-hold circuit; (*d*) output of filter.

$$f(t) = a_0 + a_1 \cos \omega_0 t + a_2 \cos 2\omega_0 t + \cdots + a_n \cos n\,\omega_0 t + \cdots$$

$$+ b_1 \sin \omega_0 t + b_2 \sin 2\omega_0 t + \cdots + b_n \sin n\omega_0 t + \cdots \qquad (3.3\text{-}15)$$

where
$$\omega_0 = 2\pi f_0 = \frac{2\pi}{T} \qquad \text{rad/s}$$

$$T = \text{period, s}$$

The series consists in general of an infinite sum of sinusoids, each one of which has a frequency that is an integral (harmonic) multiple of the fundamental frequency, $\omega_0/2\pi$. Thus the terms with coefficients a_1 and b_1 constitute the *fundamental* component, those with a_2 and b_2 the *second-harmonic* component, etc. The constant term a_0 represents the dc (average) value of $f(t)$. The sequence of numbers $a_0, a_1, a_2, \ldots,$

$a_n, \ldots, b_1, b_2, \ldots, b_n, \ldots$ which completely define the periodic function can be found from the formulas

$$a_0 = \frac{1}{T} \int_0^T f(t) \, dt \qquad (3.3\text{-}16a)$$

$$a_n = \frac{2}{T} \int_0^T f(t) \cos n\omega_0 t \, dt \qquad (3.3\text{-}16b)$$

and

$$b_n = \frac{2}{T} \int_0^T f(t) \sin n\omega_0 t \, dt \qquad (3.3\text{-}16c)$$

Let us use these formulas to find the Fourier series for the square wave of Fig. 3.3-9a.

The average value a_0 is zero by inspection. For the a_n coefficients we have

$$a_n = \frac{2}{T} \left(\int_0^{T/4} \cos \frac{n2\pi}{T} t \, dt - \int_{T/4}^{3T/4} \cos \frac{n2\pi}{T} t \, dt + \int_{3T/4}^{T} \cos \frac{n2\pi}{T} t \, dt \right)$$

$$= \frac{1}{n\pi} \left(2 \sin \frac{n\pi}{2} - 2 \sin \frac{3n\pi}{2} \right) \qquad (3.3\text{-}17)$$

Using this general form, we find all even a_n coefficients are zero. For the odd coefficients

$$a_1 = \frac{4}{\pi}$$

$$a_3 = \frac{-4}{3\pi} \qquad (3.3\text{-}18)$$

$$a_5 = \frac{4}{5\pi}$$

$$a_7 = \frac{-4}{7\pi}$$

For the b_n coefficients we find $b_n = 0$ for all n. Thus the Fourier series for the square wave is

$$f(t) = \frac{4}{\pi} \left(\cos \omega_0 t - \frac{1}{3} \cos 3\omega_0 t + \frac{1}{5} \cos 5\omega_0 t - \frac{1}{7} \cos 7\omega_0 t + \cdots \right) \qquad (3.3\text{-}19)$$

The first three terms and their sum are sketched in Fig. 3.3-9b. As more terms are added, the "ripple" decreases in amplitude and increases in frequency, and the curve more closely resembles the original square wave.

As noted previously, the coefficients of the various harmonic terms contain all the information required to construct the function. This information is often exhibited as a "spectrum," or plot of amplitude and phase vs. frequency. The amplitude

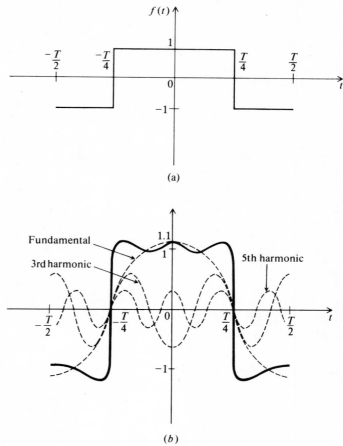

FIGURE 3.3-9
Fourier series. (*a*) Square wave; (*b*) sum of fundamental and third and fifth harmonics.

spectrum for the square wave is shown in Fig. 3.3-10, and is seen to consist of discrete lines occurring at the frequencies of the fundamental and nonzero harmonics. For this reason it is often called a "line spectrum."

3.3-5 Power; the Effective Value

It is often necessary to find the average power dissipated in a circuit by a periodic current or voltage. In Sec. 3.4-2 we will find that *instantaneous* power is proportional to the *square* of the current or voltage. Thus, to find the *average* power dissipated by a

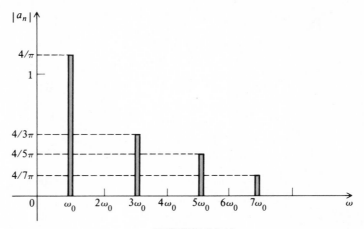

FIGURE 3.3-10
Amplitude spectrum for the square wave.

periodic current, we must average the square of the instantaneous current. It is sufficient to average over one cycle because the average over any integral number of cycles will be the same.

Using these facts, we can find the value of dc current which will produce the same heating effect as the periodic current. If we call the equivalent dc current I and the periodic current $i(t)$, we must have, for the same power from both,

$$I^2 = \frac{1}{T} \int_0^T i^2(t)\, dt \qquad (3.3\text{-}20)$$

where the right-hand side is the time average (mean) of $i^2(t)$ over one cycle of period T.
Thus, finally,

$$I = \sqrt{\frac{1}{T} \int_0^T i^2(t)\, dt} \qquad (3.3\text{-}21)$$

This is called the *effective*, or *root-mean-square* (rms), value of the current. If the current is sinusoidal,

$$i(t) = I_m \cos \omega t$$

it can be shown (Prob. 3.3-11) that

$$I = \frac{I_m}{\sqrt{2}} = 0.707 I_m$$

Thus $0.707I_m$ is the effective value of the *sinusoid* as far as power-transforming capability is concerned.

Sinusoidal voltages and currents are usually specified in terms of their rms values. For example, domestic power is usually specified as "110 volt 60 Hz." The 110 V is the rms value, so that the actual voltage is $v(t) = \sqrt{2}(110) \cos 2\pi \times 60t$ V.

3.4   CIRCUIT ELEMENTS

In this section we consider the basic elements from which digital and analog circuits are formed. The basic signals will be applied to these elements, and we shall consider the resulting response.

3.4-1   Digital Components

Since digital signals are *discrete*, they can be considered simply as sequences of numbers. The basic arithmetic operations required of digital networks which process these signals are those of addition (or subtraction) and multiplication. In addition, a delay element which delays any given pulse exactly one period, Δt, is required.

Digital adders (and subtractors) were discussed in Chap. 2 and are readily available. The circuit symbol we shall use to represent a digital adder (or subtractor) is shown in Fig. 3.4-1a. Digital multipliers will be represented as shown in Fig. 3.4-1b (note that these multipliers are essentially scalers, since they multiply by a fixed constant). The delay elements are simply single-input, single-output shift registers, as discussed in Sec. 2.3-1 and shown schematically in Fig. 3.4-1c.

These three elements are interconnected as desired to form digital networks. A basic network using one of each type of element, is shown in Fig. 3.4-2.

The input to the network is the sequence of numbers $x(n \Delta t)$, and the output is the sequence $y(n \Delta t)$. The present value of the output $y(n \Delta t)$ is delayed by Δt, at which time it becomes $y[(n-1) \Delta t]$. This is then multiplied by the constant K and added to the present value of the input, $x(n \Delta t)$. Thus the output can be written

$$y(n \Delta t) = Ky[(n-1) \Delta t] + x(n \Delta t) \qquad (3.4\text{-}1)$$

This is a first-order linear *difference* equation and should be thought of as an *algorithm*, i.e., a systematic, step-by-step process for solving a particular digital signal-processing problem. The digital network of Fig. 3.4-2 is the implementation of the algorithm which provides the solution. Some typical responses are found in the following examples.

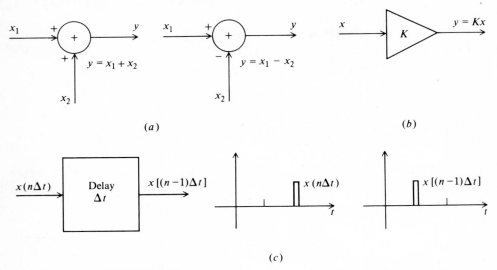

FIGURE 3.4-1
Digital components. (a) Adder and subtractor; (b) multiplier; (c) delay element.

EXAMPLE 3.4-1 Find the output of the network of Fig. 3.4-2 if the input is a single unit pulse at $t = 0$ and if $y(-\Delta t) = 0$. This type of circuit is called a *first-order digital system*.

SOLUTION   The unit input pulse at $t = 0$ indicates that

$$x(n\,\Delta t) = \begin{cases} 1 & n = 0 \\ 0 & n \neq 0 \end{cases}$$

We write Eq. (3.4-1) for increasing values of n as follows:

$$n = 0: y(0) = Ky(-\Delta t) + x(0)$$
$$n = 1: y(\Delta t) = Ky(0) + x(\Delta t) \qquad (3.4\text{-}2)$$
$$n = 2: y(2\Delta t) = Ky(\Delta t) + x(2\Delta t)$$
$$n = 3: y(3\Delta t) = Ky(2\Delta t) + x(3\Delta t)$$

$$\cdots\cdots\cdots\cdots\cdots\cdots\cdots\cdots\cdots$$

In the first equation, $y(-\Delta t) = 0$ and $x(0) = 1$ are the given initial conditions; thus $y(0) = 1$. Using this in the second equation with $x(\Delta t) = 0$, we find $y(\Delta t) = K$.

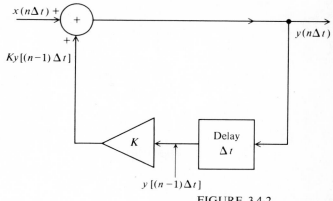

FIGURE 3.4-2
First-order digital network.

Continuing in this way, we obtain the following sequence:

n	$y(n\,\Delta t)$
0	1
1	K
2	K^2
3	K^3
⋮	⋮

By induction, we have the general solution

$$y(n\,\Delta t) = K^n$$

This solution is shown in Fig. 3.4-3 for various values of K. Note that if $K > 1$, the output of the network increases without bound. This is an *unstable* condition and is generally undesirable. However, if $K < 1$, the output decays. This is a *stable* condition; consequently most digital systems are designed with $K < 1$.

EXAMPLE 3.4-2 Find the output of the network of Fig. 3.4-2 if the input is a constant-amplitude unit pulse train beginning at $t = 0$. The initial condition is $y(-\Delta t) = 0$.

SOLUTION. For the unit pulse train (Fig. 3.4-4a)

$$x(n\,\Delta t) = 1 \qquad n \geq 0$$

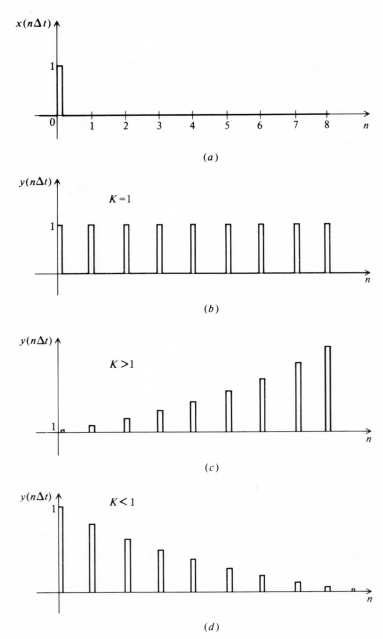

FIGURE 3.4-3
Digital-network response. (*a*) Input; (*b*) output for $K = 1$; (*c*) output for $K > 1$; (*d*) output for $K < 1$.

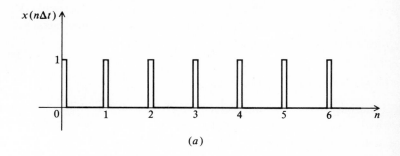

(a)

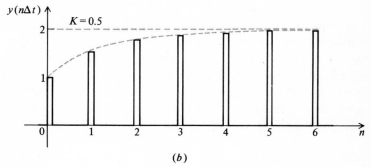

(b)

FIGURE 3.4-4
Digital-network response. (a) Constant-amplitude pulse-train input; (b) output for $K = 0.5$.

Substituting in (3.4-2), we get

$$y(0) \quad = 1$$
$$y(\Delta t) \quad = 1 + K$$
$$y(2\Delta t) = K(K + 1) + 1 = 1 + K + K^2$$
$$y(3\Delta t) = K(K^2 + K + 1) + 1 = 1 + K + K^2 + K^3$$
$$\cdots\cdots\cdots\cdots\cdots\cdots\cdots\cdots\cdots\cdots\cdots\cdots\cdots\cdots\cdots\cdots$$

Thus
$$y(n\,\Delta t) = \frac{K^{n+1} - 1}{K - 1}$$

Once again we have the possibility of instability for $|K| \geq 1$. Figure 3.4-4b shows the response for $K = 0.5$, and we see that it approaches a steady-state value, $y(n \to \infty) \to 1/(1 - K) = 2$. Thus $y(n\,\Delta t)$ increases from 1 to $1/(1 - K)$ as n increases, and a steady state is reached as long as $|K| < 1$.
////////

We have considered the response of a simple digital network to two basic signals. In the next section we shall describe the basic analog elements and consider their response to analog signals.

3.4-2   Analog Components

The basic linear analog elements are the resistor, inductor, capacitor, and current and voltage sources. In many respects their behavior is similar to the digital components described in the preceding section. However, the analog elements are not necessarily *equivalent* to the corresponding digital element.

The resistor   We are going to assume that the basic elements of interest can be considered to be "lumped," in the sense that their behavior is completely specified by the voltage and current as measured at their terminals. Refer to Fig. 3.4-5a. The circuit shown can be used to measure the *vi* characteristic of the two-terminal element. If the resulting curve is a straight line (or almost a straight line) through the origin, as shown in Fig. 3.4-5b, the element is called a *resistor*. For the straight line which we fit to the experimental points, the voltage and current are in direct proportion, and we write

$$v = Ri \qquad (3.4\text{-}3)$$

where i = current through the element, A

v = voltage across the element, V, always positive at the terminal at which i enters

R = inverse of the slope of the straight line; called *resistance*, and measured in ohms (Ω)

This is called *Ohm's law* after George Ohm, who first published this relation in 1826.

Note that the resistance can also be defined in terms of the inverse slope of the *vi* characteristic of Fig. 3.4-5b as

$$R = \frac{dv}{di} \qquad (3.4\text{-}4)$$

This definition will be used later when we consider nonlinear elements for which resistance must be defined at each point of the *vi* characteristic.

We can also describe the straight line by writing

$$i = Gv \qquad (3.4\text{-}5)$$

Here G is called the conductance, measured in mhos ($\mho$). Note that *mho* is *ohm* spelled backward and that $\mho$ is an upside-down Ω. Clearly, for a given resistance element,

$$G = \frac{1}{R} \qquad (3.4\text{-}6)$$

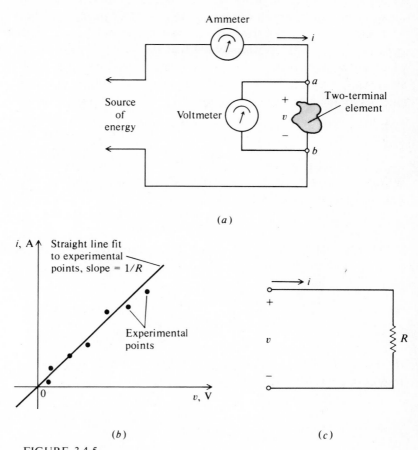

FIGURE 3.4-5
Resistance. (*a*) A circuit for measuring voltage across and current through an element; (*b*) experimental results for a resistance element; (*c*) symbol for model of a resistance.

The model   When we fit a straight line to the experimental points, we depart from the actual measured characteristic of the element in order to find a representation (the straight line) which we can describe in simple mathematical terms. The straight line is an abstraction, called a *model*. When we use the mathematical representation of the model to predict circuit behavior under different conditions, we rely on the accuracy of the model. If the model is not accurate enough, we have to refine it, sometimes by using more than one line segment, sometimes by adding other kinds of model elements, sometimes by extending the mathematics used, or by any other available means. In any case, the ultimate measure of model accuracy is determined by physical measurements in the laboratory; it cannot be determined by purely analytical means.

The circuit symbol used to represent the model for the resistance element is shown in Fig. 3.4-5c. Note carefully that the voltage is positive at the terminal at which the current enters, so that the power is always positive. Thus the resistance is an element which dissipates electric power, converting it into heat. Using (3.4-3) and (3.4-5), the power can be expressed in a variety of ways.

$$p = vi = \frac{v^2}{R} = Gv^2 = Ri^2 = \frac{i^2}{G} \qquad (3.4\text{-}7)$$

Note that if $R = 0$, we have $v = Ri = 0$, regardless of the current magnitude. We call this a *short circuit*. Similarly, if $R \to \infty$, $i = v/R \to 0$, regardless of the voltage. This is called an *open circuit*.

EXAMPLE 3.4-3   In Fig. 3.4-6, find the indicated unknowns in each circuit.

SOLUTION

(a)
$$i = \frac{v}{R} = \frac{6}{3} = 2 \text{ A}$$

$$P = i^2 R = 2^2(3) = 12 \text{ W}$$

(b) The double-subscript notation $v_{ab} = 100$ V implies that point a is positive with respect to point b. Thus

$$i = \frac{100}{20} = 5 \text{ A}$$

$$P = 5^2(20) = 500 \text{ W}$$

(c) The reference direction for i is out of the $+$ terminal. Thus

$$i = \frac{-6}{3,000} = -2 \times 10^{-3} \text{ A} = -2 \text{ mA}$$

$$P = (2 \times 10^{-3})^2(3 \times 10^3) = 12 \times 10^{-3} \text{ W} = 12 \text{ mW}$$

////////

Returning to Eq. (3.4-3), let us consider that the current i is the input signal and the voltage v is the output signal. If the input is a step function $i(t) = I_0 u(t)$, then the output is

$$v(t) = Ri(t) = RI_0 u(t)$$

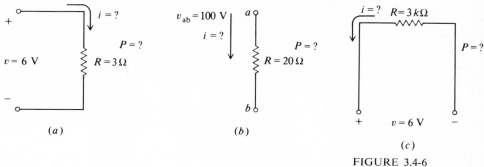

FIGURE 3.4-6
Circuits for Example 3.4-3.

Since R is a constant, this is simply a *scaled* replica of the input waveform, and a similar conclusion holds for any input waveform. Thus, in this sense, the resistance element is similar to the digital multiplier described in the preceding section. The digital multiplier has the advantage that it can multiply by a negative number, if required. It also has the further advantage of being able to attain much higher *precision* than typical analog circuits. For example, suppose we are required to multiply by 10.084. This is easily done digitally to the required number of significant figures. However, to multiply by 10.084 in an analog circuit and maintain five significant figures requires extremely sophisticated and expensive circuitry.

Sources The signals we have been discussing come from sources of energy in the form of either voltages or currents. In our networks, we use voltage- or current-source models to represent these signals.

Current sources The ideal, independent current-source model has the circuit symbol shown in Fig. 3.4-7*a*. From its *vi* characteristic, shown in Fig. 3.4-7*b*, we see that the source produces a fixed current regardless of the voltage across its terminals; i.e., the current is independent of the circuit external to the source. The ideal current source is an abstraction, as is clearly evident if we consider what happens when its terminals are open-circuited. In this case, the voltage drop across the current source is $v = Ri \rightarrow \infty$, since $R \rightarrow \infty$ and the power $p = vi \rightarrow \infty$. In a real system, infinite power is not available; so it is clear that the ideal current source must be modified before it can satisfactorily represent the model for a real current source. The required modification consists in adding a resistor permanently in parallel with the ideal source, as shown in Fig. 3.4-7*c*. When this is done, the voltage drop across the source can no longer approach infinity. The combination of an ideal current source and parallel resistor is found to model most practical current sources satisfactorily, and we shall consider its characteristics further in Sec. 4.1.

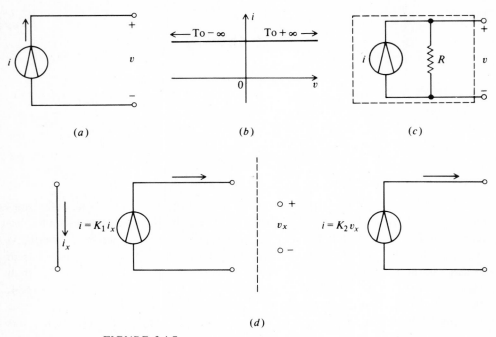

FIGURE 3.4-7
(*a*) Circuit symbol for ideal current source. (*b*) *vi* characteristic. (*c*) Practical current-source model. (*d*) Controlled current sources.

Controlled current sources   Figure 3.4-7*d* shows sources where the value of the current *i* is proportional to either a current i_x which flows in another part of the circuit or a voltage v_x across two other points in the circuit. Such sources are called *controlled* (or *dependent*) sources, since the current flowing from the source depends on a current or voltage at some other point in the circuit. This type of source arises naturally in the study of active devices such as transistors.

Voltage sources   Figure 3.4-8 shows the ideal independent voltage-source circuit symbol, the *vi* characteristic, and controlled-source representations. The polarity is always specified on the circuit symbol, and from the *vi* characteristic we see that this source maintains a fixed voltage regardless of the current required by the circuit external to the source. The ideal voltage source suffers from the same type of practical difficulty as the ideal current source. Since a resistance placed across the voltage source draws a current $i = v/R$ from the source, then if $R \to 0$, the current $i \to \infty$, resulting in theoretically infinite power.

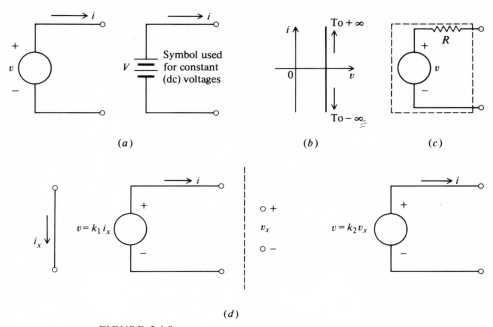

FIGURE 3.4-8
(*a*) Symbols for ideal voltage sources. (*b*) *vi* characteristics. (*c*) Model for practical voltage source. (*d*) Controlled voltage sources.

The modification required to model a practical source consists in adding a resistor permanently in series with the ideal source, as shown in Fig. 3.4-8*c*. This will be discussed further in Sec. 4.1. Controlled voltage sources are shown in Fig. 3.4-8*d*.

Inductance and capacitance   Up to this point we have considered only the resistance element, and have assumed that all *vi* curves were reasonably straight lines so that they could be modeled by linear resistors obeying Ohm's law. In an earlier section we pointed out that the resistance element dissipates electric energy in the form of heat. Now we turn our attention to capacitors and inductors, which, in their ideal form, cannot dissipate energy but can only store it.

Capacitance   An actual capacitor as used, for example, in a transistor radio, usually consists of a pair of metal plates or foil separated by an insulating material with special properties, called a *dielectric*, as shown in Fig. 3.4-9. To achieve reasonable values of capacitance, a large surface area is required; so the assembly is often rolled in cylindrical form to conserve space. If a constant voltage is applied to the terminals of the

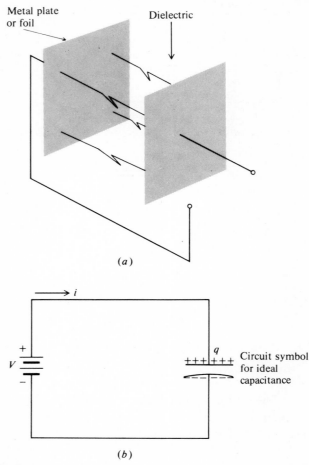

FIGURE 3.4-9
Capacitance. (*a*) Pictorial representation of a capacitor; (*b*) circuit symbol.

capacitor as in Fig. 3.4-9*b*, it is found experimentally that, after the initial instant, no current flows, and the plate connected to the positive battery terminal carries a charge $+q$, while the opposite plate carries a charge $-q$. The charge is found to be directly proportional to the voltage even if the voltage is time-varying. Thus the defining relation for the *ideal* capacitance is

$$q = Cv \qquad (3.4\text{-}8)$$

where the proportionality constant C is called the *capacitance* and is measured in farads (abbreviated F).

Charge is usually an inconvenient variable to work with in circuit analysis. If we return to the definition of current, we see that it is possible to convert (3.4-8) to the more convenient current and voltage variables. To accomplish this, we differentiate (3.4-8) with respect to time. This yields

$$\frac{dq}{dt} = C \frac{dv}{dt} \qquad (3.4\text{-}9)$$

From (3.1-1), $i = dq/dt$. Thus

$$i = C \frac{dv}{dt} \qquad (3.4\text{-}10)$$

This is the desired vi relation for the capacitor. The presence of the time derivative indicates that circuit equations involving capacitors will be differential equations rather than the simple algebraic equations we have encountered up to this point.

It is often desirable to express the voltage explicitly in terms of the current. To accomplish this, we return to (3.4-8) and write

$$v(t) = \frac{q(t)}{C} \qquad (3.4\text{-}11)$$

But

$$dq(t) = i(t)\,dt \qquad (3.4\text{-}12)$$

To find the charge at the present time t, we integrate from $t = -\infty$ to t. Thus

$$q(t) = \int_{-\infty}^{t} i(x)\,dx \qquad (3.4\text{-}13)$$

where the dummy variable x has been used instead of t on the right-hand side to avoid confusion. For convenience the integral on the right-hand side is separated into two integrals. Thus

$$q(t) = \int_{-\infty}^{0} i(x)\,dx + \int_{0}^{t} i(x)\,dx \qquad (3.4\text{-}14)$$

The first integral is a constant and represents the net charge deposited on the plates in the time interval $t = -\infty$ to $t = 0$, which we designate as Q_0. (We assume no charge at $t = -\infty$.) Finally, then,

$$q(t) = Q_0 + \int_{0}^{t} i(x)\,dx \qquad (3.4\text{-}15)$$

Substituting (3.4-15) into (3.4-11), we obtain the vi relation for the capacitor, with voltage expressed in terms of current:

$$v(t) = \frac{Q_0}{C} + \frac{1}{C} \int_{0}^{t} i(x)\,dx$$

$$= V_0 + \frac{1}{C} \int_{0}^{t} i(x)\,dx \qquad (3.4\text{-}16)$$

where
$$V_0 = \frac{Q_0}{C} = \frac{1}{C} \int_{-\infty}^{0} i(x)\, dx \quad (3.4\text{-}17)$$

represents the voltage across the capacitor at time $t = 0$.

The limits on the integral in (3.4-17) indicate that the capacitor's voltage depends on the complete past history of the current. Thus the capacitor has, in a sense, a "memory."

EXAMPLE 3.4-4a A 10-μF capacitor is to carry a constant current of 1 mA. At what rate must the voltage across it change in order that it carry this current?

SOLUTION   From (3.4-10)

$$\frac{dv}{dt} = \frac{i}{C} = \frac{10^{-3}}{10 \times 10^{-6}} = 100 \text{ V/s}$$

EXAMPLE 3.4-4b A constant current of 1 mA is applied to the positive terminal of a 10-μF capacitor which has an initial voltage of 10 V across it at $t = 0$. Find the capacitor voltage at $t = 100$ ms.

SOLUTION   From (3.4-16)

$$v(t) = V_0 + \frac{1}{C} \int_{0}^{t} i(x)\, dx$$

$$V_0 = 10 \text{ V (given)}$$
$$t = 0.1 \text{ s}$$
$$i(t) = 1 \text{ mA} = 10^{-3} \text{ A}$$
$$C = 10 \times 10^{-6} = 10^{-5} \text{ F}$$

$$v(0.1) = 10 + 10^5 \int_{0}^{0.1} 10^{-3}\, dx = 10 + \left[10^5 (10^{-3}x) \right]_{0}^{0.1} = 10 + 10^5(10^{-4})$$

$$= 10 + 10$$
$$= 20 \text{ V}$$

////////

Step-function response   In this section we consider the response of the ideal capacitor to a step function of current and a modified step function of voltage. Consider first the step of current as shown in Fig. 3.4-10a. The voltage across the capacitor, $v(t)$, is the response of this simple circuit to the current-source input. This voltage can be found using Eq. (3.4-16). Assuming $V_0 = 0$, we have $v(t) = 0$ for $t < 0$ and, for $t > 0$,

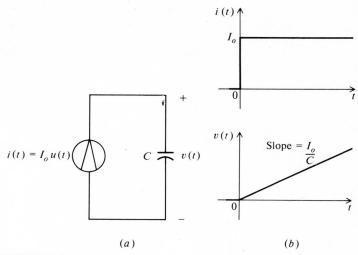

FIGURE 3.4-10
Step-function response. (*a*) Circuit; (*b*) input current and output voltage.

$$v(t) = \frac{1}{C} \int_0^t i(x)\, dx$$

$$= \frac{1}{C} \int_0^t I_0\, dx$$

$$= \frac{I_0}{C} t \qquad (3.4\text{-}18)$$

The current and voltage are sketched in Fig. 3.4-10*b*. The voltage waveform increases linearly with time, and is called a *ramp* function. Clearly, the ramp is non-physical because it theoretically increases without bound. However, ramp functions which last for a finite time are easily generated and are used to form "sawtooth" waveforms, which are often used in electronic circuits.

The student should view the voltage waveform as the *time integral* of the current waveform in this example. The voltage waveform can be obtained graphically by adding incremental areas of the current waveform while moving to the right along the time axis. Since the incremental areas under the step function are always positive, the voltage waveform continuously increases.

It is interesting to note that the constant-amplitude pulse train used as a digital input signal in Example 3.4-2 is analogous to the unit step. The output $y(n\,\Delta t)$ of the digital circuit of the example increases linearly with time for $K = 1$. Thus, for this

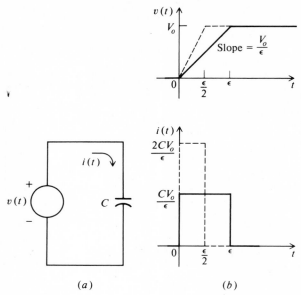

FIGURE 3.4-11
Step-function response. (*a*) Circuit; (*b*) modified voltage step input and current output.

particular value of K, the digital circuit is similar to the capacitor. In fact, the circuit of Fig. 3.4-2 is called a *digital integrator*. The capacitor with current as the input and voltage as the output is an *analog integrator*.

Now let us consider the response of the capacitor when the voltage is the input and the current is the output, as shown in Fig. 3.4-11*a*. For reasons which will shortly become apparent, we use the input-voltage waveform shown in Fig. 3.4-11*b*.

To find $i(t)$, we use (3.4-10). It is useful to do this graphically; so we plot the *slope* of $v(t)$ starting from a small negative value of t and proceeding to positive values. Before $t = 0$, the slope is zero. At $t = 0$, the slope suddenly jumps to the value V_0/ε and remains at that value until $t = \varepsilon$, at which point it suddenly drops back to zero, as shown in Fig. 3.4-11*b*. Thus the current waveform is a pulse. Now, if we reduce the voltage rise time to $\varepsilon/2$ as shown in dashed lines, the resulting current pulse will have twice the amplitude and half the width of the first pulse. If we continue to decrease the rise time of the voltage, the pulse amplitude approaches infinity and the pulse width approaches zero. If the limit exists, as $\varepsilon \to 0$, it will be the derivative of the step function. It can be shown that this limit does exist, although not in the usual mathematical sense, and it is called the impulse, or *delta function*, represented by the symbol $\delta(t)$. Thus

$$\delta(t) \equiv \frac{d}{dt} u(t) \qquad (3.4\text{-}19)$$

Although the impulse is clearly not physically realizable as a voltage or current, it is extremely important in network analysis, and indeed the response of a linear system for any input can be found if the response to an impulse is known. For experimental determination of the impulse response, it is approximated in the laboratory by a pulse having a large amplitude and a narrow width. Such a pulse is easily generated using transistor circuits to be described in Chap. 5.

It is important to note that the capacitor is a *differentiator* when voltage is the input and current is the output. The *digital differentiator* will be analyzed in Prob. 3.4-4.

Continuity conditions If the voltage across a capacitor were to have a *step* discontinuity, the current would be an impulse. Since real currents cannot be infinite, we conclude that in a real circuit the voltage across a capacitor cannot have a step discontinuity, i.e., *the voltage across a capacitor cannot change instantaneously in a real physical system.* Thus, unless infinite current is available, *the voltage across a capacitor must be continuous.*

The same conclusion can be reached by considering the physical nature of the capacitance element. To produce a change in the voltage across a capacitor, a redistribution of the charge on the plates must take place. This means that there will be actual physical motion of the charges. Since each charge has associated with it a mass, and we know that a mass cannot change its position instantaneously, we conclude that the voltage across a capacitor cannot change instantaneously.

Note that the *current through* the capacitor can change instantaneously. (What voltage waveform applied to a capacitor will produce a step change of current?)

Sine-wave response In this section we find the sine-wave response of the capacitor. Consider that the voltage is the input and is given by

$$v(t) = V_m \cos \omega t \qquad (3.4\text{-}20)$$

The current is then

$$i(t) = C \frac{dv}{dt} = -\omega C V_m \sin \omega t \qquad (3.4\text{-}21)$$

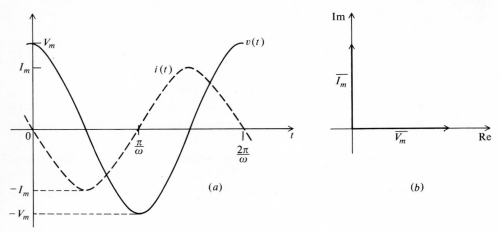

FIGURE 3.4-12
Sinusoidal response of a capacitor. (*a*) Waveforms; (*b*) phasor diagram.

The waveforms of the current and voltage are shown in Fig. 3.4-12*a*. We say that the current *leads* the voltage by 90°, or alternatively, that the voltage *lags* the current by 90°.

Now let us see how this calculation would be carried through using phasors. From (3.3-13) we have

$$v(t) = \text{Re } \overline{V}_m e^{j\omega t} \qquad (3.4\text{-}22a)$$

where the phasor voltage is

$$\overline{V}_m = V_m \angle 0° \qquad (3.4\text{-}22b)$$

The current is

$$i(t) = C\frac{d}{dt}\text{Re } \overline{V}_m e^{j\omega t}$$

$$= C \text{ Re }\frac{d}{dt}\cdot \overline{V}_m e^{j\omega t}$$

$$= \text{Re } j\omega C\overline{V}_m e^{j\omega t} \qquad (3.4\text{-}23a)$$

Thus the phasor current is

$$\overline{I}_m = j\omega C\overline{V}_m$$

$$= \omega C\overline{V}_m \angle 90° \qquad (3.4\text{-}23b)$$

Using the fact that $j = e^{j\pi/2}$, (3.4-23) becomes

$$i(t) = \text{Re } \omega C V_m e^{j(\omega t + \pi/2)}$$

$$= \omega C V_m \cos\left(\omega t + \frac{\pi}{2}\right)$$

$$= -\omega C V_m \sin \omega t \qquad (3.4\text{-}24)$$

and we get exactly the same result as in (3.4-21). Most of the steps required can be omitted if we use Ohm's law in phasor form, i.e.,

$$\overline{V}_m = Z\overline{I}_m \qquad (3.4\text{-}25)$$

where Z, called the *impedance*, has the dimension of ohms and plays the same role as resistance in our original statement of the law, except that Z is complex. The reciprocal of Z is called the *admittance* $Y = 1/Z$. Admittance has the units of mhos and is similar to conductance.

Comparing (3.4-25) with (3.4-23*b*), we find that, for the capacitor,

$$Z_c = \frac{1}{j\omega C} = -\frac{j}{\omega C} = \frac{1}{\omega C} \angle -90°$$

The phasor voltage and current are usually plotted in the complex plane as shown in Fig. 3.4-12*b*. Except for the frequency, this plot contains all the information in the time-function plot of Fig. 3.4-12*a*.

EXAMPLE 3.4-5   A 5-pF capacitor carries a current $i(t) = 2 \cos (\omega t + 30°)$ mA with $\omega = 10^6$ rad/s. Find the voltage across the capacitor in phasor form and as a time function.

SOLUTION

$$Z_c = \frac{1}{j\omega C} = \frac{1}{\omega C} \angle -90° = \frac{1 \angle -90°}{(10^6)(5)(10^{-12})} = 0.2 \times 10^6 \angle -90° \ \Omega$$

From the problem statement,

$$\overline{I}_m = 2 \times 10^{-3} \angle 30° \text{ A}$$

Then the phasor voltage is

$$\overline{V}_m = Z_c \overline{I}_m = (0.2 \times 10^6 \angle -90°)(2 \times 10^{-3} \angle 30°)$$
$$= 0.4 \times 10^3 \angle -60° \text{ V}$$

and the time function is

$$v(t) = 400 \cos(10^6 t - 60°) \qquad \text{V}$$

////////

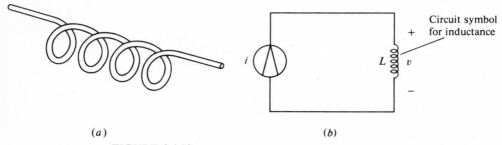

(a)   (b)

FIGURE 3.4-13
Inductance. (a) Pictorial representation of inductance element; (b) circuit symbol.

Inductance   The inductance element consists of a coil of wire, as shown in Fig. 3.4-13a. If a current i is applied to the inductance, it is found that the resulting voltage across the coil is proportional to the time rate of change of the current; i.e.,

$$v(t) = L \frac{di(t)}{dt} \qquad (3.4\text{-}26)$$

The constant L is called the *inductance* and is measured in henrys, abbreviated H.

Note the similarity to (3.4-10), which describes the capacitor. Interchanging v and i, and L and C, takes us from one relation to the other. This is an example of *duality*. Using duality, we can find $i(t)$ in terms of $v(t)$.

The expression for current in terms of voltage is [Eq. 3.4-16]

$$i(t) = I_0 + \frac{1}{L} \int_0^t v(x)\, dx \qquad (3.4\text{-}27)$$

where

$$I_0 = \frac{1}{L} \int_{-\infty}^0 v(x)\, dx \qquad (3.4\text{-}28)$$

is the current through the coil at $t = 0$. In this case, the current at $t = 0$ depends on the complete past history of the voltage across the inductor.

Because of the duality in the vi relations of the inductor and the capacitor, all the relations derived for the capacitor apply to the inductor with a simple change of symbols. Applications of the theory as applied to inductors will be left for the problems.

PROBLEMS

3.1-1   A 12-V automobile battery discharges at the rate of 300 A for 2 s in order to start the auto. If the alternator which charges the battery can provide a maximum charging current of 15 A, how long will it take to return the battery to its original condition?

3.1-2 In Prob. 3.1-1, how much power is dissipated or supplied during the charge and discharge intervals?

3.3-1 Express the waveform of Fig. P3.3-1 in terms of step functions and linear functions.

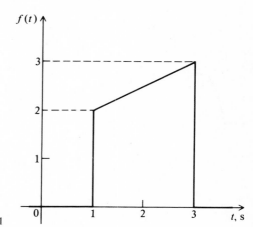

FIGURE P3.3-1

3.3-2 Sketch the functions (a) $u(t-2)$, (b) $u(2-t)$, (c) $t^2 u(t-3)$.

3.3-3 Sketch the following neatly on graph paper, carefully dimensioning both axes.

(a) $f(t) = 2 \sin\left(2\pi \times 10t - \dfrac{\pi}{6}\right)$

(b) $f(t) = 3 \times 10^{-3} \cos\left(2\pi \times 10^6 t + \dfrac{\pi}{4}\right)$

3.3-4 Consider two complex numbers
$z_1 = 4 + j3$ and $z_2 = 5 + j7$
Find analytically and graphically
(a) $z_1 + z_2$ (b) $z_1 - z_2$ (c) $3z_1 - 2z_2$

3.3-5 For z_1 and z_2 of Prob. 3.3-4, find
(a) $z_1 z_2$ (b) z_1/z_2 (c) $z_1 z_2^*$ where $z_2^* = r_2 \angle -\theta_2$
Express your answers in both polar and rectangular forms.

3.3-6 Prove Euler's identity, Eq. (3.3-9).

3.3-7 Given $z_1 = x_1 + jy_1$ and $z_2 = x_2 + jy_2$.
Find $z_1 z_2$ and z_1/z_2 in rectangular form without making use of the polar form.

3.3-8 Given two currents
$i_1(t) = 2 \times 10^{-3} \cos(2\pi \times 10^6 t - 28°)$
$i_2(t) = 3 \times 10^{-3} \cos(2\pi \times 10^6 t - 34°)$
Find $i(t) = i_1(t) + i_2(t)$ using the phasor method.

3.3-9   Show that the Fourier series of (3.3-15) can be written in the form

$$f(t) = c_0 + c_1 \sin(\omega_0 t + \theta_1) + c_2 \sin(\omega_0 t + \theta_2) + \cdots$$

and find the relations connecting c_i and θ_i to a_i and b_i.

3.3-10   Find the Fourier series, and plot amplitude spectra for the waveforms of Fig. P.3.3-10.

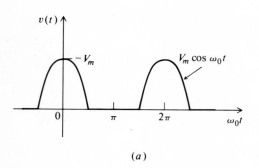

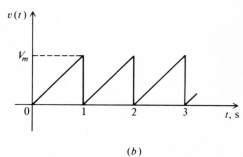

(a)   (b)

FIGURE P3.3-10

3.3-11   Prove, using Eq. (3.3-21), that the effective value of a sinusoid is $I_m/\sqrt{2}$.

3.3-12   A periodic current is given by

$$i(t) = \sqrt{2}\, I_1 \cos \omega t + \sqrt{2}\, I_2 \cos 2\omega t$$

Show that its effective value is

$$I = \sqrt{I_1{}^2 + I_2{}^2}$$

Extend this to a general current given in the form of a Fourier series.

3.4-1   Find the output of the digital network of Fig. 3.4-2 if the input is as shown in Fig. P3.4-1 and $K = \frac{1}{2}$.

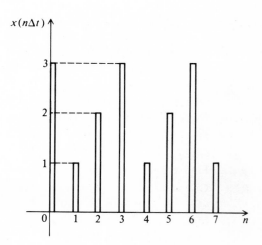

FIGURE P3.4-1

3.4-2   Repeat Prob. 3.4-1 of the circuit if Fig. P.3.4-2 is used. Compare results.

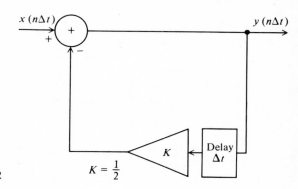

FIGURE P3.4-2

3.4-3   A light bulb is rated at 120 V, 100 W. Find the current and resistance. How much energy in kilowatthours is required to keep the bulb lit for 24 h?

3.4-4   The circuit shown in Fig. P3.4-4 is analogous to a differentiator. Show that this is so by finding the response to a constant-amplitude pulse train.

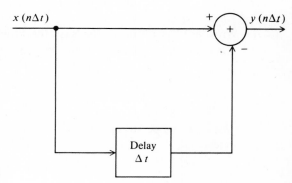

FIGURE P3.4-4

3.4-5   A 50-pF capacitor carries a total charge of 460 μC. Find the voltage across the capacitor.

3.4-6   At a certain instant of time, the voltage across a 10-μF capacitor is 20 V and is changing at the rate of 560 V/s. What is the current through the capacitor at this instant?

3.4-7   At a certain instant of time, a 1-μF capacitor is charged to 10 V. If a constant current is applied, what is the amplitude of the current that is required to increase the voltage to 100 V after 10 μs?

3.4-8   For steady-state sinusoidal calculations, the *reactance* X_c of a capacitor is defined as

$$X_c = \frac{1}{\omega C}$$

 Thus $$Z_c = -jX_c$$

Find the reactance of a 0.047-μF capacitor at 10 kHz. If a 1-V peak sine wave is applied to the capacitor, find the current.

3.4-9   The graph of Fig. P3.4-9 represents the current flowing through a 2-H inductor. Plot the resulting voltage.

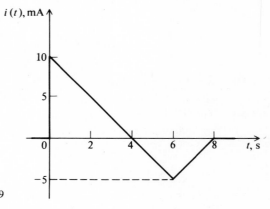

FIGURE P3.4-9

3.4-10 Write the phasor form of Ohm's law for the inductance, and use it to find the phasor voltage across a 100-mH inductor carrying a phasor current of 10 $\angle$ $-30°$ mA.

3.4-11 Using the relations

$$v = L\frac{di}{dt} \quad \text{and} \quad i = C\frac{dv}{dt}$$

explain the statement that "inductors are short circuits and capacitors are open circuits in the dc steady state, i.e., when only *constant* voltages and currents are present."

REFERENCES

HAMMOND, S. B., and D. K. GEHMLICH: "Electrical Engineering," 2d ed., McGraw-Hill Book Company, New York, 1971.

HAYT, W., and J. KEMMERLY: "Engineering Circuit Analysis," 2d ed., McGraw-Hill Book Company, New York, 1971.

SMITH, R. J.: "Circuits, Devices, and Systems," John Wiley & Sons, Inc., New York, 1966.

4

CIRCUITS AND RESPONSES

INTRODUCTION

In the preceding chapter we considered the elements that are interconnected to form both digital and analog networks and the basic signals which are applied to these networks.

In this chapter we shall consider the laws which govern the voltage and current distributions in networks. The general problem of circuit analysis consists of formulating a set of equations for the circuit under study and obtaining their solution. The solution will include all the unknown currents and voltages in the circuit. The actual mechanics of solution are more and more being handled by the digital computer. One popular computer program, ECAP, will be discussed and applied to a variety of problems. The circuits considered in Sec. 4.1 are simple enough so that computer solution is not warranted.

4.1   THE BASIC LAWS OF ELECTRIC CIRCUITS

Virtually all the theory of electric circuits is built on a foundation consisting of two laws relating to current and voltage. These laws were originally established experimentally, but have been established theoretically from basic physical principles, i.e., conservation of charge and conservation of energy. In this chapter we will accept these laws as valid and use them in our analysis of electric circuits.

In addition to these two laws involving circuit variables, we have from the preceding chapter three additional laws which govern the volt-ampere characteristics of the basic elements: resistance, capacitance, and inductance. These five laws will enable us to analyze any circuit, whether it contains only a single resistor or an entire radar transmitter.

4.1-1   The Current Law

The first law of electric circuits we consider is known as *Kirchhoff's current law* (henceforth abbreviated KCL), after Gustav Robert Kirchhoff (1824–1887), who established it experimentally. The law can be stated in a variety of ways. One way is:

> The algebraic sum of the currents entering (or leaving) a junction must add up to zero at every instant of time.

This law follows directly from the principle of conservation of charge.

We can obtain a physical "picture" of KCL by referring to Fig. 4.1-1. Here a junction has connected to it four conductors. Each conductor carries a current whose *reference direction* as indicated by the arrow is positive *into* the junction. These reference directions are chosen arbitrarily, since we have no advance knowledge of the actual directions. According to KCL as stated above, the four currents must obey the relation

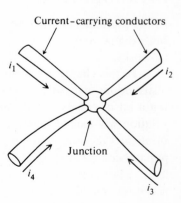

FIGURE 4.1-1
Illustrating Kirchhoff's current law.

$$\sum i = i_1 + i_2 + i_3 + i_4 = 0 \qquad (4.1\text{-}1)$$

A moment's thought will show that it is impossible for all four currents to be positive in this equation. Suppose, for example, that i_1, i_2, and i_3 are actually measured and found to be $+2$ A each. Then, from the equation, $i_4 = -i_1 - i_2 - i_3 = -6$ A; current i_4 has a magnitude of 6 A and flows *out* of the junction, i.e., in a direction opposite to its arbitrarily chosen reference direction.

4.1-2 The Voltage Law

Kirchhoff's voltage law (KVL) imposes a constraint on the voltages measured around a closed loop. As in the case of the current law, it was originally stated as a consequence of experimental observations. but it can be proved from the basic principle of conservation of energy. The law is:

The algebraic sum of the voltages around a closed loop at every instant of time is zero.

Referring to Fig. 4.1-2, the voltage v_1, for example, gives the magnitude and sign of the voltage from a to b (the *reference polarity*). Applying KVL around the loop *abc* (counterclockwise), we find, adding voltage *drops*,

$$\sum_{\substack{\text{Closed} \\ \text{loop}}} v = v_1 + v_2 - v_3 = 0 \qquad (4.1\text{-}2)$$

Suppose we trace around the loop *cba* clockwise and again add voltage drops. We then find

$$-v_2 - v_1 + v_3 = 0 \qquad (4.1\text{-}3)$$

which is identical with (4.1-2) multiplied by -1.

If double-subscript notation is used, the reference $+$ and $-$ signs on the diagram may be omitted because v_{ab} implies a drop from a to b. Again, referring to Fig. 4.1-2,

$$v_{ab} + v_{bc} + v_{ca} = 0 \qquad (4.1\text{-}4)$$

where

$$v_{ab} = v_1$$
$$v_{bc} = v_2 \qquad (4.1\text{-}5)$$
$$v_{ca} = -v_3$$

4.1-3 Applications of Kirchhoff's Laws; the Node-voltage Method

There are several ways to apply Kirchhoff's laws to networks which consist of many elements. In this section we consider the *node-voltage* method, which is based on KCL and forms the basis of several computer programs used for the solution of networks.

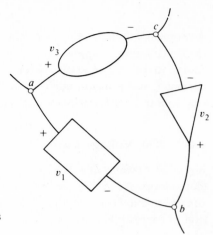

FIGURE 4.1-2
A closed loop illustrating Kirchhoff's
voltage law.

To illustrate the method, we consider the network of Fig. 4.1-3. In this network, the source and three conductances are said to be in *parallel* because they share common terminals. These terminals are called *nodes*. In this network node O is taken as the reference node (often called ground), and all voltages are arbitrarily assigned *positive* polarities with respect to it. Inspection of the circuit indicates that there is only one other node, that at *a*. We assign the voltage v_a to node *a* and tacitly understand that its *reference* polarity is positive with respect to ground. Note that v_a is shorthand for v_{a0}, the voltage drop from *a* to 0. If v_a is actually negative, our method of writing the circuit equations will automatically lead to a negative value.

Observe that there are four unknowns: the three currents i_1, i_2, and i_3 and the node voltage v_a. The known source current i enters node *a*. In accordance with Ohm's law, the currents in the three conductances are shown flowing from the *assumed* higher voltage point to the reference. It is this observance of the true current direction that ensures correct polarities in the result. In the node-voltage method, we write KCL at each independent node (not counting the reference node) in terms of the assigned node voltages and the element *vi* relations (Ohm's law), so that the node voltages are the independent variables. For the circuit of Fig. 4.1-3, we have one independent node at *a*, and KCL yields

$$i = i_1 + i_2 + i_3 \qquad (4.1\text{-}6)$$

By Ohm's law

$$i_1 = G_1 v_a \qquad i_2 = G_2 v_a \qquad i_3 = G_3 v_a \qquad (4.1\text{-}7)$$

Substituting (4.1-7) in (4.1-6), we obtain

$$i = (G_1 + G_2 + G_3)v_a \qquad (4.1\text{-}8)$$

This equation is solved for v_a, and i_1, i_2, and i_3 can be found from (4.1-7). It is interest-

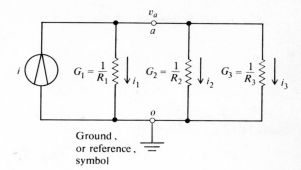

FIGURE 4.1-3
The single node-pair network.

Ground,
or reference,
symbol

ing to note that if only the voltage v_a is required, we can replace the three parallel conductances by a single conductance of value

$$G = G_1 + G_2 + G_3 \quad (4.1\text{-}9)$$

Thus G is the *equivalent conductance* connected to the source i.

In terms of *equivalent resistance*, we have, for three parallel resistances,

$$G = \frac{1}{R} = \frac{1}{R_1} + \frac{1}{R_2} + \frac{1}{R_3} \quad (4.1\text{-}10a)$$

or in general, for n parallel resistances,

$$\frac{1}{R} = \sum_{j=1}^{n} \frac{1}{R_j} \quad (4.1\text{-}10b)$$

If only two conductances were present, the equivalent conductance would be $G = G_1 + G_2$. For this case, the equivalent resistance is

$$R = \frac{1}{G} = \frac{1}{G_1 + G_2} = \frac{1}{1/R_1 + 1/R_2} = \frac{R_1 R_2}{R_1 + R_2} \quad (4.1\text{-}10c)$$

This result is used so often that it should be memorized. Henceforth we will abbreviate this result as $R = R_1 || R_2$, which should be read as "R_1 in parallel with R_2" and which implies the calculation of (4.1-10c).

EXAMPLE 4.1-1   In Fig. 4.1-3

$$i = 10 \text{ A}$$
$$G_1 = 1 \text{ ℧}$$
$$G_2 = 2 \text{ ℧}$$
$$G_3 = 0.5 \text{ ℧}$$

Find v_a and all currents.

SOLUTION   Solving (4.1-8) for v_a,

$$v_a = \frac{i}{G_1 + G_2 + G_3}$$

$$= \frac{10}{1 + 2 + 0.5} = 2.86 \text{ V}$$

Using (4.1-7),

$$i_1 = G_1 v_a = (1)(2.86) = 2.86 \text{ A}$$
$$i_2 = G_2 v_a = (2)(2.86) = 5.72 \text{ A}$$
$$i_3 = G_3 v_a = (0.5)(2.86) = 1.43 \text{ A}$$

Checking, using KCL,

$$i_1 + i_2 + i_3 = 10.01 \text{ A}$$

Note that the check is in error by 0.01 A, or 0.1 percent. This is well within slide-rule accuracy.

Another method for finding the currents proceeds as follows:
We write (4.1-8) in the form

$$v_a = \frac{i}{G_1 + G_2 + G_3} = \frac{i}{G}$$

This expression is now substituted into (4.1-7) to obtain

$$i_1 = \frac{G_1}{G} i \qquad i_2 = \frac{G_2}{G} i \qquad i_3 = \frac{G_3}{G} i \qquad (4.1\text{-}11)$$

Using these formulas (called *current-divider* formulas), the individual currents can be found without the intermediate step of finding v_a.
////////

The voltage divider   The circuit of Fig. 4.1-4*a* provides an interesting application of the node-voltage method. This circuit is used often and is called a *voltage divider*. The source v_1 and resistors R_1 and R_2 are said to be connected in *series* because the same current flows through each of them. The input is v_1, and the output is v_2. The *voltage ratio* $A_v = v_2/v_1$ is the ratio of output to input, often called the *voltage gain*, or *transfer function*. The circuit has two nodes in addition to the reference; however, only the voltage at node *b* is an independent variable, because the voltage at *a* is known. We proceed by writing KCL at the independent node *b*. Since we have no

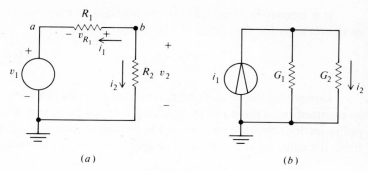

FIGURE 4.1-4
(a) The voltage divider. (b) The current divider.

advance knowledge of the relative values of the voltages, we assume i_1 in the direction shown. This fixes the reference polarity of v_{R1}. Current i_2 must flow in the indicated direction because v_2 has a positive polarity with respect to ground.

Then, at node b,

$$i_1 + i_2 = 0 \quad (4.1\text{-}12)$$

Now we must express i_1 and i_2 in terms of v_1 and v_2. For i_2, Ohm's law applies and $i_2 = v_2/R_2$. For i_1 we must be careful in applying Ohm's law to use the voltage *across* R_1, with the indicated reference polarity. (The student should work this problem assuming the reverse reference polarity for v_{R1}. The final answer must, of course, be the same.)

Thus, applying Ohm's law,

$$i_1 = \frac{v_{R1}}{R_1} = \frac{v_2 - v_1}{R_1} \quad (4.1\text{-}13)$$

Using this in (4.1-12), we obtain

$$\frac{v_2 - v_1}{R_1} + \frac{v_2}{R_2} = 0 \quad (4.1\text{-}14)$$

Collecting terms,

$$v_2\left(\frac{1}{R_1} + \frac{1}{R_2}\right) - v_1\left(\frac{1}{R_1}\right) = 0$$

Solving,

$$A_v = \frac{v_2}{v_1} = \frac{R_2}{R_1 + R_2} \quad (4.1\text{-}15)$$

It is interesting to compare the *voltage-divider* relation (4.1-15) with the *current-divider* formula for the circuit of Fig. 4.1-4b, where

$$A_i = \frac{i_2}{i_1} = \frac{G_2}{G_1 + G_2} \qquad (4.1\text{-}16)$$

Comparing the circuits and formulas (4.1-15) and (4.1-16), we note that one can be obtained from the other by replacing v by i, i by v, and R by G. As noted in an earlier section, the networks are said to be *dual* to each other, and the solution of one yields the solution of the other by simply interchanging symbols.

EXAMPLE 4.1-2   In the circuit of Fig. 4.1-4a, $R_1 = 1$ kΩ, $R_2 = 3$ kΩ, and $v_i = 20$ V. Find v_2.

SOLUTION   From (4.1-15)

$$\frac{v_2}{v_1} = \frac{3}{1+3} = \frac{3}{4}$$

Thus $v_2 = (\frac{3}{4})(20) = 15$ V.

////////

4.1-4   Equivalent Elements

In Eqs. (4.1-9) and (4.1-10) we found the equivalent resistance of any number of resistors connected in parallel. An equally important case arises when resistors are connected in series as shown in Fig. 4.1-5a. Note that the current flowing through each of the resistors must be the same in order to satisfy KCL at nodes a and b. For this case we find the equivalent resistance by applying KVL. The polarities of the voltage drops across the resistors are fixed by the direction of i as shown, so that KVL applied around the loop yields

$$-v + iR_1 + iR_2 + iR_3 = 0$$

from which the equivalent resistance is

$$\frac{v}{i} = R_{eq} = R_1 + R_2 + R_3 \qquad (4.1\text{-}17)$$

This is easily extended to any number of resistors in series.

Thus the three resistors in series are equivalent at terminals cd to a single resistance equal to the *sum* of the individual resistances.

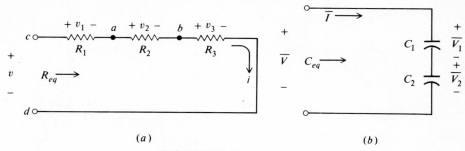

(a)   (b)

FIGURE 4.1-5
Equivalent elements. (a) Series resistors; (b) series capacitors.

Series and parallel connection of capacitors and inductors   To find the equivalent capacitance of two capacitors in series, we use KVL in phasor form. Noting Fig. 4.1-5b, we have

$$-\bar{V} + \bar{I}Z_{C1} + \bar{I}Z_{C2} = 0$$

from which

$$\frac{\bar{V}}{\bar{I}} = Z_{eq} = Z_{C1} + Z_{C2} = \frac{1}{j\omega}\left(\frac{1}{C_1} + \frac{1}{C_2}\right) = \frac{1}{j\omega C_{eq}}$$

Thus Z_{eq} is the impedance of a capacitor C_{eq}, where

$$C_{eq} = \frac{C_1 C_2}{C_1 + C_2} \qquad (4.1\text{-}18)$$

Thus capacitors in series add like resistors in parallel.

The relations for capacitors in parallel and inductors in series and parallel are given below, their derivation being left to the reader.

Capacitors in parallel: $C_{eq} = C_1 + C_2 + \cdots + C_n$

Inductors in parallel: $\dfrac{1}{L_{eq}} = \dfrac{1}{L_1} + \dfrac{1}{L_2} + \cdots + \dfrac{1}{L_n}$

Inductors in series: $L_{eq} = L_1 + L_2 + \cdots + L_n$

Equivalent sources   It is sometimes convenient to replace two or more sources by a single equivalent source. This can often be done as shown in the example which follows.

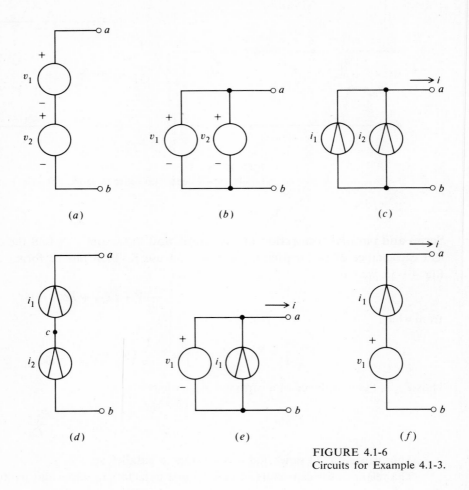

FIGURE 4.1-6
Circuits for Example 4.1-3.

EXAMPLE 4.1-3   Six possible combinations of two independent sources are shown in Fig. 4.1-6. For each configuration find, if it exists, a single source which will be indistinguishable from the two sources as far as terminals ab are concerned.

   SOLUTION   (*a*) Applying KVL, $v_{ab} = v_1 + v_2$. Thus a single voltage source of strength $v_1 + v_2$ will replace the two separate sources.
   (*b*) This situation is impossible because KVL is violated, unless $v_1 = v_2$.
   (*c*) Applying KCL at node a, $i = i_1 + i_2$. Thus a single current source of strength $i_1 + i_2$ will replace the two separate sources.
   (*d*) This situation is impossible because KCL is violated at node c, unless $i_1 = i_2$.

(e) In this circuit $v_{ab} = v_1$ regardless of the magnitude of i_1 or i. The current i is determined completely by v_1 and the circuit to be connected to the terminals. Current i_1 flows through the voltage source. Thus the current source can be removed from the circuit without affecting the behavior *at the terminals*.

(f) Here $i = i_1$, regardless of the magnitude of v_1, so v_{ab} will be determined completely by i_1 and the circuit to be connected to the terminals. Thus the voltage source can be replaced by a short circuit without affecting the terminal behavior.
////////

4.1-5 Models for Practical Sources, the Thévenin and Norton Equivalent Circuits

In this section we shall make use of KCL and KVL to find an equivalent circuit model for a *practical source* which can only be characterized by voltage and current measurements at its terminals. The equivalent circuit model can then be used to calculate in advance the effect of connecting a load to the terminals of the practical source.

Measurements made on the practical source of Fig. 4.1-7a will usually yield a set of experimental points, as shown in Fig. 4.1-7b. If these points can be approximately fitted by a straight line in a given region of the vi plane, we can derive a *linear model* from the experimental data. If one straight line will not yield an adequate fit, two or more straight lines can be used, as shown in Fig. 4.1-7c: this results in different models, each of which can be used only over the range of v and i covered by the corresponding line segment.

Consider the vi characteristic of Fig. 4.1-7b. The equation for the straight line is

$$i = mv + k \qquad (4.1\text{-}19)$$

The constant k is I_0, the intercept on the i axis when $v = 0$. This is the *short-circuit current*, since $v = 0$ implies a short circuit across the terminals. The constant m is the slope of the line, which is seen to be simply $-I_0/V_0$. We define $I_0/V_0 = G_0$ and write (4.1-19) in the form

$$i = I_0 - G_0 v \qquad (4.1\text{-}20)$$

This is the vi relation for the linear model of the practical source.

Note that we could have written the equation for the straight line in the form

$$v = m'i + k' \qquad (4.1\text{-}21)$$

Here k' is the terminal voltage V_0 when the current i is zero (this is called the *open-circuit voltage*), and m' is the slope $-V_0/I_0 = -R_0$. Then

$$v = V_0 - R_0 i \qquad (4.1\text{-}22)$$

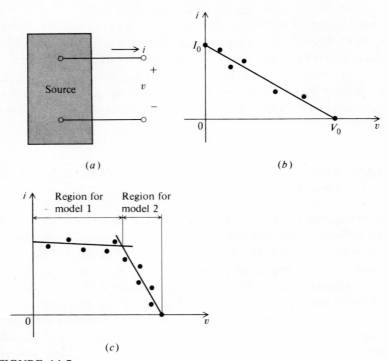

FIGURE 4.1-7
(*a*) Practical source. (*b*) *vi* characteristic approximated by a straight line. (*c*) Two-segment *vi* characteristic.

If we solve for i, there results

$$i = \frac{V_0}{R_0} - \frac{v}{R_0} \qquad (4.1\text{-}23)$$

Since (4.1-20) and (4.1-23) describe the current from the same source, they must be equal. Comparing the two equations, we find the important relations

$$I_0 = \frac{V_0}{R_0} \qquad \text{and} \qquad R_0 = \frac{1}{G_0} = \frac{V_0}{I_0} \qquad (4.1\text{-}24)$$

Now that we have the equations which describe linear mathematical models for our practical source, it ‑s useful to try to find a *circuit* model consisting of resistors and ideal sources. Consider (4.1-20) and compare it with KCL as given in (4.1-1). Each term of (4.1-20) represents a current, with i the current leaving the source. Now

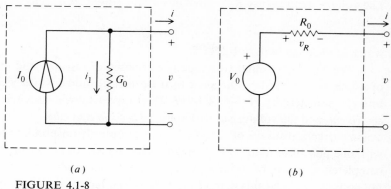

(a)   (b)

FIGURE 4.1-8
Circuit models for practical source. (a) Norton equivalent; (b) Thévenin equivalent.

consider the circuit of Fig. 4.1-8a and apply KCL at the upper node. Taking note of the reference directions on the figure, we have

$$I_0 - i_1 - i = 0$$

Rearranging,

$$i = I_0 - i_1 \qquad (4.1\text{-}25)$$

The voltage drop across G_0 is v, so that Ohm's law applies, and

$$i_1 = G_0 v$$

Thus

$$i = I_0 - G_0 v$$

which is identical with (4.1-20). The circuit enclosed in dashed lines in Fig. 4.1-8a has the same vi characteristic as the original source, and the circuits are therefore said to be equivalent as far as their external terminals are concerned. This means that if we were to enclose both circuits in "black boxes," there is no way that voltage or current measurements at the external terminals could distinguish between them.

To find a circuit model that fits (4.1-22), note that each term represents a voltage, and a *sum* of voltages is reminiscent of KVL as given by (4.1-2). Consider the circuit of Fig. 4.1-8b and apply KVL around the complete loop. Noting the reference directions on the figure and tracing the loop in a clockwise direction, adding voltage *drops* as we go around the loop,

$$-V_0 + v_R + v = 0$$

Rearranging terms,

$$v = V_0 - v_R \qquad (4.1\text{-}26)$$

The voltage drop across R_0 is, by Ohm's law, simply $R_0 i$. Thus

$$v = V_0 - R_0 i$$

which is identical with (4.1-22).

We have now found two circuits composed of resistors and ideal sources, both of which are terminally equivalent to the practical source which yielded the straight-line vi characteristic of Fig. 4.1-7b. The current-source circuit is called a *Norton equivalent*, and the voltage-source circuit a *Thévenin equivalent*. Note carefully that the original practical source of Fig. 4.1-7a was completely unspecified; it was a black box with one pair of terminals available for measurement of voltage and current. We are completely unaware of the complexity of the circuit within the box, and actually are not concerned about this complexity because we have found two circuits which yield the same terminal behavior. It is clear that the Thévenin and Norton circuits must also be terminally equivalent to each other.

It is important to note that the preceding development is quite general and shows that, for direct current, a complicated network can be replaced, as far as one pair of terminals is concerned, by an ideal source and a single resistor. This is known as Thévenin's theorem and is a powerful tool in network analysis.

EXAMPLE 4.1-4 Measurements on an automobile battery yield a short-circuit current of 200 A and an open-circuit voltage of 12 V. Find the Thévenin and Norton parameters, V_0, I_0, R_0, and G_0 for the battery.

SOLUTION From Eqs. (4.1-24), with $V_0 = 12$ V and $I_0 = 200$ A,

$$R_0 = \frac{V_0}{I_0} = \frac{12}{200} = 0.06 \ \Omega$$

$$G_0 = \frac{1}{R_0} = 16.7 \ \mho$$

EXAMPLE 4.1-5 The battery of Example 4.1-4 overheated during the short-circuit current test, and so additional data were taken. A variable resistor was connected to the battery, and the following readings were obtained:

(1) When $v = 11$ V; $i = 17$ A
(2) When $v = 6$ V; $i = 110$ A

Using these data, find V_0 and R_0, and compare with the results of Example 4.1-4.

SOLUTION   We substitute the two sets of data into (4.1-22) and solve the resulting simultaneous equations for V_0 and R_0

(1) $11 = V_0 - 17 R_0$
(2) $6 = V_0 - 110 R_0$

Solving, we find

$$R_0 = \frac{5}{93} = 0.054 \ \Omega$$

$$V_0 = 11.9 \ \text{V}$$

The worst discrepancy between the results of the two tests lies in the values of R_0, which differ by about 10 percent. The probable cause of this discrepancy is that the excessive heat caused a change in the internal resistance of the battery.
////////

4.1-6   Linearity and Superposition

In this section we present the *superposition* theorem. This is an extremely useful tool in network analysis which provides us with a simple scheme for solving networks with more than one source.

Consider that we are analyzing a network of resistors containing two current sources i_a and i_b, and that there are two unknown voltages v_a and v_b. Analysis of the network will then yield the pair of equations

$$v_a = k_1 i_a + k_2 i_b \qquad (4.1\text{-}27)$$
$$v_b = k_3 i_a + k_4 i_b \qquad (4.1\text{-}28)$$

The coefficients k_1, k_2, k_3, and k_4 depend only on the resistances in the network. If these are linear elements, whose values are independent of any current or voltage in the network, then the k's will be constants. The voltages v_a and v_b are then *linear* functions of i_a and i_b, and the network is said to be linear. One immediate consequence of the property of linearity is that the responses (v_a and v_b) are proportional to the excitations (i_a and i_b). Thus, if the excitations are both doubled, the responses will double. This is true not only of v_a and v_b, but also of all other currents and voltages in the network. This principle can be extended to a linear network of any number of resistances, and voltages as well as current sources. In the general case, the *linearity principle* states that

If all independent sources are multiplied by a constant, then all the responses (dependent variables) in the network will be multiplied by the same constant.

In mathematical terms, the response at any point is called a *homogeneous* function of the sources. For example, consider a network with sources i_a, i_b, v_a, v_b and response i_1. Then, in general,

$$i_1 = f(i_a, i_b, v_a, v_b) \qquad (4.1\text{-}29)$$

If now all sources are multiplied by a constant c, then the new current will be i_1', where

$$i_1' = f(ci_a, ci_b, cv_a, cv_b) \qquad (4.1\text{-}30)$$

Since the network is assumed to be linear, the constant c will factor out of the right-hand side of (4.1-30), yielding

$$\begin{aligned} i_1' &= cf(i_a, i_b, v_a, v_b) \\ &= ci_1 \end{aligned} \qquad (4.1\text{-}31)$$

Thus the response is multiplied by the same constant as the sources.

Returning to the response equation (4.1-27), let us consider each source separately. If we pretend to open-circuit the current sources one at a time so that first i_b is zero and then i_a, we have

$$v_a' = v_a|_{i_b=0} = k_1 i_a \qquad (4.1\text{-}32)$$
$$v_a'' = v_a|_{i_a=0} = k_2 i_b \qquad (4.1\text{-}33)$$

Adding these two equations,

$$\begin{aligned} v_a' + v_a'' &= k_1 i_a + k_2 i_b \\ &= v_a \end{aligned} \qquad (4.1\text{-}34)$$

Thus the response v_a can be found as the *sum* of two components, each due to one source *acting alone*, the other being set to zero. This is the principle of superposition applied to the network under consideration. Its great utility lies in the fact that it reduces a complicated problem to a series of simpler problems. A general statement of the *superposition principle* is as follows:

> In a linear network containing more than one independent source (current or voltage), any response can be found by adding the responses due to each source acting alone, all others being set to zero (short circuits for voltage sources, open circuits for current sources).

The utility of this theorem is demonstrated in the examples which follow.

EXAMPLE 4.1-6   In the circuit of Fig. 4.1-9a, v_1 and i_1 are independent sources. Find the response v_2 by two methods: (*a*) application of the superposition theorem, and (*b*) successive Thévenin-Norton conversion.

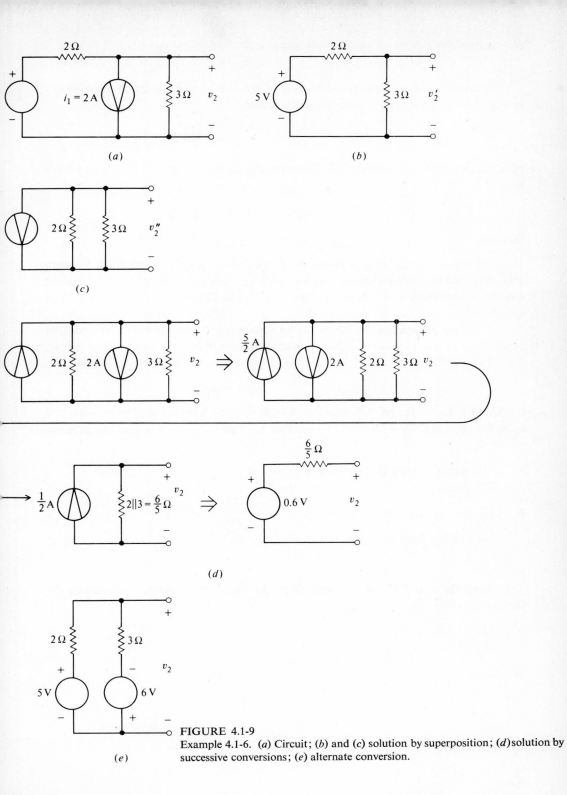

FIGURE 4.1-9
Example 4.1-6. (a) Circuit; (b) and (c) solution by superposition; (d)solution by successive conversions; (e) alternate conversion.

SOLUTION   (a) v_2' is the response to v_1 with $i_1 = 0$. The resulting circuit is shown in Fig. 4.1-9b. Using the voltage-divider formula

$$v_2' = 5\left(\frac{3}{2+3}\right) = 3 \text{ V}$$

v_2'' is the response to i_1 with $v_1 = 0$. The circuit is shown in Fig. 4.1-9c. Using Ohm's law,

$$v_2'' = -2(2 \| 3) = -2 \times \tfrac{6}{5} = -\tfrac{12}{5} \text{ V}$$

Finally,
$$v_2 = v_2' + v_2'' = 3 - \tfrac{12}{5} = 0.6 \text{ V}$$

(b) There are two ways to attack the successive-conversion solution. If we begin by converting the voltage source and the series resistance to their Norton equivalent circuit, the sequence is as shown in Fig. 4.1-9d. The final step shows $v_2 = 0.6$ V, as expected.

If, on the other hand, we had begun by converting the current source and parallel resistance to their Thévenin equivalent circuit, we arrive at the circuit of Fig. 4.1-9e. To find v_2 by further conversion would lead directly to the sequence of Fig. 4.1-9d.

EXAMPLE 4.1-7   In the circuit of Fig. 4.1-10, v_1 and i_1 are independent sources, and v_2 is the response. A voltmeter is connected to read v_2, and the following data are observed:

(1) When $v_1 = 10$ V and $i_1 = 1$ A; $v_2 = 5$ V
(2) When $v_1 = 0$ V and $i_1 = 1$ A; $v_2 = 3$ V

Find v_2 when $v_1 = 6$ V and $i_1 = 10$ A.

SOLUTION   Since the network is linear, we can write

$$v_2 = Av_1 + Bi_1$$

The constants A and B can be found from the experimental data. Substituting the measured values,

(1) $5 = 10A + 1B$
(2) $3 = 0A + 1B$

Solving, $B = 3 \quad \text{and} \quad A = \tfrac{1}{5}$

Thus

$$v_2 = \frac{v_1}{5} + 3i_1$$

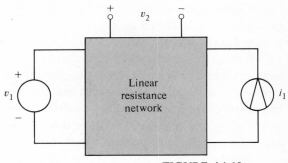

FIGURE 4.1-10
Circuit for Example 4.1-7.

For the desired conditions, $v_1 = 6$ V and $i_1 = 10$ A, we get

$$v_2 = \tfrac{6}{5} + 30 = 31.2 \text{ V}$$

////////

4.2   CIRCUIT RESPONSES

Circuit-analysis problems usually fall into one of two classifications: steady state or transient. Under the heading of steady-state calculations we have response to dc sources and to sinusoidal sources. The two problems are handled in much the same way, the difference being that the sinusoidal steady-state response involves the use of phasors and complex impedances rather than simply constant currents, voltages, and resistances, as in the dc case. The steady-state sinusoidal response leads naturally to the *frequency response*, i.e., the variation of amplitude and phase as a function of frequency. This is often used as a specification for the design of networks.

Under the heading of transient response, we have the response to a step function and other aperiodic signals.

In the following sections, we shall consider the more important of these types of response as applied to relatively simple networks. In all cases numerical calculations will be carried through using the ECAP digital computer program.

4.2-1   ECAP, the IBM Electronic Circuit Analysis Program

The ECAP program utilizes the large data-handling capability and speed of the digital computer to reduce the solution of a large class of network-analysis problems to the point where the engineer does little more than convert the schematic diagram of the circuit under study to a standard ECAP equivalent circuit form. The information from this circuit is transferred to a coding sheet, using the ECAP language, and then to punched cards. When the computer receives the information from the card deck, the ECAP program automatically formulates the network node equations, obtains their solution, and prints or otherwise displays the results. Using ECAP, the drudgery involved in setting up the equations and solving them is done by the computer. The engineer receives a printout of the results, and can thus spend his time more profitably interpreting and utilizing them. The time saving becomes even more dramatic when one is informed that ECAP can handle networks with as many as 50 nodes!

The program not only solves very complicated problems, but can also be used to determine changes in the currents and voltages when the circuit elements vary. With this capability the program can be used to find element values which will lead to a specified voltage or current. This is extremely important in practice, where element values and other parameters are seldom known accurately.

In this section we present a brief introduction to the language of ECAP and an example of its use in the analysis of networks containing resistors and dc current and voltage sources. The user of ECAP does not have to be concerned with the internal mechanics of the program, but he must know the ECAP language so that he can communicate with the computer.

The ECAP standard branch (simplified)   The circuit *branch* is the basic unit in ECAP analysis. As we shall see, the programmer completely specifies all the circuit branches, and the program automatically formulates and solves the node equations from this information.

To ensure uniformity, a *standard branch* is specified for use with ECAP, a simplified form of which is shown in Fig. 4.2-1. (The complete standard branch differs from the simplified version in that it includes controlled sources.) The simplified branch *must* contain a resistance and *may* contain independent current and/or voltage sources.

The various features in the diagram are:

Branches   Each branch b contains a resistance R, or conductance G, which must be nonzero. If independent sources are present, they are designated by E and/or I as shown.[1] The branches may be numbered in any order, using consecutive numbers beginning with 1. The branch number b is placed in a box, with an arrow on the box indicating the preassigned positive current direction.

Nodes and node voltages   Nodes are numbered in any order, using consecutive numbers beginning with 0 (d and e in the figure). The program always assumes

---

[1] We have been using the symbol V for voltage sources up to now, but must use E for ECAP.

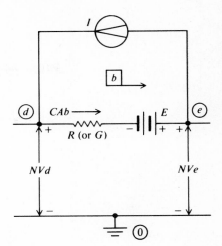

FIGURE 4.2-1
The simplified ECAP standard branch.

that node 0 is the reference (or ground) node. To distinguish node numbers from branch numbers, node numbers should be encircled.

Node voltages are specified with respect to ground (node 0) as NVd and NVe in the figure.

Element currents   The element current in branch b (designated CAb in the figure) is the current flowing through R from the initial node d to the final node e. Note that the choice of current direction determines which is the initial and which the final node. The choice of current direction is arbitrary but should, to avoid minus signs, correspond to actual current directions if they are known in advance.

To prepare a circuit for ECAP analysis, simply number all branches and nodes and choose assumed current directions on the circuit diagram. This information is transferred to a standard coding sheet and then to punched cards. The procedure is illustrated in the example which follows.

EXAMPLE 4.2-1   Analyze the circuit of Fig. 4.2-2*a* using ECAP.

SOLUTION   The ECAP circuit is shown in Fig. 4.2-2*b*. The circuit contains four branches, one of which contains a voltage source, and one a current source. There are two independent nodes, 1 and 2.

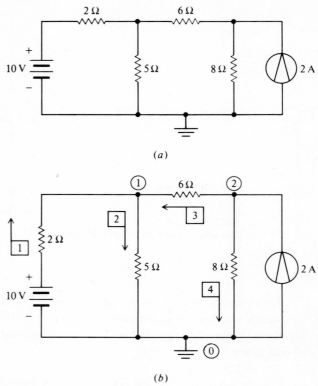

FIGURE 4.2-2
(*a*) Circuit to be analyzed for Example 4.2-1. (*b*) Circuit prepared for ECAP.

The coding sheet is shown in Fig. 4.2-3, and an explanation of the numbered lines of input data on the sheet follows.

Line 1   Several cards are usually required by the computer center to identify the user, program desired (ECAP in this case), etc.

Line 2   A command statement which tells the computer that an ECAP dc analysis is desired.

Line 3   The letter *c* in column 1 specifies a comment card. Any comment on this line is printed as part of the output but has no other effect. As many comment cards as desired may be used anywhere in the program. The comment printed on line 3 identifies the example number. A blank comment card is inserted after line 5 to provide a space in the printout.

Line 4   Specifies branch 1: initial node 0, final node 1, resistance of 2 Ω, and voltage source of 10 V. If the voltage source were reversed, we would write $E = -10$.

An easy way to determine the proper sign for a branch voltage source is to pretend to *short-circuit* the branch. If the resulting current flow through the resistance is in the same direction as the preassigned reference arrow, the sign is positive; otherwise it is negative. For branch current sources, we pretend to *open-circuit* the branch.

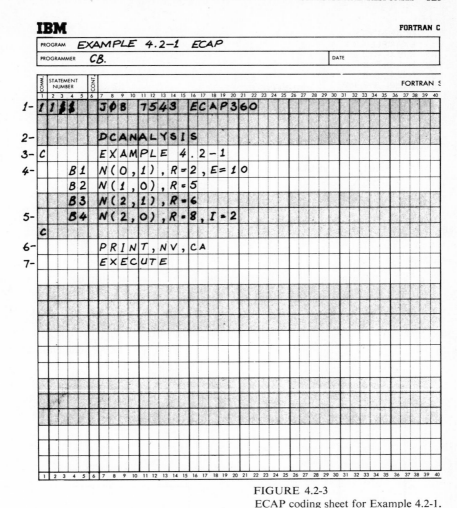

FIGURE 4.2-3
ECAP coding sheet for Example 4.2-1.

If the current from the branch source flows through the resistance in the same direction as the preassigned reference arrow, it is positive; otherwise it is negative.

Line 5 Specifies branch 4: initial node 2, final node 0, resistance of 8 Ω, current source of 2 A. If the current source were reversed, we would write $I = -2$.

Line 6 Indicates that all node voltages and element currents are to be printed as the output.

Line 7 Command statement indicating that the program is to be executed.

Figure 4.2-4 shows the computer printout. The node voltages and branch currents are listed in rows according to the numbering scheme used on the ECAP circuit. All numerical answers are in standard computer "floating-point" form. The

```
        DCANALYSIS
C       EXAMPLE 4.2-1
   B1   N (0,1), R=2, E=10
   B2   N (1,0), R=5
   B3   N (2,1), R=6
   B4   N (2,0), R=8, I=2
C
        PRINT, NV, CA
        EXECUTE
```

NODE VOLTAGES

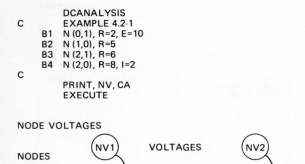

NODES   NV1   VOLTAGES   NV2

  1— 2   0.79629630D 01   0.11407408D 02

ELEMENT CURRENTS

BRANCHES

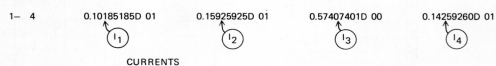

  1— 4   0.10185185D 01   0.15925925D 01   0.57407401D 00   0.14259260D 01

                                    I_1 I_2 I_3 I_4

                        CURRENTS

FIGURE 4.2-4
ECAP solution to Example 4.2-1.

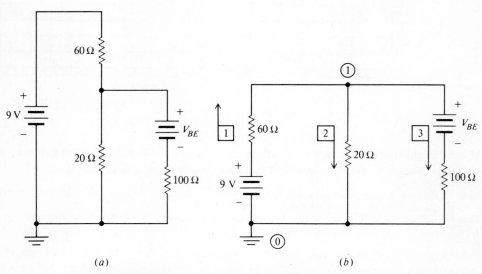

(a)   (b)

FIGURE 4.2-5
(a) Circuit to be analyzed for Example 4.2-2.   (b) Circuit prepared for ECAP.

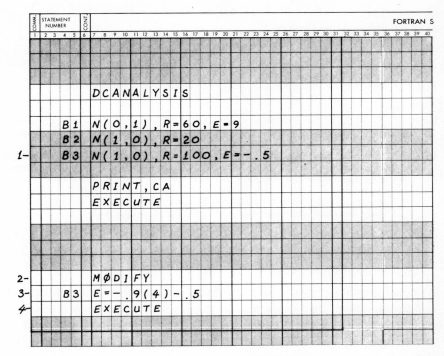

FIGURE 4.2-6
ECAP coding sheet for Example 4.2-2.

number following the D (sometimes E is used) indicates the power of 10 by which the number preceding the D is to be multiplied. Thus $I_4 = 0.14259260\ D\ 01 = 1.425926 \approx 1.43$ A.

EXAMPLE 4.2-2   This example illustrates the ECAP program's capability of changing element values in a circuit so that the effects can be evaluated. The circuit shown in Fig. 4.2-5a represents a circuit model for a transistor amplifier in which the voltage V_{BE} is a function of temperature. The effect of variations in V_{BE} on the current in the 100-Ω resistor is to be determined for values of V_{BE} in the range 0.5 to 0.9 V, in increments of 0.1 V. Provision for this is available in the ECAP MODIFY routine. The ECAP circuit is shown in Fig. 4.2-5b, and the coding sheet in Fig. 4.2-6. Noting the coding sheet, we see that a conventional analysis is done first, and then the MODIFY command given, with the desired changes. The steps which differ from the preceding example are explained below.

Line 1   Here the sign of V_{BE} is negative to be consistent with the assigned current direction in branch 3. (See Example 4.2-1 for an explanation of the signs to be used for branch voltage and current sources.)

Line 2   Commands the computer to modify the immediately preceding routine in accordance with the succeeding instructions. Up to 50 parameters may be changed, and the new solutions computed.

Line 3   Specifies the desired modification in branch 3. This type of modification is called *parameter iteration*, and the program automatically computes the solution for four equal steps between -0.9 and -0.5 V.

Line 4   Commands the computer to execute the program. The PRINT command is not required again unless it is desired to print more data than were requested in the original routine. Figure 4.2-7 shows the computer printout for this example. Note that $E = -0.9$ in the first iteration is carried through the computer as $E = -0.89999998$. This is because the computer operates in the binary system and cannot represent decimal numbers exactly. Clearly, the error involved is negligible for all practical purposes.

////////

4.2-2 AC Analysis

As noted previously, steady-state ac calculations are carried through basically like dc calculations except that all the quantities dealt with are complex rather than real, so that both magnitudes and angles must be found (Example 3.4-5). The arithmetic can become very tedious, and the chance of making an error becomes high when the slide rule is used.

The ECAP program can be used to perform steady-state ac analysis of circuits in essentially the same manner as it does for dc circuits. We illustrate this by means of the example which follows.

```
:
        DCANALYSIS
:
    B1  N(0,1),R=60,E=9
    B2  N(1,0),R=20
    B3  N(1,0),R=1C0,E=-.5
:
        PRINT,CA
        EXECUTE


ELEMENT CURRENTS


    BRANCHES              CURRENTS

      1-  3       0.11630434D 00      0.10108694D 00      0.15217387D-01
```

FIGURE 4.2-7

Computer printout for Example 4.2-2.

```
C
C
      MODIFY
   B3 E=-.9(4)-.5
      EXECUTE


E    = -0.89999998E 00

ELEMENT CURRENTS

BRANCHES            CURRENTS

   1-  3      0.11543478D 00      0.10369564D 00      0.11739126D-01

E    = -0.80000001E 00

ELEMENT CURRENTS

BRANCHES            CURRENTS

   1-  3      0.11565217D 00      0.10304346D 00      0.12608691D-01

E    = -0.70000005E 00

ELEMENT CURRENTS

BRANCHES            CURRENTS

   1-  3      0.11586956D 00      0.10239129D 00      0.13478256D-01

E    = -0.60000008E 00

ELEMENT CURRENTS

BRANCHES            CURRENTS

   1-  3      0.11608695D 00      0.10173912D 00      0.14347820D-01

E    = -0.50000012E 00

ELEMENT CURRENTS

BRANCHES            CURRENTS


   1-  3      0.11630434D 00      0.10108694D 00      0.15217385D-01
```

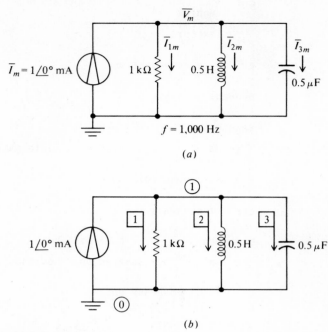

FIGURE 4.2-8
ECAP ac analysis. (a) Circuit for Example 4.2-3; (b) ECAP circuit.

EXAMPLE 4.2-3   Use ECAP to find the node voltage and branch currents in the circuit of Fig. 4.2-8a.

SOLUTION   Again an ECAP circuit with previously described branch and node numbering is prepared, as shown in Fig. 4.2-8b. The printout which includes the program is shown in Fig. 4.2-9a, and differences between it and previous examples are as follows:

Line 1   Tells the computer that an ECAP ac analysis is desired.
Line 2   The resistor and current source constitute branch 1. The resistance value is given in standard computer floating-point form. The number following the E indicates the power of 10 by which the number preceding the E is to be multiplied. Thus $R = 1E03$ means $R = 1 \times 10^3$ ($= 1$ kΩ). The current source is specified as $1E - 03 = 1 \times 10^{-3}$ A in magnitude followed by a slash (/) and a phase angle of zero degrees. The phase angle of all sources *must* be specified (in degrees) even if they are zero.
Line 3   Floating-point notation is used to specify the capacitance

$$C = 0.5E - 06 = 0.5 \times 10^{-6} = 0.5 \ \mu F$$

Line 4   A frequency card must be included for ac analysis. The frequency must be nonzero and is specified in units of hertz.

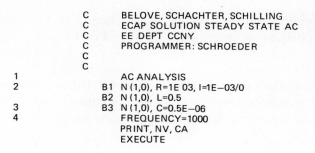

```
C        BELOVE, SCHACHTER, SCHILLING
C        ECAP SOLUTION STEADY STATE AC
C        EE DEPT CCNY
C        PROGRAMMER: SCHROEDER
C
C
1        AC ANALYSIS
2        B1  N (1,0), R=1E 03, I=1E-03/0
         B2  N (1,0), L=0.5
3        B3  N (1,0), C=0.5E-06
4            FREQUENCY=1000
             PRINT, NV, CA
             EXECUTE


FREQ = 0.99999976E 03



             NODES              NODE VOLTAGES

MAG     1—  1    0.33387309E 00
PHA             —0.70495956E 02



        BRANCHES            ELEMENT CURRENTS

MAG     1—  3    0.33387309E-03   0.10627507E-03   0.10488930E-02
PHA             —0.70495956E 02 —0.16049594E 03   0.19504013E 02
```

(a)

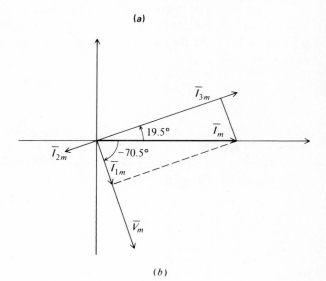

(b)

FIGURE 4.2-9
ECAP ac analysis. (a) Computer printout for Example 4.2-3; (b) phasor diagram.

The results printed after the program include both magnitude and phase (in degrees). A phasor diagram of the results is shown in Fig. 4.2-9b.

////////

The ECAP ac analysis program has the same MODIFY capability as the dc analysis. In addition, the frequency can be varied in either a logarithmic or linear manner. This will be considered further when we study frequency response, in the next section.

4.2-3   Frequency Response

Very few signals of practical importance are pure sine waves. Most signals contain many frequency components, usually concentrated in a certain frequency band. By using a generalized Fourier analysis, similar to the analysis presented in Sec. 3.3-4, it has been found, for example, that human speech can be adequately represented as the sum of sine waves of many frequencies, in the range from about 100 to 3,300 Hz. Thus it is important to determine how circuits respond to all frequencies in order to find their effect on the signal.

Consider the circuit of Fig. 4.2-10a. This represents the simplest possible *low-pass filter*, a circuit that passes low frequencies and rejects high frequencies. Our objective is to display and interpret the response of this circuit to signals of different frequencies.

The quantity of interest is the ratio of output voltage to input voltage expressed as a function of frequency. This is called the *transfer function H(jω)*. To find the transfer function for the circuit, we apply the voltage-divider relation in phasor form as follows:

$$\frac{\overline{V}_{2m}}{\overline{V}_{1m}} = H(j\omega) = \frac{Z_C}{R + Z_C} = \frac{1/j\omega C}{R + 1/j\omega C}$$

$$= \frac{1}{1 + j\omega RC} = \frac{1}{1 + j\omega/\omega_1} \qquad (4.2\text{-}1)$$

where $\omega_1 = 1/RC$.

To exhibit the frequency dependence of this equation, we first manipulate it so as to separate the amplitude and phase. Thus, using the polar form

$$H(j\omega) = |H(\omega)| \angle \theta \qquad (4.2\text{-}2a)$$

we have

$$|H| = \frac{1}{\sqrt{1 + (\omega/\omega_1)^2}} \qquad (4.2\text{-}2b)$$

and

$$\theta = -\arctan \frac{\omega}{\omega_1} \qquad (4.2\text{-}2c)$$

It is important to understand the meaning of these equations. Equation (4.2-2b) gives the amplitude response, i.e., the ratio of the output sine-wave amplitude to the input sine-wave amplitude (both at angular frequency ω), and (4.2-2c) is the phase

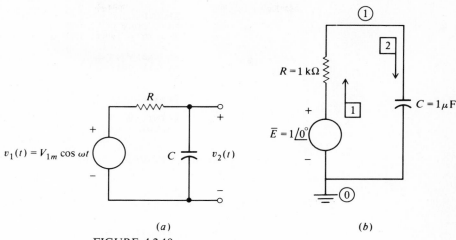

FIGURE 4.2-10
ECAP frequency response. (*a*) Circuit for Example 4.2-4; (*b*) ECAP circuit.

response, i.e., the phase difference between the output and the input sine waves. These two quantities are usually plotted against frequency on a logarithmic scale. We shall postpone this plotting for the ECAP example to be presented next.

EXAMPLE 4.2-4 Use the ECAP program to determine the frequency response (amplitude and phase) of the circuit of Fig. 4.2-10*a* with $R = 1$ kΩ and $C = 1$ μF. Cover the frequency range 40 to 300 Hz and plot the results on a logarithmic frequency scale.

SOLUTION The ECAP circuit is shown in Fig. 4.2-10*b*, and the program in Fig. 4.2-11*a*. The only significant difference between this and Example 4.2-3 is the MODIFY routine, which requests a frequency iteration, i.e., a calculation repeated at different frequencies. Two types of iteration are available:

Multiplicative This is used for *logarithmic* frequency response. An example of the required frequency modification card is

$$\text{FREQ} = 40 \ (1.1) \ 300$$

Here 40 Hz is the lower frequency limit, and 300 Hz the upper limit. The number 1.1 in parentheses is a *multiplication* factor. This card requests calculation at the frequencies 40 Hz, (1.1)(40) Hz, $(1.1)^2(40)$ Hz, $(1.1)^3(40)$ Hz, ..., up to the nearest step greater than 300 Hz.

Additive This is used for *linear* frequency response calculation as in this example. The frequency card is shown in Fig. 4.2-11*b* after the MODIFY card. The

```
C       BELOVE, SCHACHTER, SCHILLING
C       FREQUENCY RESPONSE
C       NEW YORK INSTITUTE OF TECHNOLOGY
C
        AC ANALYSIS
    B1 N(0,1),R=1E 03,E=1E 00/0
    B2 N(1,0),C=1F-06
C
        FREQUENCY=40
C
        PRINT,NV
        EXECUTE


FREQ =  0.40000000E 02



        NODES              NODE VOLTAGES


MAG     1-  1  0.96983886E 00
PHA            -0.14107789E 02
```

                            (a)

```
C
C
        MODIFY
        FREQUENCY=40(+13)300
        EXECUTE


FREQ =  0.40000000E 02



        NODES              NODE VOLTAGES


MAG     1-  1  0.96983886E 00
PHA            -0.14107789E 02


FREQ =  0.59999985E 02



        NODES              NODE VOLTAGES


MAG     1-  1  0.93571538E 00
PHA            -0.20655960E 02
```

                            (b)

FIGURE 4.2-11
Example 4.2-4. (*a*) Program; (*b*) partial printout.

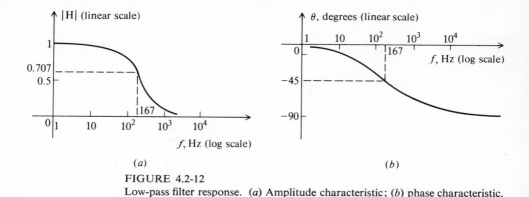

FIGURE 4.2-12
Low-pass filter response. (*a*) Amplitude characteristic; (*b*) phase characteristic.

lower frequency limit is 40 Hz, and the upper limit is 300 Hz. The +13 in parentheses requests calculations in 13 equal frequency steps between 40 and 300 Hz, i.e., at intervals of 20 Hz.

Note that the presence or absence of the plus (+) sign in the parentheses tells the computer which type of iteration is desired.

A partial printout is shown in Fig. 4.2-11*b*, and a plot of the results is shown in Fig. 4.2-12 using semilog coordinates.

To compare different low-pass filters we define a *cutoff frequency* which separates those frequencies which are *passed* from those which are *rejected*. The cutoff frequency is defined as the frequency at which the amplitude response is $1/\sqrt{2}$ times its low-frequency value. This is often referred to as the "half-power" frequency because, if the voltage is $1/\sqrt{2}$ times the low-frequency value, the power is $\frac{1}{2}$ times the low-frequency value. From (4.2-2*b*) we have, at the cutoff frequency,

$$\frac{1}{\sqrt{2}} = \frac{1}{\sqrt{1 + (\omega/\omega_1)^2}}$$

Solving, we find the cutoff frequency at $\omega = \omega_1 = 1/RC$. For the response of Fig. 4.2-12, the cutoff frequency is 1,000 rad/s, or 167 Hz. From the amplitude plot of Fig. 4.2-12, we see there is no sharp distinction between those frequencies which are passed and those which are rejected for this simple filter. However, the cutoff frequency does provide a useful means for categorizing low-pass filters. The frequency range between zero frequency (dc) and the cutoff frequency is called the *bandwidth B* of the filter. For the filter of Example 4.2-4 the bandwidth is

$$2\pi B = \omega_1 = \frac{1}{RC} = 1{,}000 \text{ rad/s}$$

$$B = 167 \text{ Hz} \qquad (4.2\text{-}3)$$

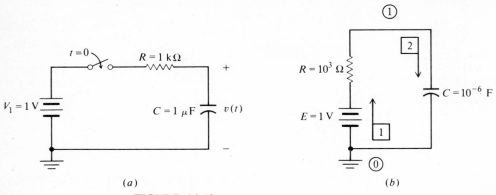

FIGURE 4.2-13
ECAP transient analysis. (a) Circuit for Example 4.2-5; (b) ECAP circuit.

4.2-4 Transient Response

In the last section we considered the response of a circuit to sine waves of different frequencies. This is a convenient method of analysis when the signals of interest are described in terms of sine waves, as, for example, by a Fourier series, and is called *frequency-domain* analysis.

As noted in Sec. 3.3, another important class of signals are nonperiodic in nature, e.g., step functions. When considering the circuit response to such signals, we use transient analysis, often called *time-domain* analysis. This involves the solution of the circuit differential equation.

Consider the low-pass-filter circuit of Fig. 4.2-13a. With the capacitor initially uncharged, the switch is closed at time $t = 0$. This applies a step function of 1 V to the *RC* circuit. We wish to find the voltage across the capacitor after the switch is closed, i.e., for $t > 0$. Since, as noted in Sec. 3.4-2, capacitor voltage must be continuous, the voltage just *after* the switch is thrown remains at 0.

To analyze the network, we write a node equation which holds for $t > 0$ as follows:

$$C\frac{dv}{dt} + \frac{v - V_1}{R} = 0 \qquad (4.2\text{-}4)$$

We also have the known initial condition $v(0) = 0$. Equation (4.2-4) is a *first-order linear differential equation*. Its solution can be shown to be, for $t > 0$,

$$v(t) = V_1(1 - e^{-t/\tau}) \qquad (4.2\text{-}5)$$

where $\tau = RC$ is called the *time constant* of the circuit. We shall discuss the physical interpretation of (4.2-5) after the following example, in which the numerical solution is obtained using ECAP.

EXAMPLE 4.2-5   Find the response of the circuit of Fig. 4.2-13a using the ECAP transient analysis capability. Plot the results.

SOLUTION   As in all other ECAP problems, the first step is to draw an ECAP circuit, as shown in Fig. 4.2-13b, with appropriate branch and node numbering. The program and printout are shown in Fig. 4.2-14. Those parts of the program which differ from previous examples are as follows:

Line 1   Command statement calling for ECAP transient analysis.
Line 2   The $E = 1$ value specifies a step function $E = 1u(t)$, which is equivalent to the switching operation indicated in Fig. 4.2-13a.
Line 3   The time step is the Δt interval used by the program (Sec. 2.9). In this example it is chosen to be 10 μs, which is $\frac{1}{100}$ of the circuit time constant. This ratio of $\Delta t/T$ usually provides sufficien t accuracy.
Line 4   This specification tells the computer to print the results at intervals of 50 time steps, i.e., every 0.5 ms.
Line 5   This tells the computer that the last calculation should be made at $t = 5$ ms. This choice is made because we know the transient will essentially disappear after four or five time constants.
Line 6   Since NV1 is the only required response, we indicate that only node voltages are to be printed.

A plot of the results is shown in Fig. 4.2-15a.

It should be noted that the ECAP transient analysis program does not have the MODIFY capability that the dc program has. However, it is capable of handling source waveforms of much greater complexity than the step function used in this example.

/////////

The waveform of Fig. 4.2-15a as determined by the ECAP program is, as expected, a plot of Eq. (4.2-5). To interpret the solution physically, we separate it into two parts. Referring to (4.2-5), the first part consists of the constant term V_1. This is called the *steady-state* part of the solution, and we write

$$v_{ss}(t) = V_1 \qquad (4.2-6)$$

The second part of the solution, called the *transient*, is

$$v_{tr}(t) = -V_1 e^{-t/\tau} \qquad (4.2-7)$$

These are plotted separately in Fig. 4.2-15b.

The physical significance of the steady-state voltage is that it is the value which the output voltage assumes as $t \to \infty$. Thus, since the initial voltage is known to be

```
C        BELOVE, SCHACHTER, SCHILLING
C        TRANSIENT RESPONSE
C        NEW YORK INSTITUTE OF TECHNOLOGY
C
C
1 →      TRANSIENT ANALYSIS
C
2 →   B1 N(0,1),R=1E 03,E=1
      B2 N(1,0),C=1E-06
C
C
3 →      TIME STEP=1E-05
4 →      OUTPUT INTERVAL=50
5 →      FINAL TIME=5E-03
6 →      PRINT,NV
         EXECUTE
```

T =   0.0

NODES   NODE VOLTAGES

  1-   1   0.99998970E-05

T =   0.4999957E-03

NODES   NODE VOLTAGES

  1-   1   0.39196748E 00

T =   0.9999878E-03

NODES   NODE VOLTAGES

  1-   1   0.63029277E 00

T =   0.1499980E-02

NODES   NODE VOLTAGES

  1-   1   0.77520376E 00

T =   0.1999972E-02

NODES   NODE VOLTAGES

  1-   1   0.86331522E 00

```
         T  =     0.2499964F-02

NODES                    NODE VOLTAGES
   1-   1        0.91689038E 00


         T  =     0.2999956E-02

NODES                    NODE VOLTAGES
   1-   1        0.94946611E 00


         T  =     0.3499949E-02

NODES                    NODE VOLTAGES
   1-   1        0.96927345E 00


         T  =     0.3999930E-02

NODES                    NODE VOLTAGES
   1-   1        0.98131704E 00


         T  =     0.4499864E-02

NODES                    NODE VOLTAGES
   1-   1        0.98864001E 00


         T  =     0.4999798E-02

NODES                    NODE VOLTAGES
   1-   1        0.99309272E 00


         T  =     0.5009796F-02

NODES                    NODE VOLTAGES
   1-   1        0.99316108E 00
```

FIGURE 4.2-14
Program and printout for Example 4.2-5.

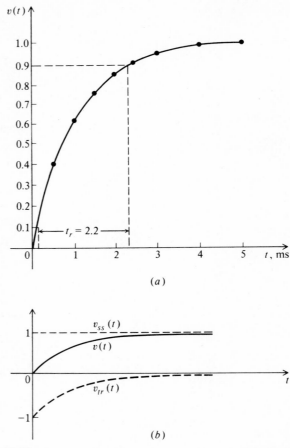

FIGURE 4.2-15
Example 4.2-5. (*a*) Plot of step response; (*b*) components of response.

zero and the final voltage, or steady state, is known to be 1, we see that the transient part *takes the solution from the initial condition to the steady state.*

All circuit problems which lead to linear differential equations are characterized by this same type of solution, i.e., a steady state plus a transient which provides the transition from the initial condition to the steady state. In our example, the steady state is a constant, and has the same form as the input voltage. In general, it is found that the steady-state response has the same form as the input signal, whether it be a step function, sine wave, or some other waveform.

In our example, the transient response is a decaying exponential of the form $Ae^{-\alpha t}$. In more complicated circuits it has the form $Ae^{-\alpha t}\cos(\omega t + \theta)$. For linear circuits, the transient part of the solution consists of such exponentials, the number of exponentials depending on the complexity of the circuit.

Rise time and bandwidth   Let us return to the waveform of Fig. 4.2-15a. We are often concerned with the speed with which $v(t)$ rises toward its steady-state value. For our example, the time constant $\tau = 1$ ms. Substituting this value in (4.2-5), we find

$$v(\tau) = V_1(1 - e^{-1}) \approx 0.63\ V_1 \qquad (4.2\text{-}8)$$

Thus the rising exponential reaches 63 percent of its final value after one time constant has elapsed. A similar calculation shows that after five time constants, $v(t)$ is within 1 percent of its final value. Thus the time constant can be used as a measure of the speed of response of this circuit.

A criterion more often used for such circuits is the time it takes for $v(t)$ to rise from 10 to 90 percent of its final value. This is called the rise time t_r and can be shown to be (Prob. 4.2-11)

$$t_r = 2.2\tau = 2.2RC \qquad (4.2\text{-}9)$$

It turns out that for this simple low-pass filter the rise time and bandwidth are related. Comparing (4.2-9) and (4.2-3), we find

$$t_r = 2.2RC = \frac{2.2}{2\pi B} \qquad (4.2\text{-}10)$$

For the circuit of Example 4.2-5, $t_r = 2.2/10^3 = 2.2$ ms. This is shown in Fig. 4.2-15a.

Although the bandwidth and rise-time relations were derived only for the simple RC low-pass filter, they are often applied to other networks in order to obtain "ball-park" estimates.

4.3   MORE COMPLICATED CIRCUITS

In this section we shall consider circuits which are more complex than the RC low-pass filter considered previously. Again the ECAP program will be used to find numerical answers.

In addition to the analog circuit, a digital circuit will also be considered.

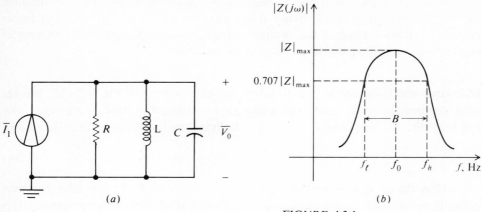

FIGURE 4.3-1
Bandpass filter. (*a*) Circuit; (*b*) response.

4.3-1   The *RLC* Bandpass Filter

Frequency response   The parallel "tuned" circuit of Fig. 4.3-1*a* is often used as a bandpass filter when the signal occupies a narrow band of frequencies around a center frequency f_0. For this case there are two cutoff frequencies, f_h and f_l (above and below the center frequency f_0) at which the response is $1/\sqrt{2}$ times the center-frequency value, as shown in Fig. 4.3-1*b*. The object of our analysis is to find these frequencies, and hence the bandwidth, in terms of *R*, *L*, and *C*.

We begin by writing the transfer function

$$\frac{\overline{V}_0}{\overline{I}_i} = Z(j\omega) = \frac{1}{1/R + j\omega C + 1/j\omega L} \qquad (4.3\text{-}1a)$$

Note that the transfer function of interest is the impedance. To put this in a form suitable for interpretation, we first multiply numerator and denominator by *R* to get

$$Z(j\omega) = \frac{R}{1 + j\omega RC + R/j\omega L}$$

$$= \frac{R}{1 + jRC(\omega - 1/\omega LC)} \qquad (4.3\text{-}1b)$$

Noting that *LC* must have the dimensions of seconds squared, we define

$$\omega_0{}^2 = \frac{1}{LC} \qquad (4.3\text{-}2)$$

Substituting (4.3-2) into (4.3-1b),

$$Z(j\omega) = \frac{R}{1 + jRC(\omega - \omega_0^2/\omega)}$$

$$= \frac{R}{1 + j\omega_0 RC(\omega/\omega_0 - \omega_0/\omega)} \qquad (4.3\text{-}3)$$

It is convenient to define a normalized frequency

$$x = \frac{\omega}{\omega_0} \qquad (4.3\text{-}4)$$

and a *quality factor* (to be explained shortly)

$$Q = \omega_0 RC = \omega_0^2 \frac{RC}{\omega_0} = \frac{1}{LC} \frac{RC}{\omega_0} = \frac{R}{\omega_0 L} \qquad (4.3\text{-}5)$$

With these definitions, the transfer function becomes

$$H(jx) = \frac{Z(jx)}{R} = \frac{1}{1 + jQ(x - 1/x)} \qquad (4.3\text{-}6)$$

where we have normalized with respect to R.

Inspection of (4.3-6) indicates that the maximum amplitude of $H(jx)$ occurs at $x = 1$, that is, $\omega = \omega_0$. Thus $\omega_0/2\pi$ is the *center frequency*, and at this frequency the magnitude of H is unity and the impedance is simply R, a pure resistance. (Note that at $\omega = \omega_0$, the equivalent impedance of the inductor in parallel with the capacitor is infinite. Why?)

To find the cutoff frequencies, we look for those values of x for which the magnitude of $H(jx) = 1/\sqrt{2}$, that is,

$$|H(jx)| = \frac{1}{|1 + jQ(x - 1/x)|} = \frac{1}{\sqrt{2}} \qquad (4.3\text{-}7)$$

Since $|1 \pm j1| = \sqrt{2}$, we see that the solution to this equation occurs where

$$\pm Q\left(x - \frac{1}{x}\right) = 1 \qquad (4.3\text{-}8a)$$

Multiplying through by x and collecting terms yields

$$x^2 \mp \frac{x}{Q} - 1 = 0 \qquad (4.3\text{-}8b)$$

Solving for x,

$$x = \pm \frac{1}{2Q} \pm \sqrt{\frac{1}{(2Q)^2} + 1} \qquad (4.3\text{-}8c)$$

Thus there are four distinct values of x which satisfy (4.3-8c).

Since Q must be positive, we will have, for all Q,

$$\sqrt{\frac{1}{(2Q)^2} + 1} > \frac{1}{2Q}$$

Also, $x = \omega/\omega_0$ must always be positive, so that we can discard the two negative values, leaving

$$x_h = \frac{\omega_h}{\omega_0} = \sqrt{1 + \frac{1}{(2Q)^2}} + \frac{1}{2Q} \qquad (4.3\text{-}9a)$$

$$x_l = \frac{\omega_l}{\omega_0} = \sqrt{1 + \frac{1}{(2Q)^2}} - \frac{1}{2Q} \qquad (4.3\text{-}9b)$$

These yield the required upper and lower cutoff frequencies.

The *bandwidth B* of the circuit is defined as the *difference* between the upper and lower cutoff frequencies. Thus, subtracting (4.3-9b) from (4.3-9a), we have

$$\omega_h - \omega_l = \frac{\omega_0}{Q} \qquad \text{rad/s} \qquad (4.3\text{-}10a)$$

The bandwidth in hertz is then

$$B = \frac{\omega_0}{2\pi Q} = \frac{f_0}{Q} \qquad \text{Hz} \qquad (4.3\text{-}10b)$$

The meaning of *quality factor* can now be explained. It is a measure of the *sharpness* of the filter. Higher values of Q lead to smaller relative bandwidths, B/f_0, or what is the same thing, sharper filters. Systems which exhibit the type of frequency response shown in Fig. 4.3-1b are often called *resonant* systems, and the response curve is called a *resonance* curve. The phenomenon of resonance is not significant unless the Q is at least 5 or more. For conventional *RLC* networks, values of Q in the range 10 to 100 are typical, while much higher Qs can be obtained by using transistors.

Specifications for the design of this type of network usually include f_0 and B. From (4.3-2)

$$f_0 = \frac{1}{2\pi\sqrt{LC}} \qquad \text{Hz} \qquad (4.3\text{-}11)$$

and using (4.3-2) and (4.3-5),

$$B = \frac{1}{2\pi RC} = \frac{R}{2\pi L} \qquad \text{Hz} \qquad (4.3\text{-}12)$$

These may be used as design equations, as shown in the example which follows.

EXAMPLE 4.3-1   Design an *RLC* bandpass filter with a bandwidth of 3.5 kHz which is centered at 100 kHz. At the center frequency, the impedance is to be 10 kΩ.

SOLUTION   At the center frequency, Eq. (4.3-3) indicates that $Z(j\omega) = R$. Thus we choose $R = 10$ kΩ to meet the specification on impedance. Next, the bandwidth requirement of 3.5 kHz when substituted into (4.3-12) yields an *RC* product

$$RC = \frac{1}{2\pi B} = \frac{1}{2\pi(3.5)(10^3)} \approx 0.045 \times 10^{-3}$$

Thus

$$C = \frac{0.045 \times 10^{-3}}{10^4} = 0.0045 \; \mu F$$

Finally, from (4.3-2)

$$L = \frac{1}{\omega_0^2 C} = \frac{1}{(2\pi \times 10^5)^2 (0.0045)(10^{-6})}$$
$$= 560 \; \mu H$$

The circuit *Q* is, from (4.3-10a),

$$Q = \frac{f_0}{B} = \frac{10^5}{3.5 \times 10^3} = 29$$

This value is readily achieved with standard components.

EXAMPLE 4.3-2   Use the ECAP program to determine the frequency response of the circuit designed in Example 4.3-1. Cover the frequency range 95 to 105 kHz on a linear scale.

SOLUTION   The ECAP circuit is shown in Fig. 4.3-2a, and the coding sheet in Fig. 4.3-2b. The program is essentially the same as that used in Example 4.2-4. Since a *linear* frequency response calculation is required in this example, the additive iteration frequency card is shown on the coding sheet after the MODIFY card. The lower

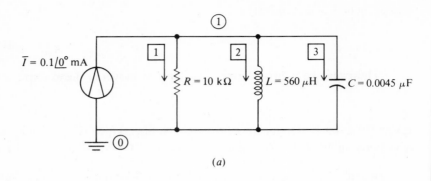

(a)

IBM   FORTRAN C

PROGRAM			
PROGRAMMER		DATE	

COMM.	STATEMENT NUMBER	CONT.	FORTRAN S
C			BELØVE, SCHACHTER, SCHILLING
C			ECAP SØLUTIØN FREQUENCY RESPØNSE
C			CCNY
C			PRØGRAMMER: SCHRØEDER
C			
C			
			AC ANALYSIS
	B1		N(1,0), R=1E 04, I=1E-04/0
	B2		N(1,0), L=0.56E-03
	B3		N(1,0), C=0.45E-08
			FREQUENCY=0.95E 05
			PRINT, NV
			EXECUTE
C			
			MODIFY
			FREQ=0.96E 05(+9)0.105E 06
			EXECUTE

(b)

FIGURE 4.3-2
Example 4.3-2. (a) ECAP circuit; (b) coding sheet.

frequency limit is 0.96 E 05 (96 kHz)—95 kHz was done in the original analysis—and the upper limit is 0.105E 06 (105 kHz). The +9 in parentheses requests calculations in nine equal frequency steps between 96 and 105 kHz, i.e., at intervals of 1 kHz.

   The printout and a plot of the results are shown in Fig. 4.3-3. The center frequency is very close to 100 kHz, and the half-power frequencies occur at approximately 98.5 and 102 kHz. This agrees well with the original design values of Example 4.3-1, that is, $f_0 = 100$ kHz and $B = 3.5$ kHz.

////////

Transient response   In Sec. 4.2-4 we studied the step-function response of a simple *RC* network and found that it consisted of two parts, steady state and transient. In this section we investigate the step response of the *RLC* circuit of Fig. 4.3-1*a*. To find the transient response of the *RLC* filter we write the differential equation for the circuit. Using KCL, we have, assuming zero initial conditions,

$$C \frac{dv_0}{dt} + \frac{v_0}{R} + \frac{1}{L} \int_0^t v_0(x) \, dx = i_1(t) \qquad (4.3\text{-}13)$$

This is actually an integrodifferential equation, and to solve it is beyond the scope of this course. However, since we have numerical values for the parameters, we can find the response using the ECAP program as shown in the example which follows.

EXAMPLE 4.3-3   Use the ECAP program to find the response of the circuit of Fig. 4.3-2*a* to a current step of 0.1 mA.

   SOLUTION   The ECAP program is shown in Fig. 4.3-4 along with a portion of the printout. The program follows that of Example 4.2-5, except that the time step is chosen as approximately $0.001(2\pi\sqrt{LC}) \approx 10^{-8}$ s in accordance with recommended procedures for an *RLC* circuit.[1]

   A plot of the results is given in Fig. 4.3-5, and the oscillatory nature of the response is evident. The period of the oscillations is seen to be about 10 μs, which agrees well with the period of the center frequency of 100 kHz. The decay time constant of the envelope is ≈ 90 μs. This agrees with the theoretical value which can be shown to be $1/\pi B$.

[1] R. W. Jensen and M. D. Lieberman, "IBM Electronic Circuit Analysis Program," Prentice-Hall, Inc., Engelwood Cliffs, N. J., 1968, p. 89

```
C        BELOVE, SCHACHTER, SCHILLING
C        ECAP SOLUTION FREQUENCY RESPONSE
C        CCNY
C        PROGRAMMER SCHROEDER
C
C
         AC ANALYSIS
B1       N (1,0), R=1E 04,I=IE—04/0
B2       N (1,0), L=0.56E—03
B3       N (1,0), C=0.45E—08
         FREQUENCY=0.95E 05
         PRINT, NV
         EXECUTE
```

FREQ = 0.94999937E 05

	NODES	NODE VOLTAGES

MAG   1— 1   0.31102085E 00
PHA   0.71879211E 02

```
         MODIFY
         FREQ=0.96E 05 (+9) 0.105E 06
         EXECUTE
```

FREQ = 0.95999937E 05

	NODES	NODE VOLTAGES

MAG   1— 1   0.37639797E 00
PHA   0.67889236E 02

FREQ = 0.96999937E 05

	NODES	NODE VOLTAGES

MAG   1— 1   0.47089422E 00
PHA   0.61907623E 02

FREQ = 0.97999937E 05

	NODES	NODE VOLTAGES

MAG   1— 1   0.61215973E 00
PHA   0.52254150E 02

FREQ = 0.98999937E 05

	NODES	NODE VOLTAGES

MAG   1— 1   0.81306171E 00
PHA   0.35603836E 02

(a)

FREQ = 0.99999937E 05

NODES   NODE VOLTAGES

MAG   1— 1   0.98947954E 00
PHA   0.83183126E 01

FREQ = 0.10099994E 06

NODES   NODE VOLTAGES

MAG   1— 1   0.92266446E 00
PHA   −0.22681213E 02

FREQ = 0.10199994E 06

NODES   NODE VOLTAGES

MAG   1— 1   0.71545058E 00
PHA   −0.44319855E 02

FREQ = 0.10299994E 06

NODES   NODE VOLTAGES

MAG   1— 1   0.54715031E 00
PHA   −0.56828262E 02

FREQ = 0.10399994E 06

NODES   NODE VOLTAGES

MAG   1— 1   0.43365639E 00
PHA   −0.64300156E 02

FREQ = 0.10499994E 06

NODES   NODE VOLTAGES

MAG   1— 1   0.35648561E 00
PHA   −0.69115448E 02

(a)

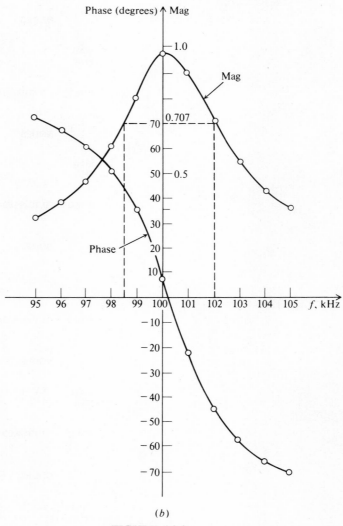

(b)

FIGURE 4.3-3
Example 4.3-2. (a) Printout; (b) plot of results.

```
C       BELOVE, SCHACHTER, SCHILLING
C       TRANSIENT RESPONSE
C       NEW YORK INSTITUTE OF TECHNOLOGY
C
C
        TRANSIENT ANALYSIS
C
   B1 N(1,0),R=1E 04,I=1E-04
   B2 N(1,0),L=0.56E-03
   B3 N(1,0),C=0.45E-08
C
C
        TIME STEP=1E-08
        OUTPUT INTERVAL=100
        FINAL TIME=150E-06
        PRINT,NV
        EXECUTE



        T =    0.0


NODES                       NODE VOLTAGES

   1-   1       0.99999852E-06



        T =    0.9999949E-06

NODES                       NODE VOLTAGES

   1-   1       0.20530529E-01



        T =    0.1999984E-05

NODES                       NODE VOLTAGES

   1-   1       0.32783471E-01



        T =    0.2999974E-05

NODES                       NODE VOLTAGES

   1-   1       0.32311141E-01



        T =    0.3999963E-05

NODES                       NODE VOLTAGES

   1-   1       0.19596949E-01
```

FIGURE 4.3-4
RLC transient program and portion of printout.

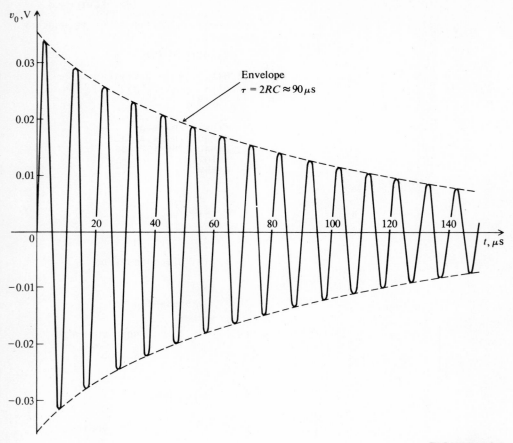

FIGURE 4.3-5
RLC transient.

4.3-2   A Second-order Digital Filter

In Sec. 3.4-1 we considered a simple first-order digital filter which yielded responses similar to the *RC* filter, a first-order analog circuit. A second-order digital filter, as shown in Fig. 4.3-6, can be adjusted to give an oscillatory response similar to the *RLC* second-order analog filter of Sec. 4.3-1. From the circuit, we note that the output, $y(n\,\Delta t)$ is the sum of the three signals feeding the summing network. Thus the difference equation for the circuit is

$$y(n\,\Delta t) = x(n\,\Delta t) + k_1 y[(n-1)\,\Delta t] + k_2 y[(n-2)\,\Delta t] \qquad (4.3\text{-}14)$$

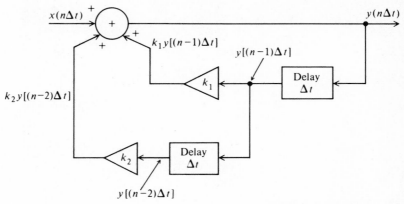

FIGURE 4.3-6
Second-order digital filter.

Consider that $k_1 = 0.5$, $k_2 = -0.5$, $x(0) = 1$, and $x(n \, \Delta t) = 0$ for $n \neq 0$; that is, the input is a single pulse occurring at $t = 0$. Then, with the initial conditions $y(-\Delta t) = y(-2\Delta t) = 0$, we get the following sequence of values:

Table 4.3-1

n	$y(n \, \Delta t)$	$x(n \, \Delta t)$	$0.5y[(n - 1) \, \Delta t]$	$-0.5y[(n - 2) \, \Delta t]$
0	1	1	0	0
1	0.5	0	0.5	0
2	−0.25	0	0.25	−0.5
3	−0.375	0	−0.125	−0.25
4	−0.063	0	−0.188	+0.125
5	+0.156	0	−0.032	+0.188
6	+0.110	0	0.078	+0.032
7	−0.023	0	+0.055	−0.078
8	−0.067	0	−0.012	−0.055

Figure 4.3-7 shows a plot of $y(n \, \Delta t)$ versus n. The response is seen to be similar to the oscillatory response of the analog *RLC* circuit (Fig. 4.3-5). It should be noted that different values for k_1 and k_2 would lead to completely different responses, ranging from nonoscillatory to unstable. This is explored further in Probs. 4.3-5 and 4.3-6.

By proper choice of the coefficients of the difference equation, the digital filter can be made to do the same signal-processing operation as the analog filter. In addition, the digital filter can handle many different signals at the same time by using a technique called *multiplexing*, in which the signals are staggered in time so that use is

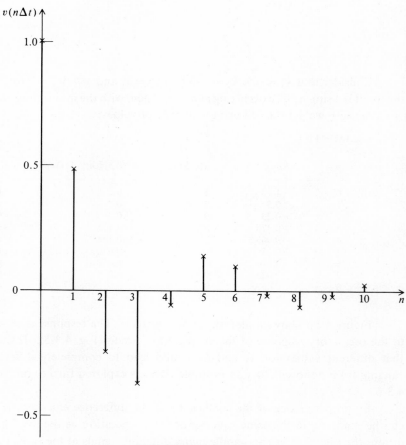

FIGURE 4.3-7
Response of second-order digital filter to a single pulse.

made of the time interval between pulses to process different signals using the same filter.

Again we should note that a digital filter can be designed to provide a desired response with much greater accuracy than an analog filter.

As digital components become more and more economical due to manufacturing improvements such as large-scale integration, we will undoubtedly find that the increased reliability and accuracy of digital circuits will cause them to supplant analog circuits in many applications, in much the same way that the transistor has replaced the vacuum tube.

4.3-3   Frequency Response of Digital Filters

In Sec. 4.2-3 we studied the response of analog filters to sinusoidal signals of different frequencies. We noted that since the filter is linear, superposition applies and our study simplifies to the determination of the response of the filter to a single sine wave at an arbitrary frequency, f.

In this section we determine the response of the linear digital filter to a sampled sinusoidal signal. This response consists of two parts: the transient solution, and the steady-state solution which has the same form as the input sinusoid. The transient response of the filter has already been studied in Sec. 3.4-1. In this section we restrict our discussion to the steady-state response.

The first-order digital filter   Consider the first-order digital filter shown in Fig. 3.4-2. This filter is characterized by the difference equation (see Sec. 3.4-1):

$$y(n \, \Delta t) = Ky[(n - 1) \, \Delta t] + x(n \, \Delta t) \qquad (4.3\text{-}15)$$

where $x(n \, \Delta t)$ is the amplitude of the input signal at the sample time $n \, \Delta t$.

To find the response of this filter to the sinusoidal input $x(t) = X_m \cos \omega t$, we first find the response to $x_1(t) = X_m e^{j\omega t}$. The desired input is then the real part of $x_1(t)$. The filter response to $x_1(t)$ will then be $y_1(t) = Y_m e^{j\omega t}$, where Y_m is a complex number. Hence the response to $x(t)$ is $y(t)$, which is the real part of $y_1(t)$ (see Secs. 3.4 and 4.2 for the corresponding theory of analog filters).

The sampled input $x_1(n\Delta t)$ is $X_m e^{j\omega n\Delta t}$. Hence, the response $y_1(n\Delta t) = Y_m e^{j\omega n \, \Delta t}$ and $y_1[(n - 1) \, \Delta t] = Y_m e^{j\omega(n-1) \, \Delta t}$. Substituting into Eq. (4.3-15) yields

$$Y_m e^{j\omega n \, \Delta t} = K Y_m e^{j\omega(n-1) \, \Delta t} + X_m e^{j\omega n \, \Delta t} \qquad (4.3\text{-}16)$$

We first cancel the term $e^{j\omega n \, \Delta t}$ from both sides of the equation. Then, the ratio Y_m/X_m is the transfer function $H(f)$ of the filter (see Eq. 4.2-1):

$$H(f) = \frac{Y_m}{X_m} = \frac{1}{1 - Ke^{-j\omega \, \Delta t}} \qquad (4.3\text{-}17)$$

The transfer function $H(f)$ is a complex function of frequency having a magnitude $|H(f)|$ and a phase, $\varphi(f)$:

$$|H(f)| = \left| \frac{1}{1 - Ke^{-j\omega \Delta t}} \right| = \left| \frac{1}{1 - K \cos \omega \Delta t + jK \sin \omega \Delta t} \right|$$

$$= \frac{1}{(1 + K^2 - 2K \cos \omega \Delta t)^{1/2}} \qquad (4.3\text{-}18)$$

and

$$\varphi(f) = -\arctan\left(\frac{K \sin \omega \Delta t}{1 - K \cos \omega \Delta t} \right) \qquad (4.3\text{-}19)$$

Note that the magnitude and the phase of the transfer function $H(f)$ are functions of K and Δt, as well as the applied frequency f.

The steady-state response

$$y(t) = \text{Re}\{Y_m e^{j\omega n \Delta t}\} \qquad (4.3\text{-}20)$$

to the sampled input $x(n \Delta t) = X_m \cos \omega n \Delta t$ is then

$$y(n \Delta t) = \text{Re}\{X_m |H(f)| e^{j\varphi(f)} e^{j\omega n \Delta t}\}$$

$$= \frac{X_m}{(1 + K^2 - 2K \cos \omega \Delta t)^{1/2}} \cos\left[\omega n \Delta t - \arctan\left(\frac{K \sin \omega \Delta t}{1 - K \cos \omega \Delta t} \right) \right] \qquad (4.3\text{-}21)$$

It is useful to plot $|H(f)|$ as a function of frequency in order to determine the frequency band passed by the filter. Since the sampling frequency is $f_s = 1/\Delta t$, we plot $|H(f)|$ vs. f/f_s:

$$|H(f)| = \frac{1}{\left(1 + K^2 - 2K \cos 2\pi \dfrac{f}{f_s} \right)^{1/2}} \qquad (4.3\text{-}22a)$$

The magnitude of the transfer function $|H(f)|$ given in Eq. (4.3-22a) is a periodic function of frequency. It has a maximum value when

$$\cos 2\pi \frac{f}{f_s} = 1 \qquad (4.3\text{-}22b)$$

which occurs when

$$\frac{f}{f_s} = 0, 1, 2, \ldots \quad (4.3\text{-}22c)$$

This maximum value is

$$|H(f)|_{max} = \frac{1}{(1 + K^2 - 2K)^{1/2}} = \frac{1}{1 - K} \quad (4.3\text{-}23)$$

The minimum value of $|H(f)|$ occurs when

$$\cos 2\pi \frac{f}{f_s} = -1 \quad (4.3\text{-}24a)$$

which results whenever

$$\frac{f}{f_s} = \frac{1}{2}, \frac{3}{2}, \frac{5}{2}, \ldots \quad (4.3\text{-}24b)$$

This minimum value is

$$|H(f)|_{min} = \frac{1}{(1 + K^2 + 2K)^{1/2}} = \frac{1}{1 + K} \quad (4.3\text{-}25)$$

Comparing Eqs. (4.3-23) and (4.3-25) we see that the difference between $|H(f)|_{max}$ and $|H(f)|_{min}$ increases as K approaches unity. Some typical values are given in Table 4.3-2.

Note that $|H|_{max} > 1$, thereby providing amplification from input to output. This is a characteristic of digital filters.

The variation of $|H(f)|$ vs. frequency is plotted in Fig. 4.3-8 for $K = 0.5$ and 0.1. Note that the filter appears to be low pass for frequencies less than one-half the sampling frequency. However, unlike its analog counterpart (an RC low-pass filter), the

Table 4.3-2

K	$|H|_{max}$	$|H|_{min}$
0.99	100	0.502
0.8	5	0.55
0.5	2	0.67
0.1	1.1	0.9

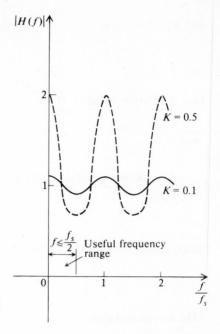

FIGURE 4.3-8
Frequency response of first-order digital filter.

digital filter is periodic and, when $f = f_s$, the signal is actually enhanced. To avoid this problem and insure that the digital low-pass filter is indeed always low pass, we set the sampling frequency f_s to be greater than or equal to twice the maximum applied signal frequency:

$$f_s \geq 2f_{max} \qquad (4.3\text{-}26)$$

Then the transfer function, as plotted in Fig. 4.3-8, is only of practical interest up to the frequency $f_{max} \leq f_s/2$. This restriction on the sampling frequency is a consequence of the *Sampling Theorem* and is discussed in detail in Sec. 6.5-1.

Higher-order digital filters The transfer function of any digital filter is easily obtained from the difference equation. To do this we first represent the sampled input as

$$x(n\,\Delta t) = X_m e^{j\omega n\,\Delta t} \qquad (4.3\text{-}27a)$$

The filter output is then

$$y(n\,\Delta t) = Y_m e^{j\omega n\,\Delta t} \qquad (4.3\text{-}27b)$$

All delays are represented in a similar manner. Thus,

$$x[(n - N)\,\Delta t] = X_m e^{j\omega(n-N)\,\Delta t} \quad (4.3\text{-}28a)$$

and

$$y[(n - N)\,\Delta t] = Y_m e^{j\omega(n-N)\,\Delta t} \quad (4.3\text{-}28b)$$

Equations (4.3-27) and (4.3-28) are substituted into the difference equation. The term $e^{j\omega n\,\Delta t}$ is cancelled, and the transfer function is

$$H(f) = \frac{Y_m}{X_m} \quad (4.3\text{-}29)$$

The output of the filter is then

$$y(n\,\Delta t) = \text{Re}\{H(f)X_m e^{j\omega n\,\Delta t}\} \quad (4.3\text{-}30)$$

This procedure is illustrated in the problems.

PROBLEMS

4.1-1 In the configuration of Fig. 4.1-1, measurements are made under various conditions and the following data are observed:
(a) When $i_1 = 2$ A, $i_2 = i_3 = 0$.
(b) When $i_1 = 6$ A, $i_2 = 3$ A and $i_3 = -3$ A.
(c) When $i_1 = 22$ A, $i_2 = -30$ A and $i_3 = 6$ A.
For each case, find the current i_4.

4.1-2 In the circuit of Fig. 4.1-2 the following conditions are found:
(a) When $v_{ab} = 10$ V, $v_{ac} = 10$ V.
(b) When $v_2 = 2 \sin t$ V, $v_1 = 4 \sin t$ V.
(c) When $v_3 = 6$ '/, $v_{ba} = -12$ V.
For each case, find the unknown voltage.

4.1-3 For the circuit of Fig. P4.1-3, find all unknown currents and voltages using node equations.

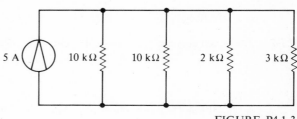

FIGURE P4.1-3

4.1-4   For the circuit of Fig. P4.1-3:

   (*a*) Find the resistance seen by the 5-A source.

   (*b*) Check the currents found in Prob. 4.1-3 using the current-divider formula.

4.1-5   In the circuit of Fig. P4.1-5, find v_2.

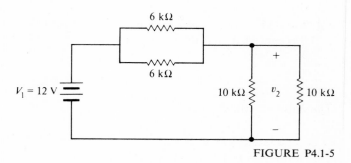

FIGURE P4.1-5

4.1-6   Find the equivalent element which will replace each of the combinations of elements shown in Fig. P4.1-6.

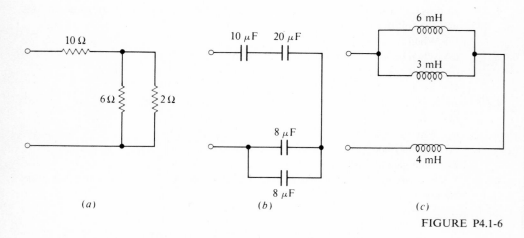

(*a*)   (*b*)   (*c*)

FIGURE P4.1-6

4.1-7   Measurements made on a certain generator yield the following data:

$$v = 80 \text{ V} \qquad i = 130 \text{ A}$$

$$v = 40 \text{ V} \qquad i = 300 \text{ A}$$

   (*a*) Find the Thévenin and Norton equivalent circuits for the generator.

   (*b*) What is the voltage when the current is 200 A?

4.1-8 In Fig. P4.1-8, find v_{ab} by two different methods.

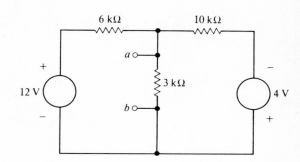

FIGURE P4.1-8

4.2-1 Check the ECAP solutions (answers in printout in Fig. 4.2-4) to Example 4.2-1 using node equations and a slide rule.

4.2-2 Use the ECAP (or similar) program to find all unknown voltages and currents in the circuit of Fig. P4.2-2.

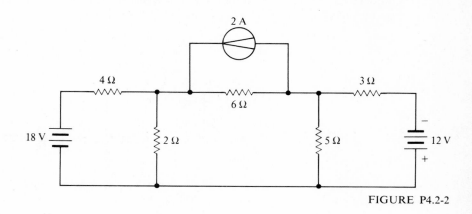

FIGURE P4.2-2

4.2-3 Check the result of Example 4.2-2 using any method.

4.2-4   Use the computer to find all currents and voltages in the circuit of Fig. P4.2-4.

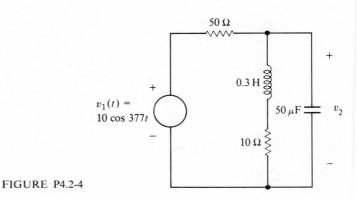

FIGURE P4.2-4

4.2-5   Check the result of Example 4.2-3 using a slide rule.

4.2-6   For the circuit of Fig. P4.2-4, find the transfer function

$$H(j\omega) = \overline{V}_2/\overline{V}_1$$

4.2-7   Use the computer to find the frequency response (amplitude and phase) for the circuit of Fig. P4.2-4 in the frequency range 4 to 500 Hz.

4.2-8   Substitute (4.2-5) into (4.2-4) to show that it is indeed a solution.

4.2-9   Write the differential equations for the circuit of Fig. P4.2-9.

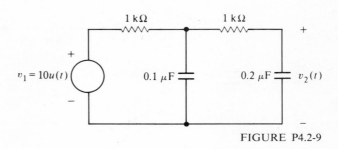

FIGURE P4.2-9

4.2-10   Use the computer to find $v_2(t)$ in the circuit of Fig. P4.2-9.

4.2-11   Prove Eq. (4.2-9).

4.3-1 Find ω_0, Q, ω_h, and ω_l for the series-tuned circuit of Fig. P4.3-1.

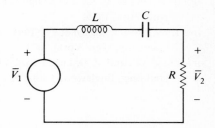

FIGURE P4.3-1

4.3-2 Use the computer to find the frequency response of the circuit of Fig. P4.3-1 if $R = 20\ \Omega$, $L = 2\ \mu\text{H}$, $C = 50\ \text{pF}$. From the results find Q, f_0, f_h, and f_l.

4.3-3 Design a parallel-tuned circuit for a broadcast-band IF stage. It should have a center frequency of 455 kHz and a bandwidth of 10 kHz. The impedance at f_0 should be 600 Ω.

4.3-4 Use the computer to find the response of the circuit of Fig. P4.2-4 to a 10-V step.

4.3-5 Find the response of the digital filter of Fig. 4.3-6 to a constant-amplitude pulse train if $k_1 = +1.2$ and $k_2 = -0.4$.

4.3-6 Find the response of the digital filter of Fig. 4.3-6 to a constant-amplitude pulse train if $k_1 = +1.5$ and $k_2 = -1.5$.

4.3-7 A first-order low-pass digital filter has $K = 0.5$ and the sampling frequency is 1 kHz.
(a) What is the maximum signal frequency that can be accommodated safely?
(b) Find the output if the input is

$$x(t) = 2 \cos 2\pi \times 100t + 3 \cos 2\pi \times 400t$$

4.3-8 The first-order filter of Prob. 4.3-7 is used to filter signals. Compare the output amplitudes of signals at 10 Hz, 100 Hz, and 500 Hz. Assume the input signals have identical amplitudes.

4.3-9 A high-pass first-order digital filter can be described by the difference equation

$$y(n\Delta t) = Ky[(n-1)\Delta t] + x(n\Delta t) - x[(n-1)\Delta t]$$

where $x(t)$ is the input signal and $y(t)$ the filter output.
(a) Synthesize a digital circuit which will produce this difference equation.
(b) Determine $|H(f)|$.
(c) Plot $|H(f)|$ vs. f/f_s for $K = 0$, 0.5, and 0.9.

4.3-10 (a) Determine the transfer function corresponding to the difference equation (Eq. 4.3-14):

$$y(n\ \Delta t) = x(n\ \Delta t) + k_1 y[(n-1)\ \Delta t] + k_2 y[(n-2)\ \Delta t]$$

(b) Let $k_1 = 0.7$ and $k_2 = -0.4$. Plot $|H(f)|$ vs. f.

REFERENCES

GOLD, B., and C. M. RADER: "Digital Processing of Signals," McGraw-Hill Book Company, New York, 1969.

HAYT, W., and J. KEMMERLY: "Engineering Circuit Analysis," 2d ed., McGraw-Hill Book Company, New York, 1971.

JENSEN, R. W., and M. D. LIEBERMAN: "IBM Electronic Circuit Analysis Program," Prentice-Hall, Inc., Englewood Cliffs, N.J., 1968.

ELECTRONIC CIRCUITS

INTRODUCTION

In this chapter we introduce two basic electronic devices, the diode and the transistor. The addition of these nonlinear elements to the linear elements of Chap. 3 provides us with the means of implementing the logic devices presented in Chap. 2. In addition, we shall consider the transistor as a linear current amplifier, and discuss some of the problems which arise because of variations in its characteristics.

5.1 THE DIODE

The diode is the most elementary of the nonlinear devices with which we are concerned. It is made in a wide variety of types and used extensively in one form or another in almost every branch of electrical technology. The list includes vacuum diodes, gas diodes, metallic rectifier diodes, semiconductor diodes, tunnel diodes, etc. In this chapter we consider the semiconductor diode because it has the widest application and because the circuit principles to be developed for this type of diode are almost directly applicable to all other diodes.

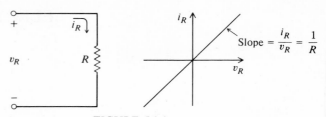

FIGURE 5.1-1
The resistance element and its vi characteristic.

5.1-1 The Ideal Diode

In the preceding chapters we began our study of circuits by considering models of linear elements, the simplest of these being the resistor. The volt-ampere (vi) characteristic of the ideal resistor can be described by such a simple relation—Ohm's law—that we sometimes lose sight of its graphical interpretation. The linear character of the resistance is evident in Fig. 5.1-1. The vi characteristic of the ideal diode is shown in Fig. 5.1-2. The nonlinear character of the diode is clearly evident here. When the source voltage v_i is positive, i_D is positive, and the diode is a short circuit ($v_D = 0$); while when v_i is negative, i_D is zero, and the diode is an open circuit ($v_D = v_i$). The diode can be thought of as a *switch* which is controlled by the polarity of the source voltage. The switch is closed for positive source voltages and open for negative source voltages.

Another way to look at this element is to note that the diode conducts current only from p to n (Fig. 5.1-2), and conduction takes place only when the source voltage is positive. The diode does not conduct when the source voltage is negative.

Physical diodes have inherent characteristics and limitations which cause them to differ from the ideal. These are discussed in succeeding sections. For the present, the diodes are considered to be ideal.

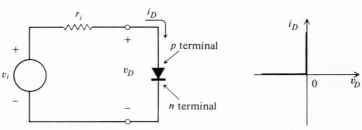

FIGURE 5.1-2
The ideal diode and its vi characteristic.

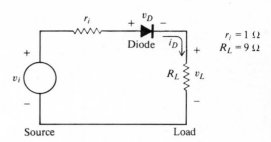

FIGURE 5.1-3
Half-wave rectifier circuit for Example
5.1-1.

The following example illustrates one of the operations on signals which is often achieved with simple diode circuits.

EXAMPLE 5.1-1   *Half-wave rectifier or clipping circuit*   One of the principal applications of the diode is the production of a dc voltage from an ac voltage source, a process called *rectification*. A typical half-wave rectifier circuit is shown in Fig. 5.1-3. (Practical rectifier circuits use two diodes for full-wave rectification. See Prob. 5.1-1.)

   (*a*) The source voltage is sinusoidal, $v_i = V_{im} \cos \omega_0 t$, where $V_{im} = 10$ V. Find and sketch the waveform of the load voltage. Find its average (dc) value.

   (*b*) Repeat (*a*) if $v_i = -5 + 10 \cos \omega_0 t$.

   SOLUTION   (*a*) Kirchhoff's voltage law (KVL) applied to the circuit of Fig. 5.1-3 yields

$$v_i = i_D r_i + v_D + i_D R_L$$

or

$$i_D = \frac{v_i - v_D}{r_i + R_L}$$

This equation contains two unknowns, v_D and i_D. They in turn are related by the diode *vi* characteristic. The solution for i_D or v_D thus requires "substitution" of the *vi* curve into the equation. This can be done in the following way: The diode characteristic indicates that only positive current, in the reference direction, can flow in this circuit. This requires that $v_i > v_D$. However, when the diode is conducting, $v_D = 0$, so that current flows in the positive direction only when $v_i > 0$.

   When v_i is negative, current flow should be opposite to the reference direction; but the diode cannot conduct current in this direction; thus $i_D = 0$ when $v_i < 0$.

   This discussion can be summarized by drawing two circuits, one of which holds

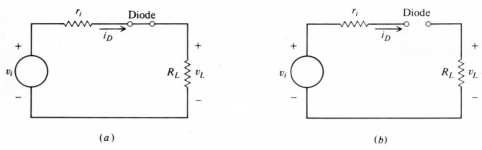

(a)   (b)

FIGURE 5.1-4
Conducting and nonconducting states of the diode rectifier.
(a) $v_i > 0$. (b) $v_i < 0$.

for $v_i > 0$ and one for $v_i < 0$, as shown in Fig. 5.1-4. Using the circuits in this figure, the unknowns v_D and i_D can be found. Thus the diode current i_D is

$$i_D = \begin{cases} \dfrac{V_{im}}{r_i + R_L} \cos \omega_0 t & \text{when } v_i > 0 \\ 0 & \text{when } v_i < 0 \end{cases}$$

and the load voltage v_L is

$$v_L = i_D R_L$$

The load voltage v_L and the signal voltage v_i are sketched in Fig. 5.1-5. Note that the current waveform has the same shape as the load voltage v_L. This is a *half-wave-rectified* sine wave. Its average value (Sec. 3.3-4) is obtained by dividing the area, contained between $v_L(t)$ and the $\omega_0 t$ axis, by the period 2π.

$$V_{L,\text{dc}} = \frac{1}{2\pi} \int_{-\pi/2}^{\pi/2} (V_{Lm} \cos \omega_0 t) d(\omega_0 t) = \frac{V_{Lm}}{\pi} = \frac{9}{\pi} = 2.86 \text{ V} \qquad (5.1\text{-}1)$$

(b) The waveform of v_i is sketched in Fig. 5.1-6. In this case a negative *bias* has been added to the signal. The waveform for v_L is obtained by noting that current will flow only when v_i is positive. The exact time $\pm t_1$ at which the current flow starts and stops is found by setting $v_i = 0$; then

$$-5 + 10 \cos \omega_0 t_1 = 0$$

$$\cos \omega_0 t_1 = 0.5$$

and

$$\omega_0 t_1 = \pm \frac{\pi}{3}$$

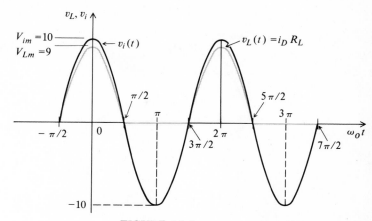

FIGURE 5.1-5
Waveforms in the rectifier circuit of Example 5.1-1.

From the symmetry of the cosine function, the diode is seen to conduct current when

$$2\pi n - \frac{\pi}{3} \le \omega_0 t \le 2\pi n + \frac{\pi}{3}$$

Thus the load voltage is

$$v_L = \begin{cases} -4.5 + 9 \cos \omega_0 t & 2\pi n - \frac{\pi}{3} \le \omega_0 t \le 2\pi n + \frac{\pi}{3} \\ 0 & 2\pi n + \frac{\pi}{3} \le \omega_0 t \le 2\pi n + \frac{5\pi}{3} \end{cases}$$

The average value of v_L is found as before:

$$V_{L,\mathrm{dc}} = \frac{1}{2\pi} \int_{-\pi/3}^{\pi/3} (-4.5 + 9 \cos \omega_0 t) \, d(\omega_0 t)$$

$$= (-4.5)\left(\frac{1}{3}\right) + \frac{9}{\pi}\left(\sin \frac{\pi}{3}\right)$$

$$= -1.5 + \frac{9}{\pi}\left(\frac{\sqrt{3}}{2}\right) \approx 0.98 \ V$$

////////

A simple power supply   In many engineering applications we require sources of dc voltage. An extremely important application is in the use of transistor amplifiers.

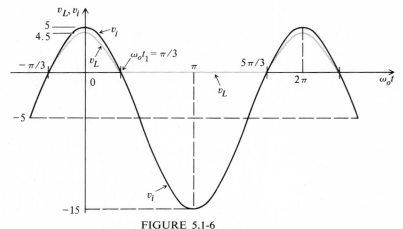

FIGURE 5.1-6
Rectifier-circuit waveforms with bias added to signal.

These devices amplify signals in our radios, televisions, computers, etc., by converting dc voltage to signal voltage.

One source of dc voltage is a battery, which is used in portable electronic equipment, such as radio and television. However, batteries have relatively short lives and must be replaced or recharged quite often. Thus, for nonportable electronic equipment, we convert the 110-V ac line voltage entering our home and business into a dc voltage source. This conversion can be effected using the half-wave-rectifier circuit of Example 5.1-1. (It should again be pointed out that while the half-wave rectifier is easier to analyze, the full-wave rectifier is commonly used in practice. See Prob. 5.1-1.)

The waveform of $v_L(t)$, shown in Fig. 5.1-5, is not a constant, however, even though it has an average value [Eq. (5.1-1)]. To convert $v_L(t)$ into a pure dc voltage requires that all waveform variations, called *ripple*, be eliminated. To see how this may be accomplished we expand $v_L(t)$ into a Fourier series (Sec. 3.3-4). Since

$$v_L(t) = \begin{cases} 9 \cos \omega_0 t & -\dfrac{\pi}{2} \le \omega_0 t \le \dfrac{\pi}{2} \\[2mm] 0 & \dfrac{\pi}{2} \le \omega_0 t \le \dfrac{3\pi}{2} \end{cases} \qquad (5.1\text{-}2)$$

and $v_L(t)$ is periodic with $T = 2\pi/\omega_0$, $v_L(t)$ can be expanded into the Fourier series.

$$v_L(t) = a_0 + \sum_{n=1}^{\infty} a_n \cos n\omega_0 t + \sum_{n=1}^{\infty} b_n \sin n\omega_0 t \qquad (5.1\text{-}3)$$

where

$$a_0 = \frac{1}{2\pi} \int_{-\pi}^{\pi} v_L(\omega_0 t)\, d(\omega_0 t) \qquad (5.1\text{-}4a)$$

$$a_n = \frac{1}{\pi} \int_{-\pi}^{\pi} v_L(\omega_0 t) \cos n\omega_0 t\, d(\omega_0 t) \qquad (5.1\text{-}4b)$$

$$b_n = \frac{1}{\pi} \int_{-\pi}^{\pi} v_L(\omega_0 t) \sin (n\omega_0 t)\, d(\omega_0 t) \qquad (5.1\text{-}4c)$$

Substituting (5.1-2) into (5.1-4) and performing the required integrations (Prob. 5.1-2) yields

$$v_L(t) = \frac{9}{\pi} + \frac{9}{2} \cos \omega_0 t + \frac{6}{\pi} \cos 2\omega_0 t - \frac{6}{5\pi} \cos 4\omega_0 t + \cdots \qquad (5.1\text{-}5)$$

This expression shows that the effect of the diode has been to generate not only the dc term and a term at the same frequency as the source, but also terms at harmonic frequencies not present in the source voltage.

If the circuit is to produce a dc voltage, the dc component of $v_L(t)$ must be separated from the harmonics of $v_L(t)$ by *filtering*. A filter suitable for this purpose is shown in Fig. 5.1-7. To show that this RC circuit can substantially reduce the harmonics of $v_L(t)$, we call the amplitude of the output voltage, at the frequency nf_0, V_{On}, and call the amplitude of the load voltage at the frequency nf_0, V_{Ln}. Then V_{On} and V_{Ln} are given by the equation (Sec. 4.2-3)

$$V_{On} = \frac{V_{Ln}}{\sqrt{1 + (n\omega_0 RC)^2}} \qquad (5.1\text{-}6a)$$

Since we want $V_{On} \ll V_{Ln}$ for every value of n, we select $\omega_0 RC \gg 1$. For example, if we choose $\omega_0 RC = 100$,

$$V_{On} = \frac{V_{Ln}}{\sqrt{1 + 10^4 n^2}} \approx \frac{V_{Ln}}{100n} \qquad (5.1\text{-}6b)$$

where we have used the fact that $10^4 n^2 \gg 1$ for all $n \geqslant 1$.

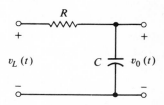

FIGURE 5.1-7
An *RC* power supply filter.

The amplitude of the filter output $v_L(t)$ at the frequency f_0 is reduced by a factor of 100 compared with the voltage at the input to the filter. Referring to (5.1-5), we see that the result of filtering $v_L(t)$ has been to reduce significantly the amplitudes of all the harmonics without attenuating the dc component. The output voltage $v_0(t)$ is therefore approximately constant and is used to supply the dc voltage to our transistors.

Another circuit, often used to produce a dc voltage when an ac voltage is given, is shown in Fig. 5.1-8a. Comparing this circuit with the circuit shown in Fig. 5.1-3, we note that r_i has been set equal to zero (to simplify the analysis) and that a capacitor C has been placed directly across R_L.

If the capacitor C were not present, the half-wave-rectified waveform shown in Fig. 5.1-5 would result. Now let us consider the output waveform of $v_L(t)$ when C is inserted. Referring to Fig. 5.1-8b, we see that at $t = 0$, $v_i(t)$ becomes positive. We will assume that $v_L(t)$ is also zero at $t = 0$. Thus the diode conducts current and $v_L(t) = v_i(t)$. Finally, $v_i(t)$ reaches its maximum positive value $+V$ and begins to decrease. However, when $v_i(t) = +V$, $v_L(t) = +V$. Now, as soon as $v_i(t)$ begins to decrease, $v_i(t)$ becomes less than $v_L(t)$, since the voltage across a capacitor cannot change instantaneously (Sec. 3.4-2), and the diode becomes reverse-biased ($v_D < 0$). No diode current flows.

During the time interval that $v_i(t)$ decreases from $+V$, becomes negative, and then becomes positive again, the parallel $R_L C$ circuit is disconnected from the ac input source. This is illustrated in Fig. 5.1-8c. Since a voltage $v_L(t)$ exists, a current will flow in R_L, as shown. From Kirchhoff's current law we know that the same current must flow in the capacitor C. Thus, using (3.4-10),

$$i(t) = \frac{v_L(t)}{R_L} = -C \frac{dv_L(t)}{dt} \qquad v_L(t_1) = +V \qquad (5.1\text{-}7a)$$

where t_1 is the time at which the diode becomes reverse-biased. Thus

$$\frac{dv_L}{dt} + \frac{1}{R_L C} v_L = 0 \qquad (5.1\text{-}7b)$$

This first-order differential equation was studied in Sec. 4.2-4. The solution was shown there to be

$$v_L(t) = V e^{-(t - t_1)/R_L C} \qquad t \geq t_1 \qquad (5.1\text{-}7c)$$

This equation is plotted in Fig. 5.1-8b.

We see from the figure that $v_L(t) = v_i(t)$ until $t = t_1$. Then $v_L(t)$ decreases exponentially more slowly than does $v_i(t)$. The rate of decrease is controlled by the product $R_L C$. When $v_L(t)$ again intersects $v_i(t)$, at $t = t_2$, $v_L(t)$ again is equal to $v_i(t)$, until $t = t_3$, when the process repeats. The resulting $v_L(t)$ is seen to have a finite average value with some variation about the average. This variation can be made as small as desired by increasing the time constant $R_L C$.

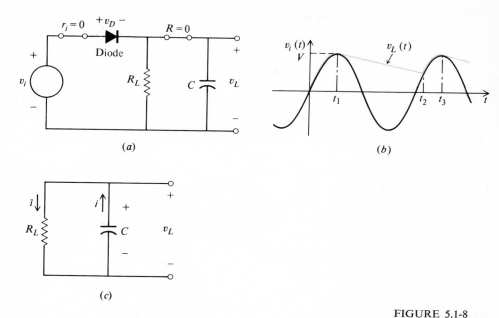

FIGURE 5.1-8
A dc power supply.

5.1-2 Diode Characteristics

The diode can be considered to be analogous to the thermocouple switch used in many home heating units. A thermocouple consists of two dissimilar metals which expand at different rates with increasing temperature. If the heating unit is adjusted for 70°F and the temperature reaches 72°F (for example), the thermocouple opens, disconnecting the electric current operating the heating unit. When the temperature drops below, say, 68°F, the two pieces of metal touch, and current is made available to operate the heating unit. In this chapter we study silicon-type semiconductor diodes. Two different types of silicon are employed, p-type and n-type (see Chap. 9 for a detailed description of the fabrication of semiconductor diodes). When the voltage drop from p to n, called v_D, is positive, current flows. When the voltage drop is negative, no current flows.

The ideal diode vi characteristic shown in Fig. 5.1-2 only approximates the characteristic of a real semiconductor diode. A physical analysis (Sec. 9.5-3) of the semiconductor diode shows that the current and voltage are related by the equation

$$i_D = I_0 \exp(qv_D/mkT) - I_0 \qquad (5.1\text{-}8a)$$

where i_D = current through diode, A

$\qquad v_D$ = voltage across diode, V

$\qquad I_0$ = a constant of proportionality, A

$\qquad q$ = electron charge, 1.6×10^{-19} C

$\qquad k$ = Boltzmann's constant, 1.38×10^{-23} J/°K

$\qquad T$ = absolute temperature, °K

$\qquad m$ = empirical constant which lies between 1 and 2

At room temperature (300°K),

$$\frac{kT}{q} \approx 25 \text{ mV} \qquad (5.1\text{-}8b)$$

Equation (5.1-8a) states that if the diode voltage v_D is negative with magnitude much greater than mkT/q, the current i_D is the *reverse saturation current* $-I_0$. This reverse current $-I_0$ is a function of material, geometry, and temperature and is of the order of 10^{-12} A. If, however, v_D is positive and greatly exceeds mkT/q, the forward current is

$$i_D \approx I_0 \exp(qv_D/mkT) \qquad (5.1\text{-}9)$$

Equation (5.1-8a) is sketched in Fig. 5.1-9a.

The actual characteristic of a typical diode (Fig. 5.1-9b) differs from the exponential curve (Fig. 5.1-9a) because of various effects. At relatively large forward currents the ohmic resistance of the contacts and the semiconductor material effectively increase the forward resistance. In the reverse direction *surface leakage*, which is the current along the surface of the material rather than through the material, effectively decreases the reverse resistance.

At large negative voltages, $v_D \ll 0$, the diode *breaks down*. When this occurs, the current increases negatively by a very large amount for a very small change in v_D. The breakdown is commonly called an *avalanche* breakdown because of the physical process involved; the actual breakdown mechanism will be studied in Chap. 9. Note that the diode equation (5.1-8a) is not valid in this region.

A photograph of the vi characteristic of a typical diode is shown in Fig. 5.1-9b. The photograph was taken from an oscilloscope display generated by a curve-tracing circuit. Note that the diode current is approximately zero until $v_D \approx 0.7$ V, after which the current rises sharply for further increases in v_D. This is a characteristic of silicon diodes. Engineers usually refer to the diode when $v_D \geq 0.7$ V as "turned on," or "forward-biased," and when $v_D < 0.7$ V, it is said to be "turned off," or "back-biased."

It is often convenient to approximate the vi curve by the piecewise-linear characteristic shown in Fig. 5.1-9c. From this curve we see that if $v_D < 0.7$ V, the diode has *infinite* resistance, while for $v_D > 0.7$ V, the diode resistance, called r_d, is the inverse

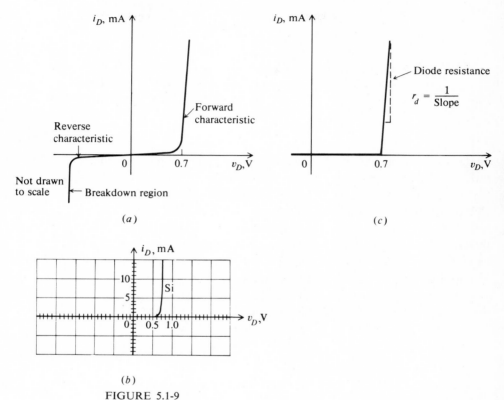

FIGURE 5.1-9
Sketch of diode characteristics. (*a*) Actual characteristic; (*b*) experimentally determined diode characteristic; (*c*) straight-line (piecewise-linear) characteristic.

of the slope of the straight-line characteristic. Comparing Fig. 5.1-9*c* with the ideal diode characteristic of Fig. 5.1-2, we see that they are similar, the break in the ideal diode characteristic occurring at $v_D = 0$ and the ideal diode resistance being either *infinite* or *zero*.

5.1-3   An Equivalent Circuit

The piecewise-linear characteristic of Fig. 5.1-9*c* which is an approximation to that of the real diode is the same as the *vi* characteristic of the equivalent circuit model shown in Fig. 5.1-10*a*. We see from this circuit and Fig. 5.1-2 that if $v_D > 0.7$ V, the ideal

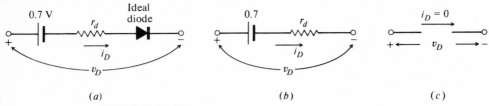

FIGURE 5.1-10
A piecewise-linear equivalent circuit for a real diode. (*a*) Equivalent circuit of
real diode; (*b*) equivalent circuit when $v_D > 0.7$ V; (*c*) equivalent circuit when
$v_D < 0.7$ V.

diode will turn on. When this happens, the voltage drop across the ideal diode is
zero and the resulting circuit is that shown in Fig. 5.1-10*b*. Similarly, if $v_D < 0.7$ V,
the voltage across the ideal diode is negative, so that it is turned off, and hence $i_D = 0$.
The equivalent circuit then takes the form shown in Fig. 5.1-10*c*.

The question now arises as to what numerical value to use for r_d. If we recall
that r_d represents the inverse slope of the straight-line approximation to the exponential diode curve of Fig. 5.1-9*b*, it is clear that any constant value for r_d must be a
compromise. A reasonable range of values can be found by calculating the inverse
slope of the exponential curve. To do this we use Eq. (5.1-9), which is valid for v_D
greater than a few tenths of a volt. The slope is

$$\frac{di_D}{dv_D} = \frac{q}{mkT} I_0 \exp(qv_D/mkT) = \frac{q}{mkT} i_D \qquad (5.1\text{-}10)$$

The resistance r_d is equal to the inverse of the slope. Thus

$$r_d \equiv \frac{mkT/q}{i_D} \qquad (5.1\text{-}11)$$

In practice, we set $m = 1$ (which is a good approximation when i_D is small).
Then, using (5.1-8*b*), we have

$$r_d \approx \frac{25 \times 10^{-3}}{i_D} \qquad (5.1\text{-}12)$$

If i_D is a constant, the value of r_d is fixed. However, if i_d varies over a narrow range, we
replace i_D by its average value I_D, so that

$$r_d = \frac{25 \times 10^{-3}}{I_D} \qquad (5.1\text{-}13)$$

Thus, if $I_D = 1$ mA, $r_d = 25$ Ω. If i_D varies over a wide range, the equivalent circuit given in Fig. 5.1-10b cannot be used because r_d is not a constant. In this case a graphical analysis can be employed. Computer analysis is also possible if we approximate the diode current-voltage characteristic by an equation.

It is important to note that regardless of the value we use for I_D, the voltage drop across r_d is negligible compared with the 0.7-V battery since, from (5.1-12), $i_D r_d \approx 0.025$ V. It is for this reason that r_d is always neglected in dc calculations.

5.2 DIODE GATES

One of the most important uses of diodes is in the construction of logical OR and AND gates. In this section we describe the principles of operation of diode gates.

5.2-1 The OR gate

A two-input OR gate is shown in Fig. 5.2-1a. This gate employs two diodes, one for each input. However, gates are commercially available with many inputs, a typical number being 12.

The operation of the diode OR gate is as follows: Let us assume that the two inputs v_1 and v_2 can either be zero volts (logic 0) or 5 V (logic 1). If both v_1 and v_2 are zero volts, the circuit is as shown in Fig. 5.2-1b. Since there is no voltage being applied to the circuit, $v_0 =$ zero volts.

Now consider that either $v_1 = +5$ V and $v_2 = 0$ V or $v_1 = 0$ V and $v_2 = +5$ V. This case is illustrated in Fig. 5.2-1c. Note that the p terminal of diode D_1 goes to $+5$ V, while the p terminal of the other diode, D_2, goes to 0 V. If, for the moment, we assume that diodes D_1 and D_2 are *ideal*, we see that D_1 is forward-biased regardless of the state of D_2. Thus $v_{D1} = 0$ and $v_0 = v_1 = 5$ V. Note that, as a result of this, D_2 is actually reverse-biased, since v_{D2} is negative and thus $i_{D2} = 0$.

The third possible combination of v_1 and v_2 is $v_1 = v_2 = 5$ V. This possibility is illustrated in Fig. 5.2-1d. In this circuit both diodes, D_1 and D_2, are seen to be forward-biased so that they both have a voltage drop of zero volts across them, and thus $v_0 = 5$ V.

Let us now consider the results of our analysis. They are: $v_0 = 0$ V if v_1 and $v_2 = 0$ V, and $v_0 = 5$ V if v_1 or v_2 are 5 V, as shown in the truth table of Fig. 5.2-1e. Thus the circuit of Fig. 5.2-1a is indeed an OR gate where 5 V corresponds to a logic 1 and zero volts corresponds to a logic 0.

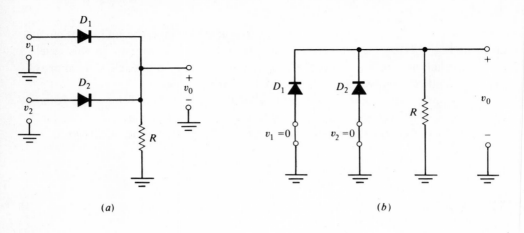

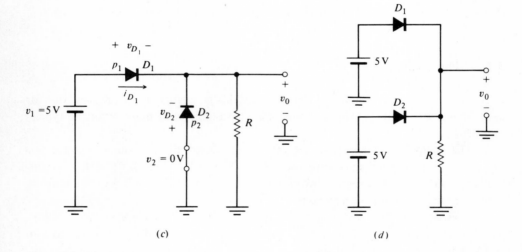

v_1	v_2	v_0
0	0	0
0	5	5
5	0	5
5	5	5

(e)

FIGURE 5.2-1
Diode OR gate. (a) A two-input OR gate using diode logic; (b) circuit when
$v_1 = v_2 = 0$ V; (c) circuit when $v_1 = 5$ V and $v_2 = 0$ V; (d) equivalent circuit when
$v_1 = v_2 = 5$ V; (e) truth table.

5.2-2   The AND Gate

A logical AND operation can be performed using the diode configuration shown in Fig. 5.2-2a. As before, only two inputs are shown and ideal diodes are assumed. In practice, 12 input gates can also be obtained. The operation of the gate can be explained using Fig. 5.2-2b and c. Figure 5.2-2b shows the case when $v_1 = v_2 = 5$ V. Then the voltage drop across each diode, D_1 and D_2, is zero, and $v_0 = 5$ V. (Note that if we had assumed that v_{D1} and v_{D2} were negative, no diode current would flow. Hence $i_A = i_B$ and $v_0 = 5$ V. However, this also yields $v_{D1} = v_{D2} = 0$.)

   If either v_1 or v_2 is zero, we now show that v_0 is zero. Figure 5.2-2c illustrates the case where $v_1 = 0$ and $v_2 = 5$ V. Using KVL around the closed loop, including the supply voltage and diode D_1, yields

$$10 = i_A R + v_{D1} + v_1 = i_A R + v_{D1} \qquad (5.2\text{-}1)$$

Since v_{D1} cannot be positive, $v_{D1} = 0$ and $i_A R = 10$ V. Thus $v_0 = 10 - i_A R = 10 - 10 = 0$ V. Note that D_2 is back-biased. Hence $i_{D2} = 0$. As a consequence of this,

$$i_A = i_{D1} = \frac{10}{R} \qquad (5.2\text{-}2)$$

Thus D_1 is ON while D_2 is OFF. Most important is that $v_0 = 0$.

   The truth table illustrating all the logical possibilities is shown in Fig. 5.2-2d.

5.2-3   Diode Logic; Effects of Nonideal Diodes

For the ideal diode the diode current is zero when the diode voltage is negative, and the diode voltage is zero when the diode current is positive. The power dissipated by the ideal diode is therefore $P_d = v_d i_d = 0$. The vi characteristic of a real diode can be approximated by the curve shown in Fig. 5.1-9c. In this case, when i_D is positive, v_D is also positive, and power is dissipated in the diode.

   As a result of the finite voltage required to obtain a positive current, the output-voltage levels of a diode gate are less than the input levels. Often the output of one OR gate must be used as the input to one or more other gates. After using several stages in this manner the voltage levels may become so small as to preclude proper operation of the last gate in the chain. This drawback to the use of diode logic is illustrated using the OR gate of Fig. 5.2-1a, which is redrawn in Fig. 5.2-3a.

   Figure 5.2-3a shows a two-diode OR gate. To assess the effect of nonideal diodes we let $v_1 = 5$ V and $v_2 = 0$ V. With ideal diodes, v_0 would be 5 V. However, this is not the case here. Figure 5.2-3b shows the equivalent circuit which holds for these conditions. In this circuit i_{D1} is positive and i_{D2} is zero. We have therefore

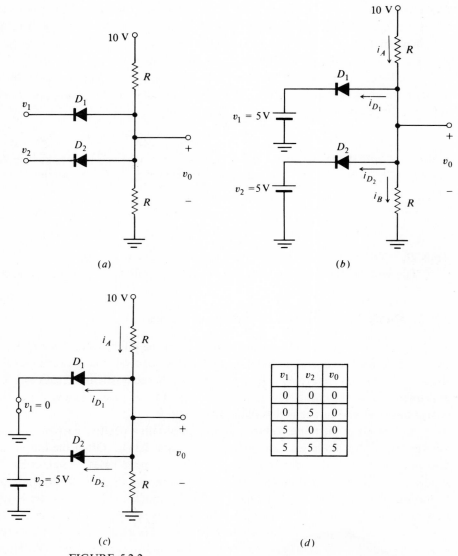

FIGURE 5.2-2
Diode AND gate. (a) An AND gate using diode logic; (b) circuit when
$v_1 = v_2 = 5\,\text{V}$; (c) circuit when $v_1 = 0$ and $v_2 = 5\,\text{V}$; (d) truth table.

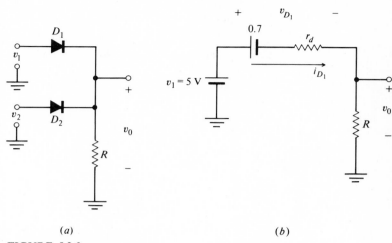

(a)   (b)

FIGURE 5.2-3
Diode OR gate using nonideal diodes. (a) A diode OR gate; (b) equivalent
circuit when $v_1 = 5$ V and $v_2 = 0$ V. D_2 is omitted from the circuit since $i_{D2} = 0$.

replaced D_1 by its equivalent circuit and have omitted D_2 completely since it is back-
biased and no current flows. The output voltage v_0 is

$$v_0 = Ri_{D1} \qquad (5.2\text{-}3)$$

where

$$i_{D1} = \frac{5 - 0.7}{r_d + R} \qquad (5.2\text{-}4)$$

Combining (5.2-3) and (5.2-4), we have

$$v_0 = \frac{4.3}{1 + r_d/R} \qquad (5.2\text{-}5)$$

To ensure that the OR gate acts as closely as possible to an ideal OR gate, we
adjust the resistance R so as to maximize v_0. Thus we design so that $R \gg r_d$. Then
$v_0 \approx 4.3$ V, which is less than the 5 V of the ideal gate by the amount of the diode
turn-on voltage.

5.2-4   Loading

Now consider that the output of this OR gate is connected to the input of another OR
gate, as shown in Fig. 5.2-4a. This is called a *cascade connection*. The logical function
performed by these two gates is

$$v_0 = v_3 \text{ OR } (v_1 \text{ OR } v_2) \qquad (5.2\text{-}6)$$

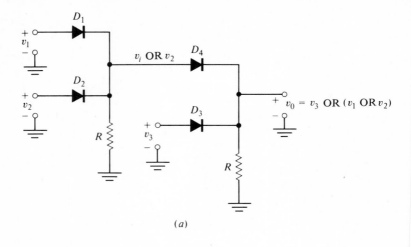

(a)

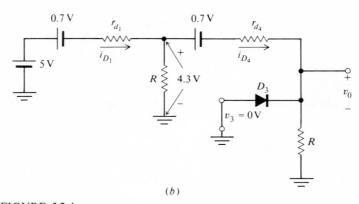

(b)

FIGURE 5.2-4
A cascade of two OR gates. (a) An OR gate followed by a second OR gate to generate $v_0 = v_3 + (v_1 + v_2)$; (b) equivalent circuit when $v_1 = 5$ V and $v_2 = 0$ V.

To illustrate the problem that arises when cascading gates using diode logic, we assume that $v_1 = 5$ V and $v_2 = 0$ V. If $v_3 = 0$ V, diode D_3 is back-biased so that $i_{D3} = 0$, while diodes D_1 and D_4 conduct current. The resulting circuit is shown in Fig. 5.2-4b. Then, using (5.1-12), we have

$$i_{D1} r_{d1} = i_{D4} r_{d4} = 25 \text{ mV} \qquad (5.2\text{-}7)$$

Taking KVL around the loop, including D_1 and D_4, yields

$$v_0 = 5 - 0.7 - 0.025 - 0.7 - 0.025$$
$$= 3.55 \text{ V} \qquad (5.2\text{-}8)$$

Since each OR gate in the chain drops the input voltage an additional 0.725 V, only six OR gates can be cascaded, at which point the output voltage is $5 - 4.35 = 0.65$. If this voltage were used as the input to another OR gate, the diode to which the voltage is applied would not conduct current, since the input voltage is less than the required 0.7 V.

To avoid this difficulty, we use transistors to *amplify* the output voltage to each gate so that it is high enough to ensure proper operation of the next gate. Gates using diodes and transistors will be discussed in Sec. 5.4.

5.3   AN INTRODUCTION TO THE OPERATION OF THE TRANSISTOR

In this section attention is focused on the device which in the past few decades has caused a revolution in the electronics field. This is, of course, the *transistor*. Conceptually, the transistor is a device that acts as a *current amplifier*, and in this section we consider a very useful circuit model for this type of amplifier.

5.3-1   Current Flow in the Transistor

In this chapter we shall not be concerned with the internal structure or physics of the transistor, but rather with its terminal properties. Thus, for our purposes, it is sufficient to describe the transistor as a three-terminal device which has one of two basic forms, called *pnp* and *npn*. The physical configuration and properties of transistors will be taken up in Sec. 9.6.

The circuit symbol for the transistor is shown in Fig. 5.3-1. As seen from the figure, the three external terminals are called the emitter, base, and collector. In a *pnp* transistor the direction of positive dc emitter current is *into* the emitter, while the dc collector and base currents are *out of* the collector and base terminals. In an *npn* transistor the dc current directions are reversed. Note that the arrow on the emitter terminal indicates the normal direction for positive dc emitter current.

Both *pnp* and *npn* transistors are used in practice. However, *npn* transistors are easier to fabricate for *integrated circuits* (ICs) and are generally used, unless the increased versatility obtained using both types of transistors is required.

Applying Kirchhoff's current law (KCL) to the transistors shown in Fig. 5.3-1, we find that

$$i_E = i_B + i_C \qquad (5.3\text{-}1)$$

where, in normal operation, i_E, i_B, and i_C are all positive currents. The transistor is normally operated by varying the input current i_B, which then changes the output

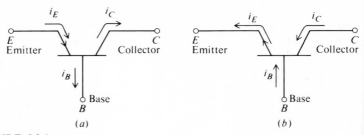

FIGURE 5.3-1
The transistor symbol used in circuit diagrams. (a) The *pnp* transistor; (b) the *npn* transistor.

currents i_C and i_E. It is therefore useful to express i_C and i_E in terms of i_B. It is found experimentally that the ratio of collector current i_C to base current i_B is approximately constant. The constant of proportionality is given the symbol β, so that

$$i_C \equiv \beta i_B \qquad (5.3\text{-}2)$$

Typical values of β are between 40 and 300, although values as high as 2,000 are found in some ICs. It can be shown that (5.3-2) is only an approximate relationship and that β varies with the average value of the collector current. In addition, it can be shown that when $i_B = 0$, the collector current is not actually zero but a very small value, typically 10^{-12} A. We will neglect these second-order effects and consider (5.3-2) as the definition of β, assuming that β is constant for a given transistor and dependent only on the transistor construction.

Combining (5.3-2) with (5.3-1), we find that the emitter current i_E and base current i_B are related by the equation

$$i_E = (\beta + 1)i_B \qquad (5.3\text{-}3)$$

Equations (5.3-1), (5.3-2), and (5.3-3) may be visualized by representing the transistor by an equivalent circuit.

5.3-2 An Equivalent Circuit for the Transistor

Throughout the remainder of this text we restrict our discussion to consideration of the *npn* transistor. An equivalent circuit for the device is shown in Fig. 5.3-2.

The base-emitter circuit The circuit between the base and emitter terminals in a transistor is essentially a semiconductor diode D_1. Thus, in order that base current

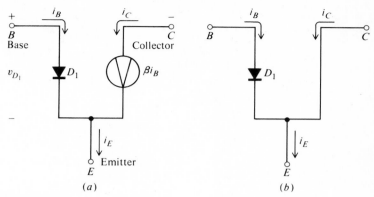

FIGURE 5.3-2
Equivalent circuit of an *npn* transistor. (*a*) Circuit valid for $v_{CE} \geq 0$; (*b*) circuit valid for $v_{CE} = 0$.

flow, the diode must be forward-biased. Since the base current is the current in diode D_1, we have from (5.1-9) that

$$i_B \approx I_0 \exp(v_{BE}/V_T) \qquad (5.3\text{-}4)$$

where $v_{BE} = v_{D1}$, and assuming $m = 1$, $V_T = kT/q = 25$ mV at room temperature.

Current relations The collector current i_C is seen from the figure to be equal to βi_B. This satisfies (5.3-2). The emitter current i_E is seen to be

$$i_E = i_B + i_C = (\beta + 1)i_B \qquad (5.3\text{-}5)$$

as expected from (5.3-3). Thus (5.3-1), (5.3-2), and (5.3-3) are all satisfied by the equivalent circuit shown in Fig. 5.3-2*a*.

Limitation of the equivalent circuit The equivalent circuit in Fig. 5.3-2*a* is valid for all the basic circuits shown in this text. However, it is not valid for all conceivable circuit arrangements. For example, the circuit is not valid at very high frequencies. In addition, the circuit model requires that the collector-emitter voltage $v_{CE} > 0$. If $v_{CE} = 0$, the transistor is said to be *saturated* (Sec. 5.4-1). The equivalent circuit for saturation is shown in Fig. 5.3-2*b*.

5.3-3 Current Amplification

Let us analyze the circuit shown in Fig. 5.3-3*a*, so that we can show that a transistor acts as a current amplifier. The transistor amplifier shown here is called a *common-emitter amplifier*, since the emitter is connected to both the *base* and *collector* through resistors, etc.

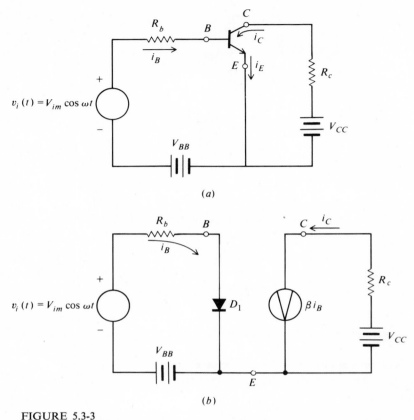

FIGURE 5.3-3
(*a*) A common-emitter amplifier. (*b*) An equivalent circuit for (*a*) valid for $v_{CE} \geq 0$.

The battery V_{BB} and the resistor R_b are inserted in series with the base-emitter diode D_1 to forward-bias D_1 and provide a specified dc current I_B. The battery V_{CC} and the resistor R_c are inserted in the collector-emitter circuit to ensure that under all operating conditions $v_{CE} \geq 0$.

Under these conditions the transistor can be replaced by its equivalent circuit (Fig. 5.3-2*a*). The resultant circuit is shown in Fig. 5.3-3*b*. If the signal $v_i(t)$, which is amplified, is initially assumed to be equal to zero, we see from KVL, taken around the base-emitter circuit, that the dc base current, called the *quiescent* base current, is

$$I_{BQ} = \frac{V_{BB} - V_{D1}}{R_b} \qquad (5.3\text{-}6a)$$

With I_{BQ} positive, the base-emitter diode D_1 can be replaced by a 0.7-V battery. Then

$$I_{BQ} = \frac{V_{BB} - 0.7}{R_b} \qquad (5.3\text{-}6b)$$

The total base current, found by using KVL around the base-emitter loop and representing D_1 by a 0.7-V battery (we assume that D_1 is always forward-biased) is

$$i_B = I_{BQ} + \frac{V_{im} \cos \omega t}{R_b} \qquad (5.3\text{-}7)$$

Equation (5.3-7) is plotted in Fig. 5.3-4 for three different values of V_{im}. In Fig. 5.3-4a and b, $V_{im} \leqslant I_{BQ} R_b$. Note that the ac base current $i_b(t)$ is sinusoidal and directly proportional to $v_i(t)$. In Fig. 5.3-4c, where $V_{im} > I_{BQ} R_b$, $i_b(t)$ is no longer proportional to $v_i(t)$, since i_B cannot become negative due to the presence of D_1 (Fig. 5.3-3b).

Using (5.3-2), we now see that $i_c(t)$ is proportional to $i_b(t)$, and hence proportional to $v_i(t)$, only if $V_{im} \leq I_{BQ} R_b$. If we are required to *linearly amplify* $v_i(t)$, this condition must be satisfied. The condition need not be satisfied when designing logic gates, since the output of a gate is a logic 1 or 0 and other voltage values are not important. This will be discussed in detail in Sec. 5.4.

Notation It is often convenient to separate the time-varying component of the current (and voltage) from its dc (quiescent) value. Thus, in Fig. 5.3-4, we see that i_B consists of a dc current I_{BQ} and a time-varying component which we define as $i_b(t)$, so that

$$i_B(t) \equiv I_{BQ} + i_b(t) \qquad (5.3\text{-}8)$$

This definition is usually restricted to the case where $i_b(t)$ has an average value of zero. Hence Eq. (5.3-8) may be used to describe i_B in Fig. 5.3-4a and b, and is not used for Fig. 5.3-4c.

Linear current amplification We now restrict the problem to the case where the base-emitter diode is always forward-biased. The collector current is [(5.3-2) and (5.3-7)]

$$i_C(t) = \beta i_B(t)$$

$$= \beta I_{BQ} + \frac{\beta V_{im}}{R_b} \cos \omega t \qquad (5.3\text{-}9a)$$

The current βI_{BQ} is the dc collector current which would exist if $v_i(t)$ were zero. This current is called the *quiescent* collector current

$$I_{CQ} \equiv \beta I_{BQ} \qquad (5.3\text{-}9b)$$

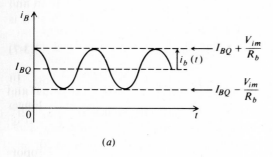

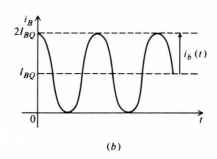

(a)

(b)

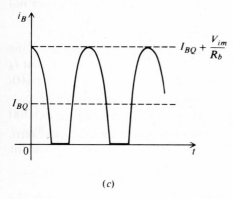

(c)

FIGURE 5.3-4

(a) $V_{im} < I_{BQ} R_b$. (b) $V_{im} = I_{BQ} R_b$. (c) $V_{im} > I_{BQ} R_b$.

Following (5.3-8), we write

$$i_C(t) = I_{CQ} + i_c(t) \qquad (5.3\text{-}10a)$$

Hence

$$i_c(t) = \beta \frac{V_{im}}{R_b} \cos \omega t \qquad (5.3\text{-}10b)$$

For completeness we note, in passing, that the quiescent emitter current is

$$I_{EQ} = I_{BQ} + I_{CQ} = (\beta + 1)I_{BQ} \qquad (5.3\text{-}11)$$

Equation (5.3-9) is a direct result of (5.3-2) and Fig. 5.3-3. However, it is valid only for $v_{CE} \geq 0$. Thus, referring to Fig. 5.3-3, we have

$$v_{CE} = V_{CC} - R_c i_C \geq 0 \qquad (5.3\text{-}12)$$

Hence
$$i_C \leq V_{CC}/R_c \qquad (5.3\text{-}13)$$

From (5.3-9) we can find the largest possible value of i_C (which, of course, is the product of β and the largest possible value of i_B). Thus, letting $i_C = i_{C,\max}$ and employing (5.3-13) yields

$$i_C = i_{C,\max} = \beta \left(I_{BQ} + \frac{V_{im}}{R_b} \right) \leq \frac{V_{CC}}{R_c} \qquad (5.3\text{-}14)$$

This equation tells us how large V_{CC} must be to ensure linear operation, i.e., to ensure that the collector current is proportional to the base current. When this condition is met, the transistor is said to be "operating within its linear region." Note that linear here means "nearly linear," since any active device is basically nonlinear.

5.3-4   Graphical Analysis

To visualize the conditions required for linear amplification, it is convenient to plot a volt-ampere characteristic for the transistor. While it is possible, theoretically, to plot several different vi characteristics, the plot most often made is of i_C versus v_{CE}. A typical plot, with the input current i_B as a parameter, is shown in Fig. 5.3-5 for the particular value of $\beta = 100$. This family of curves is sometimes supplied by the transistor manufacturer.

Equation (5.3-12) is also plotted in Fig. 5.3-5. This equation relates i_C and v_{CE}. Thus the intersection of (5.3-12), which is called the *load line*, and the vi characteristic yields i_C and v_{CE} for a given value of i_B.

The *linear region* of operation of the transistor is the region bounded by

$$0 \leq v_{CE} \leq V_{CC} \qquad [(5.3\text{-}12)] \quad (5.3\text{-}15a)$$

and
$$0 \leq i_C \leq \frac{V_{CC}}{R_c} \qquad [(5.3\text{-}13)] \quad (5.3\text{-}15b)$$

We also note that for this particular plot (Fig. 5.3-5), i_B can vary between 0 and 0.07 mA. The base current cannot exceed 0.07 mA in linear operation, since the maximum collector current ($v_{CE} = 0$) is 7 mA. A further increase in i_B does not result in an increase in i_C. From Fig. 5.3-4 we observe that a maximum symmetrical variation (this is called the *swing*) in i_B occurs when $V_{im} = I_{BQ} R_b$, in which case i_B

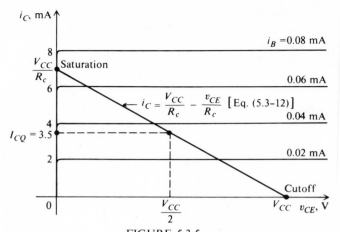

FIGURE 5.3-5
Idealized common-emitter vi characteristic.

varies from 0 to $2I_{BQ}$. Thus, from Fig. 5.3-5, we see that a maximum swing in i_B occurs if

$$2I_{BQ} = 0.07 \text{ mA} \qquad (5.3\text{-}16a)$$

and

$$I_{BQ} = 0.035 \text{ mA} \qquad (5.3\text{-}16b)$$

The corresponding quiescent collector current is [(5.3-10)]

$$I_{CQ} = \beta I_{BQ} = 100(0.035 \text{ mA}) = 3.5 \text{ mA} \qquad (5.3\text{-}17)$$

A sketch of $i_C(t)$ is shown in Fig. 5.3-6 for the three cases of base current illustrated in Fig. 5.3-4, for a transistor having the vi characteristic given in Fig. 5.3-5, and for $I_{BQ} = 0.035$ mA and $i_{C,\,max} = V_{CC}/R_c = 7$ mA.

Figure 5.3-6a and b shows that when $V_{im} \leq I_{BQ} R_b$, the transistor operates in its linear region. In this example a maximum symmetrical peak-to-peak swing of $2I_{CQ} = 7$ mA is possible. If $V_{im} > I_{BQ} R_b$, the base-emitter diode cuts off ($i_B = 0$) for a portion of each cycle. This results in $i_C = 0$ (and hence $v_{CE} = V_{CC}$; Fig. 5.3-3) during this time interval, which is called the *transistor cutoff*. Also we see that, as a result of an excessively large V_{im}, $i_C(t)$ is limited to $2I_{CQ}$ for a finite time interval in each cycle. This interval corresponds to $v_{CE} = 0$, and the transistor is here said to be *saturated*, since no additional current flows (Fig. 5.3-6c).

To summarize, we have defined the linear region as the region in Fig. 5.3-5 where $0 < v_{CE} < V_{CC}$ and where $0 < i_C < V_{CC}/R_c$, the *saturation* condition by $v_{CE} = 0$ and $i_C = i_{C,\,max} = V_{CC}/R_c$, and *cutoff* by $i_C = 0$ and $v_{CE} = V_{CC}$.

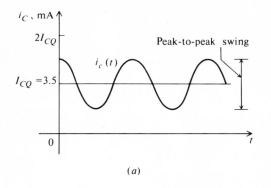

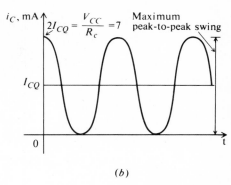

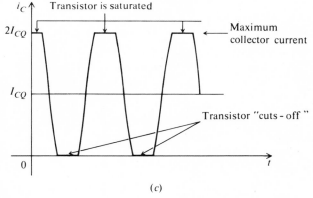

FIGURE 5.3-6
Collector-current waveforms.
(a) $V_{im} < I_{BQ} R_b$; (b) $V_{im} = I_{BQ} R_b$; (c) $V_{im} > I_{BQ} R_b$.

The effect of V_{BB} on the maximum peak-to-peak swing   We note in Fig. 5.3-5 that when $I_{CQ} = 3.5$ mA and $V_{CC}/R_c = 7$ mA, a *maximum symmetrical swing* results. That is, if $V_{CC}/R_c = 7$ mA, increasing or decreasing I_{CQ} ($= \beta I_{BQ}$) by appropriately adjusting V_{BB} results in a smaller symmetrical swing. For example, if $I_{CQ} = 2$ mA, the collector current $i_C(t)$ could still swing from 0 to 7 mA, but the swing is symmetrical only from 0 to 4 mA. Similarly, we find that if $I_{CQ} = 5$ mA, a 4-mA peak-to-peak symmetrical swing is possible.

Since

$$I_{CQ} = \beta I_{BQ} = \beta \frac{V_{BB} - 0.7}{R_b} \qquad (5.3\text{-}18)$$

we select V_{BB} to provide the correct value of I_{CQ}. This point is discussed further in Example 5.3-1.

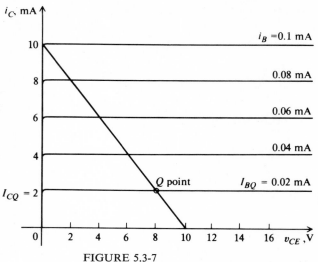

FIGURE 5.3-7
vi characteristic and load line for Example 5.3-1.

EXAMPLE 5.3-1 A certain transistor has the vi characteristics shown in Fig. 5.3-7. This transistor is used in the circuit of Fig. 5.3-3a.

(a) Find the quiescent collector current. Let $V_{BB} = 2.7$ V, $R_b = 100$ kΩ, $R_c = 1$ kΩ, and $V_{CC} = 10$ V. $\beta = 100$.

(b) Find the maximum value of V_{im} to ensure linear operation; i.e., that the time-varying component of the collector current is proportional to $v_i(t)$.

SOLUTION (a) The dc load line equation, Eq. (5.3-12), is

$$V_{CC} = v_{CE} + i_C R_c$$
$$10 = v_{CE} + 1{,}000i_C$$

This equation is plotted on the vi characteristics of Fig. 5.3-7.

The quiescent base current can be obtained from (5.3-18) or directly from Fig. 5.3-3b with V_{im} set equal to zero. Using KVL around the emitter-base circuit yields

$$V_{BB} = i_B R_b + v_{BE}$$
$$2.7 = 10^5 i_B + 0.7$$

Hence
$$i_B = I_{BQ} = 0.02 \text{ mA}$$

From Fig. 5.3-7, $I_{CQ} = 2$ mA. Hence the time-varying component of i_C is limited to a 4-mA peak-to-peak swing. If a peak-to-peak swing greater than 4 mA is attempted, by increasing V_{im} sufficiently, the transistor will *cut off.* The student should verify this by referring to Fig. 5.3-7 and noting that while a maximum positive peak swing of $i_C - I_{CQ} = 8$ mA is possible, a negative peak swing of only $|i_C - I_{CQ}| = 2$ mA can be attained.

(b) The time-varying component of the base current can be found from (5.3-8) or directly from Fig. 5.3-3b:

$$i_b = \frac{V_{im}}{R_b} \cos \omega_m t$$

In this problem, i_b is limited to 0.02 mA; thus

$$\frac{V_{im}}{R_b} \leq 0.02 \times 10^{-3}$$

and since $R_b = 10^5 \, \Omega$,

$$V_{im} \leq 2 \text{ V}$$

This solution indicates that the full current-swing capability of the transistor is not being utilized. If V_{BB} could be adjusted, we might set it so that $I_{BQ} = 0.05$ mA. This would require that

$$V_{BB} = R_b I_{BQ} + 0.7 = 10^5(0.05 \times 10^{-3}) + 0.7 = 5.7 \text{ V}$$

Under these conditions, the ac component of i_B can swing 0.05 mA, and the input voltage is restricted to values

$$V_{im} \leq 5 \text{ V}$$

an increase in input voltage, and output current, by a factor of 2.5.
////////

Current gain   Current gain in a transistor is defined as the ratio of the ac output current to the ac input current. In this section, it refers to the ratio of i_c to i_b. Using (5.3-8) and (5.3-9), the current gain A_i is

$$A_i = \frac{i_c}{i_b} = \beta$$

For this reason β is called the *current amplification factor.* It is shown in Sec. 5.6 that β is actually the maximum possible current gain, and that current gains obtained in practice are often significantly less than β.

5.4   TRANSISTOR GATES

In this section we show how the gates used in computer circuits are designed. These gates are of two basic varieties, those using both diodes and transistors, which are called *diode-transistor logic* (DTL) gates, and those employing transistors only. These latter gates are of several different types. We shall discuss emitter-coupled logic (ECL), which is used extensively when extremely high speed is required.

5.4-1   The Transistor Logic States, Saturation and Cutoff

Saturation and *cutoff* are two extreme states of transistor operation. As explained in Sec. 5.3, saturation occurs when $v_{CE} = 0$, while cutoff occurs when $i_C = 0$. The operation of a transistor in saturation is illustrated by means of the following example.

EXAMPLE 5.4-1   The behavior of the transistor in the saturation region becomes important in the design of switching circuits. To illustrate this, consider the circuit shown in Fig. 5.4-1 with $V_{CC} = 10$ V, $R_b = 10$ kΩ, and $R_c = 1$ kΩ. The transistor has $\beta = 100$ and $V_{BE} = +0.7$ V. Find the operating conditions when (*a*) $V_{BB} = 1.5$ V and (*b*) 10.7 V.

SOLUTION   (*a*) For $V_{BB} = 1.5$ V, application of KVL around the base-emitter loop yields

$$-V_{BB} + I_B R_b + V_{BE} = 0$$

Then

$$I_B = \frac{V_{BB} - V_{BE}}{R_b} = \frac{1.5 - 0.7}{10^4} = 0.08 \text{ mA}$$

$$I_C = \beta I_B = (100)(0.08) = 8 \text{ mA}$$

$$I_E \approx I_C = 8 \text{ mA}$$

$$V_{CE} = V_{CC} - I_C R_c = 10 - (8)(1) = 2 \text{ V}$$

Thus the transistor is operating within the linear region ($V_{CE} > 0$ V). This is illustrated in Fig 5.4-1*b*.

(*b*) For $V_{BB} = 10.7$ V,

$$I_B = \frac{10.7 - 0.7}{10^4} = 1 \text{ mA}$$

If the basic relation $I_C = \beta I_B$ were to hold here, we should have $I_C = 100$ mA

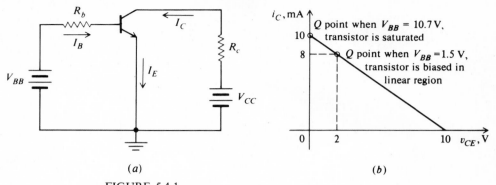

FIGURE 5.4-1
Figures for Example 5.4-1. (a) Circuit for Example 5.4-1; (b) load line.

and $V_{CE} = 10 - 100 = -90$ V, an impossible situation. Thus the transistor is in saturation, as shown in Fig. 5.4-1b, and

$$V_{CE} = 0 \text{ V}$$

The collector current is

$$I_C = \frac{V_{CC} - V_{CE}}{R_c} = \frac{10 - 0}{10^3} = 10 \text{ mA}$$

and

$$I_E = I_C + I_B = 11 \text{ mA}$$

Note that the effective β in this particular saturation condition is $I_C/I_B = 10$. Also, further increases in V_{BB} will affect only I_B, with I_C remaining at 10 mA. This is the saturation current.

This example shows that saturation is evidenced by a reduction in the effective β of the transistor, and occurs when $V_{CE} = 0$.

////////

5.4-2 The NOT Gate

We stated in Sec. 5.2 that NOT gates can be constructed using transistors, but not with diodes alone. The reason for this is that *inversion* is possible with a transistor. This will be seen from the following discussion.

The transistor NOT gate shown in Fig. 5.4-2 operates between cutoff and saturation. Here the input signal varies between 0 and 5 V. When $v_i = 0$ V, no base current flows; therefore no collector current flows, and the transistor is at cutoff. The collector voltage v_C is

$$v_C = V_{CC} - i_C R_c = V_{CC} \qquad (5.4\text{-}1)$$

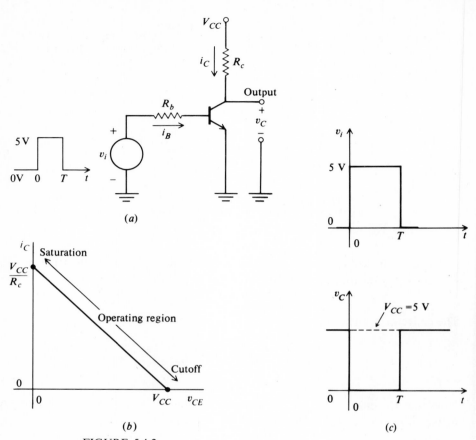

FIGURE 5.4-2
The transistor switch. (a) A transistor switch; (b) operating path of the NOT gate; (c) waveforms.

When $v_i = 5$ V, the base current is, assuming $V_{BE} \approx 0.7$ V,

$$i_B = \frac{5 - V_{BE}}{R_b} = \frac{4.3}{R_b} \qquad (5.4\text{-}2)$$

This value of base current is usually large enough to result in saturation. Then

$$v_C = 0 \qquad (5.4\text{-}3a)$$

and

$$i_C = \frac{V_{CC}}{R_c} \qquad (5.4\text{-}3b)$$

Thus $v_C = 0$ V when $v_i = 5$ V.

The operating path of the NOT gate is shown in Fig. 5.4-2b, and the results are summarized in Fig. 5.4-2c. Here we see that the transistor is an *inverter*, or NOT, gate. The logical 1 is represented by 5 V (we set $V_{CC} = 5$ V), and the logical 0 is represented by 0 V.

5.4-3 Diode-Transistor Logic (DTL)

In Sec. 5.2 we found that the main drawback when using diode gates was that the signal voltage was attenuated due to the 0.7-V drop across each conducting diode. If the diode gate is followed by a transistor amplifier, the attenuation problem is eliminated. This is the underlying philosophy of *diode-transistor logic*.

The most commonly used DTL gate is the NAND (NOT-AND) gate, a diode AND gate followed by a transistor NOT gate which also acts as an amplifier. Thus, if the two inputs to a NAND gate are x_1 and x_2, the output y is

$$y = \overline{(x_1 \cdot x_2)} \qquad (5.4\text{-}4)$$

A two-input NAND gate is shown in Fig. 5.4-3a. The inputs x_1 and x_2 first go to the diode AND gate. This is followed by the transistor which inverts the signal, thereby performing the NOT function.

To explain the operation of this gate, let us assume that each diode can be replaced by a 0.7-V battery when current flows. Also assume that x_1 and x_2 are either 0 or 5 V. The first case to be considered is x_1 OR x_2 equal to 0 V. If x_1 is 0 V, we have $v_1 = 0.7$ V, since D_1 is turned on. The circuit for this condition takes the form shown in Fig. 5.4-3b. Since D_3 and D_4 are in series directly across v_1, we must have (assuming $V_{BE} = 0$)

$$v_1 = v_{D3} + v_{D4} = 0.7 \text{ V} \qquad (5.4\text{-}5)$$

and for identical diodes,

$$v_{D3} = v_{D4} = 0.35 \text{ V} \qquad (5.4\text{-}6)$$

Since this is not enough to turn the diodes on, the diode current $i_D \approx 0$. Note that for i_D to be positive, v_{D3} and v_{D4} must each be 0.7 V. This is impossible because $v_1 = 0.7$ V. Since $i_D \approx 0$, the base-emitter voltage at the transistor is indeed

$$v_{BE} = i_D(5 \text{ k}\Omega) \approx 0 \text{ V} \qquad (5.4\text{-}7)$$

Finally, since $v_{BE} = 0$, no base current flows. Consequently, no collector current flows, and thus $v_C = 5$ V.

The second case to consider is $x_1 = x_2 = 5$ V. In this case, we will show that $v_1 < 5$ V. Thus the voltages v_{D1} and v_{D2} are negative (D_1 and D_2 are reverse-biased). Hence D_1 and D_2 are turned off, and $i_{D1} = i_{D2} = 0$. To prove this we use indirect reasoning. First, assume that the statement is correct. Then we need only show that v_1 is indeed less than 5 V. This is done using Fig. 5.4-3c, where D_1 and D_2 have

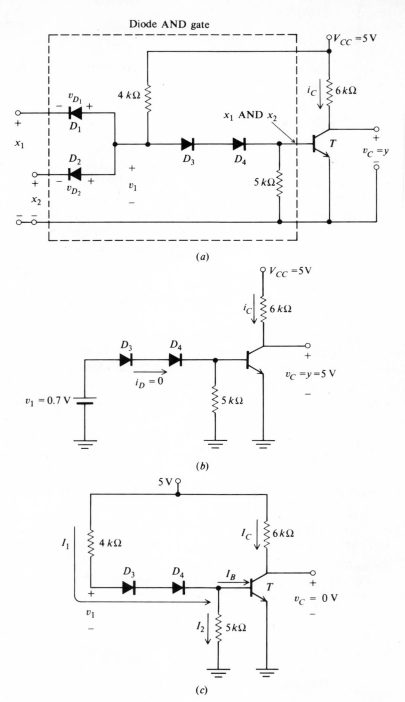

FIGURE 5.4-3
(a) A DTL NAND gate. (b) DTL gate when x_1 or x_2 equals 0 V. (c) Circuit when $x_1 = x_2 = 5$ V.

been omitted because we have assumed that they are turned off. The voltage v_1 is found from KVL:

$$v_1 = v_{D3} + v_{D4} + v_{BE} \qquad (5.4\text{-}8)$$

Since each of the voltages v_{D3}, v_{D4}, and v_{BE} are diode voltages, they are less than or equal to 0.7 V. Thus $v_1 \le 2.1$ V < 5 V, which proves the original statement. The student can prove that assuming $v_1 \ge 5\,^\bullet$V leads to a contradiction.

We must now prove that when $x_1 = x_2 = 5$ V, current flows in D_3, D_4, and in the transistor. To be rigorous, we must again use an indirect proof (Prob. 5.4-4). However, let us assume the statement correct. Then from Fig. 5.4-3c, since $v_1 = 2.1$ V,

$$I_1 = \frac{5 - 2.1}{4{,}000} \approx 0.725 \text{ mA}$$

The current I_2 is

$$I_2 = \frac{V_{BE}}{5{,}000} = \frac{0.7}{5{,}000} = 0.14 \text{ mA}$$

Hence the base current I_B, found using KCL, is

$$I_B = I_1 - I_2 = (0.725 - 0.14) \text{ mA} = 0.585 \text{ mA}$$

This is usually sufficient base current to cause the transistor to saturate. To show this, we assume saturation ($v_C = 0$ V). Then the collector current at saturation is

$$I_{C,\,\text{sat}} = \frac{5 - v_C}{6{,}000} = \frac{5}{6{,}000} = 0.83 \text{ mA}$$

This corresponds to a β of

$$\beta = \frac{I_C}{I_B} = \frac{0.83}{0.585} \approx 1.4$$

However, typical values of β far exceed this value; typical values of β are between 40 and 300. We therefore conclude that the transistor is saturated (Example 5.4-1), so that v_C is indeed equal to 0 V.

These results are best summarized by the truth table below. (Note that $v_C = 5$ V corresponds to $y = 1$.)

x_1	x_2	y	$\bar{y}$
0	0	1	0
0	1	1	0
1	0	1	0
1	1	0	1

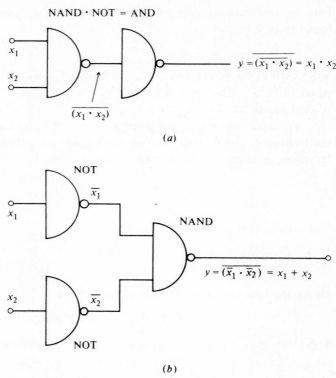

FIGURE 5.4-4
(a) An AND gate using DTL. (b) An OR gate using DTL.

From the truth table

$$\bar{y} = x_1 \cdot x_2 \qquad (5.4\text{-}9)$$

so that

$$\bar{\bar{y}} = y = \overline{x_1 \cdot x_2} \qquad (5.4\text{-}10)$$

Thus the circuit of Fig. 5.4-3 does indeed function as a NAND gate. The output logic 1 level is 5 V, so that there is no problem driving succeeding gates.

Other logic functions So far we have seen that NOT and NAND (NOT-AND) gates can be constructed using DTL. To implement the logic AND function, we follow the NAND gate by a NOT gate, as shown in Fig. 5.4-4a.

An OR gate can be constructed by noting that in (5.4-10), using De Moivre's theorem,

$$y = \overline{x_1 \cdot x_2} = \bar{x}_1 + \bar{x}_2 \qquad (5.4\text{-}11)$$

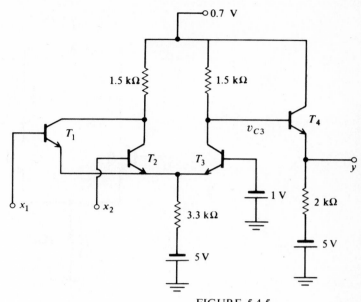

FIGURE 5.4-5
A two-input OR gate using ECL.

Thus, if the inputs to the NAND gate were $\bar{x}_1$ and $\bar{x}_2$ instead of x_1 and x_2, the output would be $x_1 + x_2$. This is illustrated in Fig. 5.4-4*b*.

Since the OR, NOT, and AND functions can all be implemented using NAND gates, NAND logic is extremely popular (note also that a single-input NAND gate is equivalent to a NOT gate).

5.4-4 Emitter-coupled Logic

Emitter-coupled logic (ECL) is a system using only transistors, which can produce the logic functions OR and NOR. A NOR gate is an OR gate followed by a NOT gate. In this section we consider only the two-input OR gate shown in Fig. 5.4-5.

Each input x_1 and x_2 is either 0 or -1.5 V. A logic 1 corresponds to $x = 0$ V, and for a logic 0, x is -1.5 V. To see how ECL operates, consider the circuit of T_2 and T_3. This is called a *comparator*, or difference amplifier, and is redrawn in Fig. 5.4-6. We shall now show that when x_2 is greater than the -1-V reference voltage, $v_{C3} = 0.7$ V, and when x_2 is less than the -1-V reference voltage, $v_{C3} = -0.8$ V.

Consider that $x_2 = 0$ V. Which transistor, T_2 or T_3, is conducting current? We

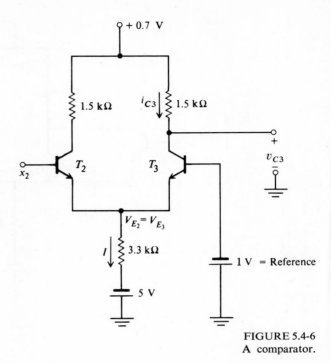

FIGURE 5.4-6
A comparator.

know that when a transistor is turned on so that it conducts current, its base-emitter voltage is 0.7 V. Assume that T_2 conducts; then the emitter of T_2 is

$$v_{E2} = v_{B2} - v_{BE2} = 0 - 0.7 = -0.7 \text{ V}$$

Note that T_3 is not conducting since its base-emitter voltage is

$$v_{BE3} = v_{B3} - v_{E3} = v_{B3} - v_{E2} = -1 - (-0.7) = -0.3 \text{ V}$$
$$v_{E3} = v_{E2}$$

·which is less than the +0.7 V required to turn on the transistor.

If we had assumed T_3 conducting, we would have found

$$v_{E3} = v_{B3} - v_{BE3} = -1 - (+0.7) = -1.7 \text{ V}$$
$$T_3 \text{ assumed on}$$

and therefore

$$v_{BE2} = v_{B2} - v_{E2} = v_{B2} - v_{E3} = 0 - (-1.7) = +1.7 \text{ V}$$
$$v_{E2} = v_{E3}$$

which is not possible since a conducting transistor can have a base-emitter voltage of only $+0.7$ V. Hence this assumption is incorrect.

Since T_3 is not conducting (turned off), $i_{C3} = 0$ and $v_{C3} = 0.7$ V. The student can verify that as long as $x_2 > -1$ V, $v_{C3} = 0.7$ V.

We have just considered the possibility that $x_2 = 0$ and have found that T_2 is ON while T_3 is OFF. Let us now consider that $x_2 < -1$ V, and specifically, $x_2 = -1.5$ V. In this case T_3 is ON and conducts current. Hence, referring to Fig. 5.4-6, we have

$$v_{E2} = v_{E3} = v_{B3} - v_{BE3} = -1 - (0.7) = -1.7 \text{ V}$$

Hence

$$v_{BE2} = v_{B2} - v_{E2} = -1.5 - (-1.7) = 0.2 \text{ V}$$

This voltage is less than the 0.7 V required to turn on T_2, and as a result no current flows in T_2.

Since current flows in T_3 and not in T_2, all the current I comes from T_3. Thus

$$I = i_{C3} \qquad (5.4\text{-}12)$$

But from KVL

$$V_{E3} = 3{,}300I - 5 \qquad (5.4\text{-}13)$$

Setting $V_{E3} = -1.7$ V yields

$$I = 1 \text{ mA} = i_{C3} \qquad (5.4\text{-}14)$$

Thus

$$v_{C3} = 0.7 - 1{,}500i_{C3} = -0.8 \text{ V} \qquad (5.4\text{-}15)$$

We now see that as a result of using the comparator shown in Fig. 5.4-6, the voltage levels of x_1 and x_2 are shifted from 0 V and -1.5 V to 0.7 V and -0.8 V. The advantage of this circuit is that this shift is accomplished in several nanoseconds, orders of magnitude faster than when using other techniques.

In the circuit shown in Fig. 5.4-5, we have T_1 and T_2 connected in parallel (the emitters and collectors are connected together). Thus, if x_1 OR x_2 is 0 V, the collector voltage of v_{C3} is $+0.7$ V. If however, both x_1 AND x_2 are -1.5 V, then $v_{C3} = -0.8$ V.

The output y of the OR gate is taken from the emitter of T_4. Since the emitter voltage is 0.7 V less than the base voltage,

$$y = \begin{cases} 0 \text{ V} & \text{if } x_1 \text{ OR } x_2 \text{ equals 0 V } (v_{C3} = 0.7 \text{ V}) \\ -1.5 \text{ V} & \text{if } x_1 \text{ AND } x_2 \text{ equal } -1.5 \text{ V } (v_{C3} = -0.8 \text{ V}) \end{cases}$$

Thus T_4 shifts the level back to that of the original x_1 and x_2. Using this result, we obtain the truth table below for ECL, where we have represented 0 V as a logic 1 and -1.5 V as a logic 0.

x_1	x_2	y
0	0	0
0	1	1
1	0	1
1	1	1

Thus we have proved that ECL performs the logic functions of an OR gate.

A NOR gate can be constructed by connecting the base of T_4 to the collector of T_2 rather than to the collector of T_3 (Prob. 5.4-6). It is left as an exercise for the reader to show that, as in the case of DTL, all three logic operations OR, AND, and NOT can be obtained using NOR logic.

5.4-5   Cascading Transistor Gates

In Fig. 5.2-4 we showed two diode OR gates in cascade. The analysis of this circuit indicated that cascading this type of gate was not practical because the output voltage decreased with the number of gates cascaded. In this section we consider cascading DTL NAND gates and show that there is no attenuation when several gates are cascaded. However, we shall see that the output of one NAND gate can be connected to only a limited number of other NAND gates. This number is called the *fan-out* of the gate.

Figure 5.4-7 shows two two-input NAND gates in cascade. One input of the second gate (diode D_5) is connected to the collector of T_1. The second gate therefore will operate properly if v_{C1} is either 0 or 5 V. We see that if T_1 is at cutoff, that is, $i_1 = 0$, then $v_{C1} = 5$ V, whether or not D_5 is connected.

However, consider that x_1 and x_2 are each 5 V, so that T_1 is in saturation. Our previous calculations, in Sec. 5.4.3, showed that a base current $i_{B1} = 0.585$ mA resulted for this condition. To maintain transistor T_1 in saturation (Sec. 5.4-1),

$$\beta i_{B1} \geq i_{C1} = i_1 + i_2 \qquad (5.4\text{-}16)$$

For example, if $\beta = 20$, $\beta i_{B1} = 11.7$ mA. If D_5 were not connected, $i_{C1} = i_1 = V_{CC}/6{,}000 = 0.83$ mA. Hence T_1 is saturated as in Sec. 5.4-3.

Now consider that D_5 is connected to T_1. Then, with T_1 saturated, $v_{C1} = 0$ V, D_5 is turned on, and $v_7 = 0.7$ V. The current i_7 is therefore

$$i_7 = \frac{V_{CC} - v_7}{4{,}000} = \frac{5 - 0.7}{4{,}000} \approx 1.1 \text{ mA} \qquad (5.4\text{-}17)$$

How much of this current flows in D_5? Since $v_7 = 0.7$ V, no current flows in D_7 and

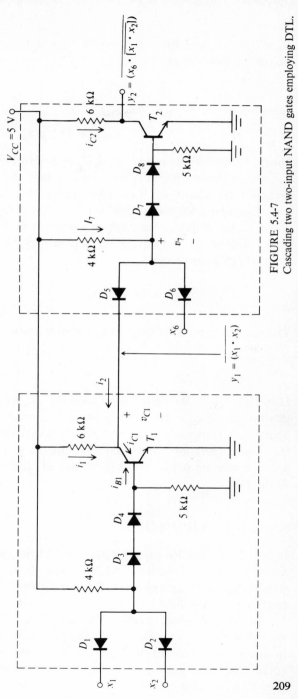

FIGURE 5.4-7
Cascading two two-input NAND gates employing DTL.

209

D_8. Thus all the current i_7 flows in D_5 and D_6. If $x_6 = +5$ V, D_6 is off, and all the current flows in D_5. Then

$$i_2 = i_7 = 1.1 \text{ mA} \qquad (5.4\text{-}18)$$

Substituting into (5.4-16) yields

$$\beta i_{B1} = 11.7 \geq i_{C1} = 0.83 + 1.1 = 1.93 \text{ mA}$$

Thus the inequality is still satisfied, T_1 is in saturation, and $v_{C1} = 0$.

We have shown that v_{C1} will take on only the value 0 or 5 V whether or not D_5 is connected. Thus there is no loading effect when cascading DTL gates.

Consider a somewhat different problem, that of connecting, not a single diode D_5 to T_1, but N diodes representing the inputs to N NAND gates. Now, instead of a single current $i_2 = 1.1$ mA, we might possibly have a current $Ni_2 = N(1.1)$ mA. Equation (5.4-16) becomes

$$\beta i_{B1} \geq i_{C1} = i_1 + Ni_2$$

or
$$11.7 \geq 0.83 + N(1.1) \qquad (5.4\text{-}19)$$

The inequality must be satisfied in order to ensure that T_1 is saturated. Thus

$$N \leq \frac{11.7 - 0.83}{1.1} = 9.9 \qquad (5.4\text{-}20)$$

Hence T_1 can be connected simultaneously to no more than nine NAND gates. If this number is exceeded, T_1 will not be saturated, a condition required for proper operation. Thus, connecting more than one gate to the output of any gate can affect the system operation. The maximum number of gates N which can be paralleled is a very important parameter in the design of digital systems, and is called the fan-out of the gate.

5.5   THE FLIP-FLOP

In Sec. 2.3 we studied the logic operation of the *flip-flop*, and we found that it had a memory capable of storing one binary digit. It was also shown that a flip-flop can be constructed using logic gates. In this section we shall discuss a flip-flop which employs NOR logic (Prob. 5.5-1).

A basic flip-flop circuit is shown in Fig. 5.5-1a. The outputs are Q_1 and Q_2. We will show that when $Q_1 = 5$ V, then $Q_2 = 0$ V, and when $Q_1 = 0$ V, then $Q_2 = 5$ V. In this particular circuit the logic 1 is represented by 5 V and the logic 0 by 0 V. To obtain these voltages, the circuit is designed so that when T_1 is cut off ($Q_1 = 5$ V), then T_2 is in saturation ($Q_2 = 0$ V), and vice versa.

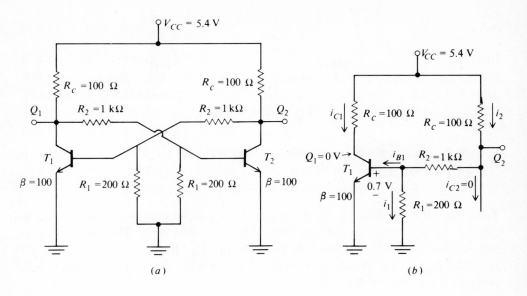

(a)

(b)

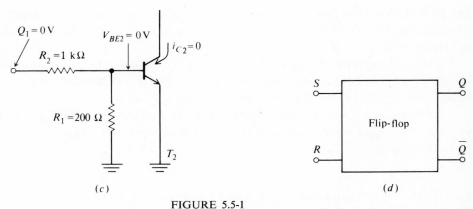

(c)

(d)

FIGURE 5.5-1
(a) A flip-flop. (b) T_1 is in saturation. (c) T_2 is cut off ($i_{C2} = 0$).
(d) Logic block for SET RESET flip-flop.

To show that this is the case, assume T_1 is saturated and T_2 is at cutoff. Then $Q_1 = 0$ V and $i_{C2} = 0$, as shown in Fig. 5.5-1b. In addition, $v_{BE1} = 0.7$ V. Then

$$i_{C1} = \frac{V_{CC} - v_{C1}}{R_c} = \frac{5.4 - 0}{100} = 54 \text{ mA} \qquad (5.5\text{-}1)$$

$$i_1 = \frac{v_{BE1}}{R_1} = \frac{0.7}{200} = 3.5 \text{ mA} \qquad (5.5\text{-}2)$$

and

$$i_2 = \frac{V_{CC} - v_{BE1}}{R_c + R_2} = \frac{5.4 - 0.7}{1.1 \times 10^3} \approx 4.3 \text{ mA} \qquad (5.5\text{-}3)$$

Thus

$$i_{B1} = i_2 - i_1 = 0.8 \text{ mA} \qquad (5.5\text{-}4)$$

Assume that the transistors selected each have a $\beta = 100$. Multiplying i_{B1} by $\beta = 100$ yields an $i_{C1} = \beta i_{B1} = 80$ mA. This is larger than the calculated value given in (5.5-1). Thus T_1 is saturated, and $i_{C1} = 54$ mA. The voltage Q_2 is found using KVL.

$$Q_2 = V_{CC} - R_c i_2 = 5.4 - 0.43 \approx 5 \text{ V} \qquad (5.5\text{-}5)$$

If T_2 is cut off, its base-emitter voltage must be less than 0.7 V. Refer to Fig. 5.5-1c. Here we see that since T_1 is in saturation, $Q_1 = 0$ V; hence $v_{BE2} = 0$ V. Thus we have proved that T_2 is indeed at cutoff.

Triggering the flip-flop   If Q_2 is initially at 0 V and we want to *set* the flip-flop so that $Q_2 \approx 5$ V, we apply a positive voltage pulse to the base of T_1. The applied voltage pulse should exceed 0.7 V. Then T_1 turns on and Q_1 "flips" to 0 V. This cuts off T_2, making $Q_2 = 5$ V. Similarly, to make $Q_1 = 5$ V when Q_2 is initially equal to 5 V, we apply a positive voltage to the base of T_2.

The SET-RESET flip-flop   We now establish the relationship between the flip-flop shown in Fig. 5.5-1a and the SET-RESET (logic block) flip-flop discussed in Sec. 2.3 and shown in Fig. 5.5-1d.

The logic performed by the device shown in Fig. 5.5-1d is as follows. A positive voltage pulse applied at the S (set) input makes $Q = 1$ and $\bar{Q} = 0$. Similarly, a positive voltage pulse applied at the R (reset) input makes $Q = 0$ and $\bar{Q} = 1$.

Comparing this with the logic operation of the flip-flop shown in Fig. 5.5-1a, we note that the set input is the base of T_1, the reset input is the base of T_2, and $Q_1 = Q$, while $Q_2 = \bar{Q}$.

5.6   THE TRANSISTOR AS A SMALL-SIGNAL LINEAR AMPLIFIER

In Sec. 5.3 we considered the equivalent circuit of the transistor (Fig. 5.3-2) and used this circuit to determine the large-signal performance of an amplifier. In that section we represented the base-emitter diode as a 0.7-V battery when the diode was on.

In this section we are concerned with amplification of very small signals. These signals exist at the input to every AM and FM radio, television, etc. When amplifying small signals, approximating a diode by only a battery is not sufficient. It is found that the diode resistance r_d, shown in Fig. 5.1-10, must also be considered since the small ac voltage drop across this resistor may be comparable with the small ac input signal.

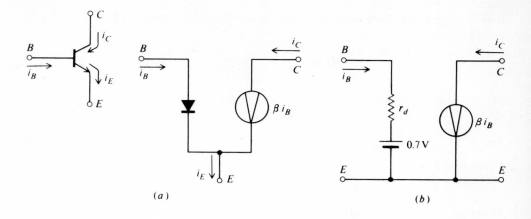

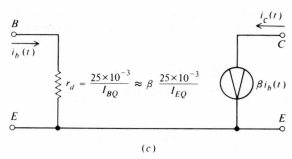

(c)

FIGURE 5.6-1
Small-signal equivalent circuit of a transistor. (*a*) Basic equivalent circuit with
$v_{CB} < 0.7$ V; (*b*) a refined equivalent circuit; (*c*) an equivalent circuit for small-
amplitude, time-varying signals.

5.6-1   An Equivalent-circuit Model for Small-signal Amplification

In Sec. 5.3 we found that the transistor could be modeled by the equivalent circuit
shown in Fig. 5.6-1*a*. In this circuit we assumed that $v_{CE} \geq 0$ V. We now replace
the base-emitter diode by its equivalent circuit (Fig. 5.1-10), which includes the 0.7-V
battery considered earlier and the diode resistance [(5.1-13), with I_D replaced by I_{BQ}].

$$r_d = \frac{25 \times 10^{-3}}{I_{BQ}} \qquad (5.6\text{-}1)$$

The resulting equivalent circuit is shown in Fig. 5.6-1*b*.

For small-signal linear operation, it is convenient to write i_B, v_{BE}, v_{CE}, and i_C
in terms of a dc and a time-varying component. Since we have assumed that the

time-varying component is small, r_d can be considered constant. Then from (5.3-8) and (5.3-10a)

$$i_B = I_{BQ} + i_b(t) \qquad (5.6\text{-}2a)$$

$$i_C = I_{CQ} + i_c(t) \qquad (5.6\text{-}2b)$$

We can also use this notation for voltages. Thus

$$v_{BE} = V_{BEQ} + v_{be}(t) \qquad (5.6\text{-}2c)$$

and

$$v_{CE} = V_{CEQ} + v_{ce}(t) \qquad (5.6\text{-}2d)$$

From Fig. 5.6-1b

$$V_{BEQ} = r_d I_{BQ} + 0.7 \qquad (5.6\text{-}3)$$

However, from (5.6-1), $r_d I_{BQ} = 25$ mV. In what follows we shall neglect this small voltage for dc calculations so that $V_{BEQ} = 0.7$ V as before.

The definitions given in (5.6-2) can be used with Fig. 5.6-1b to obtain an equivalent circuit for the time-varying currents and voltages. Thus, going around the base-emitter circuit, we have

$$v_{BE} = V_{BEQ} + v_{be}(t) = r_d i_B + 0.7 = r_d I_{BQ} + 0.7 + r_d i_b(t) \qquad (5.6\text{-}4a)$$

Hence, separating dc and ac terms, we obtain Eq. (5.6-3) for the dc components and

$$v_{be}(t) = r_d i_b(t) \qquad (5.6\text{-}4b)$$

for the ac components. Similarly, using KCL in the collector-emitter circuit,

$$i_C = I_{CQ} + i_c(t) = \beta i_B = \beta I_{BQ} + \beta i_b(t) \qquad (5.6\text{-}5a)$$

Thus, for the ac component of the collector current, we have

$$i_c(t) = \beta i_b(t) \qquad (5.6\text{-}5b)$$

Equations (5.6-4b) and (5.6-5b) can be modeled by the equivalent circuit for time-varying signals shown in Fig. 5.6-1c. This is called a *hybrid* equivalent circuit, and r_d and β are called *hybrid parameters*. Standard symbols for these parameters are

$$h_{fe} \approx \beta \qquad (5.6\text{-}6a)$$

and

$$h_{ie} \approx r_d \approx \beta \, \frac{25 \times 10^{-3}}{I_{EQ}} \approx \frac{h_{fe}(25 \times 10^{-3})}{I_{EQ}} \qquad (5.6\text{-}6b)$$

since $I_{BQ} \approx I_{EQ}/\beta$. The utility of the circuit of Fig. 5.6-1c is seen from the following example.

EXAMPLE 5.6-1   The circuit of Fig. 5.6-2 is a single-stage, common-emitter amplifier. The transistor has $h_{fe} \approx \beta = 100$. All capacitors are assumed to have zero

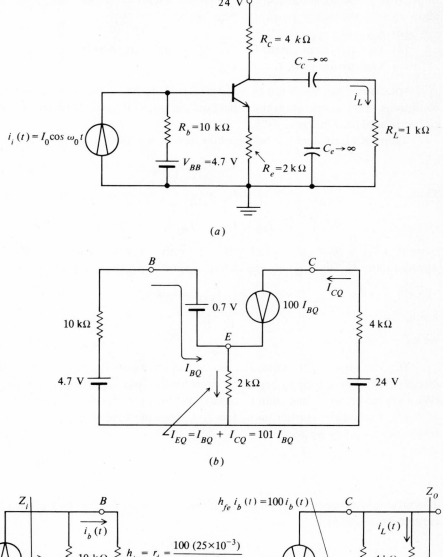

FIGURE 5.6-2
(a) Circuit for Example 5.6-1. (b) DC equivalent circuit. (c) Small-amplitude equivalent circuit.

impedance at the signal frequency, f_0. They are used to "block" the dc components, allowing only the ac component to pass. Find:

(a) I_{CQ} and V_{CEQ}.

(b) The equivalent circuit for the small-amplitude, time-varying signals.

(c) The current gain $A_i = i_L(t)/i_i(t)$.

SOLUTION   (a) We begin by setting $i_i(t) = 0$ to find the dc (quiescent) operating conditions. For dc operation the capacitors are open circuits. Thus the dc equivalent circuit is as shown in Fig. 5.6-2b.

Using KVL around the base-emitter circuit, we have

$$4.7 = 10,000 I_{BQ} + 0.7 + 2,000(101 I_{BQ})$$

Thus
$$I_{BQ} \approx \frac{4.7 - 0.7}{10^4 + 2 \times 10^5} \approx 0.02 \text{ mA}$$

Hence
$$I_{EQ} \approx I_{CQ} = \beta I_{BQ} = 100(0.02) \text{ mA} = 2 \text{ mA}$$

Note that $I_{EQ} = (\beta + 1)I_B$, which differs by only 1 percent from I_{CQ}. We therefore approximate I_{EQ} by I_{CQ}. Using KVL around the collector-emitter circuit yields

$$V_{CEQ} = -4,000 I_{CQ} + 24 - 2,000 I_{EQ}$$

Using
$$I_{EQ} \approx I_{CQ} = 2 \text{ mA}$$

we have
$$V_{CEQ} = +12 \text{ V}$$

(b) The small-signal equivalent circuit is shown in Fig. 5.6-2c. It is obtained directly from Fig. 5.6-2a by replacing each battery and capacitor by a short circuit. (Why are dc batteries and infinite capacitors short circuits for alternating current?)

(c) To find the current gain $A_i = i_L/i_i$, we note that i_L and i_i are both related to i_b. We therefore write

$$A_i = \frac{i_L}{i_i} = \frac{i_L}{i_b} \frac{i_b}{i_i}$$

The ratio i_L/i_b is found by application of the current-divider formula to the collector-emitter circuit. Thus

$$\frac{i_L}{i_b} = -100 \times \frac{4}{4 + 1} = -80$$

where all resistances are in kilohms. The ratio i_b/i_i is found using the current-divider formula in the base-emitter circuit.

$$\frac{i_b}{i_i} = \frac{10}{10 + 1.25} \approx 0.9$$

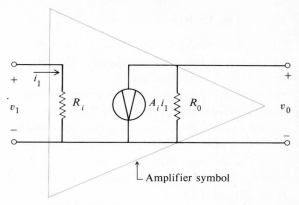

FIGURE 5.6-3
Small-amplitude equivalent circuit of an amplifier.

Thus the small-signal ac current gain A_i is

$$A_i = (-80)(0.9) = -72$$

This means that the load current is 72 times larger than the ac input current. The negative sign indicates a reversal of phase between input and output.
////////

5.6-2 Impedances—Input and Output

When analyzing or designing circuits containing more than one stage of amplification, the mathematics is considerably simplified by using Thévenin and Norton equivalents to reduce the complexity of the circuit. This procedure also makes it an easy matter to take into account the interaction between stages. A convenient form for the equivalent circuit of a transistor amplifier includes an input impedance, controlled current source, and output impedance, as shown in Fig. 5.6-3. These impedances are found using the methods of Sec. 4.1-5.

As an example, consider the circuit of Fig. 5.6-2c. In this circuit $R_i = 10 \text{ k}\Omega \| h_{ie} \approx 1 \text{ k}\Omega$. The output impedance R_0 is found from the output circuit to be

$$R_0 = 4 \text{ k}\Omega \| 1 \text{ k}\Omega = 800 \ \Omega$$

where R_L is included in the output impedance. The short-circuit gain A_i is simply h_{fe} for this case. Note the similarity to the Norton equivalent circuit.

5.6-3   The Emitter Follower

An amplifier configuration which has a high input impedance and a very low output impedance is the *emitter follower*. The device is used extensively to approximate an almost ideal voltage source. The basic configuration is shown in Fig. 5.6-4a. In this circuit the output is taken from the emitter. Comparing this circuit with the emitter-coupled logic circuit (Fig. 5.4-5), we see that the emitter follower is used as the output stage for ECL. In this section we consider the response of the emitter follower to small-amplitude signals.

The dc equivalent circuit is shown in Fig. 5.6-4b. This circuit is obtained by letting $v_i(t) = 0$ and replacing the base-emitter diode by a 0.7-V battery. Then, using KVL around the base-emitter circuit yields

$$V_{BB} = r_i I_{BQ} + 0.7 + (\beta + 1)R_e I_{BQ}$$

Solving, we have

$$I_{EQ} = (\beta + 1)I_{BQ} = \frac{V_{BB} - 0.7}{R_e + r_i/(\beta + 1)} \qquad (5.6\text{-}7)$$

The collector-emitter voltage is found from Fig. 5.6-4b:

$$V_{CEQ} = V_{CC} - R_e I_{EQ} \qquad (5.6\text{-}8)$$

EXAMPLE 5.6-2   The emitter follower shown in Fig. 5.6-4a has the following circuit parameters: $V_{BB} = 2.7$ V, $r_i = 10$ kΩ, $R_e = 1$ kΩ, $V_{CC} = 10$ V, and $\beta = 100$. Find I_{EQ} and V_{CEQ}.

SOLUTION   Using (5.6-7),

$$I_{EQ} = \frac{2.7 - 0.7}{1{,}000 + (10{,}000/101)} \approx 1.8 \text{ mA}$$

From (5.6-8)

$$V_{CEQ} = 10 - 10^3 \times (1.8 \times 10^{-3}) = 8.2 \text{ V}$$

////////

The small-signal equivalent circuit is shown in Fig. 5.6-4c. It is obtained from Fig. 5.6-4a by replacing each battery by a short circuit and replacing the base-emitter diode by its dynamic resistance h_{ie}. Two modified equivalent circuits can be obtained by writing KVL around the base-emitter circuit.

$$v_i(t) = r_i i_b + h_{ie} i_b + (h_{fe} + 1)R_e i_b \qquad (5.6\text{-}9)$$

The last term represents the voltage which would appear across a resistor $(h_{fe} + 1)R_e$ having a current i_b flowing through it. This is shown in Fig. 5.6-5a. The voltage v_e in the circuit of Fig. 5.6-4c is exactly the same as that of Fig. 5.6-5a. In the latter circuit the controlled current source has been eliminated. Since the current i_b flows through $(h_{fe} + 1)R_e$, we state that R_e, which is in the emitter circuit, has been *reflected* into

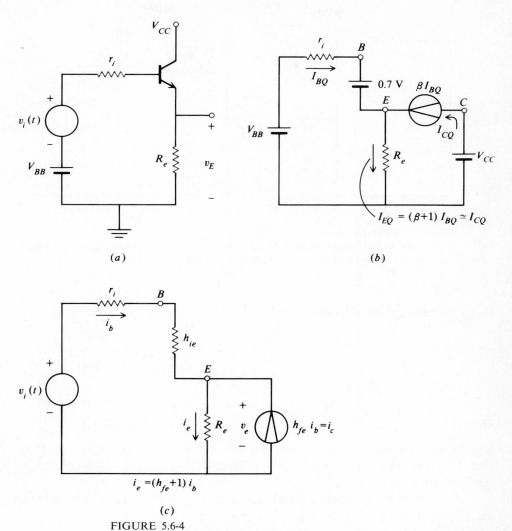

FIGURE 5.6-4
(a) The emitter follower. (b) DC equivalent circuit. (c) Small-signal equivalent circuit.

the base circuit where it "looks like" $(h_{fe} + 1)R_e$. The *input impedance* of the amplifier is then

$$R_i = \frac{v_i}{i_b} = r_i + h_{ie} + (h_{fe} + 1)R_e \qquad (5.6\text{-}10)$$

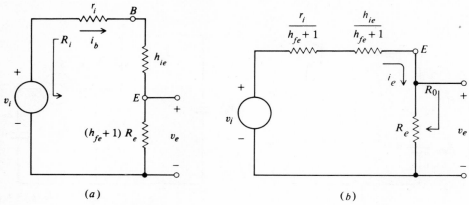

(a)   (b)

FIGURE 5.6-5
(a) Equivalent circuit obtained by reflecting R_e into the base circuit. (b) Equivalent circuit obtained by reflecting v_i, r_i, and h_{ie} into the emitter circuit.

Using the values given in Example 5.6-2

$$r_i = 10 \text{ k}\Omega$$

$$h_{ie} = h_{fe} \frac{25 \times 10^{-3}}{I_{EQ}} = 100 \times \frac{25}{1.8} = 1,400 \ \Omega$$

$$(h_{fe} + 1)R_e = 101 \text{ k}\Omega$$

Thus

$$R_i \approx 112 \text{ k}\Omega$$

Comparing this value with the R_i obtained for the common-emitter amplifier (Sec. 5.6.2), $R_i \approx 1 \text{ k}\Omega \approx h_{ie}$, we see that the input impedance is increased significantly using the emitter follower.

An alternative equivalent circuit is shown in Fig. 5.6-5b. This is obtained from Eq. (5.6-9) by replacing $(h_{fe} + 1)i_b$ by i_e. Then

$$v_i = \frac{r_i}{h_{fe} + 1} i_e + \frac{h_{ie}}{h_{fe} + 1} i_e + R_e i_e \qquad (5.6\text{-}11)$$

Once again the voltage v_e is the same as in the previous circuit. From this circuit we calculate the voltage gain

$$A_v = \frac{v_e}{v_i} = \frac{i_e R_e}{v_i} = \frac{R_e}{(r_i + h_{ie})/(h_{fe} + 1) + R_e} \qquad (5.6\text{-}12)$$

Usually, $R_e \gg (r_i + h_{ie})/(h_{fe} + 1)$, so that $A_v \approx 1$.

The output impedance is (setting $v_i = 0$)

$$R_0 = R_e \| \frac{r_i + h_{ie}}{h_{fe} + 1} \quad (5.6\text{-}13)$$

EXAMPLE 5.6-3 Using the values of Example 5.6-2, calculate A_v and R_0.

SOLUTION From (5.6-12)

$$A_v = \frac{1,000}{\dfrac{(10,000 + 1,400)}{101} + 1,000} \approx 0.9$$

and

$$R_0 = 1,000 \| \frac{10,000 + 1,400}{101} \approx 100 \ \Omega$$

These results should be compared with the results of Example 5.6-1, which shows a *current* gain of -72. Thus we see that the emitter follower is used to provide a *voltage* gain of approximately 1, while the common-emitter amplifier is used to provide a large *current* gain. Comparing impedances, we see that $R_i = 112 \ \text{k}\Omega$ for the emitter follower, while for the current amplifier, R_i is $1 \ \text{k}\Omega$ and $R_0 = 100 \ \Omega$ for the emitter follower, while $R_0 = 800 \ \Omega$ for the current amplifier.

EXAMPLE 5.6-4 Verify the gain A_v found in Example 5.6-3 using ECAP.

SOLUTION The small-signal equivalent circuit of Fig. 5.6-4c is redrawn in Fig. 5.6-6a as an ECAP circuit. We shall carry out the solution using the ECAP dc analysis, since the small-signal circuit contains no frequency-sensitive elements. The only difference between this example and previous ECAP examples is that we have a controlled source in this circuit. Referring to line 8 of the program shown in Fig. 5.6-6b, we see that the controlled source is accounted for by a "T card." The designation T1 B(1, 2) specifies controlled source number 1. The designation B(1, 2) indicates that the controlling current is the current in branch 1 and the controlled source is connected across branch 2. Branch 1 is called the *from-branch*, and branch 2 the *to-branch*. They are connected by a dashed line for clarity. The strength of the controlled source is βI_1. The sign to be used with β can be determined by short-circuiting the to-branch. If the current from the controlled source flows in the same direction as that preassigned to the to-branch, the sign is *negative*, as in this example.

We set the input voltage equal to 1 V so that the node voltage $NV1$ is numerically equal to the voltage gain. The printout is shown in Fig. 5.6-6b, and the result is seen to agree closely with that of Example 5.6-3.

////////

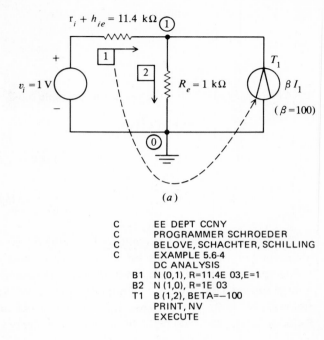

(a)

```
C        EE DEPT CCNY
C        PROGRAMMER SCHROEDER
C        BELOVE, SCHACHTER, SCHILLING
C        EXAMPLE 5.6-4
         DC ANALYSIS
B1       N (0,1), R=11.4E 03,E=1
B2       N (1,0), R=1E 03
T1       B (1,2), BETA=−100
         PRINT, NV
         EXECUTE
```

NODE VOLTAGES

NODES	VOLTAGES
1− 1	0.89857648D 00

(b)

FIGURE 5.6-6
ECAP solution for Example 5.6-4. (a) ECAP circuit; (b) computer printout.

5.7 PARAMETER VARIATION

Transistors present one major difficulty to the engineer: parameter variation. One cannot, in general, replace one transistor by another of the same type and have the same β in each. Manufacturers often specify a $3:1$ variation in β, for a given type, and a $7:1$ variation is not unusual, In addition, the base-emitter voltage of 0.7 V changes with temperature, according to the relation

$$\Delta V_{BE} = -2.5 \times 10^{-3} \Delta T \text{ V}$$

where ΔT is temperature change in degrees Celsius.

The β variation is due to the fact that all transistors of the "same type" are not identical. This is a fabrication problem which, in time, may be reduced to the point where β may vary, say, by only 15 percent rather than 300 or 700 percent. The change in base-emitter voltage due to a change in temperature is a physical phenomenon associated with semiconductor devices, and is not a manufacturing problem as such.

Both the β variation from unit to unit and the variation in V_{BE} due to temperature changes may result in a considerably different quiescent collector current in the amplifier we build than in the amplifiers we have designed on paper. Unless proper precautions are taken in the design, the shift in quiescent current may be so large that the amplifier is at cutoff or saturation. In this section we point out several methods for reducing these undesirable effects.

5.7-1 β Variation

We now show that the quiescent collector current can be stabilized against unit-to-unit β variation by using an emitter resistor and maintaining a certain relationship between the base-and emitter-circuit resistances. This relation is given by the inequality

$$R_e \gg \frac{R_b}{\beta + 1} \qquad (5.7\text{-}1)$$

When this inequality is satisfied, the Q point is essentially independent of the transistor characteristics. The circuit employed for this illustration is shown in Fig. 5.7-1.

Note that if a large capacitor, $C_e \to \infty$, is placed across resistor R_e, then Fig. 5.7-1 resembles Fig. 5.6-2a. If, instead, we adjust R_c to be zero, then Fig. 5.7-1 is similar to Fig. 5.6-4a. Thus the dc circuits of both the amplifier and emitter follower are represented by Fig. 5.7-1, and all the results which follow apply equally well to the two configurations studied previously.

Using results obtained in Secs. 5.3 and 5.6, we have

For the collector current:

$$I_C = \beta I_B \qquad (5.7\text{-}2)$$

For the collector circuit using KVL:

$$V_{CC} = I_C R_c + I_E R_e + V_{CE} \qquad (5.7\text{-}3)$$

For the base circuit using KVL:

$$V_{BB} = I_B R_b + V_{BE} + I_E R_e \qquad (5.7\text{-}4)$$

From (5.3-3):

$$I_B = \frac{I_E}{\beta + 1} \qquad (5.7\text{-}5)$$

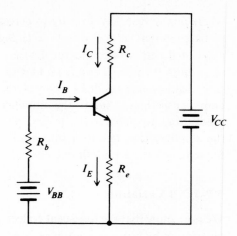

FIGURE 5.7-1
Common-emitter circuit.

Combining (5.7-4) and (5.7-5), we obtain

$$V_{BB} = V_{BE} + I_E\left(R_e + \frac{R_b}{\beta + 1}\right) \qquad (5.7\text{-}6)$$

Now using

$$I_C \approx I_E \qquad (5.7\text{-}7)$$

in (5.7-6), the quiescent collector current becomes

$$I_{CQ} \approx \frac{V_{BB} - V_{BE}}{R_e + R_b/(\beta + 1)} \qquad (5.7\text{-}8)$$

The quiescent collector-emitter voltage V_{CEQ} can be obtained by combining (5.7-3), (5.7-7), and (5.7-8). The result is

$$V_{CC} \approx V_{CE} + I_C(R_c + R_e) \qquad (5.7\text{-}9)$$

If the inequality (5.7-1) is satisfied, (5.7-8) simplifies to

$$I_{CQ} \approx \frac{V_{BB} - V_{BE}}{R_e} \approx \frac{V_{BB} - 0.7}{R_e} \qquad (5.7\text{-}10)$$

since V_{BE} is assumed equal to 0.7 V for silicon units.

The location of the Q point as given by (5.7-8) is seen to be relatively independent of β when the inequality of (5.7-1) is satisfied. This is illustrated in the following example.

EXAMPLE 5.7-1 In the circuit of Fig. 5.7-1 let $V_{CC} = 10$ V, $V_{BB} = 1.75$ V, $I_{CQ} = 10$ mA, $V_{CEQ} = 5$ V, $R_c = 400$ Ω, and $40 \leq \beta \leq 120$.

Find suitable values for (a) R_e and (b) R_b. (c) Calculate the variation in Q point as β varies over its total indicated range.

SOLUTION The specifications give enough information to determine the load line and locate the Q point shown in Fig. 5.7-2.

(a) From the load line

$$R_c + R_e = \frac{10}{20 \times 10^{-3}} = 500 \ \Omega$$

and since $R_c = 400$ Ω,

$$R_e = 100 \ \Omega$$

(b) From (5.7-1)

$$R_b \ll (\beta + 1)R_e$$

We use the minimum value of β in the inequality; thus $\beta_{min} = 40$ and $R_b \ll 4.1$ kΩ. We next employ a "rule of thumb" and let a factor of 10 represent "much less than." This leads to a value of $R_b = 400$ Ω.

(c) To calculate the effect of β on the Q point, we use (5.7-8).

When $\beta = 40$:

$$I_{CQ} = \frac{1.75 - 0.7}{100 + 400/40} = \frac{1.05}{110} \approx 9.5 \ \text{mA}$$

When $\beta = 120$:

$$I_{CQ} = \frac{1.75 - 0.7}{100 + 400/120} \approx 10.2 \ \text{mA}$$

Thus a 3 : 1 variation in β produces a 7.3 percent shift in the Q point.
////////

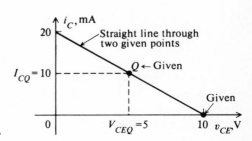

FIGURE 5.7-2
Load lines for Example 5.7-1.

5.7-2   Effect of Temperature on the Q Point

In the preceding section we discussed the variation of Q-point position with respect to unit-to-unit variations in β, and a biasing arrangement which minimized these variations. Another important cause of Q-point variation is the transistor operating temperature. In this section we study the variation of the Q point due to the dependence of V_{BE} on temperature.

We begin the analysis with the expression for the quiescent collector current given by Eq. (5.7-10). This expression assumes that we have stabilized against variations of β, and is the desired relation between collector current and the temperature-dependent variable V_{BE}.

The variation of I_{CQ} with temperature can be found from (5.7-10). Assuming that only V_{BE} varies,

$$\frac{\Delta I_{CQ}}{\Delta T} = -\frac{1}{R_e}\frac{\Delta V_{BE}}{\Delta T} \qquad (5.7\text{-}11)$$

where

$$\frac{\Delta V_{BE}}{\Delta T} = -2.5 \times 10^{-3} \text{ V/°C} \qquad (5.7\text{-}12)$$

Substituting (5.7-12) into (5.7-11), we get

$$\frac{\Delta I_{CQ}}{\Delta T} = \frac{2.5 \times 10^{-3}}{R_e} \qquad (5.7\text{-}13)$$

from which

$$\Delta I_{CQ} = \frac{2.5 \times 10^{-3} \, \Delta T}{R_e} \qquad (5.7\text{-}14)$$

In the example to follow, a typical value will be calculated.

EXAMPLE 5.7-2   Consider the circuit of Fig. 5.7-1, with $R_b = 400 \; \Omega$, $R_e = 100 \; \Omega$, and $I_{CQ} = 10 \text{ mA}$, at room temperature (25°C). Calculate the change in I_{CQ} if the temperature increases to 125°C.

SOLUTION   Substituting the given values in (5.7-14) with $\Delta T = 100$°C,

$$\Delta I_{CQ} = \frac{(2.5)(10^{-3})(100)}{100}$$

$$= 2.5 \text{ mA}$$

We see from this example that I_{CQ} changed by 25 percent over the 100°C change in temperature. For many applications, this variation is permissible.

////////

The techniques discussed in this section are used in practice in the design of transistor circuits. They ensure, for example, that if a company mass-produces radios for people living in cold and warm climates, then all the radios will operate properly, even though the β variation in the transistors used might be 3 : 1 and the temperature might vary from 100 to $-32°$F.

PROBLEMS

5.1-1 A full-wave rectifier is shown in Fig. P5.1-1. Note that the full-wave rectifier can be considered to be two half-wave rectifiers connected across the same load resistance.

  (a) Sketch $v_L(t)$ if $v_i(t) = V_{im} \cos \omega_0 t$. Compare your result with the result given in Fig. 5.1-5.

  (b) Calculate the average value of $V_L(t)$ and show that it is $2V_{im}/\pi$. Note that if the circuit were a half-wave rectifier, the average value would be V_{im}/π.

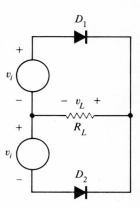

FIGURE P5.1-1

5.1-2 (a) Show that substituting Eq. (5.1-2) into (5.1-4b) yields

$$a_n = \frac{9}{\pi} \int_{-\pi/2}^{\pi/2} \cos x \cos nx \, dx \qquad \text{where } x = \omega_0 t$$

$$= \frac{9}{\pi} \left[\frac{\sin \dfrac{(n-1)}{2}\pi}{n-1} + \frac{\sin \dfrac{(n+1)}{2}\pi}{n+1} \right]$$

and

$$b_n = \frac{9}{\pi} \int_{-\pi/2}^{\pi/2} \cos x \sin nx \, dx = 0$$

  (b) Using the results of (a), verify (5.1-5).

5.1-3 The input to an *RC* series circuit is the voltage

$$v_i(t) = \cos t + \tfrac{1}{2} \cos 2t + \tfrac{1}{3} \cos 3t + \tfrac{1}{4} \cos 4t$$

If the *RC* product is 1, calculate the voltage drop across the capacitor.

5.1-4 Tabulate i_D/I_0 as a function of v_D (Eq. 5.1-8a). Let v_D vary from -5 to $+1$ V. Assume that $mkT/q = 25\text{mV}$.

5.1-5 The equivalent circuit in Fig. 5.1-10a can be improved upon when $v_D < 0$ (in the reverse region) by inserting a resistor *R* as shown in Fig. P5.1-5.

    (a) If $r_D = 25\ \Omega$ and $R = 100\ \text{M}\Omega$, plot the *vi* characteristic of the diode for $0 < v_D \leq 2$ V.

    (b) Repeat (a) on a new set of axes for $-10 \leq v_D \leq 0$.

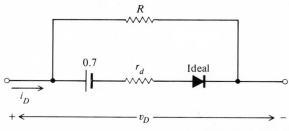

FIGURE P5.1-5

5.1-6 A real diode having the equivalent circuit shown in Fig. 5.1-10a, with $r_d = 25\ \Omega$, is used in the circuit shown in Fig. P5.1-6.

    (a) Using ECAP, determine V_L when *E* varies between 0 and 5 V in 1-V steps. That is, find V_L when $E = 0, 1, 2, 3, 4,$ and 5 V.

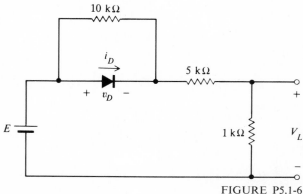

FIGURE P5.1-6

5.1-7 The circuit shown in Fig. P5.1-7 is used to approximate the equation $1,000i = v^2$. Sketch on the same set of axes the equation $1,000i = v^2$ and the relation between i and v obtained from Fig. P5.1-7 for $v \geq 0$. Compare results.

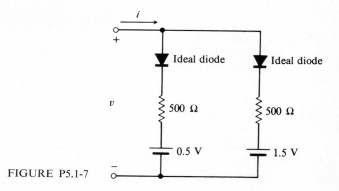

FIGURE P5.1-7

5.2-1 A diode AND gate can be constructed as shown in Fig. P5.2-1. If v_1 and v_2 are either 0 or 5 V and the diodes are *ideal*, show that $v_0 = 5$ V only if v_1 AND v_2 are 5 V.

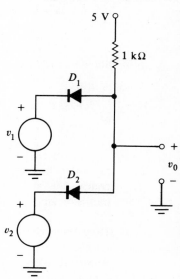

FIGURE P5.2-1

5.2-2 A diode OR gate (Fig. 5.2-3a) uses nonideal diodes having the equivalent circuit shown in Fig. 5.1-10 ($r_d = 25\ \Omega$). If $v_2 = 0$ and

$$v_1(t) = \begin{cases} 10t & 0 \leq t \leq 1 \\ 10 & t > 1 \end{cases}$$

sketch $v_0(t)$, $0 \leq t \leq 1$, if (a) $R = 1\text{k}\,\Omega$ and, (b) $R = 25\ \Omega$.

5.2-3   The two-input diode AND gate shown in Fig. 5.2-2a is built using real diodes. These diodes can be approximated by the equivalent circuit shown in Fig. 5.1-10 with $r_d = 25\ \Omega$. If $R = 1\ k\Omega$, sketch $v_0(t)$ if $v_2(t) = 5$ V and

$$v_1(t) = \begin{cases} 10t & 0 \leq t \leq \tfrac{1}{2} \\ 5 & t > \tfrac{1}{2} \end{cases}$$

5.3-1   The circuit in Fig. 5.3-3 is used to transform the input voltage $v_i(t)$ into an output current i_c. $\beta = 100$. If $R_b = 1\ k\Omega$ and $V_{BB} = 1.4$ V:

(a)   Determine the maximum value of V_{im} in order that $i_B(t)$ be sinusoidal.

(b)   If $V_{im} = 1.35$ V, sketch $i_B(t)$.

(c)   If $V_{im} = 0.5$ V, sketch $i_B(t)$ and $i_C(t) = \beta i_B(t)$.

5.3-2   Refer to Prob. 5.3-1. Let $V_{CC} = 10$ V.

(a)   If $V_{im} = 675$ mV, find the maximum value that R_c can have for i_C to remain sinusoidal.

(b)   If $V_{im} = 1$ V and $R_c = 100\ \Omega$, sketch $i_C(t)$.

5.3-3   The collector current in a transistor is a function of the base current i_B and the collector-emitter voltage v_{CE}. Thus we can write

$$i_C = f(i_B, v_{CE})$$

(a)   Show that, using a Taylor series expansion about the point $i_C = I_{CQ}$, $i_B = I_{BQ}$ and $v_{CE} = V_{CEQ}$ yields

$$i_C = I_{CQ} + \left[\frac{\partial i_C}{\partial i_B} \bigg|_{v_{CE} = V_{CEQ}} \right] \Delta i_B + \left[\frac{\partial i_C}{\partial v_{CE}} \bigg|_{i_B = I_{BQ}} \right] \Delta v_{CE} + \text{other terms}$$

(b)   Show that this expression reduces to $i_c = \beta i_b$ when

(1) $\dfrac{\partial i_C}{\partial i_B} \bigg|_{v_{CE} = V_{CEQ}} \equiv \beta$

(2) $\Delta i_B = i_b$

(3) $\dfrac{\partial i_C}{\partial v_{CE}} \bigg|_{i_B = I_{BQ}} = 0$

i.e., the collector current *does not change* when v_{CE} changes. This result is, of course, not valid in saturation.

5.3-4   The transistor amplifier in Fig. 5.3-3a has $R_b = 2\ k\Omega$, $R_c = 3\ k\Omega$, and $V_{CC} = 15$ V. $\beta = 50$.

(a)   Draw the vi characteristics for the transistor.

(b)   On the same set of axes, plot the load line equation.

(c)   Select V_{BB} to obtain a maximum symmetrical swing in i_C. What is the maximum symmetrical swing in i_C, i_B, and v_{CE}?

(d)   Find the maximum value of V_{im} to ensure linear operation, i.e., avoid cutoff and saturation.

5.4-1   Transistor NOR gates can be constructed using resistor-transistor logic (RTL). A typical two-input NOR gate is shown in Fig. P5.4-1.

(a)   Explain the operation of the gate and calculate all pertinent currents and voltages.

(b)   Show, using a truth table, that the circuit is a NOR gate.

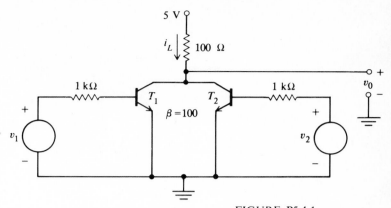

FIGURE P5.4-1
v_1 and v_2 are either 0 or 5 V.

5.4-2 The circuit shown in Fig. 5.4-2 is a NOT gate. If $V_{CC} = 5$ V and $R_b = 1$ kΩ, find the minimum value of R_c to ensure that the transistor saturates. Assume a transistor with $\beta = 40$.

5.4-3 The statement "saturation occurs in a transistor if i_C gets so large that $v_{CE} = 0$" is only approximate. Actually, a better approximation of the equivalent circuit in the saturation region is shown in Fig. P5.4-3.

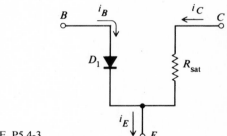

FIGURE P5.4-3

Refer to the NOT gate in Fig. 5.4-2a. Let $\beta = 20$, $R_b = 1$ kΩ, $R_c = 400$ Ω, and $V_{CC} = 5$ V. If the equivalent circuit in saturation is as shown in Fig. P5.4-3, with $R_{\text{sat}} = 100$ Ω, sketch $v_C(t)$ when $v_i(t)$ is a 5-V pulse.

5.4-4 Refer to Fig. 5.4-3a. Let $x_1 = x_2 = 5$ V.
(*a*) Show that diodes D_1 and D_2 are reverse-biased.
(*b*) Using (*a*), show that $v_1 = 2.1$ V.

5.4-5 Show that an AND gate can be synthesized using NOR gates.

5.4-6 A two-input NOR gate is shown in Fig. P5.4-6. x_1 and x_2 are either -1.5 V or 0 V.
(*a*) Explain the operation of the gate.
(*b*) Verify, using a truth table, that the circuit is a NOR gate.

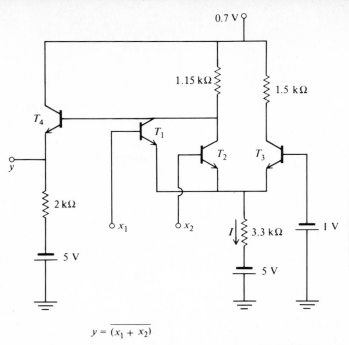

$$y = \overline{(x_1 + x_2)}$$

5.4-7 Calculate the fan-out of the RTL NOR gate in Fig. P5.4-7. Assume $\beta = 100$. v_1, v_2, v_{21}, ..., v_{2N} are either 0 or 5 V.

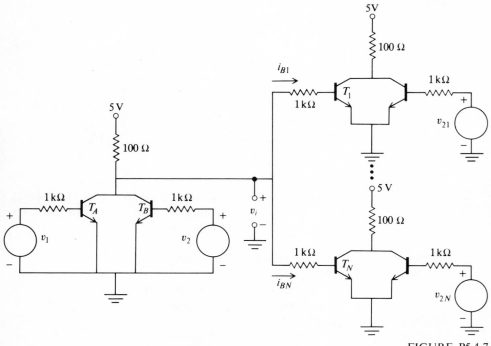

5.5-1 A flip-flop used in integrated circuits consists of an interconnection of RTL NOR gates as shown in Fig. P5.5-1. Explain the operation of the flip-flop.

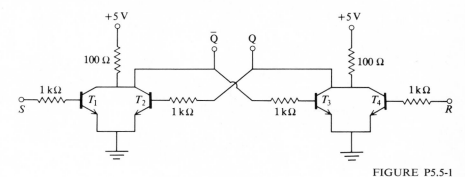

FIGURE P5.5-1

5.6-1 For the transistor amplifier shown in Fig. P5.6-1 find:
- (*a*) The dc equivalent circuit.
- (*b*) I_{CQ}, V_{CEQ}, I_{BQ}, and I_{EQ}.
- (*c*) The small-amplitude equivalent circuit.
- (*d*) The current gain i_L/i_i (check your answers by using ECAP).
- (*e*) The input resistance R_i.
- (*f*) The output resistance R_0.

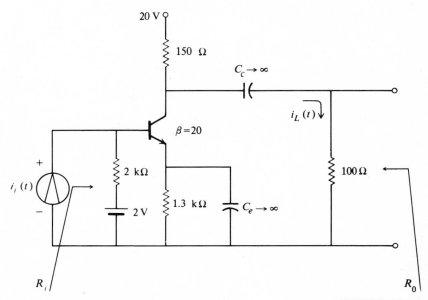

FIGURE P5.6-1

5.6-2   Repeat parts (*a*) to (*f*) of Prob. 5.6-1 using the amplifier shown in Fig. P5.6-2.

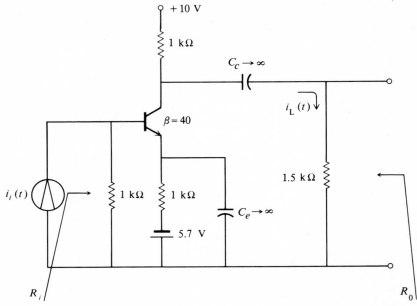

FIGURE P5.6-2

5.6-3   For the emitter follower shown in Fig. P5.6-3, find:

(*a*)   The dc equivalent circuit.

(*b*) I_{CQ}, V_{CEQ}, I_{BQ}, and I_{EQ}.

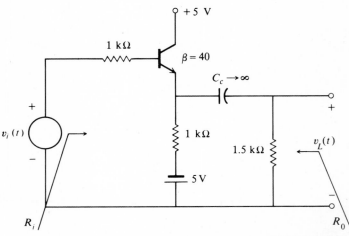

FIGURE P5.6-3

(c) The small-amplitude equivalent circuit.

(d) The voltage gain v_L/v_i (check your answer by using ECAP).

(e) The input resistance R_i.

(f) The output resistance R_o.

5.7-1 Refer to Example 5.7-1. Using ECAP, determine I_{CQ} and V_{CEQ} as β varies from 40 to 120 in increments of 10.

5.7-2 Refer to Example 5.7-1. If V_{CC} can vary between 9 and 11 V and β can have any value between 40 and 120, determine, using ECAP, the variation in I_{CQ}.

5.7-3 Refer to Example 5.7-1. Assume that V_{CC} can vary between 10 and 12 V and that V_{BB} can vary between 1.65 and 1.75 V. Then, with $40 \le \beta \le 120$, determine the maximum and minimum values of I_{CQ}.

5 7-4 Repeat Prob. 5.7-1 if the temperature can vary from 25 to 125°C.

5.7-5 Repeat Prob. 5.7-2 if the temperature can vary from -55 to 25°C.

REFERENCES

SCHILLING, D. L. and C. BELOVE: "Electronic Circuits: Discrete and Integrated," McGraw-Hill Book Company, New York, 1968.

STRAUSS, L.: "Wave Generation and Shaping," McGraw-Hill Book Company, New York, 1970.

6

COMMUNICATIONS SYSTEMS

6.1 INTRODUCTION

The purpose of any communication system is to transmit information from one location to another. The quality of the system is measured by the clarity or preciseness of this information transfer.

For example, suppose that two people separated by a considerable distance wish to communicate with each other. One method of transmission is to install a pair of copper wires (these wires are called a *transmission line*) extending from one location to another. If each location is equipped with a microphone and an earpiece, the communication system is complete. The microphone transforms the *acoustic wave* resulting from the voice into an *electric signal* voltage. This signal voltage is applied to one end of the transmission line and is eventually received at the other end. At this end, the earpiece transforms the electric voltage back into an acoustic wave which is heard by the listener.

The received signal, however, will have associated with it an erratic, random, unpredictable voltage called *thermal noise*. A major source of thermal noise is a resistor, which can be found in all receivers (and hence in the earpiece). The thermal noise is produced by electrons present in the resistor, which are free to wander randomly throughout its entire volume. Thus, at each instant of time, the velocity of electrons present at any point in the resistor varies. This variation results in a random voltage at the terminals of the resistor. In addition to resistor noise, we find that transistors are also sources of noise. These two devices account for much of the noise associated with a received signal voltage.

Another important factor affecting the transmitted signal is *attenuation*. As a result of the length of the wire link, the received message signal voltage will be greatly attenuated in comparison with its level at the transmitting end of the link. Hence the message signal voltage may not be much larger than the noise voltage generated in the receiver, and the message may be distinguished from the noise only with difficulty, or possibly not at all. An amplifier placed at the receiving end will not alleviate our problem, since the amplifier will amplify signal and noise alike, and also because the amplifier is itself a source of noise.

The above discussion centered on communication between two persons. However, similar problems arise when communicating between a computer and a man, or between two computers. Thus a principal concern in the study of communications systems is the study of methods which suppress the effect of noise. In this chapter we shall compare several types of communications systems and shall see that it is often better not to transmit the original signal (the microphone output in our above discussion) directly. Instead, the original signal is used to generate a different signal waveform which is then applied to the line. This processing of the signal at the transmission end of the communication link is called *encoding*, or *modulation*. At the receiving end, an inverse process called *decoding*, or *demodulation*, is employed to recover the original signal.

In particular, we shall discuss analog communications systems such as *amplitude modulation* (AM) and *frequency modulation* (FM), as well as digital communications systems such as *pulse-code modulation* (PCM) and the use of *error-correcting codes*. These systems will be compared on the basis of *noise suppression*. It will be shown that to obtain an increase in noise suppression requires an increased use of *bandwidth*. Thus, in ordinary broadcast-band AM radio, the bandwidth is 10 kHz and the noise suppression is small. On the other hand, the bandwidth required in broadcast-band FM radio is 200 kHz and the noise suppression is greatly increased.

6.1-1 Direct-wire Communications

The first problem we shall consider is that which arises when a signal voltage is transmitted directly over a very long pair of wires. Assume that the received signal is significantly smaller than the transmitted signal, and that the noise at the receiver is comparable with the signal.

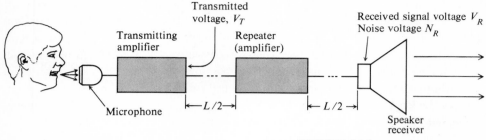

FIGURE 6.1-1
A telephone system using one repeater.

An obvious way of solving the problem is to amplify the signal prior to transmission. Such a solution turns out to be impractical because the required voltage at the transmitter is usually astronomical, beyond the power capabilities of available transistor amplifiers. For example, the attenuation in a typical telephone cable is approximately 10 percent per mile of cable. Thus, for a 1,000-mi length of cable, the transmitted signal will be attenuated by $(0.9)^{1,000} \approx 10^{-46}$. Hence, if a received signal level of 10^{-3} V is required, a transmitted signal of 10^{+43} V must be supplied at the sending end. Typical signal voltages are often less than 10 V, although 1,000-V signals are possible. The required signal level is completely impractical.

An amplifier inserted in the receiver will not help the above situation, since at this point in the system the received signal and the noise are amplified together.

One solution to the problem is to insert amplifiers at various points along the cable. This procedure is employed in practice, and each amplifier is called a *repeater*. To understand the operation of a repeater, consider that a single repeater is used and placed midway between the transmitting and receiving ends of a cable L mi in length. This system is illustrated in Fig. 6.1-1. Let us assume that the transmitted voltage is V_T. Then, at the input to the repeater, the voltage is $(0.9)^{L/2}V_T \approx 10^{-0.025L}V_T$. If the gain of the repeater is $10^{+L/40}$, the voltage leaving the repeater will be V_T, the voltage originally transmitted. In this case the signal voltage received at the speaker is $10^{-(L/40)}V_T$. The transmitted voltage V_T is adjusted to ensure that the received signal voltage is much greater than the noise voltage present at the speaker. This point is further illustrated in Example 6.1-1.

EXAMPLE 6.1-1 A telephone system is 100 mi long. The transmitted voltage V_T is 1 V. The noise voltage at the receiver is $N_R = 10^{-5}$ V. To obtain a "clear" signal voltage, the received voltage V_R must be 100 times greater than the noise. Three repeaters are to be used. Each repeater has a gain K, and they are equally spaced along the telephone line (every 25 mi).

Find the required gain K for each repeater.

SOLUTION   The voltage present at the input to the first repeater is $1(0.9)^{25}$. This voltage is amplified to a level $1(0.9)^{25}K$ and then transmitted over the second 25 mi. The voltage received by the second repeater is then $[1(0.9)^{25}K](0.9)^{25}$. Similarly, we can show that the voltage transmitted by the third repeater is $\{[1(0.9)^{25}K](0.9)^{25}K\}$ $(0.9)^{25}K$. Hence the final received voltage is $V_R = 1(0.9)^{100}K^3$.

Our requirement is that $V_R = 100N_R = 10^{-3}$ V to obtain clarity, so that we must have

$$10^{-3} = (0.9)^{100}K^3$$

$$K^3 = \frac{10^{-3}}{(0.9)^{100}} = \frac{10^{-3}}{10^{-4.6}} = 10^{+1.6}$$

Thus $K = 10^{0.53} = 3.4$, which is readily obtained using integrated circuits.
////////

It is interesting to note that in Example 6.1-1 no advantage was gained by spacing the repeaters. In practice, there is an advantage because the repeaters, being amplifiers, *saturate*; i.e., if all the repeaters were placed one after the other, the signal being amplified by the last repeater would greatly exceed the capability of a transistor amplifier.

In this example we neglected the noise contributed to the system by the transistor amplifiers (repeaters). To include the effect of this noise in the above example would only have complicated our solution. To reduce the effect of the additional noise, a somewhat larger value of K would be employed.

6.1-2   The Overcrowded Spectrum

A second major problem is the efficient use of the frequency spectrum. Throughout the world many companies, as well as individuals, wish to transmit information simultaneously. We have, for example, telephone systems; cable TV; AM, FM, and TV broadcasting; intercontinental telephone service (this is often operated by transmitting to a satellite which relays the messages from one country to another); amateur radio operation and shipboard communication; and specific services which allow private communications such as petroleum industry, railroads, taxis, police, fire, highway maintenance, etc.

We could go on and on, since almost everyone throughout the day uses some form of communication system. The problem is to permit the simultaneous transmission of information by each of these users without having them interfere with each

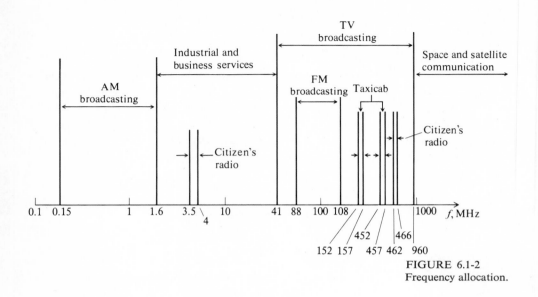

FIGURE 6.1-2
Frequency allocation.

other. One answer is to provide a separate wire link or equivalent between all users. This is done in local telephone operation and cable TV. However, transmission lines are expensive, and new lines must constantly be laid for new users. Furthermore, some applications preclude the use of cables, an example being communication between a NASA satellite and earth.

The Federal Communications Commission (FCC) was formed to ensure interference-free simultaneous transmission of signals. This was accomplished by taking the entire frequency spectrum from dc to infinite frequency and dividing it among all users, depending on their special requirements. The reasons behind the frequency allocations are quite complex and will not be discussed here. A few of the more commonly employed frequency bands are shown in Fig. 6.1-2.

It is interesting to note that approximately 1.5 MHz is allocated to AM broadcasting. However, each AM station requires 10 kHz of bandwidth. Thus 150 stations can operate simultaneously. There are more than 150 stations operating in the United States. This is accomplished by limiting the transmitting power of each station. Thus two or more stations can transmit using the same frequency range if they are located in different parts of the country. The FCC regulates the number of stations permitted to broadcast and specifies their frequency allocation and their maximum transmitting power.

It is also interesting to observe that, due to the complexity and cost of building communications systems at microwave frequencies (frequencies over 1,000 MHz), the FCC was forced to overlap the FM broadcast band, the TV band, and the taxicab, citizen's radio, and other user bands. This presents problems on occasion when a citizen's radio transmitter frequency changes slightly so as to fall directly into the frequency range used by a TV station. This type of interference is observed by almost everyone from time to time.

We note from the above discussion that there are many users of the frequency spectrum. This has resulted in an *overcrowded spectrum* and the necessity for communication in the *microwave* and *optical* frequency regions. In this chapter we discuss the various methods of modulating a signal in order to *frequency-translate* the signal to its appropriate frequency band.

6.1-3   The Decibel, a Logarithmic Measure

In the analysis of communications systems, we often find that, given a voltage $v(t)$, we are interested in V_{rms}, the root-mean-square value of $v(t)$, and often in the square of this value,

$$V_{rms}^2 = \frac{1}{T} \int_{-T/2}^{T/2} [v(t)]^2 \, dt \qquad (6.1\text{-}1)$$

In the case of periodic voltages, the time T is the period of the waveform; if the voltage $v(t)$ is not periodic, T is chosen to be large compared with the time of observation of the voltage.

Suppose that in a particular system we wish to measure the signal and the noise at a given location. If the rms signal voltage is V_{rms} and the rms noise voltage is N_{rms}, it is often convenient to know the ratio V_{rms}/N_{rms}. Thus, in Example 6.1-1, we were told that the rms signal voltage was to be 100 times the rms noise voltage; i.e., $V_{rms}/N_{rms} = 100$. It frequently turns out to be more convenient not to specify this ratio directly, but instead to specify the quantity

$$D = 20 \log \frac{V_{rms}}{N_{rms}} \qquad (6.1\text{-}2)$$

Equation (6.1-2) gives the logarithmic measure of the ratio of a signal and a noise voltage. However, this representation can be used for ratios of two signal voltages or two noise voltages, if desired.

A useful alternative expression for (6.1-2) is

$$D = 10 \log \frac{V_{rms}^2}{N_{rms}^2} \qquad (6.1\text{-}3)$$

where we have applied the formula

$$\log x^2 = 2 \log x \qquad (6.1\text{-}4)$$

    The units of D are called *decibels* (dB). They are extremely useful for computational purposes since logarithms convert multiplication to addition. To illustrate this, consider Example 6.1-1. In this example it was pointed out that the cable introduced an attenuation of 10 percent per mile. Thus the ratio of the voltage at a distance x mi to the voltage at a distance $x + 1$ mi is

$$\text{Attenuation/mile} = 20\log\frac{V_{x+1}}{V_x} = 20\log\frac{9}{10} = 20(0.954 - 1) = -0.92\,\text{dB/mi}$$

The attenuation in 100 mi is therefore -92 dB. Thus the ratio of the received voltage to the transmitted voltage ($V_T = 1$ V) is

$$20\log\frac{V_R}{V_T} = 20\log V_R = -92\text{ dB} + 20\log K^3$$

We are told that $V_R = 100N_R = 10^{-3}$. Thus

$$20\log V_R = 20\log 10^{-3} = -60\text{ dB}$$

Hence
$$-60 = -92 + 60\log K$$

and
$$\log K = \frac{32}{60} = 0.53$$

Thus
$$K = 3.4$$

    Another important reason for using decibels is that a voltage ratio of, say, 10,000/1 becomes 80 dB; thus we are dealing with smaller numbers in our calculations, a decided convenience in many instances.

6.1-4   Mathematical Representation of Thermal Noise

In a communication system the frequency spectrum of the received signal is usually known a priori. Thus it is common practice to pass the received signal which is embedded in thermal noise through a *filter*. The filter is designed to pass the signal without distortion and simultaneously to eliminate as much noise as possible.

    Filters are usually described in terms of their characteristics in the frequency domain. Hence, to determine the influence of these filters on the noise, it is convenient to have a *frequency-domain characterization* of the noise. We shall now establish, using heuristic arguments, such a characterization.

    A noise voltage is one which varies in a random, unpredictable manner. Such a waveform is sketched in Fig. 6.1-3a. What distinguishes the noise waveform from a deterministic signal, such as a sine wave, is that the amplitude of the noise at any specified time is unknown. In addition, the noise is not a periodic function of time, while the sine wave is.

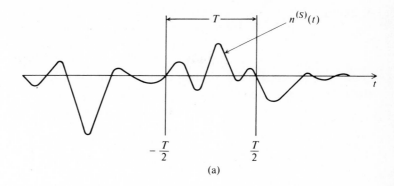

(a)

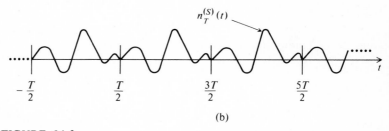

(b)

FIGURE 6.1-3

(a) A noise waveform $n(t)$ showing the T-second truncated noise $n^{(s)}(t)$. (b) The truncated noise waveform $n^{(s)}(t)$ repeated every T s to form a periodic waveform $n_T^{(s)}(t)$.

Let us consider a noise waveform for an interval of time T extending, say, from $t = -T/2$ to $t = +T/2$. Such a truncated representation of the noise we shall call $n^{(s)}(t)$; it is shown in Fig. 6.1-3a. Next we generate, as in Fig. 6.1-3b, a waveform in which the truncated noise waveform in the selected interval is repeated periodically. This periodic waveform $n_T^{(s)}(t)$ can be expanded in a Fourier series, and such a series will properly represent $n^{(s)}(t)$ in the interval $-T/2 \leq t \leq T/2$. The fundamental frequency of the series is $1/T$, which we shall define as

$$v \equiv \frac{1}{T} \qquad (6.1\text{-}5)$$

Thus the Fourier series is

$$n_T^{(s)}(t) = \sum_{k=1}^{\infty} (a_k \cos 2\pi k v t + b_k \sin 2\pi k v t) \qquad (6.1\text{-}6)$$

or alternatively,

$$n_T^{(s)}(t) = \sum_{k=1}^{\infty} c_k \cos(2\pi k v t + \theta_k) \qquad (6.1\text{-}7)$$

in which a_k, b_k, c_k are the constant coefficients of the spectral terms and θ_k is a phase angle. The two representations are related by

$$c_k^2 = a_k^2 + b_k^2 \qquad (6.1\text{-}8a)$$

and

$$\theta_k = -\arctan \frac{b_k}{a_k} \qquad (6.1\text{-}8b)$$

Note that $n_T^{(s)}(t)$ has no dc component. The dc component was removed since, in practice, communications systems are constructed to eliminate dc components of signal and noise. This permits a less expensive system design without any degradation in performance.

Referring to (6.1-6), we see that if $n_T^{(s)}(t)$ is known, the a_k and b_k can be found from the equations [Eq. (3.3-16)]

$$a_k = \frac{1}{T} \int_{-T/2}^{T/2} n_T^{(s)}(t) \cos 2\pi k v t\, dt \qquad (6.1\text{-}9a)$$

and

$$b_k = \frac{1}{T} \int_{-T/2}^{T/2} n_T^{(s)}(t) \sin 2\pi k v t\, dt \qquad (6.1\text{-}9b)$$

However, in the region $-T/2 \le t \le T/2$, $n_T^{(s)}(t) = n^{(s)}(t)$, the truncated noise wave-form. If we had chosen another segment of T from Fig. 6.1-3a and called that segment $n^{(s)}(t)$, we would find that different values of a_k and b_k would result. This is a further illustration of what we mean when we say that the thermal noise is *random* and *unpredictable*.

We are concerned mainly with a noise whose variation is such that, although the values of a_k and b_k vary, depending on the starting time of the T-second interval, the rms thermal noise voltage is a constant; i.e.,

$$n_{\text{rms}} = \left[\frac{1}{T} \int_{t_0-T/2}^{t_0+T/2} n^2(t)\, dt \right]^{1/2} = \text{constant} \qquad (6.1\text{-}10)$$

independent of the starting time t_0. An important corollary to this result is obtained by substituting (6.1-7) into (6.1-10). The result is

$$n_{\text{rms}}^2 = \sum_{k=1}^{\infty} \frac{\overline{c_k^2}}{2} = \text{constant} \qquad (6.1\text{-}11)$$

independent of the starting time t_0. In Eq. (6.1-11) $\overline{c_k^2}$ is the average of c_k^2 taken over all possible values of t_0.

We saw in Chap. 4 that if the input to a filter characterized by $H(f)$ was sinusoidal with a frequency f_k and an amplitude c_k, then the output of the filter was also sinusoidal with a frequency f_k and a peak amplitude $|H(f=f_k)|c_k$. The mean-square amplitude $n^2_{k,\,\mathrm{rms}}$ is therefore equal to one-half of the square of the amplitude.

$$n^2_{k,\,\mathrm{rms}} = \tfrac{1}{2}|H(f=f_k)|^2 \overline{c_k^2} \qquad (6.1\text{-}12)$$

If thermal noise $n(t)$, which is characterized by an infinite number of sinusoidal components [Eq. (6.1-7)], is the input to a filter $H(f)$, then the output of the filter consists of an infinite number of sine waves, each having a mean-square value given by (6.1-12). The total mean-square output noise is therefore

$$(n_0)^2_{\mathrm{rms}} = \frac{1}{2}\sum_{k=1}^{\infty}|H(f=f_k=kv)|^2 \overline{c_k^2} \qquad (6.1\text{-}13)$$

an expression similar to that presented in (6.1-11). The rms output thermal-noise voltage is therefore

$$(n_0)_{\mathrm{rms}} = \left[\sum_{k=1}^{\infty}|H(kv)|^2 \frac{\overline{c_k^2}}{2}\right]^{1/2} \qquad (6.1\text{-}14)$$

Equation (6.1-14) indicates that the rms noise present at the output of a filter depends on the magnitude of the transfer function of that filter.

EXAMPLE 6.1-2   Thermal noise $n(t)$ is passed through a bandpass filter having the transfer function

$$H(f) = \begin{cases} 1 & f_1 \le f \le f_2 \\ 0 & \text{elsewhere} \end{cases}$$

Obtain an expression for the rms output noise. Comment on the change in value of the rms output noise when f_2 increases, with f_1 remaining the same (i.e., the bandwidth increases).

SOLUTION   Referring to (6.1-14), we let

$$k_1 v = f_1$$

and

$$k_2 v = f_2$$

Then

$$(n_0)^2_{\mathrm{rms}} = \left(\sum_{k=k_1=f_1/v}^{k_2=f_2/v}|1|^2 \frac{\overline{c_k^2}}{2}\right)^{1/2}$$

$$= \left(\sum_{k=k_1}^{k_2} \frac{\overline{c_k^2}}{2}\right)^{1/2} \qquad (6.1\text{-}15)$$

As f_2 increases, $k_2 = f_2/v$ also increases. This results in an increase in the number of terms in (6.1-15); hence $(n_0)_{rms}^2$ increases. Thus, for this case, the mean-square output noise is directly proportional to the *bandwidth* of the filter.

The mean-square output noise power measured per unit bandwidth is called the *power spectral density* η and has the units V^2/Hz.

EXAMPLE 6.1-3   Thermal noise $n(t)$ is passed through a bandpass filter having a bandwidth of 10 kHz. A true rms meter attached to the filter output reads 3 V rms. If the bandwidth of the filter were 30 kHz, calculate the rms voltage that would be read by the meter.

SOLUTION   Since the mean-square noise is proportional to the filter bandwidth, we can set up the ratio

$$\frac{(n_0)_{rms}^2}{30 \times 10^3} = \frac{3^2}{10 \times 10^3}$$

Hence

$$(n_0)_{rms}^2 = 9 \times 3 = 27 \text{ V}^2$$

and the rms voltage read by the meter is

$$(n_0)_{rms} = \sqrt{27} = 5.2 \text{ V}$$

////////

6.2   AMPLITUDE MODULATION (AM)

One of the basic problems of communications engineering is the design of systems which allow many signals to be transmitted simultaneously. Consider commercial radio broadcasting, where the receiver must be capable of choosing from among many programs which occur simultaneously. These programs could be transmitted to each home using separate cables. However, the expense of having perhaps 50 cables brought into each house, added to the expense of the required repeaters, makes such a procedure impractical.

One way of solving this problem is to separate the signals in frequency so that only one transmission path is required. This is done by allocating to each broadcasting station a certain bandwidth. For example, one station transmits from 90 to 100 kHz, while another station can transmit from 100 to 110 kHz, etc. The voice signal voltage is then *modulated* so that it will occupy the prescribed frequency range. In this section we discuss one often used modulation technique, called *amplitude modulation*. We shall show that amplitude modulation results in *frequency translation* of the voice signal. However, it does not result in noise suppression. The AM system depends on very large transmitter power to ensure clarity of the received signal.

In Sec. 6.4 we shall consider frequency modulation (FM) systems. An FM system requires a much wider bandwidth than is required for AM. However, noise suppression is considerably greater, and lower transmitter power can be employed.

6.2-1   Frequency Translation

The frequency components of a signal may be translated uniformly along the frequency axis by *multiplying* the signal with an auxiliary sinusoidal signal. This process is illustrated in Fig. 6.2-1. Referring to Fig. 6.2-1*a*, we see that a typical voice signal has frequency components from 0 to f_M. Note that the strongest amplitudes exist at frequencies near f_p, which is found experimentally to be 800 Hz. The maximum frequency f_M is typically 3 kHz for telephone systems and 5 kHz for AM radio broadcasting.

Figure 6.2-1*b* shows the multiplication process whereby the voice signal $v_m(t)$ is multiplied by the auxiliary sinusoidal signal $v_c(t)$. $v_c(t)$ is called the *carrier signal*. Figure 6.2-1*c* illustrates the character of the resulting frequency-translated signal. Note that the voice signal is linearly shifted by the frequency f_c. Note also that frequencies also appear from $f_c - f_M$ to f_c. The form of the frequency spectrum shown in Fig. 6.2-1*c* may be found by assuming that the signal $v_m(t)$ is sinusoidal:

$$v_m(t) = A_m \cos \omega_m t \qquad (6.2\text{-}1)$$

where A_m is the peak signal amplitude and $\omega_m/2\pi = f_m$ is a signal frequency, between 0 and f_M.

If we multiply $v_m(t)$ by the auxiliary sinusoidal signal (the carrier signal) $v_c(t)$, given by

$$v_c(t) = A_c \cos \omega_c t \qquad (6.2\text{-}2)$$

we obtain

$$v_m(t)v_c(t) = A_m A_c \cos \omega_m t \cos \omega_c t$$

$$= \frac{A_m A_c}{2} [\cos(\omega_c - \omega_m)t + \cos(\omega_c + \omega_m)t] \qquad (6.2\text{-}3)$$

In obtaining (6.2-3) we have made use of the trigonometric identity

$$\cos \alpha \cos \beta = \tfrac{1}{2}\cos(\alpha + \beta) + \tfrac{1}{2}\cos(\alpha - \beta) \qquad (6.2\text{-}4)$$

Comparing (6.2-1) and (6.2-3), we see that (6.2-1) has a single frequency component at the frequency $f_m = \omega_m/2\pi$, while the product signal $v_m(t)v_c(t)$ has two components, one at the *difference frequency* $f_c - f_m$, and the second at the *sum frequency* $f_c + f_m$.

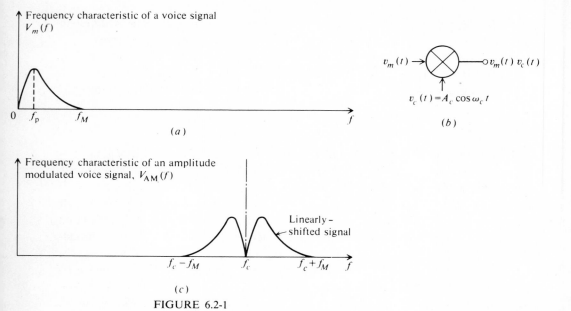

(a)

(b)

(c)

FIGURE 6.2-1
Illustrating the process of frequency translation using AM. (a) The voice signal;
(b) the multiplier; (c) the amplitude-modulated signal.

This simple result is easily extended to the case where $v_m(t)$ consists of many sine waves having frequency components f_m between 0 and f_M.

$$v_m(t) = \sum_{m=1}^{M} A_m \cos \omega_m t \qquad (6.2\text{-}5)$$

where $f_1 = \omega_1/2\pi$ can be as close to zero as required, and $f_M = \omega_M/2\pi$ is the maximum frequency contained in the signal. Then the product signal is

$$v_m(t)v_c(t) = \sum_{m=1}^{M} \frac{A_m A_c}{2} [\cos (\omega_c - \omega_m)t + \cos (\omega_c + \omega_m)t] \qquad (6.2\text{-}6)$$

Note that now the product signal has frequency components which extend from $f_c - f_M$ to $f_c + f_M$, as shown in Fig. 6.2-1c, while $v_m(t)$ has frequency components which extend from 0 to f_M. A voice signal typically has frequency components extending up to 5 kHz. If the voice signal is multiplied by a carrier with $f_c = 100$ kHz, the product signal will have frequency components extending from 95 to 105 kHz.

6.2-2 Generation of AM Signal

To design the frequency translation system so that an inexpensive receiver can be used to recover the original signal, we add $v_c(t)$ to the voltage produced by the product signal $v_m(t)v_c(t)$.

The voltage produced by the product is

$$v_p(t) = Pv_m(t)v_c(t) \qquad (6.2\text{-}7)$$

where the constant of proportionality P has the units of (volts)$^{-1}$.

The resulting AM signal is

$$v_{AM}(t) = [1 + Pv_m(t)]v_c(t) = A_c[1 + Pv_m(t)] \cos \omega_c t \qquad (6.2\text{-}8)$$

This voltage $v_{AM}(t)$ is an *amplitude-modulated waveform*. The reason for this is that the amplitude of the *carrier* $\cos \omega_c t$ changes in proportion to $v_m(t)$.

This is illustrated in Fig. 6.2-2, where $v_m(t)$ is chosen, for simplicity, to be a single sine wave. In Fig. 6.2-2a we see the signal $Pv_m(t)$. Its amplitude $M = PA_m$ [where A_m is the peak value of $v_m(t)$] is often referred to as the *modulation index*, and is always made less than 1. Figure 6.2-2b shows that the carrier frequency f_c is much higher than the modulation frequency f_m. Typically $f_c/f_m > 100$. The resulting AM signal is shown in Fig. 6.2-2c for the case where $A_c = 1$ and $M = \frac{1}{2}$. (Note that A_c can have any value, while $M \leq 1$. The values $A_c = 1$, $M = \frac{1}{2}$ are chosen for purposes of illustration only.) Referring to this figure and to Eq. (6.2-8), we see that the amplitude of $\cos \omega_c t$ is $1 + Pv_m(t)$ and that its amplitude is therefore proportional to $v_m(t)$. We also see that the designation carrier for the auxiliary signal $\cos \omega_c t$ is indeed appropriate since this signal carries the information-bearing signal as its envelope.

6.2-3 Demodulation

The very great merit of the AM system is the ease with which the information-bearing signal $v_m(t)$ can be recovered. The recovery process is referred to as *demodulation*, and is accomplished with the simple diode circuit shown in Fig. 6.2-3a. This circuit was also used as a simple rectifier (Fig. 5.1-8a). The circuit acts as a rectifier here also, since the output of the diode demodulator $\hat{v}_m(t)$ is always positive. However, here the amplitude of the sinusoidal carrier is proportional to $v_m(t)$.

The operation of the rectifier-type circuit was explained in Sec. 5.1 for the case of a constant-amplitude signal. To see how the circuit operates when the signal amplitude varies slowly, we shall assume initially that the resistor R is not present. Then, as $v_{AM}(t)$ increases, the diode conducts (acts like a short circuit) and therefore $\hat{v}_m(t) = v_{AM}(t)$. When $v_{AM}(t)$ decreases, $\hat{v}_m(t)$ does not change instantaneously and the diode turns off. The voltage $\hat{v}_m(t)$ is then constant until $v_{AM}(t)$ again is larger than $\hat{v}_m(t)$. To allow $\hat{v}_m(t)$ to decrease, as well as increase, we insert the resistor R. This resistor allows the capacitor to discharge, and hence reduce its voltage during the interval when the diode is turned off.

It is seen from Fig. 6.2-3b that $\hat{v}_m(t)$ closely approximates the modulating signal $v_m(t)$, except for the sawtooth (jagged-edge) characteristic of its peaks. In practice, these jagged edges are removed by following the diode detector by a low-pass filter.

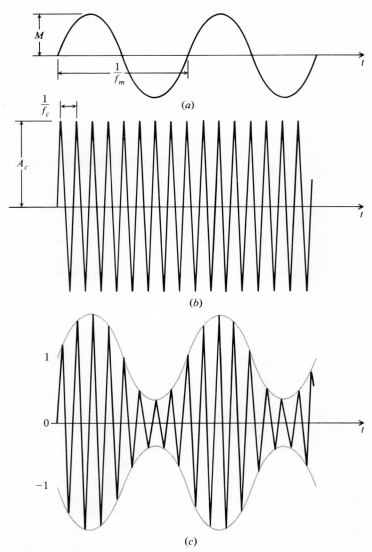

FIGURE 6.2-2
(a) Signal $Pv_m(t)$. (b) Carrier $v_c(t)$. (c) AM signal $v_{AM}(t)$ as in Eq. (6.2-8).

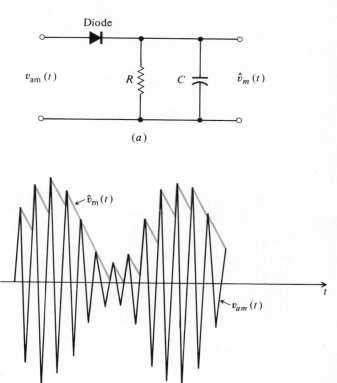

FIGURE 6.2-3
(*a*) The diode demodulator. (*b*) AM signal and the demodulated signal $\hat{v}_m(t)$.

6.2-4 Maximum Allowable Modulation

If we are to use the simple diode demodulator shown in Fig. 6.2-3*a*, we must limit the extent of the modulation of the carrier. Referring to Eq. (6.2-8), we see that if $Pv_m(t)$ is greater than unity, the amplitude can become negative. When this occurs, the resulting AM signal is distorted, as shown in Fig. 6.2-4. Figure 6.2-4*a* and *b* shows the modulating and carrier signals. Here $M = 2$ while $A_c = 1$. The resulting AM signal is shown in Fig. 6.2-4*c*. Also shown in Fig. 6.2-4*c* is the output of the diode demodulator, after filtering of the jagged edges. Note that since the diode demodulator is a rectifier, its output consists of the peaks of the positive portion of the carrier amplitude. This is not the desired output. Hence we always restrict $|Pv_m(t)| \le 1$. This ensures that the carrier amplitude $A_c[1 + Pv_m(t)]$ remains positive.

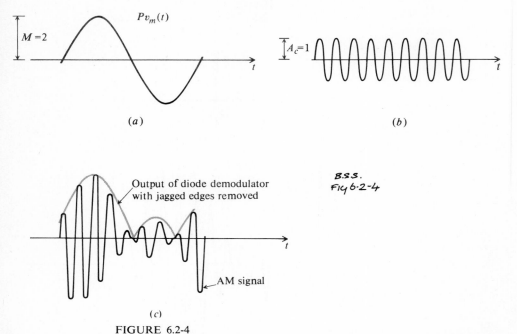

(a)

(b)

B.S.S.
FIG 6·2-4

(c)

FIGURE 6.2-4
(a) The modulating signal $Pv_m(t)$. (b) The carrier signal $v_c(t)$. (c) AM signal and filtered output of diode detector.

6.3   SINGLE-SIDEBAND COMMUNICATION

In Eq. (6.2-6) we showed that an AM signal consisted of *sum-frequency* terms such as $f_c + f_m$ and *difference-frequency* terms such as $f_c - f_m$. The sum-frequency terms result in a frequency characteristic extending from $f_c + f_1$ to $f_c + f_M$, called an *upper sideband*, while the difference-frequency terms result in a frequency characteristic extending from $f_c - f_M$ to $f_c - f_1$, called the *lower sideband*. A typical AM spectrum is shown in Fig. 6.2-1c for the case $f_1 = 0$.

We note from (6.2-6) that all the information concerning the modulating signal $v_m(t)$ may be conveyed by transmitting either the upper or the lower sideband. This is called *single-sideband transmission* (SSB). If single-sideband transmission is possible, why send both sidebands? Why not send only one sideband, upper or lower, and thereby save one-half of the bandwidth?

The reason for the widespread use of AM (which is the transmission of both the upper and lower sidebands) is that the AM modulators and demodulators are very simple to construct, and hence inexpensive. On the other hand, SSB modulators and demodulators are quite complex and costly. However, when bandwidth is a problem, as in the very limited citizen's radio band, single-sideband transmission is often employed. Single sideband is also used in *television* to save bandwidth. Here the signal carrying the picture information is transmitted using a modified form of SSB called *vestigial sideband* (VSB). In SSB a bandwidth reduction of one-half is possible, while in VSB systems the bandwidth is reduced to two-thirds of the original bandwidth. The extra expense incurred with SSB systems is also warranted when *security* is required. To receive a SSB message, a listener is required to have a SSB receiver. Thus, by using an uncommon transmission procedure, we can eliminate many unwanted listeners.

6.4 FREQUENCY MODULATION

Frequency modulation (FM) is often employed when significant noise suppression is required and there is no severe bandwidth limitation. In the AM systems discussed in Secs. 6.2 and 6.3, signal information was contained in the amplitude of the carrier. In FM, the modulator output is of constant amplitude and the signal information is transmitted by variations of the carrier frequency.

Consider the signal

$$v_{FM}(t) = A \cos[\omega_c t + \phi(t)] = A \cos[\theta(t)] \qquad (6.4\text{-}1)$$

The angle $\theta(t)$ is

$$\theta(t) = \omega_c t + \phi(t) \qquad (6.4\text{-}2)$$

where $\omega_c = 2\pi f_c$ is the angular carrier frequency (a constant) and $\phi(t)$ is the instantaneous *phase deviation* (phase offset) with respect to the angle $\omega_c t$. The amplitude A is the amplitude of the FM voltage.

The *instantaneous angular frequency* $\omega(t) = 2\pi f(t)$ is defined as the rate of change of angle $\theta(t)$ with respect to time. Thus the instantaneous angular frequency of the FM voltage given in (6.4-1) is

$$\omega(t) = 2\pi f(t) = \frac{d}{dt}\theta(t) \qquad (6.4\text{-}3a)$$

$$= \frac{d}{dt}[\omega_c t + \phi(t)] \qquad (6.4\text{-}3b)$$

$$= \omega_c + \frac{d\phi(t)}{dt} \qquad (6.4\text{-}3c)$$

Thus we see that the instantaneous frequency $f(t)$ of the FM voltage consists of the sum of the carrier frequency f_c and a *frequency deviation* $v(t)$ with respect to this carrier frequency, where

$$v(t) = \frac{1}{2\pi} \frac{d\phi(t)}{dt} \qquad (6.4\text{-}4)$$

If the information to be transmitted is $v_m(t)$, then the frequency deviation $v(t)$ is made proportional to the input signal $v_m(t)$, so that

$$v(t) = \frac{kv_m(t)}{2\pi} \qquad (6.4\text{-}5)$$

where $v(t)$ has the units of hertz (cycles per second, or Hz), $v_m(t)$ has the units of volts, and k is a constant of proportionality having the units of radians per second per volt [rad/(s)(V)].   Combining (6.4-4) and (6.4-5) yields

$$\frac{d\phi}{dt} = 2\pi v(t) = kv_m(t) \qquad (6.4\text{-}6)$$

Hence

$$\phi(t) = k \int^t v_m(\lambda)\, d\lambda \qquad (6.4\text{-}7)$$

We see from (6.4-5) and (6.4-7) that in FM transmission the frequency deviation from the carrier frequency is proportional to the modulating signal, and the phase deviation from the angle $\omega_c t$ is proportional to the integral of the modulating signal. In terms of (6.4-7), (6.4-1) can now be written

$$v_{FM}(t) = A \cos \left[\omega_c t + k \int^t v_m(\lambda)\, d\lambda \right] \qquad (6.4\text{-}8)$$

This is the standard relationship between a modulating signal $v_m(t)$ and the modulated voltage $v_{FM}(t)$.

EXAMPLE 6.4-1   A modulating voltage $v_m(t)$ is shown in Fig. 6.4-1a. Sketch $v_{FM}(t)$ if the constant $k = 1,000$ rad/(s)(V) and $\omega_c = 3,000$ rad/s.

SOLUTION   The modulating signal $v_m(t)$ can take on one of two possible values: ± 1 V. This corresponds to a frequency deviation [Eq. (6.4-5)]

$$v(t) = \frac{k}{2\pi} v_m(t) = \pm \frac{1,000}{2\pi} \qquad \text{Hz}$$

Thus the total instantaneous frequency $f(t)$ of the FM signal is [Eqs. (6.4-3c) and (6.4-4)]

$$f(t) = \frac{1}{2\pi} \omega_c + v(t)$$

$$= \frac{3,000}{2\pi} \pm \frac{1,000}{2\pi}$$

$$= \begin{cases} \dfrac{4,000}{2\pi} \text{ Hz} & \text{when } v_m(t) = +1 \text{ V} \\[2ex] \dfrac{2,000}{2\pi} \text{ Hz} & \text{when } v_m(t) = -1 \text{ V} \end{cases}$$

Referring to Fig. 6.4-1a, we see that for the first $2\pi \times 10^{-3}$ s, the frequency of the FM voltage is $f(t) = 4,000/2\pi$ Hz. Thus the number of cycles completed in that time interval is

$$\text{Cycles} = Tf(t) = (2\pi \times 10^{-3}) \frac{4,000}{2\pi} = 4$$

This is shown in Fig. 6.4-1b. Similarly, we find that during the second time interval of $\pi \times 10^{-3}$ s, $f(t) = 2,000/2\pi$ Hz, and one cycle is completed. The complete FM voltage is sketched in Fig. 6.4-1b. Note how the frequency changes as $v_m(t)$ changes.
////////

In Example 6.4-1, the FM voltage stayed at a particular frequency for 4, 1, 3, etc., cycles. In addition, there were only two possible frequencies since $v_m(t)$ took on only two values. If $v_m(t)$ is an analog signal, it can usually take on *all* values between the given maximum and minimum voltages. Thus, if $-1 \le v_m(t) \le +1$, then all values between -1 and $+1$ are possible. Hence, in the context of Example 6.4-1, all frequencies between $2,000/2\pi$ and $4,000/2\pi$ Hz are possible. Furthermore, unlike Fig. 6.4-1a, $v_m(t)$ typically changes smoothly with time, so that the frequency of $v_{FM}(t)$ changes continuously, and usually does not dwell at any single frequency for more than an instant.

For example, if $v_m(t) = V_0 \cos \omega_m(t)$, then the frequency $f(t)$ produced by the modulating signal is

$$f(t) = f_c + v(t) \tag{6.4-9a}$$

$$= f_c + \frac{k}{2\pi} v_m(t) = f_c + \frac{kV_0}{2\pi} \cos \omega_m t \tag{6.4-9b}$$

In this case the frequency varies continuously between $f_c - kV_0/2\pi$, and $f_c + kV_0/2\pi$.

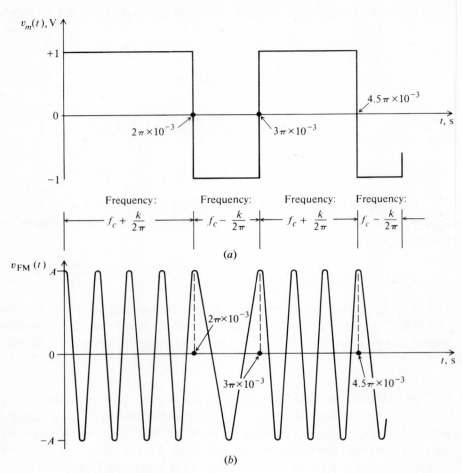

FIGURE 6.4-1
(*a*) The modulating signal $v_m(t)$. (*b*) The corresponding FM signal $v_{FM}(t)$.

For the special case of sinusoidal modulation, the frequency deviation $v(t)$ is

$$v(t) = \frac{kV_0}{2\pi} \cos \omega_m t \qquad (6.4\text{-}10)$$

It is convenient in this case to define the *maximum frequency deviation* by the symbol Δf; hence

$$\Delta f = \frac{kV_0}{2\pi} \qquad (6.4\text{-}11a)$$

and

$$v(t) = \Delta f \cos \omega_m t \quad (6.4\text{-}11b)$$

The FM signal [Eq. (6.4-1)] is

$$v_{FM}(t) = A \cos[\omega_c t + \phi(t)] \quad (6.4\text{-}12)$$

where, from (6.4-4) and (6.4-11b),

$$\phi(t) = 2\pi \int^t v(\lambda)\, d\lambda = \frac{2\pi\Delta f}{\omega_m} \sin \omega_m t = \frac{\Delta f}{f_m} \sin \omega_m t \quad (6.4\text{-}13a)$$

Thus

$$v_{FM}(t) = A \cos\left(\omega_c t + \frac{\Delta f}{f_m} \sin \omega_m t\right) \quad (6.4\text{-}13b)$$

Equation (6.4-13b) expresses the FM signal v_{FM} in terms of its basic parameters: the amplitude A, the carrier frequency f_c, the maximum frequency deviation Δf, and the frequency f_m of the modulating signal.

It is interesting to note that since $\phi(t)$ is the instantaneous phase deviation, the ratio $\Delta f/f_m$ is the *maximum phase deviation*. The often used ratio is given the symbol β:

$$\beta \equiv \frac{\Delta f}{f_m} \quad \text{rad} \quad (6.4\text{-}14a)$$

Using (6.4-14a), (6.4-13b) becomes

$$v_{FM}(t) = A \cos(\omega_c t + \beta \sin \omega_m t) \quad (6.4\text{-}14b)$$

6.4-1 Bandwidth

In AM and SSB systems, the bandwidth required to pass the signal without attenuation depended on the maximum frequency of the modulating signal. Thus, if the highest frequency component of $v_m(t)$ is f_M, then, referring to Fig. 6.2-1c, we see that the bandwidth of a filter required to pass an AM signal without attenuation is $2f_M$, while the bandwidth required to pass a SSB signal is f_M.

In FM, the frequency of the FM voltage is $f(t)$ as in (6.3-3a), and its maximum and minimum values depend, not on the frequency of the modulating signal $v_m(t)$, but primarily on the frequency deviation $v(t)$ produced by the magnitude of $v_m(t)$. Thus, in Example 6.4-1, the frequency varied between $2{,}000/2\pi$ and $4{,}000/2\pi$ Hz, and these frequencies were independent of the times at which $v_m(t)$ changed voltage, i.e., independent of the frequency of $v_m(t)$. Similarly, referring to (6.4-9b) and (6.4-11a), we see that $f(t)$ is bounded by

$$f_c - \Delta f \le f(t) \le f_c + \Delta f \quad (6.4\text{-}15a)$$

where Δf is the maximum frequency deviation produced by $v_m(t)$.

It can be shown that the bandwidth of a bandpass filter required to pass the FM signal is given approximately, in terms of the maximum frequency deviation Δf produced by a sinusoidal modulating signal and the frequency f_M of the modulating signal, by the equation

$$B_{FM} = 2(\Delta f + f_M) = 2(\beta + 1)f_M \qquad (6.4\text{-}15b)$$

since $\beta = \Delta f/f_M$.

EXAMPLE 6.4-2   The signal $v_m(t) = V_0 \cos \omega_M t$ is to be FM-modulated and also AM-modulated. Compare the bandwidth required in an AM receiver to that required in an FM receiver.

SOLUTION   In the AM system the bandwidth is

$$B_{AM} = 2f_M$$

In the FM system the bandwidth is

$$B_{FM} = 2(\Delta f + f_M) = 2(\beta + 1)f_M$$

The ratio of bandwidths is therefore

$$\frac{B_{FM}}{B_{AM}} = \frac{\Delta f}{f_M} + 1 = \beta + 1$$

Thus the bandwidth required to receive an FM signal is greater than the bandwidth required to receive an AM signal by the factor $\beta + 1$.
////////

6.4-2   Modulation, the Armstrong Method

The Armstrong method of frequency modulation is used by many commercial FM radio stations. It is based on the trigonometric identity

$$\cos[\omega_0 t + \phi_1(t)] = \cos \phi_1(t)\cos \omega_0 t - \sin \phi_1(t)\sin \omega_0 t \qquad (6.4\text{-}16a)$$

For the method to work, certain approximations must be satisfied. We note that if

$$|\phi_1(t)| \ll 1 \qquad (6.4\text{-}16b)$$

then $\qquad\qquad\qquad\qquad \cos \phi_1(t) \approx 1 \qquad$ and $\qquad \sin \phi_1(t) \approx \phi_1(t) \qquad (6.4\text{-}16c)$

If (6.4-16b) is satisfied, then (6.4-16a) becomes

$$\cos[\omega_0 t + \phi_1(t)] \approx \cos \omega_0 t - \phi_1(t)\sin \omega_0 t \qquad (6.4\text{-}16d)$$

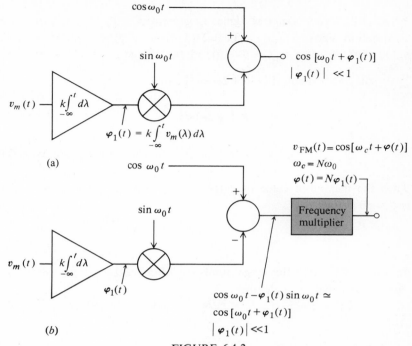

FIGURE 6.4-2
The Armstrong method of frequency modulation.

The voltage $\cos[\omega_0 t + \phi_1(t)]$ can be generated, as shown in Fig. 6.4-2a, using the approximation (6.4-16d), provided that the magnitude of the phase deviation $|\phi_1(t)| \ll 1$. Note that $\phi_1(t)$ is obtained by passing $v_m(t)$ through an amplifier which is designed to integrate the incoming signal.

In most FM applications where noise suppression is desired, the maximum value of $|\phi_1(t)|$ is required to be much greater than 1, not much less than 1. (Since the maximum phase deviation was defined to be β, we note that β should be much greater that unity and not much less than unity.) However, electronic circuits exist which have the capability of multiplying frequency by any integer N. An example of such a frequency multiplier is the diode rectifier discussed in Sec. 5.1. Equation (5.1-5) shows that as a result of rectification, all harmonics of the basic signal frequency are generated. Thus, in our example, if the signal $\cos[\omega_0 t + \phi_1(t)]$ is passed through a frequency multiplier designed to produce the Nth harmonic, the output of the multiplier is $\cos N[\omega_0 t + \phi_1(t)] = \cos[N\omega_0 t + N\phi_1(t)]$. If N is sufficiently large, the maximum value of $|N\phi_1(t)| \gg 1$ as required. The carrier frequency is now $f_c = Nf_0$. The complete Armstrong modulation system is shown in Fig. 6.4-2b.

EXAMPLE 6.4-3   An FM signal is generated using the Armstrong method. The modulation signal is $v_m(t) = 3 \cos 2\pi(3,000)t$. If $f_c = 100$ MHz and the maximum value of $\phi(t)$ is to be $\phi_{max} = \beta = 10$ rad, find N and f_0 when $k = 20\pi$ rad/(s)(V).

SOLUTION   From Fig. 6.4-2a we see that

$$\phi_1(t) = k \int^t v_m(\lambda) \, d\lambda$$

$$= 20\pi \int^t 3 \cos 2\pi(3,000)t \, dt = \frac{1}{100} \sin 2\pi(3,000)t$$

Thus the maximum value of $\phi_1(t)$ is $\beta_1 = 10^{-2}$ rad. The maximum value of $\phi(t)$ is $\beta = 10$ rad; thus

$$N = \frac{\phi_{max}}{\phi_{1,max}} = \frac{\beta}{\beta_1} = \frac{10}{10^{-2}} = 10^3$$

In practical systems this large number is obtained by using several frequency multipliers rather than a single one.

Since $f_c = 100$ MHz, $f_0 = f_c/N = 10^8/10^3 = 100$ kHz.

////////

6.4-3   Demodulation

The basic principle of FM demodulation is to apply the FM signal

$$v_{FM}(t) = 1 \cos[\omega_c t + \phi(t)] \qquad (6.4\text{-}17a)$$

to a nonlinear system which provides the output voltage

$$v_0(t) = \lambda \frac{d\phi}{dt} \qquad (6.4\text{-}17b)$$

where λ is a constant of proportionality having the dimensions volts per radian per second. Since $d\phi/dt = kv_m(t)$, $v_0(t)$ is

$$v_0(t) = \lambda k v_m(t) \qquad (6.4\text{-}17c)$$

Thus $v_0(t)$ is proportional to the modulating signal, as required.

There are many nonlinear systems capable of demodulating an FM signal. One such system is shown in Fig. 6.4-3a. Here the FM signal is applied to a frequency selective network which converts the FM signal into an AM signal. The AM signal is then demodulated using a diode demodulator. To illustrate the manner in which the FM signal is converted to an AM signal, consider that the frequency-selective

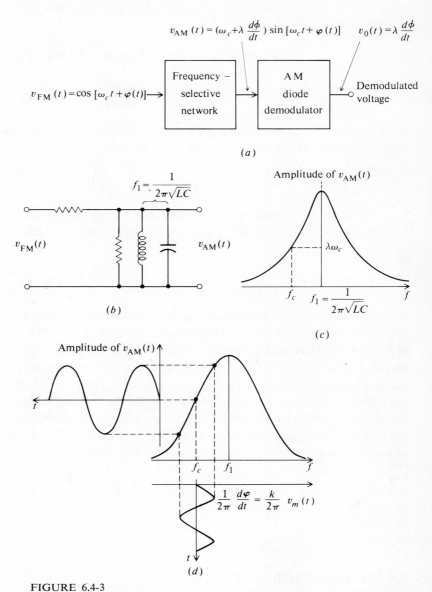

FIGURE 6.4-3

FM demodulation. (*a*) Illustrating the principle of one type of FM demodulator. (*b*) A parallel *RLC* circuit used to approximate a differentiator. (*c*) Resonance curve of the *RLC* circuit. (*d*) Input frequency and output voltage waveforms.

network is a *differentiator*, that is, $v_{out} = \lambda(dv_{in}/dt)$. Then the input to the diode demodulator is

$$v_{AM}(t) = \lambda \frac{d}{dt}[v_{FM}(t)] = \lambda \frac{d}{dt}[\cos(\omega_c t + \phi(t)] \quad (6.4\text{-}18a)$$

$$= -\lambda \left[\omega_c + \frac{d\phi(t)}{dt}\right] \sin[\omega_c t + \phi(t)] \quad (6.4\text{-}18b)$$

Note that this voltage is indeed an AM signal since the amplitude of $\sin[\omega_c t + \phi(t)]$ varies with time. Thus the output of the diode demodulator is

$$v_0(t) = \lambda\omega_c + \lambda \frac{d\phi(t)}{dt} \quad (6.4\text{-}19)$$

The term $\lambda\omega_c$ represents a dc voltage which is eliminated from the output by blocking capacitors. Thus the voltage at the output of the diode demodulator is actually

$$v_0(t) = \frac{\lambda \, d\phi(t)}{dt} \quad (6.4\text{-}20)$$

The differentiation network can be approximated by a simple *RC* circuit. However, in most practical receivers it is approximated by a parallel *RLC* circuit, as shown in Fig. 6.4-3b. Here $v_{FM}(t)$ is applied to an *RLC* circuit having a resonance peak at a frequency $f_1 = 1/2\pi\sqrt{LC}$ which is larger than the carrier frequency f_c. This is illustrated by the resonance curve shown in Fig. 6.4-3c. Note that at the frequency f_c, the output of the *RLC* circuit has the amplitude $\lambda\omega_c$. As the frequency f increases, the amplitude of the output voltage $v_{AM}(t)$ increases, and as the frequency f decreases, the amplitude of $v_{AM}(t)$ decreases. This is shown in Fig. 6.4-3d. Thus, the amplitude of $v_{AM}(t)$ is proportional to the *frequency* of the FM signal,

$$\frac{1}{2\pi} \frac{d\phi(t)}{dt} = \frac{k}{2\pi} v_m(t)$$

as desired.

6.5   PULSE-CODE MODULATION

The AM and FM systems considered up to this point are called analog modulation systems, since the analog signal $v_m(t)$ is employed directly to modulate the carrier. In the remainder of this chapter we study a pulse-code-modulation (PCM) system in which the analog signal $v_m(t)$ is first encoded, by converting it into a binary signal, and this binary signal is then modulated. The result is a system with better noise-suppression characteristics than FM (even for the *same* bandwidth). Furthermore, since the signal is in digital form, digital processing is used. This enables communications systems to be built with greater versatility and smaller size.

6.5-1 The Sampling Theorem

The basis for all pulse-code-modulation techniques is the *sampling theorem*. Before stating and proving this theorem, it is useful to illustrate the concept of sampling. Figure 6.5-1a shows a signal voltage waveform $v_m(t)$ which is to be sampled. By this we mean that the signal $v_m(t)$ is to be multiplied by the function $S(t)$ shown in Fig. 6.5-1b. $S(t)$ is seen to be a sequence of very narrow pulses, each having an amplitude of 1 unit and occurring every T. The product voltage is $v_T(t) = S(t)v_m(t)$.

Figure 6.5-1c shows the product voltage $v_{T1}(t)$ when $v_m(t)$ is sampled every T. Intuitively, we can see that $v_m(t)$ can be recovered by simply passing $v_{T1}(t)$ through an AM demodulator and filtering to remove jagged edges. Similarly, we can argue intuitively that $v_{T2}(t)$ shown in Fig. 6.5-1d can be processed to yield $v_m(t)$. What about the resulting distortion? Figure 6-5-1e shows $v_{T2}(t)$ when samples are taken every $21T$. Can $v_m(t)$ still be recovered?

These questions are answered by the sampling theorem, which in essence states that any signal having components with frequencies lying within a band f_M Hz wide must be sampled by pulses occurring more frequently than $1/2f_M$. Furthermore, the theorem states that under this condition the signal is recovered, with *no* distortion, simply by filtering $v_T(t)$ using a filter having a bandwidth f_M. No demodulator is needed!

> **Theorem** Let $v_m(t)$ be a signal having a maximum frequency component f_M. Let values of $v_m(t)$ be determined at regular intervals separated by the time $T_s \leq 1/2f_M$; that is, the signal is periodically *sampled* every T_s.
>
> Then these samples $v_m(nT_s)$, where n is an integer, uniquely determine the signal, and the signal may be reconstructed from these samples without error.

The time T_s is called the *sampling time*, and the *sampling rate* is defined as $f_s \equiv 1/T_s$. Note that the theorem states that $f_s \geq 2f_M$ and that therefore at least two samples are taken during the course of the period corresponding to the highest frequency component of $v_m(t)$. The minimum sampling frequency $f_s = 2f_M$ is called the *Nyquist rate*.

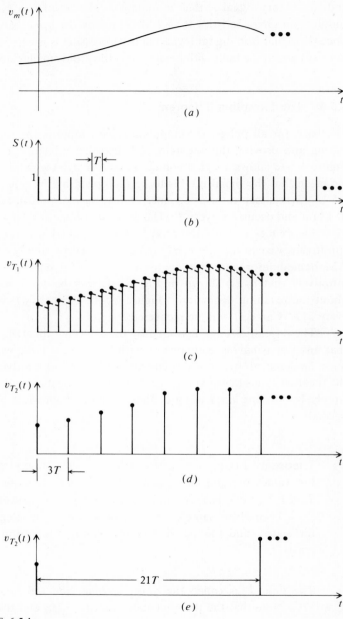

FIGURE 6.5-1
(a) The information-bearing signal $v_m(t)$. (b) The sampling function $S(t)$. (c) Transmitted pulses—sampling every T. (d) Transmitted pulses—sampling every $3T$. (e) Transmitted pulses—sampling every $21T$.

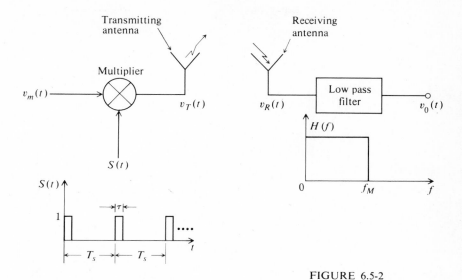

FIGURE 6.5-2
A pulse-modulation system.

Pulse modulation; an application of the sampling theorem One possible pulse-modulation technique is shown in Fig. 6.5-2. Here the input signal $v_m(t)$ is multiplied by the pulse train $S(t)$. Each pulse has a unit amplitude and a width τ which is much less than the time between pulses, $\tau \ll T_s$, where $T_s = 1/f_s = 1/2f_M$. The process of multiplying $v_m(t)$ by $S(t)$ is identical with the process of sampling $v_m(t)$. Consider that $v_m(t)$ has the waveform shown in Fig. 6.5-3a; then with $S(t)$ as shown in Fig. 6.5-3b, the product signal $v_T(t) = v_m(t)S(t)$ is as shown in Fig. 6.5-3c. Note that $v_T(t)$ consists of a pulse train, each pulse having an amplitude equal to $v_m(t)$ at the pulse instant. Thus the samples of $v_m(t)$, which are $v_m(t = nT_s)$, are the amplitudes of the pulses formed by the product $v_T(t) = v_m(t)S(t)$.

Since amplitude modulation involves the multiplication of the modulating signal $v_m(t)$ by a carrier signal, the technique shown in Fig. 6.5-2 is called *pulse-amplitude modulation* (PAM). The resulting pulses $v_T(t)$ may be transmitted directly, as shown in Fig. 6.5-2, or they may be modulated again by, say, frequency modulation. In this case the pulse height would correspond to a frequency deviation $kv(t)$ from the carrier frequency ω_c.

Referring to Fig. 6.5-2, it is seen that the transmitted signal is eventually received as $v_R(t)$. If transmission is over a long channel, the received signal is an attenuated version of the transmitted signal. In addition, the received signal will be

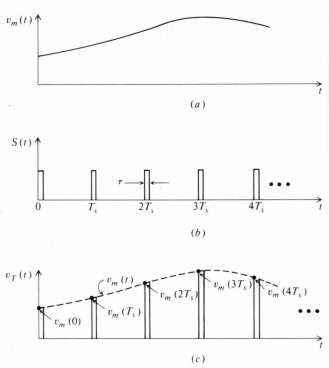

FIGURE 6.5-3
(a) The information-bearing signal $v_m(t)$. (b) The sampling voltage $S(t)$. (c) The transmitted-pulse waveform.

contaminated by noise (Sec. 6.1). Let us neglect the thermal noise in our initial discussin. Then

$$v_R(t) = \alpha v_T(t) \qquad (6.5\text{-}1)$$

where α represents the attenuation caused by the channel. The sampling theorem then states that if we pass $v_R(t)$ through a low-pass filter which rejects all frequencies above the maximum-frequency component of $v_m(t)$, which is f_M, then $v_0(t)$ is proportional to $v_m(t)$:

$$v_0(t) = \text{constant} \cdot v_m(t) \qquad (6.5\text{-}2)$$

and the received signal has exactly the same form as the modulating signal; i.e., there is no loss of information, and hence no distortion.

EXAMPLE 6.5.1   A signal $v_m(t) = \cos \omega_m t$ is sampled at four times the Nyquist frequency. The samples are equally spaced, and one sample occurs at $t = 0$. Find (a) the samples $v_T(t)$ and (b) the output of a low-pass filter which passes all frequencies less than and equal to f_m.

SOLUTION   (a) The Nyquist rate is $2f_m$; so samples are taken every $1/8f_m$. Thus the samples are

$$v_m(0) = 1 \qquad v_m\!\left(t = \frac{1}{8f_m}\right) = \frac{\sqrt{2}}{2} \qquad v_m\!\left(t = \frac{1}{4f_m}\right) = 0 \quad \cdots$$

In general, this can be written

$$v_m\!\left(\frac{k}{8f_m}\right) = \cos \frac{k\pi}{4} \qquad k = 0, 1, 2, \ldots$$

(b) The transmitted signal is $v_T(t) = v_m(t)S(t)$. The sampling signal $S(t)$ shown in Fig. 6.5-3b is a periodic function and can therefore be expressed as a Fourier series. It is left for the reader to show that, when $\tau \ll T_s$, $S(t)$ is

$$S(t) \approx \frac{\tau}{T_s} + \frac{2\tau}{T_s}\left(\cos 2\pi \frac{t}{T_s} + \cos 2 \times 2\pi \frac{t}{T_s} + \cdots\right) \qquad (6.5\text{-}3)$$

Since $v_m(t) = \cos 2\pi f_m t$ and $T_s = 1/8f_m$, the transmitted signal is

$$v_T(t) = \frac{\tau}{T_s} \cos 2\pi f_m t + \frac{2\tau}{T_s} \cos 2\pi f_m t \cos 16\pi f_m t$$

$$+ \frac{2\tau}{T_s} \cos 2\pi f_m t \cos 2 \times 16\pi f_m t + \cdots \qquad (6.5\text{-}4)$$

Using the identity

$$\cos A \cos B = \tfrac{1}{2} \cos(A + B) + \tfrac{1}{2} \cos(A - B) \qquad (6.5\text{-}5)$$

Eq. (6.5-4) becomes

$$v_T(t) = \frac{\tau}{T_s} \cos 2\pi f_m t + \frac{\tau}{T_s} \cos 14\pi f_m t + \frac{\tau}{T_s} \cos 18\pi f_m t$$

$$+ \frac{\tau}{T_s} \cos 30\pi f_m t + \frac{\tau}{T_s} \cos 34\pi f_m t + \cdots \qquad (6.5\text{-}6)$$

The received signal is $v_R(t) = \alpha v_T(t)$. This signal is now filtered by a low-pass filter which passes all frequencies less than or equal to f_m and totally rejects all higher frequencies. Thus only the first term in (6.5-6) is passed by the filter. The second term, for example, has the frequency $7f_m$ and is totally rejected by the filter. The result is

$$v_0(t) = \frac{\alpha\tau}{T_s} \cos 2\pi f_m t = \frac{\alpha\tau}{T_s} v_m(t) \qquad (6.5\text{-}7)$$

Note that the output signal $v_0(t)$ is equal to the input signal $v_m(t)$, except for the proportionality factor $\alpha\tau/T_s = 8\alpha f_m \tau$.

EXAMPLE 6.5-2 The signal $v_m(t) = \cos(2\pi \times 0.5 f_M t) + 0.3 \cos 2\pi f_M t$ is sampled at twice the Nyquist rate. A sample occurs at $t = 0$. The received signal is filtered by a low-pass filter which rejects all frequencies above f_M and passes frequencies at and less than f_M without attenuation.

(a) Show that $v_0(t)$ is proportional to $v_m(t)$.

(b) The same signal $v_m(t)$ is sampled at the frequency rate $f_s' = 1.5 f_M$. Show that $v_0(t)$ is now a distorted version of $v_m(t)$.

SOLUTION   (a) Using (6.5-3), we have

$$v_R(t) = \alpha v_T(t) = \alpha v_m(t)S(t)$$

$$= \alpha\left[\frac{\tau}{T_s}(\cos \pi f_M t + 0.3 \cos 2\pi f_M t)\right.$$

$$\left. + \frac{2\tau}{T_s}(\cos \pi f_M t + 0.3 \cos 2\pi f_M t)\left(\cos 2\pi \frac{t}{T_s} + \cos 4\pi \frac{t}{T_s} + \cdots\right)\right] \quad (6.5\text{-}8)$$

Letting $T_s = 1/4 f_M$ and using (6.5-5), we have

$$v_R(t) = \frac{\alpha\tau}{T_s}(\cos \pi f_M t + 0.3 \cos 2\pi f_M t)$$

$$+ \frac{\alpha\tau}{T_s}(\cos 7\pi f_M t + \cos 9\pi f_M t + 0.3 \cos 6\pi f_M t + 0.3 \cos 10\pi f_M t)$$

$$+ \frac{\alpha\tau}{T_s}(\cos 15\pi f_M t + \cos 17\pi f_M t + 0.3 \cos 14\pi f_M t + 0.3 \cos 18\pi f_M t)$$

$$+ \cdots \quad (6.5\text{-}9)$$

The low-pass filter removes all but the first two terms, yielding

$$v_0(t) = \frac{\alpha\tau}{T_s}(\cos \pi f_M t + 0.3 \cos 2\pi f_M t) \quad (6.5\text{-}10)$$

Thus the output signal is proportional to the input signal.

(b) Using (6.5-8), letting $T_s = 1/1.5 f_M$, and with (6.5-5), we have

$$v_R(t) = \frac{\alpha\tau}{T_s}(\cos \pi f_M t + 0.3 \cos 2\pi f_M t)$$

$$+ \frac{\alpha\tau}{T_s}(\cos 2\pi f_M t + \cos 4\pi f_M t + 0.3 \cos \pi f_M t + 0.3 \cos 5\pi f_M t)$$

$$+ \frac{\alpha\tau}{T_s}(\cos 5\pi f_M t + \cos 7\pi f_M t + 0.3 \cos 4\pi f_M t + 0.3 \cos 8\pi f_M t)$$

$$+ \cdots \quad (6.5\text{-}11)$$

The low-pass filter removes all frequencies greater than f_M. Thus

$$v_0(t) = \frac{\alpha\tau}{T_s} (\cos \pi f_M t + 0.3 \cos 2\pi f_M t)$$

$$+ \frac{\alpha\tau}{T_s} (\cos 2\pi f_M t + 0.3 \cos \pi f_M t) \quad (6.5\text{-}12)$$

Hence

$$v_0(t) = \frac{\alpha\tau}{T_s} (1.3 \cos \pi f_M t + 1.3 \cos 2\pi f_M t) \quad (6.5\text{-}13)$$

Note that by sampling at $f_s = 1.5f_M$, which is less than the Nyquist rate, the amplitudes of the transmitted frequency components are altered so that $v_0(t)$ is no longer proportional to $v_M(t)$.
////////

The above two examples were used to illustrate the sampling theorem. In each example $v_m(t)$ was chosen, for simplicity, to be sinusoidal. However, the sampling theorem applies to any bandlimited $v_m(t)$.

6.5-2 Quantization of Signals

The sampled signal $v_m(t)S(t)$ obtained in the preceding section is usually not transmitted directly, nor directly employed to modulate a carrier. The reason for this is that, if we first convert this product signal into a binary signal, the noise-suppression characteristic of this new system is significantly greater than for the original system shown in Fig. 6.5-1.

We recall from Sec. 2.3 that the decimal number V can be written, using binary notation,

$$V = \cdots a_2 2^2 + a_1 2^1 + a_0 2^0 \quad (6.5\text{-}14a)$$

where each a_i, that is, $a_0, a_1, a_2, \ldots$, can take on the value 1 or 0. The binary sequence $\cdots a_2 a_1 a_0$ then represents the number V. To relate this to our sampled signal, we let V be the sampled value at any one sampling instant. Then, instead of transmitting a pulse of amplitude V, we can transmit the sequence $\cdots a_2 a_1 a_0$. Our constraint is immediately evident. Each T_s, V changes; hence the sequence $\cdots a_2 a_1 a_0$ must change. Thus we must curtail the number of a's in our sequence or we will be unable to generate them and transmit them in the allotted time interval. Fortunately, we find that in many practical systems eight values of a suffice. That is,

$$V = a_7 a_6 a_5 a_4 a_3 a_2 a_1 a_0 \quad (6.5\text{-}14b)$$

It can be shown (Prob. 6.5-3) that, in general, an N-digit sequence permits V to attain M different values, where

$$M = 2^N \qquad (6.5\text{-}15)$$

For example, if $N = 3$, the sequence is $a_2 a_1 a_0$. This sequence can take on eight possible values, as shown in Table 6.5-1. However, the sampled signal can take on every value that $v_m(t)$ can assume, which is generally an infinite number of values. To permit the sampled voltage V to be converted to a binary sequence, we first *quantize* V; i.e., we divide V into M possible values. For simplicity, we shall assume that each value is separated from the adjacent value by the same voltage.

The process of quantization is illustrated in Fig. 6.5-4. In Fig. 6.5-4a we see that $v_m(t)$ varies from a voltage slightly less than 0 V to a voltage slightly greater than 7 V. In addition, for the purpose of illustrating the principle of quantization and *analog-to-digital* conversion, we have chosen the number of quantization levels $M = 8$.

Consider that $v_m(t)$ is sampled every T_s as shown in Fig. 6.5-4a. Then the first sample $v_m(0)$ is closest to 0 volts, the second sample $v_m(T_s)$ is closest to 1 volt, etc. In Fig. 6.5-4b we see that the sampled voltage is quantized to the voltage to which it is closest. Since there are eight possible voltages, 0 to 7, each quantized signal has an equivalent binary representation. This, too, is shown in Fig. 6.5-4b.

Figure 6.5-4c shows how binary pulses can be employed to represent the quantized signal. Note the sequence of steps leading to these binary pulses. First we sample $v_m(t)$, then we quantize, and finally we generate a sequence of binary pulses equivalent to the quantized signal.

In general, significantly more than eight quantization levels are employed. For example, good commercial-quality television pictures can be obtained with $M = 256$ quantization levels. The reason that many quantization levels are needed for good-quality pictures can be seen from Fig. 6.5-4a. Here we see that the largest difference

Table 6.5-1

| Binary sequence | | | Decimal number |
a_2	a_1	a_0	(eight values)
0	0	0	0
0	0	1	1
0	1	0	2
0	1	1	3
1	0	0	4
1	0	1	5
1	1	0	6
1	1	1	7

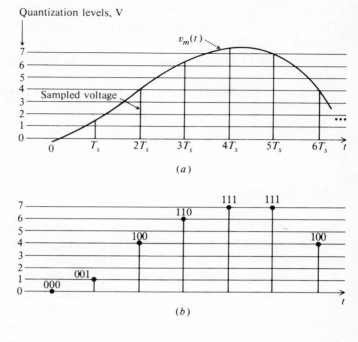

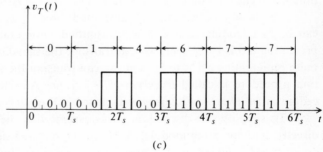

FIGURE 6.5-4
(*a*) Signal. (*b*) Quantized samples. (*c*) Binary pulses used to transmit the quantized voltages.

between the true sampled voltage and the quantized voltage is ± 0.5 V. However, if $v_m(t)$ were quantized to 256 levels, the largest difference would be ± 0.016 V.

This result can be generalized by noting that if the voltage range of $v_m(t)$ is P V, and the number of quantization levels is M, then the voltage between adjacent levels is

$$S = \frac{P}{M} \qquad (6.5\text{-}16)$$

The voltage S is called the *step size*. In the example of Fig. 6.5-4a the step size $S = 1$ V. The maximum difference between the true sampled voltage and the quantized voltage which is to be transmitted is $\pm S/2$. This is called the maximum *quantization error*. The error due to quantization, e_q, decreases as S decreases. Hence, for a fixed P, increasing M decreases S and thereby decreases the error e_q produced by quantization. In fact, it can be shown that the rms noise voltage due to quantization is

$$e_{q,\text{rms}} = \frac{S}{2\sqrt{3}} \qquad (6.5\text{-}17)$$

6.5-3 The Pulse-code-modulation System

The complete *pulse-code-modulation* (PCM) system is shown in Fig. 6.5-5. Here the signal $v_m(t)$, which has a maximum frequency f_M, is sampled at a frequency greater than or equal to the Nyquist rate $2f_M$. The sampled signal $v_{ms}(t)$ is quantized, so that at any sampling instant, $v_{ms}(t = nT_s)$ can take on one of M possible values. The quantized signal is converted into a digital signal consisting of a group of $N = \log_2 M$ [Eq. (6.5-15)] binary pulses. This grouping is called a *word*. This last operation is often called *analog-to-digital* (A-to-D) conversion. However, it is also common practice to call the combined *quantizer-converter* the A-to-D converter.

The binary pulses can be transmitted directly, as shown in Fig. 6.5-5, or they can be first modulated and then transmitted. For example, if the binary pulse representing a 0 is to be sent, we can transmit the signal $\cos \omega_1 t$, and when the binary pulse representing a 1 is to be sent, we can transmit the signal $\cos \omega_2 t$. This modulation procedure is called *frequency-shift keying*. Another common modulation procedure called *phase-shift keying* is discussed in Prob. 6.5-6.

To simplify our discussion, let us assume that the binary signal is transmitted directly, without being modulated. Then the received signal $v_R(t)$ will, in general, be an attenuated version of the transmitted signal $v_T(t)$. In this case,

$$v_R(t) = \alpha v_T(t) \qquad (6.5\text{-}18)$$

where α represents the attenuation of the channel, and v_T consists of a sequence of N bits whose values change every T_s. The digital-to-analog (D-to-A) converter shown in Fig. 6.5-5 changes the received N binary digits per word back into a voltage which can of course assume any one of $M = 2^N$ possible values. This reconstructed pulse train $v_a(t)$ is seen to be identical with the quantized signal $v_{mq}(t)$, since the A-to-D operation is essentially canceled in the receiver by the D-to-A operation.

The reconstructed signal is filtered to remove any frequency components above

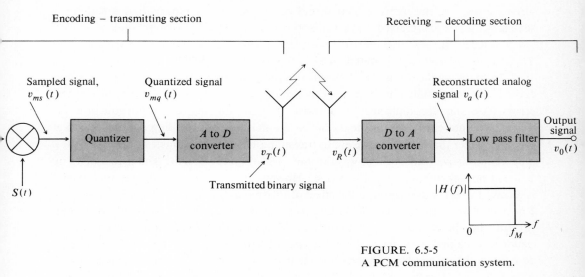

FIGURE. 6.5-5
A PCM communication system.

f_M. The output signal $v_0(t)$ then approximates $v_m(t)$, except for the quantization error $e_q(t)$.

It is convenient to represent this result by the equation

$$v_0(t) = v_m(t) + n_q(t) \qquad (6.5\text{-}19)$$

where $n_q(t)$ is a quantization noise voltage due to the quantization error $e_q(t)$. $n_q(t)$ and $e_q(t)$ are not the same, since the error $e_q(t)$, which appears at the quantizer output, is eventually filtered by the low-pass filter in the receiver. However, since $n_q(t)$ is proportional to $e_q(t)$, the rms value of n_q is proportional to the step size S [Eq. (6.5-17)]. In a well-designed communication system the rms signal voltage $(v_m)_{\text{rms}}$ is usually 30 to 40 dB greater than the rms quantization noise voltage $(n_q)_{\text{rms}}$.

6.6 CODING

In Sec. 6.5 we introduced the concept of PCM and showed that the technique consists of transmitting one of M possible waveforms as a sequence of binary digits during each sampling interval. In that section we neglected the effect of thermal noise. In a binary communication system thermal noise can affect our results by altering the polarity of one of the binary digits being received, so that if the binary digit $+1$

were transmitted, the received digit would be a 0, and if the binary digit 0 had been sent, a $+1$ would be received. The probability of this interchange occurring is typically 10^{-5}. That is, for 10^5 transmitted binary digits, one digit is in error on the average. Thus the noise produced is small and can often be neglected.

In many applications, even the small number of errors due to the thermal noise exceed system specifications. When this occurs, *coding* is employed to reduce these errors. Coding accomplishes its purpose through the deliberate introduction of *redundancy* into each *word* of the *message*. As an example of adding redundancy to a word, consider that whenever we are to transmit a 1, we transmit instead three 1s : 111; and whenever we transmit a 0, we transmit instead three 0s : 000. The triplet of 1s in 111 add no information to the message. However, if now any one of the three digits is received in error as a result of the effect of thermal noise, that error can be corrected. For if we transmitted the word 111 and received 101, 011, or 110, we would be rather certain that the message was actually 111. Thus the deliberately introduced redundancy has enabled us to detect the occurrence of a single-bit error, and in this example, to correct the error. Note, however, that if two bit errors occurred, changing a 111 to a 001, for example, we would have assumed that a 000 was transmitted. This results in an error in the word.

An essential feature which results from the introduction of redundancy is that not all sequences of symbols constitute a bona fide message. For example, with a triplet of binary digits, eight combinations are possible. However, only two of these combinations, that is, 000 and 111, are recognized as words which convey a message. The remaining combinations are not in our "dictionary." It is this fact, that certain words are not in our dictionary, that allows us to detect errors. Corrections are made on the basis of a similarity between unacceptable and acceptable words.

There is a correspondence between the redundancy deliberately introduced in coding messages prior to transmission over a channel and the redundancy which is part of language. For example, suppose that on a page of printed text we encounter the word *ekpensive*. We would immediately recognize that the printer had made an error because we know that there is no such word. If we were inclined to judge it unlikely that the printer had made an error in more than one letter, we would easily recognize the word to be *expensive*. On the other hand, there is always the possibility that more than one error was made and that the intended word was, say, *offensive*. In this latter case, of course, we would not make the proper correction.

In language, redundancy extends beyond combinations of letters in a word. It extends to entire words, and beyond to phrases and even sentences. For example, if we had come across the sentence "The army launched an ekpensive," we would not have much difficulty in recognizing that the correction of the last word is *offensive*, in spite of the fact that corrections in three letters are called for. In this case we would be taking advantage of the redundancy in the sentence.

6.6-1 Error Detection; Parity-check Coding

Computer systems employ *error detection*; i.e., the binary digits forming a message are coded so that the computer knows if an error occurs while solving a problem. If an error is detected, the computer generally prints out a statement telling where the error occurred and then stops processing the problem.

The simplest error-detecting technique consists in adding an extra binary digit at the end of each word. This extra bit is called a *parity-check bit* and is chosen to make the number of 1s in each word an *even* number. Thus, consider a case in which there are only 16 ($=2^4$) possible messages to be transmitted. These 16 messages could be encoded into 4 bits. By adding an extra bit, the fifth bit, we now have $2^5 = 32$ possible words, only 16 of which are to be recognized as messages conveying information. Thus the parity-check bit has introduced redundancy. If an odd number of the first 4 bits were 1s, we would add a 1. Thus 1011 would become 10111. If an even number of the first 4 bits were 1s, we would add a 0. Thus 1010 would become 10100.

The parity-check bit is rather universally used in digital computers for error detection. This check bit will be effective if the probability of error in a bit is low enough so that we may ignore the likelihood of more than a single-bit error in a word. If such a single error occurs, it will change a 0 to a 1 or a 1 to a 0, and the word, when received, would have an odd number of 1s. Hence it will be known that an error has occurred. We shall not, however, be able to determine which bit is in error. An error in 2 bits in a word is not detectable, since such a double error will again yield an even number of 1s.

6.6-2 Block Codes; Error Correction

The introduction of redundancy to convert a 1 to a 111 and a 0 to a 000 resulted in single-error correction. Note, however, that 2 redundant bits are added to each uncoded bit. This results in an inefficient code because in a time T we send 3 bits, but only 1 containing information. More efficient coding, i.e., where the ratio of information bits to redundant bits exceeds unity, can be obtained by adding redundancy to a group of bits called a *block*, rather than to each bit in the block.

For example, consider that 4 bits are grouped together and redundancy is then added. The uncoded words and a particular set of coded words are given in Table 6.6-1.

Since there are 4 digits in each uncoded word, there can be at most $2^4 = 16$ possible code words. However, there are 7 digits in each of the coded words. Thus there are $2^7 = 128$ possible 7-digit words, of which we have selected only 16.

If we compare each of the 16, 7-digit coded words, we see that each word differs from every other word by at least 3 digits. For example, the words 0000000 and 0001011 differ in the fourth, sixth, and seventh digits. As a result of each word differing by 3 or more digits from the other words, single-error correction results. Thus, consider that the word 0000000 was transmitted, and due to thermal noise the word 1000000 is received. A comparison of the received word with the 16 coded words given in Table 6.6-1 indicates that the closest match results with the word 0000000. Hence the error is corrected. The reader can easily show that if any of the coded words is in error by a single digit, it will differ by at least 2 digits from any other code word.

Much more sophisticated error-correcting codes are available than the block code discussed here. These codes enable signals to be rapidly transmitted over very noisy channels with a negligible number of errors.

6.6-3 Effect of Coding on Bandwidth

Consider that an analog signal $v_m(t)$ is sampled every T_s. If each sample is converted into N bits, the bandwidth needed to receive the signal can be shown to be

$$B_{PCM} = \frac{N}{2T_s} \qquad (6.6\text{-}1a)$$

If sampling is at the Nyquist rate, $T_s = 1/2f_M$. Then, using (6.6-1a),

Table 6.6-1

Uncoded words	Coded words
0000	0000000
0001	0001011
0010	0010101
0011	0011110
0100	0100110
0101	0101101
0110	0110011
0111	0111000
1000	1000111
1001	1001100
1010	1010010
1011	1011001
1100	1100001
1101	1101010
1110	1110100
1111	1111111

$$B_{\text{PCM}} = Nf_M \qquad (6.6\text{-}1b)$$

If the signal is uncoded PCM having $N = k$ bits,

$$B_{\text{uncoded PCM}} = \frac{k}{2T_s} \qquad (6.6\text{-}2)$$

while if the PCM signal is coded PCM having $N = k + r$ bits, where r is the number of redundant bits,

$$B_{\text{coded PCM}} = \frac{k + r}{2T_s} \qquad (6.6\text{-}3)$$

Thus

$$\frac{B_{\text{coded}}}{B_{\text{uncoded}}} = 1 + \frac{r}{k} \qquad (6.6\text{-}4)$$

We see that coding increases the bandwidth required to receive the PCM signal. However, it can be shown that as the number of digits k in the uncoded word increases, the extra bandwidth needed approaches unity. Thus, for $k = 1$ and $r = 2$ (the repeated code word in Sec. 6.6),

$$\frac{B_{\text{coded}}}{B_{\text{uncoded}}} = 3$$

while for $k = 4$ and $r = 3$ (Table 6.6-1),

$$\frac{B_{\text{coded}}}{B_{\text{uncoded}}} = 1.75$$

The effect of increasing the bandwidth of a PCM system without a corresponding increase in M is to increase the thermal noise and thereby increase the possibility of a bit error. For this reason, long code words are used in preference to short code words, because the bandwidth for long code words is approximately the same as the bandwidth required if no coding was employed.

6.6-4 Conclusion on Coding

Coding is used today in digital computers and in almost all digital communication systems. There are many types of coding techniques employed, in addition to the techniques discussed here. In general, the technique chosen depends on the system operation. Thus *block* codes are used when we expect the errors to be widely separated from each other. In Prob. 6.6-2 we discuss an *interleaving code* which is designed for systems where many adjacent digits can be in error.

6.7   COMPARISON OF NOISE SUPPRESSION CHARACTERISTICS OF COMMUNICATIONS SYSTEMS

In Secs. 6.2 to 6.6 we discussed the operation of several common analog and digital communications systems. In this section we compare these systems on the basis of fidelity; i.e., we compare the *noise suppression characteristics* of these systems.

A typical communications system is shown in Fig. 6.7-1. The signal $v_m(t)$, which contains frequency components between 0 and f_M, is to be transmitted. In an AM or FM system, $v_m(t)$ is modulated and then transmitted. The signal $v_m(t)$ is recovered, after reception, by using the appropriate demodulation process. However, as seen from the figure, the output of the demodulator is $v_0(t)$,

$$v_0(t) = v_m(t) + n_0(t) \qquad (6.7\text{-}1)$$

where $n_0(t)$ is noise which is added to the signal due to the presence of thermal noise in the receiver.

In a PCM system, $v_m(t)$ is first sampled and then A/D-converted in the encoder. The resulting binary waveform can then be modulated or directly transmitted. The received waveform is amplified in the receiver and then decoded. The output voltage is again expressed by (6.7-1). However, in PCM, two types of noise are present, quantization noise $n_q(t)$ and noise due to the presence of thermal noise in the receiver, $n_t(t)$.

$$n_0(t) = n_q(t) + n_t(t) \qquad (6.7\text{-}2)$$

Output signal-to-noise ratio S_0/N_0   The fidelity of a communication is experimentally found to be proportional to the ratio of the mean-square output signal voltage S_0 to the mean-square output noise voltage N_0. Using (6.1-1),

$$S_0 = \frac{1}{T} \int_{-T/2}^{T/2} [v_m(t)]^2 \, dt \qquad (6.7\text{-}3a)$$

and from Sec. 6.1-4,

$$N_0 = (n_0)^2_{\text{rms}} \qquad (6.7\text{-}3b)$$

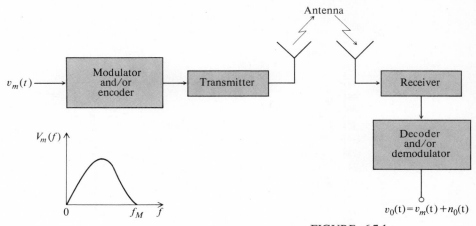

FIGURE. 6.7-1
A typical communication system.

This ratio, called the *output signal-to-noise ratio* S_0/N_0 is usually expressed in decibels (Sec. 6.1-3).

The output signal-to-noise ratio is found to be proportional to the mean-square received signal voltage S_i, inversely proportional to the bandwidth f_M of the desired signal $v_m(t)$, and inversely proportional to the noise power spectral density η measured at the demodulator input. To summarize, we find that

$$\frac{S_0}{N_0} \approx \frac{S_i}{\eta f_M} \qquad (6.7\text{-}4)$$

The exact relationship between S_0/N_0 and $S_i/\eta f_M$, for AM, FM, and PCM communications systems is extremely complicated. Thus, rather than present these relationships, we have plotted them in Fig. 6.7-2.

Referring to Fig. 6.7-2, we see that for a large range of values of $S_i/\eta f_M$, S_0/N_0 for the case of PCM is a constant. It can be shown that in this range of values, S_0/N_0 varies with N as

$$\left(\frac{S_0}{N_0}\right)_{\text{PCM}} = 2^{2N} \qquad (6.7\text{-}5)$$

Thus, for $N = 8$, $S_0/N_0 = 2^{16} = 48$ dB.

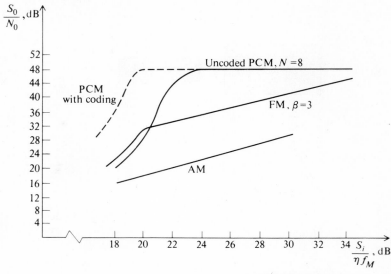

FIGURE 6.7-2
Output signal-to-noise ratio.

We also note from this figure that over a similar range of values, the S_0/N_0 for AM and FM are directly proportional to $S_i/\eta f_M$. It can be shown that

$$\left(\frac{S_0}{N_0}\right)_{FM} = \frac{3}{2}\beta^2 \frac{Si}{\eta f_M} \qquad (6.7\text{-}6)$$

and

$$\left(\frac{S_0}{N_0}\right)_{AM} \approx \frac{Si}{\eta f_M} \qquad (6.7\text{-}7)$$

Comparing the AM, FM, and PCM systems using Fig. 6.7-2 indicates that, for a given $S_i/\eta f_M$, the S_0/N_0 is largest for PCM and smallest for AM. These conclusions are not valid for very large values of $S_i/\eta f_M$; however, to obtain such a large value requires a huge transmitter and is not practical. Note that the PCM system using coding maintains a high S_0/N_0 even for very small $S_i/\eta f_M$. This is possible because the coding results in the correction of errors caused by thermal noise.

Bandwidth considerations   One must be careful about any conclusions drawn directly from Fig. 6.7-2, since no mention was made of the bandwidth required by the transmitted signal. In AM (Example 6.4-3)

$$B_{AM} = 2f_M \qquad (6.7\text{-}8)$$

while in FM [Eq. (6.4-15b)]

$$B_{FM} = 2(\beta + 1)f_M \qquad (6.7\text{-}9)$$

and in PCM [Eq. (6.6-1b)]

$$B_{PCM} = Nf_M \qquad (6.7\text{-}10)$$

Comparing (6.7-9) and (6.7-10), for $\beta = 3$ and $N = 8$, we see that

$$B_{FM} = B_{PCM} = 4B_{AM} \qquad (6.7\text{-}11)$$

Thus, while the output signal-to-noise ratio of AM shown in Fig. 6.7-2 is significantly less than that of FM and PCM, the bandwidth requirement is also significantly less.

EXAMPLE 6.7-1   A system is to be designed to provide an output signal-to-noise ratio of 30 dB. The ratio $S_i/2\eta f_M = 10$ dB is measured. Select a system using FM or PCM which is capable of meeting these specifications and which will require a minimum bandwidth.

SOLUTION   Using Eq. (6.7-6) with $S_o/N_o = 10^3$ and $S_i/2\eta f_M = 10$, we have

$$\beta^2 = \frac{100}{3} \qquad \beta = 5.8$$

or

$$B_{FM} = 2(\beta + 1)f_M = 13.6f_M$$

The result for PCM is found from (6.7-5). Since $S_o/N_o = 10^3$, we have

$$1,000 \le 2^{2N}$$

Choosing $N = 5$ satisfies this condition, and results in a bandwidth

$$B_{PCM} = Nf_M = 5f_M$$

Thus a PCM system provides the same output signal-to-noise ratio but uses only 37 percent of the bandwidth of an FM system. Hence the system selected is PCM.

////////

6.8   CONCLUSIONS

In this country, most commercial radio broadcasting uses amplitude modulation since the receiver required is extremely inexpensive and the system requires a small bandwidth. To make up for the poor noise-suppression characteristic, transmitting stations operate at very high power levels.

Frequency modulation is the second most widely used communication technique. It is used for radio broadcasting and for all satellite communication. Thus COMSAT uses FM to transmit telephone and television signals from the United States to Europe and vice versa, via a satellite. NASA also uses FM to communicate with its satellites and astronauts.

Newer communications systems are employing PCM, rather than frequency-modulating the analog signal. The PCM systems provide greater noise suppression without an increase in bandwidth. The use of coding has resulted in even greater noise suppression. The drawback to PCM has been our inability to build transistors to operate properly at the high speeds required. These fabrication problems are rapidly being solved. As a result, PCM systems will continue to become more popular.

PROBLEMS

6.1-1   A telephone system is 1,000 mi long. The transmitted voltage V_T is 1 V. If the attenuation of the line is 1 dB per 10 mi, find the minimum number of repeaters needed and their spacing if the received voltage is to be greater than or equal to 0.1 V. The maximum output voltage of a repeater is 10 V, and the voltage gain of each repeater is 40 dB.

6.1-2   A telephone system is 160 mi long. The transmitted voltage is 1 V. The attenuation of the line is 1 dB/mi. If four repeaters are used and each repeater can supply up to 10 V, find the required voltage gain of the repeaters (they each have the same gain) if the received voltage is to be 1 V.

6.1-3   Noise is inserted into a filter. The mean-square thermal-noise voltage at the filter output is 10^{-12} V^2 when

$$H_1(f) = \begin{cases} 1 & f_0 \le f \le f_0 + 1 \\ 0 & \text{elsewhere} \end{cases}$$

for any value of f_0.
Calculate the mean-square output thermal-noise voltage when

$$H_2(f) = \begin{cases} 1 & 0 \le f \le 10 \text{ kHz} \\ 0 & \text{elsewhere} \end{cases}$$

6.1-4   The mean-square output thermal noise measured at the output of a filter having a bandwidth of 20 MHz is 1 V². If the volt squared per hertz measured within the frequency range of the filter is a constant, find the mean-square voltage measured in a 1-Hz bandwidth.

6.2-1   Given an AM signal

$$v_{AM}(t) = [1 + Pv_m(t)] \cos \omega_0 t$$

$v_m(t)$ is a square wave having values of either $+5$ or -5 V. Find
(a) P to ensure diode demodulation.
(b)   Sketch $v_{AM}(t)$ if $v_m(t)$ changes polarity every time the carrier completes 3 cycles.

6.2-2   For the AM signal described in Prob. 6.2-1, sketch the demodulator output, before the jagged edges are removed.

6.4-1   A modulating voltage $v_m(t)$ is a square wave having an amplitude of ± 1 V. The square wave has a period of 0.2 μs. The carrier frequency is $f_c = 30$ MHz.
(a)   If the maximum frequency deviation is 10 MHz, calculate k.
(b)   Using this value of k, calculate the maximum phase deviation.
(c)   Sketch $v_{FM}(t)$.

6.4-2   A carrier of frequency 100 MHz and amplitude 2 V is frequency-modulated by a sinusoidal modulating waveform of frequency 1 kHz and amplitude 2 V. The "gain" $k = 2\pi \times 10^6$ rad/(V)(s).
(a)   Calculate the maximum frequency deviation Δf.
(b)   Calculate the maximum phase deviation β.
(c)   Calculate the bandwidth needed to pass the signal.

6.4-3   A carrier of frequency 30 MHz and amplitude 3 V is frequency-modulated by a sinusoidal modulating waveform of frequency 5 kHz. The gain $k = 4\pi \times 10^6$ rad/(mV)(s).
(a)   Find the amplitude of the modulating signal if $\Delta f = 3$ MHz.
(b)   Find β.
(c)   Calculate the bandwidth needed to pass the signal.

6.4-4   An FM signal is generated using the Armstrong method. The modulating signal is sinusoidal, with an amplitude of 2 V and frequency $f_m = 1$ kHz. The carrier frequency is 30 MHz, and $\Delta f = 1$ MHz. If $k = 2\pi \times 10^2$ rad/(V)(s)
(a)   Find N and f_0.
(b)   Calculate $\phi_1(t)$.

6.4-5   FM demodulation can be accomplished using the circuit shown in Fig. P6.4-5. The FM signal enters a comparator which compares $v_{FM}(t)$ with 0 V. If $v_{FM}(t) > 0$, the comparator output is $+10$ V. If $v_{FM}(t) < 0$, the comparator output is 0 V.

        The integrate-and-dump circuit consists of an RC circuit with a switch placed across the capacitor. When v_c becomes positive, the switch opens and v_d increases exponentially toward 10 V. When v_c becomes zero, the switch closes and v_d is equal to zero. The diode detector "connects" the peak values of $v_d(t)$, producing an output waveform proportional to $v_m(t)$. $v_m(t)$ is a square wave of amplitude ± 1 V and period $0.15\ \mu s$. $k = 40\ \pi \times 10^6$ rad/(V)(s). $f_c = 60$ MHz.

(a)   Sketch $v_c(t)$.

(b)   Sketch $v_d(t)$.

(c)   Sketch $v_0(t)$ and show that $v_0(t)$ is proportional to $v_m(t)$.

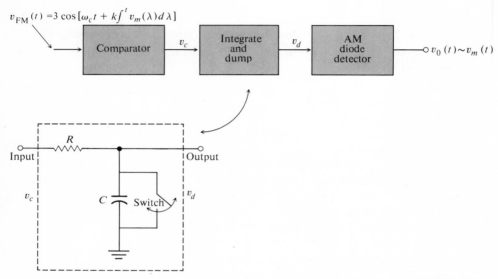

$$v_{FM}(t) = 3\cos\left[\omega_c t + k\int^t v_m(\lambda)d\lambda\right]$$

FIGURE P6.4-5

6.5-1   A signal $v_m(t) = \sin 2\pi t$ is sampled at two times the Nyquist rate. The samples are equally spaced, and one sample occurs at $t = 0$. The sampled signal is then passed through a low-pass filter which has the transfer function

$$H(f) = \begin{cases} 1 & 0 \le f \le 1.1\ \text{Hz} \\ 0 & f > 1.1\ \text{Hz} \end{cases}$$

(a)   Sketch $v_T(t) = v_m(t)S(t)$.

(b)   Calculate the output of the low-pass filter.

6.5-2   Repeat Example 6.5-2 assuming that sampling occurs at 1.1 times the Nyquist rate. Does distortion result?

6.5-3   Show that an N-digit sequence permits V to attain M different values.

6.5-4 A 7-digit sequence is often used in PCM. Calculate the number of quantization levels, M.

6.5-5 The signal $10 \sin \omega_m t$ is quantized in M levels. If 8 binary digits can be used to represent the signal:

(a) Find M.

(b) Find the step size S.

(c) Calculate the rms quantization error.

6.5-6 An often used modulation technique, called *phase-shift keying* (PSK), takes the sequence of binary digits $b(t)$, where $b(t)$ is either $+1$ V or -1 V, and multiplies it by a sinusoidal carrier $v_c(t) = \cos \omega_c t$. The transmitted signal is then

$$v_T(t) = b(t) \cos \omega_c t$$

(a) This technique is called phase-shift keying because $v_T(t)$ can be written

$$v_T(t) = \cos \left[\omega_c t + \phi(t) \right]$$

where $\phi(t) = \begin{cases} 0 & b(t) = 1 \\ \pi & b(t) = -1 \end{cases}$

Verify this statement.

(b) Prove that a possible receiver for this signal $v_T(t)$ multiplies $v_T(t)$ by $2 \cos \omega_c t$ and passes the product through a low-pass filter which rejects the frequency $2f_c$. Verify that the receiver output is $b(t)$.

6.6-1 Compare the coded words in Table 6.6-1.

(a) Find the minimum number of digits in which they differ.

(b) A word has a single bit in error. How many bits are different between this word and the correct word? Any other word?

6.6-2 In many systems errors occur in *bursts*. Let us assume that during a burst each bit in a word is in error.

(a) Can the block code of Table 6.6-1 be used if the bursts are 7 bits long?

To counteract burst errors, interleaved codes are used. To illustrate an interleaved code, assume that a burst is 7 bits long. Then, if the uncoded message were

0000 0010 0100 1000 1111 0101 1011

the block coded message would be

0000000 0010101 0100110 1000111 1111111 0101101 1011001

The interleaved code is formed by transmitting the first bit of each coded word in sequence, then the second, etc. The result is

$$|0001101|0010110|0100101| \ldots$$

(b) Show that a 7-bit burst of errors does not produce an error in the decoded words of an interleaved code.

6.7-1 A PCM system has an output signal-to-noise ratio of 36 dB. The modulating signal is $v_m = 5 \cos 2\pi (1,000)t$.

   (*a*) Calculate N.

   (*b*) Calculate B_{PCM}, assuming sampling at the Nyquist rate.

   (*c*) An FM system is to have the same output signal-to-noise ratio. Calculate $S_i/\eta f_m$ if $\Delta f = 3$ kHz.

   (*d*) Calculate the FM bandwidth.

REFERENCES

TAUB, H., and D. L. SCHILLING: "Principles of Communications Systems," McGraw-Hill Book Company, New York, 1971.

AUTOMATIC CONTROL

INTRODUCTION

Over the past thirty or so years man has learned to build machines which exhibit purposeful behavior. By this we mean that these machines can actually seek out and find a goal, just as a human being does when he reaches for an object on a table. This remarkable achievement has been brought about because man has learned to understand the concept of *feedback*.

In today's complex world the concept of *feedback*, or *automatic control*, is employed in virtually all branches of technology. Some examples which should be familiar to all include the feedback system in our radios, called an *automatic volume control*, which maintains a constant sound level from the loudspeaker, even though the signal received by the radio differs from station to station, close stations presenting strong signals and distant stations presenting weak signals; the control of temperature within our homes; the complex guidance systems by means of which a guided missile "homes in" on a target; and others too numerous to mention.

The above examples are all man-made systems. Within the human body we have many extremely complex biological feedback systems. One such system controls body temperature to a fraction of a degree, even though the outside temperature may vary over extreme ranges. Another allows us to focus our eyes almost instantaneously on any object we wish.

In this chapter we shall study feedback and its application to such diverse systems as home temperature control and the human eye.

7.1 THE BASIC CONCEPT OF FEEDBACK

Feedback can be applied to man-made systems in many different ways. The central characteristic of feedback systems which distinguishes them from other systems is that their input is determined wholly or in part by the output. This points to the origin of the word feedback, for if the input is to be determined by the output, some portion of the output must be fed back to the input.

To obtain a qualitative idea of how feedback systems operate, let us consider controlling the remote TV camera system shown in Fig. 7.1-1a. The system is designed so that the angular position of the camera is precisely the same as the angular position of a graduated knob on the operator's console. When the operator turns the knob, the camera follows as rapidly as possible. The system operates as follows: Let us assume that the camera is initially pointing at an angle of zero degrees. The operator turns his control knob to 10°. This causes a voltage to be applied to the positioning device, which then turns the camera toward the 10° position. The position sensor attached to the camera provides a voltage proportional to the actual camera angle. This voltage is fed back to the console, where it is used to modify the voltage applied to the positioning device so that the camera will point to exactly 10°.

It is interesting to note that the TV camera proper may weigh several hundred pounds, and is controlled by the operator's control knob, which may weigh only a few ounces.

A block diagram of the system is shown in Fig. 7.1-1b. In this example the input signal, called $r(t)$, is the angular position of the shaft on the operator's console, and the output signal $y(t)$ is the angular position of the actual camera. The input signal might be an electric voltage produced by a circuit such as that shown in Fig. 7.1-1c, where the voltage v changes in direct proportion to the angle of the input control knob. This signal is fed first into a *comparator*, or *error detector*. In the comparator, the input signal is compared with the fed-back output voltage, and an error signal $e(t)$ is produced. This error signal is then fed to a part of the system called the *controller*. In this system the controller is a positioning device which produces a shaft angle approximately proportional to the voltage applied to its terminals.

The controller converts the electric error signal to a mechanical force which

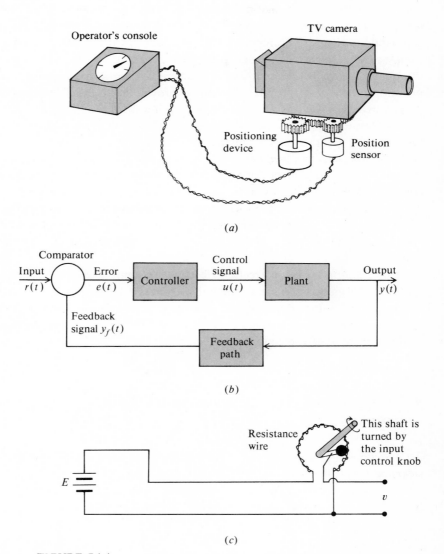

FIGURE 7.1-1
Remote TV camera positioning system. (*a*) Pictorial sketch; (*b*) block diagram;
(*c*) circuit to provide input voltage.

moves the camera in accordance with the error signal. In control parlance, the camera is called the *plant*, and for our example the plant output $y(t)$ is the angular position of the camera.

To compare the output and input, a position sensor provides a voltage proportional to the actual camera angle. This signal is fed back via the *feedback path* to the comparator, where it is compared with the input. In the simplest case the output is simply *subtracted* from the input to produce the error, so that when they are equal, the error is zero. If the input and output are not the same, an error signal will be present, and the controller is designed to provide a control force which turns the camera in a direction such that the error tends toward zero.

In this example, it is the continuous comparison of input and output that makes the feedback system unique. This uniqueness stems from the fact that such systems are self-correcting, i.e., *goal-seeking*. Consider, for example, our camera without the feedback path. If the operator were to turn the input shaft to a setting of 30°, the controller might turn the camera toward 30°, but due to the presence of inevitable mechanical imperfections, the camera might overshoot and come to rest at an angle of, say, 33°. With the feedback path present, an error signal proportional to the error is generated continuously, so that the error is corrected, and the camera moves to almost exactly 30°.

In addition to self-correction, feedback systems also display other desirable properties. Among these are considerable reduction of the effects of external disturbances on the system response and automatic compensation for changes within the system, such as ageing, temperature variation, etc. In succeeding sections we shall consider these other advantages of feedback.

7.2   QUANTITATIVE ASPECT OF BASIC FEEDBACK PROPERTIES

To put some of the notions of the preceding section on a quantitative basis, we consider the simple feedback system shown in Fig. 7.2-1.

For concreteness, assume that the comparator is a subtractor. In addition, we lump the controller and plant into one unit which has a transmission function

$$A = \frac{y}{e} \qquad (7.2\text{-}1)$$

Note that A is the transmission function which relates the output y to the error signal e; that is, $y = Ae$.

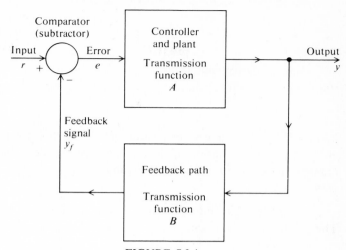

FIGURE 7.2-1
Block diagram of a general feedback system.

The output is fed back to the input via a feedback path which has a transmission function

$$B = \frac{y_f}{y} \qquad (7.2\text{-}2)$$

The comparator simply subtracts the feedback signal y_f from the input signal r; that is,

$$e = r - y_f \qquad (7.2\text{-}3)$$

Our main interest centers on the overall transmission of the system from input r to output y. We shall call this the gain A_f, so that

$$A_f = \frac{y}{r} \qquad (7.2\text{-}4)$$

The subscript f indicates gain *with* feedback.

To find A_f, we must eliminate e and y_f from Eqs. (7.2-1) to (7.2-3). If we solve (7.2-1) for e and (7.2-2) for y_f and then substitute these results into (7.2-3), we get

$$\frac{y}{A} = r - By$$

Finally, solving for the ratio y/r, we have

$$A_f = \frac{y}{r} = \frac{A}{1 + AB} \qquad (7.2\text{-}5)$$

This is the overall transmission of the feedback system and represents the starting point for a quantitative study of system behavior.

EXAMPLE 7.2-1   A certain positioning device and TV camera combination turns $360°$ for each $10°$ rotation of the shaft on the operator's console before feedback is applied. Find the feedback transmission function B required to produce an overall gain $A_f = 1$ deg/deg.

SOLUTION   The data indicate that $y = 360°$ when $r = 10°$ without feedback. Thus, using (7.2-1) and noting that $e = r$ when there is no feedback,

$$A = \frac{y}{e} = \frac{360°}{10°} = 36 \text{ deg/deg}$$

Next, using (7.2-5) with $A = 36$ and $A_f = 1$, we find

$$B = \frac{35}{36} = 0.972 \text{ deg/deg}$$

////////

7.2-1   Loop Gain

The quantity AB in the denominator of Eq. (7.2-5) deserves special consideration, and has a straightforward physical interpretation. Referring again to the circuit of Fig. 7.2-1, consider that the input r is zero. Now think of introducing an error signal at the input to the controller. This error signal will be transmitted through the controller and plant, through the feedback path, through the comparator (where it is reversed in sign), and back to the controller. During its traversal of this *loop*, it will be subject to a transmission function $-AB$. This quantity, known as the *loop gain*, is of fundamental importance in the study of feedback systems, as we shall see in the developments to follow.

In most cases of interest, the magnitude of the loop gain is much larger than unity. When this is so, we can neglect the 1 in the denominator of (7.2-5), and with this approximation, the gain A_f becomes

$$A_f \approx \frac{1}{B} \qquad (7.2\text{-}6)$$

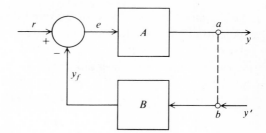

FIGURE 7.2-2
Feedback system with loop open.

Thus, when the loop gain is large, the transmission function of the plant and controller do not affect the overall transmission. In other words, the overall transmission is approximately *independent* of the controller and plant and depends *only* on the transmission function of the feedback path. This result is indeed amazing. Consider our TV camera example of the last section. Our result, in effect, states that the transmission from the operator's console to the camera position can be made independent of the characteristics of the camera. Of course, this can only be approximated in practice, and we shall consider it in more detail in a later section.

The loop gain is so important that we assign to it a symbol of its own and devise special ways of measuring it. For one possibility, consider the circuit of Fig. 7.2-2. In this diagram we have "opened" the loop so that the connection between points a and b is broken.

Now, with $r = 0$, think of introducing a signal which we shall call y' into terminal b. This signal will go through the feedback network, through the comparator, through the plant and controller, and emerge at terminal a. This is similar to the definition of loop gain used previously. Thus, if we assign the symbol T to loop gain, we can write

$$T = \frac{y}{y'}\bigg|_{r=0} = -AB \qquad (7.2\text{-}7)$$

We now have one possible method for measuring loop gain; i.e., we physically open the loop, introduce a signal y', and measure the signal returned to the output, y. Then the loop gain is simply the ratio of y to y'.

In the example of the remote TV camera, we might open the loop by physically disconnecting the position sensor from the camera. Then the position of the sensor shaft would be y'. Using the values given in Example 7.2-1, a $10°$ rotation of the sensor shaft would then produce a $350°$ rotation of the camera.

The physical opening of the loop is often conveniently carried out at the output terminal, as shown in the figure. When this is not convenient, it is clear that the loop can be broken at any point; for example, when the power level at the output is high, the output of the sensor is often a more convenient point. In any case, care must be taken to see that the transmission paths on both sides of the opening are terminated exactly the same as when the loop is closed, so that the open-loop measurements will be valid. Since the connections shown in Fig. 7.2-2 are symbolic in the sense that they may not be electrical connections but may be mechanical or hydraulic, for example, the reader will appreciate the fact that opening the loop is not always an easy task.

7.2-2   Gain without Feedback

To assess the effect of feedback on the system, we must define the gain of the system without feedback. Using Eqs. (7.2-5) and (7.2-7), we can express the external, or overall, gain of the system as

$$A_f = \frac{A}{1 + AB} = \frac{A}{1 - T} \qquad (7.2\text{-}8)$$

From this equation we see that the gain without feedback, A, is equal to the gain with feedback, A_f, when the loop gain T is zero, i.e., when the feedback path is *open*. The most convenient way to reduce the loop gain to zero is to set $y' = 0$. Then we can write, noting Fig. 7.2-2,

$$A = A_f \Big|_{y'=0} = \frac{y}{r} \Big|_{y'=0} \qquad (7.2\text{-}9)$$

Again returning to Example 7.2-1, the system without feedback consists of the positioning device and camera, which have a gain $A = 36$ deg/deg.

7.2-3   Overall Gain

Let us return to Eq. (7.2-8). As noted previously, loop gain T is usually a relatively large number (magnitude 10 or more); so if we consider the controller and plant gain A as being the gain of the system without feedback, we see that the addition of feedback has *reduced* the gain of the system without feedback by the factor $1 - T$. Thus one of the effects of applying feedback to any system is to reduce the gain of the system compared with what it would be without feedback. It should be noted at this point that this has meaning only for *negative* feedback, i.e., feedback which tends to reduce the error to zero. (For this type of feedback, T is a negative number.)

7.3   THE CONCEPT OF SENSITIVITY

We noted previously that feedback systems were capable of compensating automatically for changes within the system. In this section we shall study this characteristic quantitatively by introducing the concept of *sensitivity*. We shall include several examples to illustrate this very important characteristic of feedback systems.

Let us consider what happens if the plant transmission function A changes by an amount ΔA. This change is conveniently measured in terms of the *fractional* change in gain $\Delta A/A$. We shall determine the fractional change in the overall transmission A_f due to a given fractional change in A. The relation between these quantities is written in the form

$$\frac{\Delta A_f}{A_f} = S_A{}^{A_f} \frac{\Delta A}{A} \qquad (7.3\text{-}1)$$

where $S_A{}^{A_f}$ is called the *sensitivity* of A_f with respect to A. From (7.3-1) we see that the sensitivity is the ratio of the fractional change in A_f to the fractional change in A.

It is convenient to assume at this point that the increment ΔA is equal to the differential dA. This allows us to use ordinary differentiation to find the differentials dA and dA_f, but restricts us to small changes.

To find $S_A{}^{A_f}$ in terms of the system parameters, we first rearrange (7.3-1) so that

$$S_A{}^{A_f} = \frac{A}{A_f} \frac{dA_f}{dA} \qquad (7.3\text{-}2)$$

The derivative can be found from (7.2-8).

$$\frac{dA_f}{dA} = \frac{1}{1-T} - \frac{A}{(1-T)^2} \frac{d(1-T)}{dA} \qquad (7.3\text{-}3a)$$

From (7.2-7)

$$A \frac{d(1-T)}{dA} = A \frac{d(1+AB)}{dA} = AB = -T \qquad (7.3\text{-}3b)$$

so

$$\frac{dA_f}{dA} = \frac{1}{(1-T)^2} \qquad (7.3\text{-}3c)$$

Finally, substituting (7.3-3c) into (7.3-2) yields

$$S_A{}^{A_f} = \frac{A}{A_f} \frac{1}{(1-T)^2} = \frac{1}{1-T} \qquad (7.3\text{-}4)$$

Equation (7.3-4) is the desired relation. To interpret it, assume that $-T \gg 1$. Then a 10 percent change in the plant transmission, A, due to any cause, will appear as a change in the overall transmission, A_f, of approximately $10/T$ percent, a much smaller change. Equations (7.2-8) and (7.3-4) are extremely useful for establishing preliminary design figures. We illustrate the use of these relations in the examples which follow.

EXAMPLE 7.3-1   For the system of Example 7.2-1, use the sensitivity function to find the change in overall gain if the plant transmission A can vary from 30 to 40.

SOLUTION   From Example 7.2-1, the nominal loop gain $T = -AB = -(36)(0.972) = -35$. Therefore, from (7.3-4)

$$S_A^{A_f} = \frac{1}{1 - T} = \frac{1}{36} = 0.028$$

From the data, $dA = 40 - 30 = 10$ and $A_{\text{nominal}} = 36$. Thus $dA/A = 28$ percent. From (7.3-1)

$$\frac{dA_f}{A_f} = S_A^{A_f} \frac{dA}{A} = 0.028\left(\frac{10}{36}\right) = 0.0078 = 0.78 \text{ percent}$$

This is the fractional change in overall transmission. The differential change is (recall that $A_{f,\text{nominal}} = 1$)

$$dA_f = 0.0078 A_f = 0.0078$$

Thus a 28 percent change in forward transmission has resulted in 0.78 percent change in the overall transmission of the system. This improvement is due to the addition of the feedback. If the feedback were not present, the change in overall transmission of the system would be 28 percent over the indicated change in plant transmission. Such a large change would make the system unsuitable for accurate remote positioning of the TV camera.

Note that the price we pay for this improvement is a considerable reduction in the overall gain of the system. However, this is usually a small price to pay in return for the benefits gained.

EXAMPLE 7.3-2   A new type of remote control system is to be designed such that the angle of the camera is to be changed $10°$ for each $1°$ rotation of the control shaft.

The camera is to be used for a 10-year period. Over this time the manufacturer expects its positioning device to wear so that its change in gain may be as much as 20 percent. However, system requirements necessitate that the output position never be in error by more than 1 percent due to this change. From these specifications we have $dA/A = 20$ percent and $dA_f/A_f = 1$ percent. Thus, using Eq. (7.3-1), we see that a sensitivity of 5 percent is required.

Find the required loop gain and gain without feedback.

SOLUTION   The desired overall gain is obtained from the specifications as 10 ($10°$ output angle per $1°$ input angle). Thus, using (7.2-8), we have

$$A_f = \frac{A}{1 - T} \approx \frac{A}{-T} = 10$$

This holds when $-T \gg 1$.

From (7.3-4), the 5 percent sensitivity requirement implies

$$S_A{}^{A_f} = \frac{\text{percent change in } A_f}{\text{percent change in } A} = \frac{1}{20} = \frac{1}{1-T} \approx \frac{1}{-T}$$

so that
$$|T| \approx 20$$

and
$$|A| \approx |T|A_f = (20)(10) = 200$$

Thus, to achieve the desired overall gain of 10, we must start with a positioning system having a gain of 200. As in Example 7.3-1 this sacrifice of gain has resulted in a considerable degree of stability.
////////

7.4 REDUCTION OF DISTURBANCES

When feedback is applied to a system, another benefit results, namely, that the effects of both internal and external disturbances are often considerably reduced in the output as compared with a nonfeedback system. To illustrate this aspect of feedback, consider the system shown in block-diagram form in Fig. 7.4-1. The system is the same as that previously considered in Fig. 7.2-2, the only difference being that the controller transfer function A has been separated into two cascaded blocks with transfer functions A_1 and A_2. The disturbance r_d is introduced at the junction between the two blocks. This representation can often be used to take account of such effects as drift due to temperature, wind gusts and other externally applied forces, variations in power-supply output, etc.

We write, for the controller output,

$$y = A_1 A_2 e + A_2 r_d \qquad (7.4\text{-}1)$$

for the comparator,

$$e = r - y_f \qquad (7.4\text{-}2)$$

and for the feedback path,

$$y_f = By \qquad (7.4\text{-}3)$$

Eliminating e and y_f from these equations, we get

$$y = \frac{A_1 A_2}{1 - A_1 A_2 B} r + \frac{A_2}{1 - A_1 A_2 B} r_d \qquad (7.4\text{-}4)$$

This gives the output of the system in terms of the desired input r and the disturbance r_d. If we rearrange (7.4-4), recognizing that $T = -A_1 A_2 B$, we get

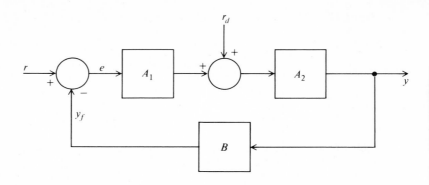

FIGURE 7.4-1
Feedback system with disturbing signal.

$$y = \frac{A}{1 - T}\left(r + \frac{r_d}{A_1}\right) \qquad (7.4-5)$$

where $A = A_1 A_2$.

This indicates that the disturbance source can be replaced by an equivalent source r_d/A_1 at the input as shown in Fig. 7.4-2. This new source represents the disturbance signal r_d *referred to the input* and has the same effect on the output as the actual disturbance signal. Equation (7.4-5) shows that the effect of the disturbance at the output depends on the point inside the system at which it is introduced. If we set $r = 0$ in (7.4-5), we get

$$y\Big|_{r=0} = \frac{A_2}{1 - T}r_d \qquad (7.4-6)$$

This last equation shows that if the disturbance occurs at a point very near the output of the system where $A_2 \approx 1$, then the effect of the disturbance is reduced in the output by the factor $1 - T$. If, on the other hand, the disturbing signal appears at the input to the controller and plant, where $A_1 \approx 1$, so that $A_2 \approx A$, then the disturbance appears in the output multiplied by $A/(1 - T)$, that is, the same as the input signal.

From this discussion we see that feedback is definitely not a cure-all, and the design of the controller and plant must be carefully carried out if disturbances are expected. For example, in electronic amplifiers to which feedback is to be applied, the amplifier takes the place of the controller and plant in our analysis. The input stages of such amplifiers must be carefully designed so that little distortion and noise are generated.

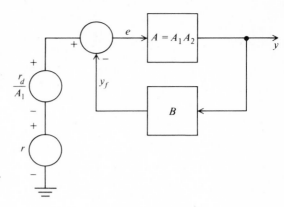

FIGURE 7.4-2
Equivalent representation of system of
Fig. 7.4-1 with voltage sources.

EXAMPLE 7.4-1   *Reduction of distortion in a transistor power amplifier.*   A certain amplifier is to be designed to take the signal from a phonograph cartridge,
amplify it, and drive a high-fidelity loudspeaker. The cartridge output is 50 mV,
and the voltage required for full power at the loudspeaker terminals is 10 V. The first
amplifier design is constructed and tested. It is found that when a 1-kHz 50-mV signal
is introduced at the input to the amplifier, the output voltage is the required 10 V at
1 kHz, but in addition there is present a signal component at 2 kHz (the second
harmonic). Measurements show that the amplitude of the second harmonic is 1 V;
so the percentage of second-harmonic distortion is $\frac{1}{10} \times 100 = 10$ percent. Also,
tests indicate that virtually all this distortion is generated due to nonlinearity in the
final stage of the amplifier (see Fig. 7.4-3a and b).

This amount of distortion is intolerable for high-fidelity reproduction. It is
therefore required that the amplifier be redesigned so that the second-harmonic
distortion will be less than $\frac{1}{2}$ percent. Work out the new design.

SOLUTION   Instead of redesigning the whole amplifier, the decision is made to
apply feedback to the original design to reduce the distortion to the required level. A
diagram of the original system with signal levels included is shown in Fig. 7.4-3a.
A schematic diagram which includes the effect of the distortion represented as a voltage
source is shown in Fig. 7.4-3b.

According to the specifications, we must reduce the distortion in the output by
a factor of 20. Thus, from (7.4-6) we see that we must design the feedback network to
provide a loop gain $|T| = 19$. The price we have to pay for this improvement can be
determined as follows: The effect of the loop gain of 19 with the original amplifier
would be to reduce the overall gain from the original value $A_v = 200$ to $A_{vf} = \frac{200}{20} = 10$.
Thus, to achieve a 10-V output signal in response to a 50-mV input signal, we add

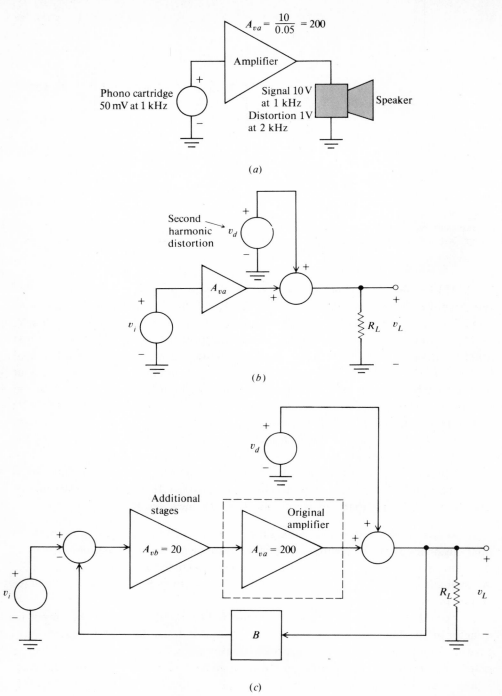

FIGURE 7.4-3
Amplifier system. (a) Original design; (b) distortion represented as a voltage source; (c) final design.

additional stages to the amplifier, as shown in Fig. 7.4-3c. To determine the gain requirements of the additional stages we use the basic feedback equation with $A_{vf} = 200$ and $1 - T = 20$. Then

$$A_v = A_{vf}(1 - T) = (200)(20) = 4{,}000$$

But $A_v = A_{va} A_{vb}$, where $A_{va} = 200$. Thus $A_{vb} = 20$. Now substituting in (7.4-4) with the proper change of variables,

$$v_L = \frac{4{,}000}{20} v_i + \frac{1}{20} v_d$$

$$= 200 \, v_i + \frac{v_d}{20} \tag{7.4-7}$$

The corresponding expression for the output of the original amplifier without feedback is

$$v_L = 200 v_i + v_d \qquad (7.4\text{-}8)$$

The amount of feedback required is easily found by noting that $|T| = |A_v B|$. Since $|T| = 19$ and $|A_v| = 4{,}000$, we have

$$B = \frac{19}{4{,}000} \approx 0.005$$

Comparing (7.4-7) and (7.4-8), we see that the distortion in the output of the feedback amplifier is reduced by a factor of 20 as compared with the amplifier without feedback. Note also that a constraint in this problem has been to achieve this reduction of the disturbance while maintaining a specified ratio of v_L/v_i.
////////

7.5 EFFECT OF FEEDBACK ON DYNAMICS

In many automatic control systems, the speed of response of the power elements of the system is a limiting factor on overall performance speed. Another benefit of feedback is that it can be used to improve the response time.

To illustrate this aspect of feedback, consider again our TV camera positioning system. Because the camera and its associated mounting are heavy, they have considerable inertia and take appreciable time to move. When a voltage is applied suddenly, the motion will, to a first approximation, increase slowly in an exponential fashion. With this assumption, the controller and plant without feedback can be described by a single time constant τ (Sec. 4.2-4). With feedback applied, it can be

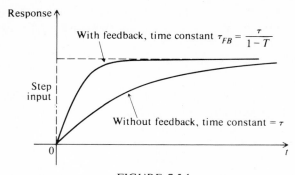

FIGURE 7.5-1
Effect of feedback on step response.

shown that the time constant τ_f is reduced by the same amount that the gain is reduced. Thus

$$\tau_f = \frac{\tau}{1 - T}$$

where T is the loop gain.

The reduction in time constant can be seen qualitatively from the following argument. When a signal is suddenly applied to the controller, the camera cannot move instantaneously. Thus the error is approximately equal to the input signal until the camera begins to move. This error signal is $|T|$ times as large as the signal that would be required at the input to the controller to yield the same output with no feedback. Because of the application of a large signal at the input to the controller when feedback is present, the camera begins to move much more quickly than if feedback were not present.

A plot showing typical step-function responses before and after application of feedback is shown in Fig. 7.5-1.

7.6   THE PROBLEM OF STABILITY

In preceding sections we have seen how feedback improves the performance of systems to which it is applied. One of the prices paid for these improvements is the loss in gain, which sometimes has to be made up in other ways. Another price we pay is that we must face the possibility of the system becoming *unstable*.

For a qualitative description of instability, consider our TV camera positioning system. Assume that a signal is applied which calls for a camera angle of 30°. Further, let us assume that the loop gain is very large. If the loop gain is large enough and friction effects are not dominant, the camera will overshoot the 30° position by a considerable amount. If we assume that the overshoot stops at 40°, then, since this is negative feedback, there will be an error signal equivalent to 10° in a direction which will reverse the camera's motion. This error signal will cause the camera to move in the opposite direction, heading back toward the desired 30° position. Because of the high gain and low friction, the camera overshoots when coming back. When it passes 30°, the error reverses in sign again, and it comes to rest at perhaps 20°. We now have a 10° error signal tending to turn the camera back toward 30°. This cycling back and forth is one form of instability, called *oscillation*, which can continue indefinitely so that the position never stabilizes at the desired 30°.

To see how instability can arise quantitatively, let us return to (7.2-8), which is repeated below for convenience.

$$A_f = \frac{A}{1 - T} \qquad (7.2\text{-}8)$$

The gain A and loop gain T are, in general, both functions of frequency. Thus, for sinusoidal input signals, both A and T will reduce to complex numbers (Sec. 4.2-3). If at some frequency f_0, the loop gain T becomes $+1 + j0$, Eq. (7.2-8) indicates that we are in serious trouble because the denominator becomes zero and A_f approaches infinity. Physically, this can be interpreted in the following way: Let us assume that T is close to $+1 + j0$. Then, because the denominator of (7.2-8) is very small, A_f will be very large. This means that a very small input signal at the appropriate frequency will result in a very large output signal. Now let us suppose that T approaches closer and closer to $+1 + j0$. Clearly, the overall gain A_f increases. If we decrease the input signal so as to maintain a constant output signal as $T \to +1 + j0$, we find in the limit that *no input signal* is required to obtain an output when $T = +1 + j0$. When this happens, the system is said to be unstable, and it will oscillate, i.e., have an output signal without any input signal.

It is not necessary for T to be exactly $1 + j0$ for instability to occur. When a system is turned on, its loop gain will increase from zero to its nominal value in the time it takes for the system to reach steady-state conditions. If the loop gain passes through the $1 + j0$ point during this "warm-up" period, the system will break into oscillation.

It should be noted that these oscillations begin to build up at some point in the warm-up period. According to the theory, they should build up to large amplitudes. However, real systems cannot support such large-amplitude signals, so that the oscillations are limited by nonlinear effects such as saturation and cutoff. In some cases the amplitude of a current or a mechanical force may become so large that the system actually undergoes physical failure.

A quantitative study of instability is beyond the scope of this text. Such investigations usually center on the denominator of (7.2-8). They seek to determine if there is a band of frequencies in which the denominator comes to within a certain distance of zero. This distance determines the degree of stability, larger distances generally corresponding to more stable systems.

If a band of frequencies is found in which stability is not adequate, *compensating networks* are added to the controller so as to modify the frequency response in that frequency band and thus ensure adequate stability. Often the stability problem limits the amount of useful loop gain that can be achieved.

7.7 A FEEDBACK EXAMPLE; TEMPERATURE CONTROL

An interesting example of feedback is provided by the thermostatically controlled heating system used in many homes today. Typically, a single heating unit supplies all the rooms of a house and is controlled by a thermostat placed in a central location. Consider the block diagram of the system shown in Fig. 7.7-1a. The reference temperature T_R is the desired temperature, which is set manually and usually lies between 65 and 75°F. The thermostat is a relay (switch) which closes when the actual house temperature T_A is a certain amount less than the reference temperature. (We assume 2° as typical.) The switch opens when the temperature T_A rises a certain amount above the reference (again 2° is typical), and the heating unit is then turned off.

When the thermostat closes, the heating unit is turned on, and when the thermostat opens, the heating unit is turned off. Therefore the heating unit in this system is either on or off. Thus the heat fed into the house (the plant) is either the full output of the furnace or no heat at all. For this reason such systems are called *bang-bang*, *on-off*, or *maximum effort*, systems.

To follow the cycle of operation, let us assume that the reference temperature is set at 72° and the thermostat operates on a $\pm 2°$ differential. If the furnace is *on* (Fig. 7.7-1b), heat is applied to the house and the temperature around the thermostat begins to rise. The rate at which it rises depends on many factors, among which are the thermal characteristics of the house, wind conditions, the outside temperature T_D (a disturbance signal), and the characteristics of the heating system.

When the actual temperature T_A reaches 74°, the thermostat opens and the heating unit is turned off. If the heating system is of the warm-air type, heat flow will stop as soon as the unit is turned off. On the other hand, if the system is of the circulating-hot-water type, heat will continue to flow into the room when the circulation is stopped until the water in the radiator cools.

As long as the outside temperature T_D remains lower than 70°, the temperature in the house will fluctuate between 70 and 74°. (In the case of the hot-water system, the temperature may actually rise a bit above the 74° thermostat upper limit.)

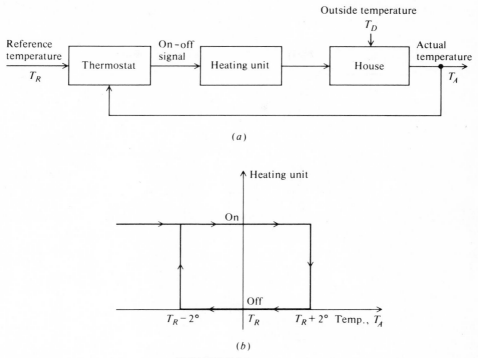

FIGURE 7.7-1
Home heating system. (*a*) Block diagram; (*b*) heating cycle.

As long as the furnace capacity is large enough, this system will be completely independent of the house characteristics and of the outside temperature. However, if the furnace capacity is not large enough and the outside temperature drops to a very low value, the inside temperature may never reach 74° or might even drop below the 70° lower limit. In such cases, of course, the furnace is never turned off.

To obtain quantitative information we shall *model* the heating system and house using an electrical analog. In this analog, the temperature difference (the *across* variable) is chosen analogous to electric voltage. Heat flow (the *through* variable) is then analogous to electric current, and electric resistance is analogous to thermal resistance. The thermal capacity of the house is directly analogous to electric capacitance.

An electrical analog of our heating system is shown in Fig. 7.7-2*a*. In the analog, voltage is directly analogous to temperature, the ground symbol representing 0 V = 0°F. As to units, we will represent 1°F by 1 V and will use the symbols T and V

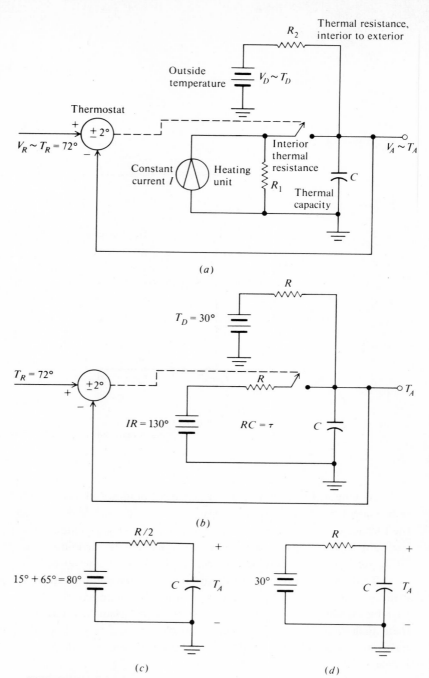

FIGURE 7.7-2
Electrical analog of home heating system. (*a*) Analog with constant current source
(*b*) Thévenin equivalent of current source; (*c*) analog when furnace is on; (*d*) analog when furnace is off.

interchangeably. The capacitance C represents the thermal capacity of the house and R_2 the thermal resistance between exterior and interior.

It seems plausible to assume that a typical home furnace can supply a *constant* heat flow to the house. Thus the furnace is analogous to a constant current source, as shown in Fig. 7.7-2a. R_1 represents the thermal losses in the heating system. For this example, we assume that the thermostat is set at $T_R = 72°$. The switch will then close when T_A drops to 70° and will open when T_A rises to 74°, according to the cycle in Fig. 7.7-1b.

The outside temperature T_D is assumed constant and unaffected by the thermal activity of the house. This temperature is represented by a battery (constant voltage = constant temperature), and for this example we assume winter conditions with $T_D = V_D = 30°$.

The first step in the analysis is to write a node equation for the circuit of Fig. 7.7-2a, assuming that the switch is closed (full heat flow from the furnace). Using KCL, we have

$$\frac{V_A - V_D}{R_2} + \frac{V_A}{R_1} + C\frac{dV_A}{dt} = I \qquad (7.7\text{-}1)$$

At this point, to simplify the analysis, we shall assume that $R_2 = R_1 = R$. Then the thermal time constant is $RC = \tau$ and (7.7-1) can be put in the form

$$2V_A - V_D - IR = -\tau\frac{dV_A}{dt} \qquad (7.7\text{-}2)$$

The constant current I (heat flow) can be found from the manufacturer's data for the furnace or, for our purposes, can be found approximately by the following argument: Consider that $T_D = V_D = 0°$ and that the temperature T_A has reached an equilibrium value. Then $dV_A/dt = 0$ and (7.7-2) yields

$$2V_A - IR = 0$$
$$IR = 2V_A|_{V_D=0°} \qquad (7.7\text{-}3)$$

Now let us assume that when the outside temperature is as low as 0°, the furnace operating continuously will maintain the house at a constant temperature of only 65°. Then from (7.7-3)

$$IR = 2 \times 65 = 130 \text{ V} (=130°) \qquad (7.7\text{-}4)$$

With this value of IR we can make a Thévenin conversion and arrive at the circuit of Fig. 7.7-2b. To make calculations, we need values for R and C, or since we are primarily interested in time intervals, the value of $\tau = RC$ will do. We assume that for the type of home heating system under discussion, a typical time constant τ might be 2 h, where the time constant is the time it would take for the furnace operating continuously to raise the inside temperature from 0 to 63 percent of its final value of 65°: $0.63 \times 65° = 41°$, with the outside temperature at 0°.

With these assumptions we are now able to calculate the time required for the temperature to rise to any desired value with the furnace on.

At this point it is convenient to combine the two battery circuits of Fig. 7.7-2*b* into the single battery and resistance of Fig. 7.7-2*c*. From this we see that when the outside temperature is 30°, the maximum inside temperature T_A subject to our assumptions is 80°F. We take as our starting point $T_A = 70°$ (thermostat just closed) at $t_1 = 0$, and we wish to find the time t_2 at which the system will reach $T_A = 74°$ (thermostat just open). Using the result of Prob. 7.7-2, we find that

$$V_A(t) = 80 - 10e^{-t} \qquad (7.7\text{-}5)$$

where t is measured in hours.

Thus

$$V_A(t_2) = 74 = 80 - 10e^{-t_2}$$
$$e^{-t_2} = 0.6$$
$$t_2 \approx 0.5 \text{ h} \qquad (7.7\text{-}6)$$

This does not appear to be an unreasonable figure.

Now, when $T_A = 74°$ and the furnace is turned off, we have $I = 0$ and the situation is as shown in Fig. 7.7-2*d*. For this circuit we have $V_A(t_2) = 74°$ and

$$T_A(t') = 30 + 44e^{-t'/2}$$

where $t' = t - t_2$ in hours. Here we wish to find the time for T_A to drop from 74 to 70°. Thus

$$V_A(t_3) = 70 = 30 + 44e^{-(t_3 - t_2)/2}$$
$$e^{-(t_3 - t_2)/2} = 0.91$$
$$\frac{t_3 - t_2}{2} = 0.09$$
$$t_3 - t_2 = 0.18 \text{ h}$$

Thus, according to our rough model, it takes about 11 min for the house to cool down from 74 to 70°. A plot of the variation of T_A with time is shown in Fig. 7.7-3.

We can also find, for our assumed system parameters, the outside temperature at which the furnace will run continuously. Consider Fig. 7.7-2*c*. If the voltage (temperature) of the battery is less than 74° the thermostat will never turn off the furnace. The battery voltage is $T_D/2 + 65°$, so that if $T_D < 18°$, the furnace will run continuously. Thus the heating plant in our example is a bit too small for a house situated in an area where temperatures may drop to this level.

It should be noted that, according to our analog, heat flow is exponential in nature. This is not strictly true but does often give good "ball-park" figures.

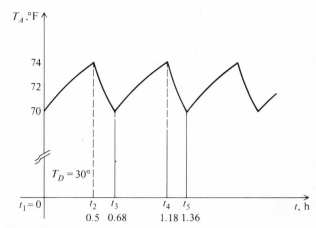

FIGURE 7.7-3
Predicted inside house temperature for outside temperature of 30°.

7.8   BIOLOGICAL CONTROL SYSTEMS

One of the most interesting areas where control theory is being applied today is in biological control systems. One type of biological control system includes *homeostatic* systems. These are control systems within the body of a living organism that tend to maintain a fixed internal environment in spite of extreme internal and external disturbances. An obvious example of such a system is the temperature-regulating mechanism in warm-blooded animals. For example, the internal temperature of the human body is maintained close to 98.6°F, even though the ambient temperature may range from 120°F to well below zero and may be accompanied by high winds. These effects are external disturbances (represented by r_d in Sec. 7.4). The internal temperature control system of the body is a *regulator*, i.e., a system that maintains a controlled output (in our case body temperature) at a constant desired reference level (in our case 98.6°F). The reference level does not usually change, as did the input to our camera positioning system of Sec. 7.1.

Within the temperature regulation system are several subsystems which control the body temperature to within 1 to 2°F of the reference level of 98.6°F. The subsystems themselves are quite complex. For example, if the sensors in the skin detect a sharp drop in outside temperature, electric signals are transmitted to the muscles (the plant), ordering them to "shiver." Shivering is uncoordinated muscular motion, and the energy of this motion is converted into heat which tends to warm the body and compensate for the original drop in temperature.

Another subsystem involves the basal metabolic rate (BMR). Here oxygen

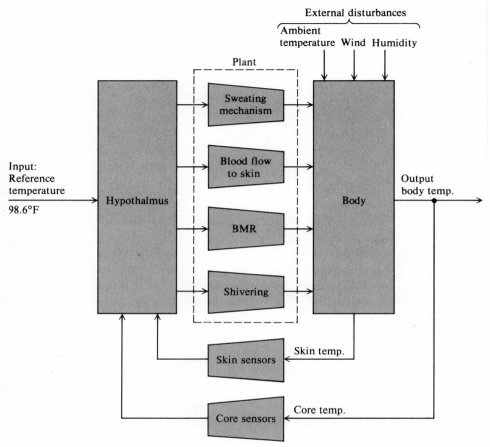

FIGURE 7.8-1
Block diagram of internal-temperature regulator.

inhaled from the atmosphere is transported by the blood to those cells where fat is stored. Oxidation of this fat results in the release of carbon dioxide to the blood, and the consequent release of heat energy. This release is triggered by electric signals sent from the brain through an endocrine gland.

Body temperature is also affected by the skin, in two different ways. First, blood flow to the surface of the skin is controlled by signals from the brain. When more heat is to flow out of the body, more warm blood is sent to the skin. The second effect involves sweating, which permits loss of heat from the body by evaporation.

These four mechanisms for exerting control over body temperature are represented by the "plant" in the feedback-system block diagram shown in Fig. 7.8-1.

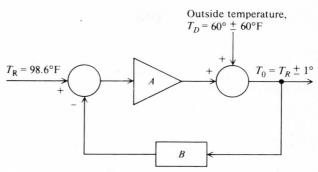

FIGURE 7.8-2
Simplified block diagram of body-temperature regulator.

The heart of any feedback system is perhaps the controller, which for body-temperature regulation comprises the temperature sensors within the skin and within the core of the body and that portion of the brain (the hypothalmus) which is thought to be the controller for thermal regulation.

In Fig. 7.8-2 we have a simplified block diagram which represents the whole system. Let us calculate the forward gain and loop gain required to maintain the output (body) temperature at $98.6°F \pm 1°F$ if the ambient temperature varies from 0 to $120°F$. Adapting (7.4-4) to this situation, we have

$$T_0 = \frac{T_D + AT_R}{1 + AB} \qquad (7.8\text{-}1)$$

Consider first the change in T_D (the ambient temperature). Since T_R does not change, we have

$$\Delta T_0 = \frac{\Delta T_D}{1 + AB} \qquad (7.8\text{-}2)$$

For $\Delta T_D = 60°$, we require a maximum $\Delta T_0 = 1°$. Substituting in (7.8-2),

$$1 = \frac{60}{1 + AB}$$

$$AB = 59$$

This is the required loop gain. Now returning to (7.8-1), the output (body) temperature is to be $98.6°F$ when the ambient is equal to its nominal value of $60°F$. Thus, substituting into (7.8-1), we have

$$98.6 = \frac{60 + 98.6A}{1 + 59}$$

$$A = 59.5$$

The next step in the analysis would be to identify A and B with the various components in Fig. 7.8-1. Then these components would be described by an appropriate transfer function, with the parameters derived either from experimental measurements on human beings or from application of the pertinent physical laws.

Needless to say, we have hardly scratched the surface of this topic. The discussion has indicated the importance of feedback in the human body and how one may at least begin to analyze its effects.

A visual tracking system   A second type of biological feedback system is similar to the camera positioning system which we studied in Secs. 7.1 and 7.2. One example is the visual tracking system, which enables the eyes to lock on to a moving target. This is a very complicated system, for the process involves simultaneous coordinated action of tracking mechanisms, focusing and converging mechanisms, eye-pupil reflex mechanisms, and various body-movement mechanisms such as motion of the head on the body and the body in space. For each of these mechanisms there is actually a separate feedback path to the "error detector" in the brain. Thus the system is exceedingly complex, and little quantitative information is available.

A much simplified diagram of the visual tracking system is shown in Fig. 7.8-3. Only one of the feedback loops has been shown, for simplicity. One complication that is evident is that the motion controlled by each of these loops must be considered in three dimensions. This adds considerable complexity to the mathematical treatment. A further complication occurs because, under certain conditions, the eye does not move smoothly, but rather moves in small jumps, called *saccades*. This happens most markedly when a scene is being viewed with the head fixed. The eye normally holds on to each portion of the scene for a period not less than about 150 ms before it jumps to the next target. This type of motion is usually modeled by a *sampled-data* system. In such a system, the error between the target and eye positions is sampled (Sec. 6.5), and corrections are made at intervals, rather than continuously.

The reason why there exists a scarcity of quantitative information on eye motion is that the system is so complicated that it is extremely difficult to obtain mathematical models for the component parts of the system. Until such models are available, it is impossible to set down an overall mathematical picture of the eye which can be used to predict performance under different conditions and varying disturbances.

Over the past decade, control engineers and physicians have gotten together and begun to learn each other's language, so that the information gained by the medical people in their research can be put on a firm mathematical basis and analyzed, using

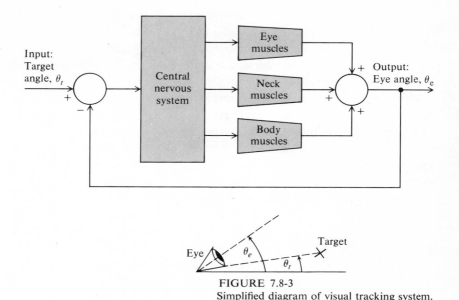

FIGURE 7.8-3
Simplified diagram of visual tracking system.

the tools already available to the control engineer. This team effort is now beginning to produce results, in that appropriate and adequate models are being developed for biological components. Thus we have here an exciting area of electrical engineering which crosses the boundaries of many other fields.

7.9   COMPUTERS IN CONTROL SYSTEMS

As in all areas of engineering, the modern digital computer is making its mark in the control field. Its influence is being strongly felt in the design, development, and operation of all manner of control systems.

Possibly the most interesting use of the digital computer is when it is incorporated as part of the control loop. Here it takes over the role of the controller. An important aspect of its operation as the controller is the fact that it has *memory* and therefore can be programmed to make control decisions based on the characteristics of a previously determined model of the process being controlled. In many instances, its computational speed is such that, using a *time-sharing* scheme, the same computer can act as the controller for a number of independent control loops. This is done routinely in the machine-tool industry, where small special-purpose computers are available which can simultaneously operate several automatic machine tools independently.

As another example of the possibilities afforded by the digital computer, consider the problem of controlling traffic at a busy intersection. The situation is illustrated in Fig. 7.9-1a. Let us assume that the flow of traffic is so heavy that there are constant traffic jams at the intersection and we wish to design a system using a digital computer to alleviate the problem. One possibility is as follows: We install traffic counters at each of the eight positions shown on the diagram. The traffic flow rate, i.e., the number of cars per minute passing the indicated points, is calculated by the computer from the traffic-counter outputs.

Before the feedback system is designed, the traffic counters are used to measure the traffic pattern in each direction. From this information, a mathematical model is constructed which includes such factors as the patterns occurring at different times of the day and the effect of different weather conditions. A *nominal* traffic model is thus determined, and a nominal traffic-signal program can be set up on the basis of this model. The feedback system is then designed to make adjustments of the nominal program to take account of varying conditions.

Later, when the feedback system is installed, the counters will become the sensors which feed input and output information to the computer-controller.

To illustrate how such a system might work, consider the following example: The system is to be designed around a nominal time interval of 1 min for each direction. For simplicity we assume that only right turns are allowed. If more than 10 cars are waiting in any direction, 20 s is to be added to the next interval during which the light is green in that direction.

A timing diagram is shown in Fig. 7.9-1b. The various *intervals* are denoted as $T_1, T_2, T_3, \ldots$, while the actual times are $t_1, t_2, t_3, \ldots$. The number of cars waiting in direction i at time t_j is easily calculated by the computer and is denoted by $N_i(t_j)$.

Flow equations similar to Kirchhoff's current law can be written for the system. Consider first the flow when the traffic lights are green in the east-west direction. From Fig. 7.9-1a and using subscripts E, W, N, and S to indicate cars turning in the subscript direction, we have

$$d_6 = d_1 - d_{1N} \qquad (7.9\text{-}1a)$$

$$d_2 = d_5 - d_{5S} \qquad (7.9\text{-}1b)$$

For those cars that have turned north,

$$d_8 = d_{1N} \qquad (7.9\text{-}1c)$$

and for those cars turning south,

$$d_4 = d_{5S} \qquad (7.9\text{-}1d)$$

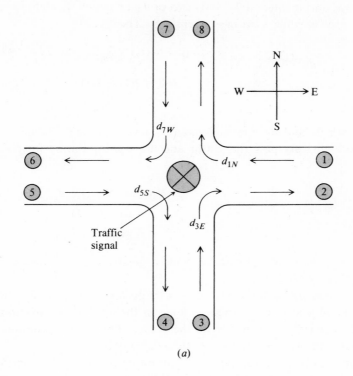

(a)

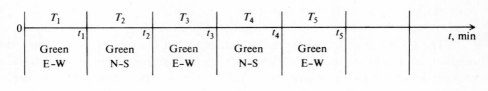

(b)

FIGURE 7.9-1
Traffic control. (a) Road map showing traffic flow; (b) timing diagram.

In these equations d_1, d_2, d_4, d_5, d_6, and d_8 represent the flow rates (number of cars per minute that pass the sensor) as determined from signals sent in by the traffic counters.

Now consider that we start at $t = 0$. At $t = t_1$ there are three cars waiting to travel west. Then $N_1(t_1) = 3$. During interval T_2, when the east-west light is red, assume five more cars pass the sensor in direction 1, so that eight cars are waiting;

i.e., $N_1(t_2) = 8$. Now, during interval T_3, only two cars go through the light for some reason, and pass sensor 6, while 1 car passes sensor 8. Then

$$N_1(t_3) = N_1(t_2) - d_6 T_3 - d_8 T_3 \qquad (7.9\text{-}2)$$

$$= 8 - 2(1) - 1(1)$$

$$= 5$$

This is compared with 10, and since it is less than 10, no adjustment is made.

Next, assume eight cars pass the sensor and are waiting during interval T_4. Then

$$N_1(t_4) = N_1(t_3) + d_1 T_4$$

$$= 5 + 8(1)$$

$$= 13$$

Now the computer compares $N_1(t_4)$ with 10, finds it greater than 10, and thus sets interval $T_5 = 1$ min 20 s $= 80$ s.

Similar calculations are made for eastbound cars during these intervals, and if a pileup occurs in that direction when there is none in the westbound direction, the nominal pattern is changed to accommodate the excess. During alternate intervals calculations are made for northbound and southbound traffic.

The computer must be programmed to make these calculations on a continuous basis and use the results to modify the traffic-signal pattern which was set up on the basis of the original model. If the program is successful, traffic will not pile up at the junction, assuming that it is not so heavy that saturation effects come into play.

The system described above is "self-adaptive" in the sense that it adapts the original model to current conditions. In control-system language, it calculates changes in the plant parameters (flow rates) and uses this information to derive optimizing control forces (traffic-light patterns).

Our analysis represents a considerable simplification of the actual traffic problem. However, it is clear that the digital computer allows the traffic engineer an almost infinite degree of flexibility for controlling the traffic according to any criterion he may wish to apply.

PROBLEMS

7.2-1 An amplifier has a gain (voltage out/voltage in) of 3×10^4 without feedback. Find the feedback transmission B required to produce gains of 1, 10, 100, and 1,000. For each case find the loop gain.

7.2-2   Measurements on a certain automatic control system show that the output and the input are identical when the feedback loop is closed. With the loop open, the output is 500 times greater than the input. Find the loop gain, the gain without feedback A, and the feedback transmission B.

7.2-3   Feedback is applied to a common-emitter amplifier (Sec. 5.6-1) by connecting a resistor R_f from the collector terminal to the base terminal. Draw the equivalent circuit and identify the comparator, sampling point, and feedback path.

7.3-1   For the system of Prob. 7.2-2 the gain without feedback can vary from 400 to 600. Find the variation in overall gain due to this range of variation in A.

7.3-2   A feedback amplifier is to be designed to have an overall gain A_f of 40 dB and a sensitivity of 5 percent to internal amplifier gain variations. Find the required loop gain, gain without feedback, and feedback transmission B.

7.3-3   A transistor amplifier has a gain $A_1 = 500$ which is subject to ± 10 percent change when transistors are replaced. Design a feedback amplifier (block diagram) which has $A_f = 500$ but a 0.1 percent change in gain due to transistor replacement. Use amplifier A_1 as part of your design.

7.4-1   An amplifier has a voltage gain of 100. When the output is 10 V, an undesired 60-Hz hum voltage of 0.5 V is superimposed on the output. Design a feedback system which will reduce this hum to 0.02 V.

7.4-2   In the remote-control TV camera system of Example 7.2-1, a 30-mi/h wind blowing on the camera without feedback produces a $2°$ change in the camera angle. What will the change be with the feedback connected?

7.4-3   A person riding a bicycle can be considered a feedback system. A slight change in the position of the balanced bicycle will cause a spill unless corrective action is taken by the rider. Draw a block diagram and indicate all the components, variables, and disturbances which occur to you.

7.4-4   Draw block diagrams for several feedback systems with which you are familiar. Identify input and output variables, plant, controller, sensors, error detectors, and feedback paths.

7.4-5   A racing-car driver tries to keep the right side of his car exactly 1 yd from the track fence. Draw a complete block diagram of this feedback system.

7.7-1   For the home heating system of Sec. 7.7 calculate the heat-up and cool-down times, assuming that $R_1 = 2R_2$, $T_D = 15°$, and $\tau = 1.5$ h.

7.7-2   Consider the RC analog circuit of Fig. 7.7-2c. Write the differential equation for the circuit and show that the solution is

$$V_A(t) = 80 + [V_A(0) - 80]e^{-2t/RC}$$

where $V_A(0)$ is the initial condition, i.e. the value of V_A at $t = 0$.

7.7-3   Recommend steps which might be taken to improve the heating system of Sec. 7.7 so that lower outside temperatures will not cause the furnace to run continuously.

7.8-1   Draw block diagrams for several biological control systems. Identify all possible variables and components.

7.9-1   Design a traffic control system for a supermarket with four checkout counters. Choose suitable control strategies, desirable maximum waiting times, and sensors.

REFERENCES

CLYNES, M., and J. H. MILSUM: "Biomedical Engineering Systems," McGraw-Hill Book Company, New York, 1970.

LYNCH, W. A., and J. G. TRUXAL: "Signals and Systems in Electrical Engineering," McGraw-Hill Book Company, New York, 1962.

ELECTROMAGNETIC THEORY AND APPLICATIONS

INTRODUCTION

In all the circuits considered up to now, changes were felt *instantaneously* at all points
in the circuit. We did not concern ourselves with the fact that, since charges move
with a finite velocity, their effect is felt at different times at different parts of the circuit.
Our reason for neglecting this seemingly important point is the relatively small
physical dimensions of the actual circuits. By physical smallness we mean that the
effects of the changes in voltages and currents traveled with such a high velocity and
the changes themselves occurred at such a low rate that it appeared as if all components of the circuit suffered the change simultaneously.

In this chapter we discard the assumption that the physical dimensions of the
circuit are negligible and consider the transmission of electric energy to distant points.
This will lead to the concepts of electric and magnetic fields and their distribution in
time and space.

Finally, we will consider some engineering applications of these concepts, such
as antenna radiation, radar, transmission lines, etc.

8.1   ENERGY AND MOMENTUM, NEWTON'S LAW

Our fundamental experience is the perception of bodies in relative motion. This motion can be explained quantitatively using the concepts of energy and momentum. Mathematically, we express the relation between the *state of motion* of a body and its energy and momentum by

$$KE = \tfrac{1}{2}m \sum v_i^2 \qquad (8.1\text{-}1)$$

and
$$p_i = mv_i \qquad (8.1\text{-}2)$$

where KE = kinetic energy of the body considered
   m = mass of the body
   v_i = velocity with which the body moves in i direction
   p_i = momentum of the body in i direction

Note that in the mks system the unit of energy is the *joule* and that of momentum the *newton-second*.

The kinetic energy and momentum of a body are continuously changing, due to interaction with all other moving bodies which exist in our universe. We express this by saying that an *exchange of energy and momentum* occurs between the body under consideration and the rest of the universe.

We represent this exchange of energy by introducing a new concept, that of *force*; i.e., we say that the change in the state of motion of a body is due to the action of a force. To summarize: The force applied to a body is the resultant of the action of all the bodies in our universe on this particular body. Quantitatively, we represent this action and the resulting change by

$$F_i = \frac{dp_i}{dt} = m\,\frac{dv_i}{dt} \qquad (8.1\text{-}3)$$

where F_i is the component of the force in the i direction acting on the body of mass m.

Equation (8.1-3) is called *Newton's law*, and it describes the relation between the applied force and the change in velocity (acceleration) of the body under consideration.

8.2   ELECTRIC AND MAGNETIC FORCES. THE CONCEPT OF CHARGE

In this section we consider the behavior of forces which act on systems of charged particles. These particles possess one other fundamental characteristic besides those of mass and motion. They have associated with them a property called *charge*.

Experimental evidence has shown that two types of charges can be associated with a system of particles: positive and negative charges. The fundamental unit of

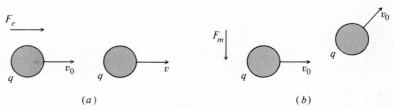

FIGURE 8.2-1
(*a*) Electric force changes the magnitude of the velocity of a charge. (*b*) Magnetic force changes direction of motion of charged particle.

charge is the coulomb (C). The coulomb is a fundamental unit, like the meter, kilogram, or second, and is therefore not expressible in terms of other units. An interesting characteristic of the amount of charge which can be associated with a particle is the existence of a *quantum* of charge. By this we mean that there is a minimum indivisible amount of charge which can be associated with a particle. This minimum charge is associated with a particle called the *electron*, and it has the experimentally determined value of -1.6×10^{-19} C.

Charged particles exchange energy continuously among themselves in a much more active way than uncharged particles. By this we mean that at a given distance the electric force between two charged particles is much stronger than the gravitational force.

Experiments have shown that there are two kinds of forces acting on charged particles. The first kind of force is called an *electric force*, and is shown in Fig. 8.2-1*a*. The electric force acts in the direction of motion of a charged particle, and tends to change the *magnitude of the velocity* of the particle. The electric force acts on charged bodies either at rest or in motion. The second type of force, shown in Fig. 8.2-1*b*, is the *magnetic force* which acts in a direction perpendicular to the direction of motion of the system. The action of the magnetic force thus tends to change the *direction* in which the system moves, and it will act only on bodies already in a state of motion.

8.3   ELEMENTARY VECTOR ALGEBRA

Forces and velocities are *vector* quantities. This means that we need two parameters to characterize them completely. For example, we say that a northwest wind is blowing at 20 km/h. To characterize the velocity of the wind we needed two quantities: the magnitude of the velocity, 20 km/h, and the direction from which it was blowing, northwest.

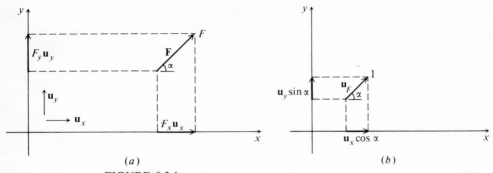

(a)   (b)

FIGURE 8.3-1
(a) Relation between a vector and its rectangular components. (b) Definition of a
unit vector.

The above parameters, magnitude and direction, are characteristics of any vector
quantity. To specify that a quantity is a vector we will use boldface type:

$$\mathbf{F}$$

Since it is much easier, numerically, to work with scalars (quantities characterized by
one parameter, magnitude), we will define a vector in terms of its components in a
system of orthogonal axes. One such system is the cartesian rectangular axes, shown
in Fig. 8.3-1. On the figure the solid line is the vector $\mathbf{F}$, with the arrow indicating its
direction. The vector is expressed in terms of its x and y components by writing it in
the form

$$\mathbf{F} = F_x \mathbf{u}_x + F_y \mathbf{u}_y \qquad (8.3\text{-}1)$$

In this equation $\mathbf{u}_x$ and $\mathbf{u}_y$ are vectors of magnitude 1 in the x and y direction, respectively; F_x and F_y are the projections of the vector $\mathbf{F}$ on the x and y axes. The magnitudes of F_x and F_y are related to the magnitude F of the vector $\mathbf{F}$ by the relations

$$F_x = F \cos \alpha \qquad (8.3\text{-}2a)$$
$$F_y = F \sin \alpha \qquad (8.3\text{-}2b)$$

where α is the angle which the direction of $\mathbf{F}$ makes with the x axis (Fig. 8.3-1). The
vector $\mathbf{F}$ can also be expressed as a magnitude multiplied by a unit vector.

$$\mathbf{F} = F\mathbf{u}_F \qquad (8.3\text{-}3)$$

Figure 8.3-1b shows the unit vector $\mathbf{u}_F$, which has a magnitude of unity and a direction
parallel to the direction of $\mathbf{F}$. $\mathbf{u}_F$ is related to the unit vectors $\mathbf{u}_x$ and $\mathbf{u}_y$ by

$$\mathbf{u}_F = \mathbf{u}_x \cos \alpha + \mathbf{u}_y \sin \alpha \qquad (8.3\text{-}4)$$

8.3-1   Addition of Vectors

The addition of two vectors **A** and **B** is defined as

$$\mathbf{A} + \mathbf{B} = (A_x + B_x)\mathbf{u}_x + (A_y + B_y)\mathbf{u}_y \qquad (8.3\text{-}5)$$

In words, we add two vectors by adding their respective projections on the x and y axes. (This is similar to phasor addition as described in Sec. 3.3-2.)

EXAMPLE 8.3-1   Given the vectors $\mathbf{A} = 3 \angle 30°$ and $\mathbf{B} = 5 \angle 45°$, find their sum

$$\mathbf{F} = \mathbf{A} + \mathbf{B}$$

SOLUTION

$$A_x = 3 \cos 30° = 2.60$$
$$B_x = 5 \cos 45° = 3.52$$
$$A_y = 3 \sin 30° = 1.5$$
$$B_y = 5 \sin 45° = 3.52$$

Using (8.3-5),

$$F_x = A_x + B_x = 2.60 + 3.52 = 6.12$$
$$F_y = A_y + B_y = 1.5 + 3.52 = 5.02$$

thus

$$\mathbf{F} = 6.12\mathbf{u}_x + 5.02\mathbf{u}_y$$

Since

$$F = \sqrt{F_x^{\,2} + F_y^{\,2}} = \sqrt{(6.12)^2 + (5.02)^2} = 7.9$$

and

$$\alpha = \arctan \frac{F_y}{F_x} = \arctan \frac{5.02}{6.12} = 39.4°$$

we have

$$\mathbf{F} = 7.9 \angle 39.4°$$

Note:

$$\mathbf{u}_F = 1 \angle 39.4°$$

////////

8.3-2   Multiplication of Two Vectors

The rule for multiplying two vectors is more complex, and depends on whether the result is a *vector* or a *scalar*.

Figure 8.3-2 shows the case when the result is a scalar. In this case the multiplication is called a *dot product*, and is defined by the equation

$$C = \mathbf{A} \cdot \mathbf{B} = AB \cos \theta = AB\mathbf{u}_A \cdot \mathbf{u}_B \qquad (8.3\text{-}6)$$

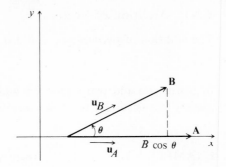

FIGURE 8.3-2
Definition of dot product.

where θ = angle between two vectors
$\quad C$ = resulting scalar

From the definition we see that since cos 0 = 1, the dot product of two *parallel* vectors is a scalar equal to the product of the magnitudes. For example,

$$\mathbf{u}_x \cdot \mathbf{u}_x = 1 \qquad (8.3\text{-}7a)$$

and the dot product of two perpendicular vectors (θ = 90°) is zero, e.g.,

$$\mathbf{u}_x \cdot \mathbf{u}_y = 0 \qquad (8.3\text{-}7b)$$

Another way of looking at the dot product is as follows: First project the vector **B** in the direction of **A** as shown in Fig. 8.3-2. Since the angle between **A** and **B** is θ . the magnitude of this projection is $B \cos \theta$. Now multiply A by the projection. The result is $A(B \cos \theta)$ as given in (8.3-6). Let us now express the dot product of two vectors **A** and **B** in rectangular coordinates. Using (8.3-7a) and (8.3-7b), we obtain

$$\mathbf{A} \cdot \mathbf{B} = (A_x \mathbf{u}_x + A_y \mathbf{u}_y) \cdot (B_x \mathbf{u}_x + B_y \mathbf{u}_y) = A_x B_x + A_y B_y \qquad (8.3\text{-}8)$$

In other words, (8.3-8) tells us that to find the dot product of two vectors we multiply the respective projections on the cartesian axes and then add the resulting magnitudes.

The cross product   The second type of multiplication is called the *cross product*, or *vector product*, and is defined as

$$\mathbf{F} = \mathbf{A} \times \mathbf{B} = AB \sin \theta \mathbf{u}_F = AB\mathbf{u}_A \times \mathbf{u}_B \qquad (8.3\text{-}9)$$

The result **F** is a vector whose magnitude is $AB \sin \theta$. The direction of **F** is perpendicular to the plane formed by the vectors **A** and **B**, as shown in Fig. 8.3-3. To enable

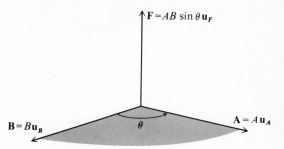

FIGURE 8.3-3
Definition of cross product. The vector
F is perpendicular to the plane formed
by the vectors **A** and **B**.

us to write (8.3-9) in rectangular coordinates, we will introduce a third direction, the z
axis. The unit vector in the z direction is defined by

$$\mathbf{u}_z = \mathbf{u}_x \times \mathbf{u}_y \quad (8.3\text{-}10a)$$

Note that

$$\mathbf{u}_x \times \mathbf{u}_x = 0 \quad (8.3\text{-}10b)$$

$$\mathbf{u}_y \times \mathbf{u}_y = 0 \quad (8.3\text{-}10c)$$

Note that $\mathbf{u}_z$ is a unit vector in a direction perpendicular to the xy plane. It is directed
so that if the x axis moves counterclockwise toward the y axis, then $\mathbf{u}_z$ is upward, as
shown in Fig. 8.3-4a. Using (8.3-10) and (8.3-9), we can express **F** as

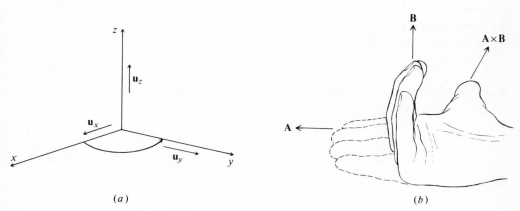

(a) (b)

FIGURE 8.3-4
(a) When the x axis moves counterclockwise toward the y axis, the z axis and $\mathbf{u}_z$
are in the upward direction. (b) Right-hand rule for cross product. The four
fingers point in the direction of **A**. As the fingers close toward **B**, the cross product
is in the direction of the thumb.

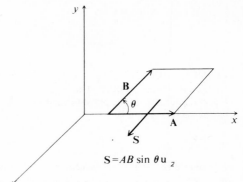

$$S = AB \sin \theta \, u_z$$

FIGURE 8.3-5
Defining the area of a parallelogram.

$$\mathbf{F} = (A_x \, \mathbf{u}_x + A_y \, \mathbf{u}_y) \times (B_x \, \mathbf{u}_x + B_y \, \mathbf{u}_y) = (A_x B_y - A_y B_x)\mathbf{u}_z \qquad (8.3\text{-}11)$$

The relation between $\mathbf{u}_x$, $\mathbf{u}_y$, and $\mathbf{u}_z$ can be expressed by the right-hand rule (Fig. 8.3-4b). In words, with the palm open, the x axis is in the direction of the four fingers. As the fingers close toward the y axis, the z axis is in the direction of the extended thumb.

The vector product is strongly associated with the concept of *area*. The vector associated with an area has a magnitude equal to that of the area and points in a direction perpendicular to the plane of the area. To show this, let us find the area of the parallelogram in Fig. 8.3-5. The side A is on the x axis, and B is in the xy plane. From elementary geometry we know that the area of a parallelogram with sides A and B and an angle θ between them is

$$S = AB \sin \theta \qquad (8.3\text{-}12)$$

But from the definition of vector product the magnitude of the vector $\mathbf{A} \times \mathbf{B}$ is $AB \sin \theta$ so that, in order for the vector $\mathbf{S}$ to be defined by

$$\mathbf{S} = \mathbf{A} \times \mathbf{B}$$

it must have a direction perpendicular to the plane of the vectors $\mathbf{A}$ and $\mathbf{B}$. This agrees with the definition previously given.

EXAMPLE 8.3-2   Given two vectors

$$\mathbf{A} = 3\mathbf{u}_x \qquad \mathbf{B} = 2\mathbf{u}_x + 5\mathbf{u}_y$$

Find the magnitude and direction of the area encompassed by the two vectors.

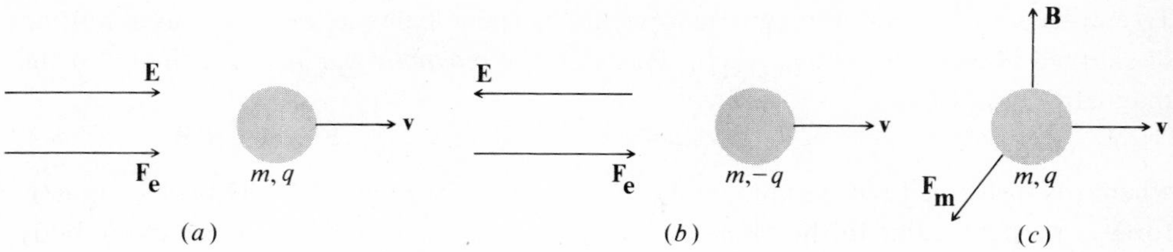

FIGURE. 8.4-1
(*a*) Electric force and electric field intensity applied to a positively charged body.
(*b*) Electric force and electric field intensity applied to a negatively charged body.
(*c*) Magnetic force due to a magnetic flux density applied to a positively charged body in motion.

SOLUTION   Using (8.3-11), we find

$$S = A \times B = (3u_x) \times (2u_x + 5u_y)$$

Solving, we obtain $\qquad\qquad\qquad\qquad\qquad\qquad\qquad S = 15u_z$

Note that the vector product **B × A** is equal to $-15u_z$. It represents a vector whose direction is opposite to **S**. The direction we choose to represent the area depends on the observer or the context of the problem.
////////

8.4   SOME USEFUL PHYSICAL CONCEPTS

Experimental evidence has shown that the acceleration of a charged body is proportional to its charge. To stress this fact in Newton's law [Eq. (8.1-3)], we will define per-unit-charge quantities for both electric and magnetic forces.

8.4-1   Electric Field Intensity

The electric field intensity **E** is defined as the force exerted on a body whose charge is one coulomb. According to this definition,

$$E = \frac{F_e}{q} \qquad (8.4\text{-}1)$$

where q is the charge of the body influenced by the force F_e. The units of **E** are newtons per coulomb, and the direction of **E** is such that it accelerates a positively charged body in the direction of the field and a negatively charged body in the opposite direction. This is illustrated graphically in Fig. 8.4-1*a* and *b*.

8.4-2   The Magnetic Flux Density

To emphasize the fact that magnetic forces act perpendicular to the direction of motion of charged bodies, we define a vector **B**, called the *magnetic flux density*, such that the magnetic force $\mathbf{F}_m$ is

$$\mathbf{F}_m = q\mathbf{v} \times \mathbf{B} \qquad (8.4\text{-}2)$$

where **v** is the velocity of the charged body. The cross product shows that the magnetic force is perpendicular to the plane defined by the velocity vector of the moving body and the magnetic flux density vector. The dimensions of the magnetic flux density are found from (8.4-2) to be

$$\text{Newtons} \times \text{seconds/coulombs} \times \text{meters}$$

For historical reasons which will be clarified later, we define

$$1\,\frac{\text{newton} \times \text{second}}{\text{coulomb} \times \text{meter}} = 1\,\frac{\text{weber}}{\text{meter}^2}$$

thus emphasizing the fact that B is a *density*. The vector relation is illustrated graphically in Fig. 8.4-1c.

Combining Eqs. (8.4-1) and (8.4-2) with Eq. (8.1-3), we write Newton's law for charged bodies as

$$\frac{\mathbf{F}}{q} = \frac{m}{q}\frac{d\mathbf{v}}{dt} = \mathbf{E} + \mathbf{v} \times \mathbf{B} \qquad (8.4\text{-}3)$$

where **F** is the total force on the body due to both electric and magnetic fields. This is called the *Lorentz-Newton law*.

EXAMPLE 8.4-1   An electron is a negatively charged particle whose mass is 9.3×10^{-31} kg and whose charge is -1.6×10^{-19} C. Let us now assume that an electron is moving along the x axis in the positive direction at a velocity of 10 m/s. An electric field of magnitude 100 N/C is applied in the same direction. How many meters will the electron travel and how much time will elapse before it stops?

SOLUTION   From (8.4-3)

$$\frac{m}{-q}\frac{dv_x}{dt} = E_x$$

Integrating, we get

$$\frac{-m}{q}\int_{v_x(0)}^{v_x(t)} dv_x = \int_0^t E_x\,dt$$

and

$$\frac{-m}{q}[v_x(t) - v_x(0)] = tE_x$$

Substituting the given values of m, q, E_x, and $v_x(0)$ yields

$$v_x(t) = -1.7 \times 10^{13}t + 10^4 \qquad (8.4\text{-}4)$$

The electron will stop when $v_x(t) = 0$. This occurs at $t = 5.9 \times 10^{-10}$ s. To find the distance traveled, note that

$$x(t) = \int_0^t v_x(t)\, dt + x(0) \qquad (8.4\text{-}5)$$

Combining (8.4-4) and (8.4-5) and integrating, we find with $x(0) = 0$

$$x(t) = -0.85 \times 10^{13}t^2 + 10^4 t \qquad (8.4\text{-}5a)$$

Substituting $t = 5.9 \times 10^{-10}$ s, we find that the electron will travel 2.95×10^{-6} m.
////////

8.4-3   Electric Potential

Another basic concept is that of electric potential. In classical mechanics we defined potential energy as the work done by a force in moving a body from r_1 to r_2

$$PE = -\int_{r_1}^{r_2} \mathbf{F} \cdot d\mathbf{s}$$

If $\mathbf{F} = q\mathbf{E}$ is the electric force on a charged body, the potential energy is

$$PE = -q \int_{\infty}^{r} \mathbf{E} \cdot d\mathbf{s} \qquad (8.4\text{-}6)$$

We then define the electric potential ϕ as

$$\phi = \frac{PE}{q} = -\int_{\infty}^{r} \mathbf{E} \cdot d\mathbf{s} \qquad (8.4\text{-}7)$$

ϕ is the potential energy necessary to bring a unit charge from infinity to a distance r from the origin. Note that this implies that the potential energy at infinity is zero. The units of ϕ are joules per coulomb and are called volts (V). With reference to these units, the units of $\mathbf{E}$ can also be expressed as volts per meter (V/m).

8.4-4   Current Density

The concept of current i was presented in Chap. 3. Current was defined as the rate of change of charge per unit time,

$$i = \frac{dq}{dt} \qquad (3.1\text{-}1)$$

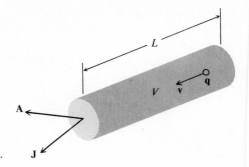

FIGURE 8.4-2
Current density in a conducting wire.

We will now define another concept, that of current density $\mathbf{J}$. The current density $\mathbf{J}$ is defined as the current per unit area passing normal to the area. $\mathbf{J}$ is a vector quantity, and the relation between current which is a scalar and current density $\mathbf{J}$ is defined mathematically as

$$i = \int_{A} \mathbf{J} \cdot d\mathbf{A} \qquad (8.4\text{-}8a)$$

In Fig. 8.4-2 we represent Eq. (8.4-8a) for the special case of a uniform current density, that is, $\mathbf{J} = $ constant. In this case (8.4-8a) becomes

$$i = \mathbf{J} \cdot \mathbf{A} \qquad (8.4\text{-}8b)$$

We now give the reason for considering $\mathbf{J}$ a vector. Consider a volume AL. If there are n particles per unit volume, the total number of particles will be nAL. If in addition each particle has a charge q, then the total charge contained in the volume is

$$Q = qnAL \qquad (8.4\text{-}9)$$

If every particle moves with a velocity v in the L direction, it will take a particle a time

$$t = \frac{L}{v} \qquad (8.4\text{-}10)$$

to traverse the volume.

The amount of charge passing through the surface A per unit time will then be

$$i = \frac{Q}{t} = qnAv \qquad (8.4\text{-}11)$$

Since A and v are actually vector quantities, we express (8.4-11) by writing

$$i = qn\mathbf{v} \cdot \mathbf{A} \qquad (8.4\text{-}12)$$

Comparing (8.4-12) and (8.4-8*b*), we see that the current density is given by

$$\mathbf{J} = qn\mathbf{v} \qquad (8.4\text{-}13)$$

and that $\mathbf{J}$ is a vector quantity. The unit of current density in the mksc system is amperes per meter squared, where an ampere (A) is defined as one coulomb per second (C/s).

8.5   SOURCES OF ELECTRIC AND MAGNETIC FORCES

A charged body changes its state of motion due to interactions with other charged bodies. The electric and magnetic forces represent the resultant of the action of all charged bodies on the body under consideration. We naturally expect that their magnitude and direction should depend on the amount of charge these bodies possess and on their relative position in space. Experimental evidence confirms this assumption. We shall discuss this further in the succeeding sections.

8.5-1   Dependence of the Electric Field and Potential on the Charge Distribution

Consider two point charges q and Q separated by a distance r. Experiments show that the force of attraction or repulsion between these two charges is given by

$$\mathbf{F}_e = \frac{qQ}{4\pi\varepsilon r^2}\,\mathbf{u}_r \qquad (8.5\text{-}1)$$

where ε is a parameter called the *dielectric constant*, and its value depends on the nature of the medium between the two charges. Figure 8.5-1 shows the case where q and Q have the same polarity. Note that the direction of the resulting force is along the axis connecting the two charges, and it is a force of repulsion. If the charges were of opposite polarity, the force would be one of attraction. Equation (8.5-1) is called *Coulomb's law*.

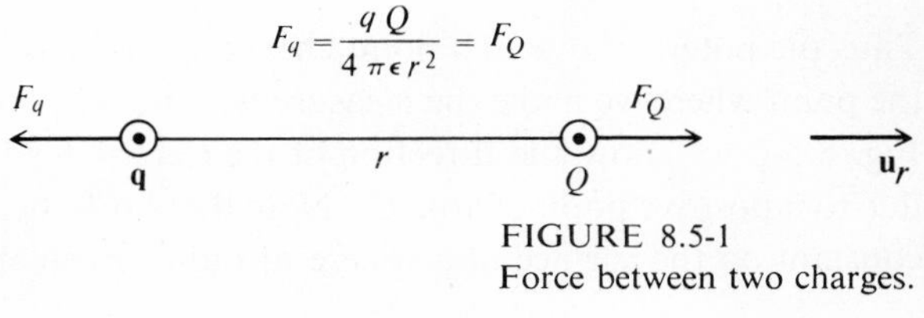

$$F_q = \frac{qQ}{4\pi\varepsilon r^2} = F_Q$$

FIGURE 8.5-1
Force between two charges.

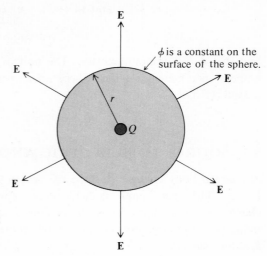

FIGURE 8.5-2
Electric field and potential due to a point
charge Q. **E** and ϕ are constant on the
surface of a sphere of radius r.

Electric field due to a point charge   Since the force on any charge q is

$$\mathbf{F}_e = q\mathbf{E}$$

it follows from (8.5-1) that the electric field at the position of the charge q is

$$\mathbf{E} = \frac{Q}{4\pi\varepsilon r^2}\,\mathbf{u}_r \qquad (8.5\text{-}2)$$

i.e., the electric field intensity, due to a point charge, is inversely proportional to
the square of the distance from the charge. Its direction is along a line away from the
charge if the charge is positive, and toward the charge if the charge is negative.

Potential due to a point charge   It usually turns out to be easier to deal mathematically with the potential than with the electric field because of the scalar nature of
potentials. Combining (8.4-7) with (8.5-2), we get

$$\phi = -\int_\infty^r \frac{Q\,dr}{4\pi\varepsilon r^2} = \frac{Q}{4\pi\varepsilon r} \qquad (8.5\text{-}3)$$

Thus the potential due to a point charge is inversely proportional to the distance from
the point where we make the measurement to the point where the charge is located. In
Fig. 8.5-2 we show the direction of the electric field and a surface of equal potential
due to a positive point charge Q. Note that both the electric field and the potential are
constant on the surface of a sphere of radius r centered at the point where the charge

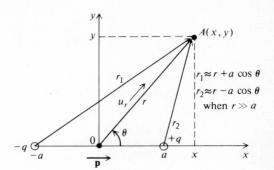

FIGURE 8.5-3
Geometry for Example 8.5-1.

is located; also the direction of **E** is along the radius of the sphere, perpendicular to the surface of the sphere.

Potential due to two point charges; the dipole Equations (8.5-2) and (8.5-3) can be easily extended to the case of many point charges if we assume that linearity, and thus superposition, hold. This is illustrated in the following example.

EXAMPLE 8.5-1   Figure 8.5-3 shows two equal charges of opposite polarity separated by a distance $2a$. If $r \gg a$ this configuration is called a dipole.

(a) Find the potential at any point in space.

(b) Find an approximate expression for ϕ when $r \gg a$.

SOLUTION   (a) Referring to Fig. 8.5-3 and Eq. (8.5-3), the potential at the point A will be

$$\phi(x, y) = \frac{q}{4\pi\varepsilon} \left(\frac{1}{r_2} - \frac{1}{r_1} \right) = \frac{q}{4\pi\varepsilon} \frac{r_1 - r_2}{r_1 r_2}$$

(b) From Fig. 8.5-3

$$r^2 = x^2 + y^2$$

$$r_1^2 = (x + a)^2 + y^2$$

$$r_2^2 = (x - a)^2 + y^2$$

thus

$$r_1^2 - r_2^2 = (r_1 - r_2)(r_1 + r_2) = 4ax$$

or

$$r_1 - r_2 = \frac{4ax}{r_1 + r_2}$$

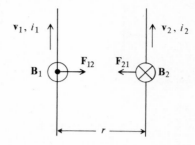

FIGURE 8.5-4
Forces between two current-carrying wires.

If $r_1, r_2 \gg a$, one can assume that

$$r_1 r_2 \approx r^2$$

$$r_1 + r_2 \approx 2r$$

Then

$$\phi \approx \frac{q}{4\pi\varepsilon} \frac{4ax}{2r^3} = \frac{2aq}{4\pi\varepsilon} \frac{x}{r^3} \qquad (8.5\text{-}4)$$

////////

Note that in (8.5-4) the potential depends on the product $2aq$: If the charge q increases and the distance $2a$ decreases, with the product $2aq$ a constant, the potential does not change value; as a matter of fact the larger q (i.e., the smaller $2a$), the better the approximation. The product $2aq$ considered in the limit when q approaches infinity and a approaches zero is called a *dipole moment*. It is a vector quantity whose direction lies on the axis connecting the two charges, pointing toward the positive charge. If we define the dipole moment by the symbol $\mathbf{p}$, then

$$\mathbf{p} = 2aq\mathbf{u}_x \qquad (8.5\text{-}5)$$

Using this notation, (8.5-4) becomes

$$\phi = \frac{\mathbf{p} \cdot \mathbf{r}}{4\pi\varepsilon r^3} \qquad (8.5\text{-}6)$$

We observe, using (8.5-5) and the geometry of Fig. 8.5-3, that

$$\mathbf{p} \cdot \mathbf{r} = px = pr \cos\theta$$

Since matter is composed of positive and negative charges, the dipole moment plays an important role in all physical problems, and we will encounter it often in our studies.

8.5-2 Dependence of Magnetic Flux Density on Current Distribution

It was stated previously that magnetic forces alter the direction of charges in motion. Since a moving charge represents a current, it would appear logical to assume that

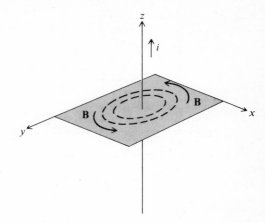

FIGURE 8.5-5
Iron filings arrange themselves in direction of magnetic flux.

a relation exists between currents and magnetic fields. Experimental evidence shows that this is indeed true.

Force between two infinitely long line currents   Figure 8.5-4 represents two infinitely long parallel wires. The currents in each wire are, respectively, i_1 and i_2. Experimental evidence shows that the force (per meter of wire) of attraction or repulsion between the two wires is given by

$$\mathbf{F}_{12} = -\frac{\mu}{2\pi} \frac{i_1 i_2}{r} \mathbf{u}_r \qquad \text{N/m} \qquad (8.5\text{-}7)$$

where μ, the *permeability*, is a constant dependent on the nature of the material. Note that when the currents are in the same direction, the force tends to pull the wires together; i.e., it is a force of attraction. If we compare (8.5-7) with (8.4-2) and let $-qv_1 = i_1$, we see that the magnetic flux density at i_1 due to i_2 will be

$$\mathbf{B}_1 = \frac{\mu}{2\pi} \frac{i_2}{r} \mathbf{u}_\phi \qquad (8.5\text{-}8)$$

with $\mathbf{B}_1$ in the ϕ direction, which is perpendicular to both the direction of the current and that of the magnetic force.

Origin of the name magnetic flux density   Consider a line current as in Fig. 8.5-5. If we place some iron filings on a table in the xy plane, they will arrange themselves as shown in Fig. 8.5-5, i.e., in the form of *flux lines*. The above incidence led the early physicists to associate magnetic fields with flux densities and gave rise to the name *magnetic flux density* for the vector $\mathbf{B}$. Note also that the lines of flux in Fig. 8.5-5

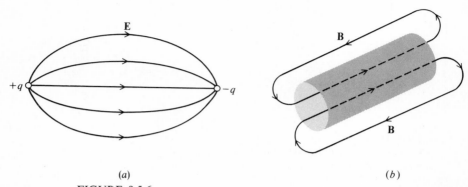

(a)   (b)

FIGURE 8.5-6
(a) Electric flux lines start at $+q$ and end on $-q$. **E** is a divergent field. (b) Magnetic flux lines form a closed path. **B** is a solenoidal field.

close on themselves. Thus, if we were to construct a cylindrical tube with its axis parallel to the lines, the number of lines of flux entering the tube would be equal to the number of lines going out: i.e., the magnetic lines of flux behave as if they have no source. The above behavior of magnetic flux lines led scientists to eliminate the possibility of magnetic charges as sources of magnetic flux lines.

Figure 8.5-6 represents a summary of the above discussion: Since electric fields have charges as sources, we represent them in Fig. 8.5-6a as starting from a positive charge and ending in a negative charge. Because they have sources, the electric fields are called *divergent fields*. Since magnetic fields have no sources, we represent them in Fig. 8.5-6b as closing on themselves. Fields of this type are called *solenoidal fields*.

8.6 THE LAWS OF ELECTROMAGNETIC PROPAGATION

The following relations based on experimental evidence were established in Sec. 8.5:

1 The distribution of electric fields in space depends on the distribution of charges considered as sources of electric forces.

2 The distribution of magnetic fields in space is associated with the existence of currents.

Further experimental evidence shows that when static conditions prevail (no time variation of charges and currents), the magnetic and the electric fields can be found independently.

On the other hand, when charges vary with time, the electric and magnetic fields, **E** and **B**, are related. This can be shown heuristically as follows: Since the electric field **E** is proportional to the charge q, a time rate of change of charge, dq/dt, will produce a change in **E**. However, the current $i = dq/dt$ produces a magnetic field **B**. Thus, **B** is proportional to the time rate of change of **E**. This and other similar results were put on a rigorous mathematical basis by Maxwell and are usually referred to as *Maxwell's equations*.

8.6-1 Differential Equations of Electromagnetic Theory; Maxwell's Equations

The laws governing the variation of electric and magnetic fields in space and time can be derived by expressing Maxwell's equations in differential form. Since the fields involved are vectors, their variation requires an understanding of vector analysis, e.g., methods of finding derivatives of vectors, which is beyond the scope of this chapter.

To understand the field variations and apply them to some engineering problems, we will simplify our assumptions. Although this will involve some loss of generality, it will not detract from the rigor of our treatment.

We will assume that **E** and **B** are always orthogonal to each other and that they vary spatially only in a direction orthogonal to their plane. For example, if **E** is in the x direction and **B** in the y direction, their only variation is in the z direction. Let us assume, then, that

$$\mathbf{B} = B(t, z)\mathbf{u}_y \qquad (8.6\text{-}1)$$

$$\mathbf{E} = E(t, z)\mathbf{u}_x \qquad (8.6\text{-}2)$$

and

$$\mathbf{J} = J(t, z)\mathbf{u}_x \qquad (8.6\text{-}3)$$

With these assumptions Maxwell's equations are

$$-\frac{\partial E(t, z)}{\partial z} = \frac{\partial B(t, z)}{\partial t} \qquad (8.6\text{-}4)$$

and

$$-\frac{\partial B(t, z)}{\partial z} = \varepsilon\mu \frac{\partial E(t, z)}{\partial t} + \mu J(t, z) \qquad (8.6\text{-}5)$$

where ε and μ are the dielectric and permeability constants of the medium; i.e., they represent the influence of the medium on the values of **E** and **B**. **J** is the current density resulting from the time variation of charge.

8.6-2   Solutions of Maxwell's Equations in a Source-free Region

Consider a region in space where $J = 0$. Taking the derivative of (8.6-4) with respect to space, z, and of (8.6-5) with respect to time t, and combining, we find

$$\frac{\partial^2 E}{\partial z^2} = \varepsilon\mu \, \frac{\partial^2 E}{\partial t^2} \qquad (8.6\text{-}6)$$

The reader is asked to show by a similar procedure (Prob. 8.6-1) that

$$\frac{\partial^2 B}{\partial z^2} = \varepsilon\mu \, \frac{\partial^2 B}{\partial t^2} \qquad (8.6\text{-}7)$$

Equations (8.6-6) and (8.6-7) are called the *wave equations*. Note that in order for (8.6-6) and (8.6-7) to be dimensionally correct, $1/\sqrt{\mu\varepsilon}$ must have the dimensions of a velocity.

The reader is asked to verify by substitution (Prob. 8.6-2) that a solution to (8.6-6) and (8.6-7) is

$$E(t, z) = Ef\!\left(t - \frac{z}{v_p}\right) \qquad (8.6\text{-}8a)$$

$$B(t, z) = \frac{E}{v_p} \, f\!\left(t - \frac{z}{v_p}\right) \qquad (8.6\text{-}8b)$$

where $f\!\left(t - \dfrac{z}{v_p}\right)$ is an arbitrary function, and
$$v_p = \frac{1}{\sqrt{\varepsilon\mu}} \qquad (8.6\text{-}8c)$$

is the velocity of propagation of electric and magnetic fields in space. The reason we call v_p the propagation velocity is now given.

An examination of (8.6-8) shows that **E** and **B** are constants when $t - z/v_p$ is a constant. That is, if we measure **E** and **B** at $t = 0$ and $z = 0$, for example, and then we measure **E** and **B** at a distance z, at a time $t = z/v_p$, we will find the same values for **E** and **B**. We then say that **E** and **B** propagate in space with a velocity v_p. The experimental value of v_p in a vacuum is 3×10^8 m/s, which is also the velocity of propagation of light. Recognition of the identity between the velocity of propagation of light and that of electromagnetic waves led Maxwell to be the first to assume that light is an electromagnetic-wave phenomenon, a fact later confirmed experimentally.

To provide the reader with a better physical feeling for the meaning of wave propagation, an analogy from water-wave propagation will be drawn. Assume that

$$f\!\left(t - \frac{z}{v_p}\right) = -\sin \pi\!\left(t - \frac{z}{v_p}\right)$$

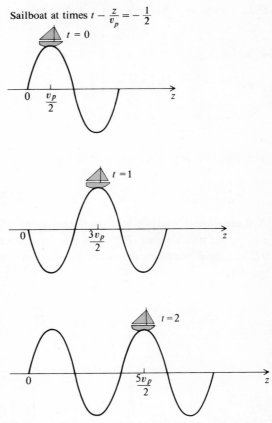

FIGURE 8.6-1
The man and the boat on the crest at $t = 0$ will stay permanently on the crest if the boat moves with velocity v_p. The man will think he is not moving. He will have the impression that the origin O is receding with a velocity $-v_p$.

In Fig. 8.6-1 visualize a person sitting in a boat on the crest of a wave at time $t = 0$ and $z = v_p/2$. If the person wants to remain on top of the wave at all times, he must travel a distance of $3v_p/2$ in 1 s. This will ensure that $t - z/v_p = -\frac{1}{2}$ for all t and z. The boat, then, must move at all times with a velocity identical with that of the water wave. If the boat stands still, $v = 0$, he will be badly rocked by the boat, which moves continuously up and down from crest to valley.

8.6-3 Energy and Power

When we say that electromagnetic fields *propagate*, we imply that electromagnetic energy varies with time and space. We will now derive some basic relations expressing these variations. Multiplying (8.6-4) by B and (8.6-5) by E yields

$$B \frac{\partial E}{\partial z} = -B \frac{\partial B}{\partial t} = -\frac{1}{2} \frac{\partial B^2}{\partial t} \qquad (8.6\text{-}9a)$$

and

$$E \frac{\partial B}{\partial z} = -\mu EJ - \mu\varepsilon E \frac{\partial E}{\partial t}$$

$$= -\mu EJ - \tfrac{1}{2}\mu\varepsilon \frac{\partial E^2}{\partial t} \qquad (8.6\text{-}9b)$$

The reader is asked to verify (Prob. 8.6-3) that by adding (8.6-9a) and (8.6-9b) we get

$$\frac{1}{\mu} \frac{\partial}{\partial z} EB = -EJ - \frac{\partial}{\partial t} \left(\frac{\varepsilon E^2}{2} + \frac{B^2}{2\mu} \right) \qquad (8.6\text{-}10)$$

A dimensional analysis will show that both $B^2/2\mu$ and $\varepsilon E^2/2$ have the dimensions of energy per unit volume, EB/μ has the dimensions of energy per unit time and area, and JE has the dimensions of energy per unit time and volume (Prob. 8.6-4). Accordingly, we define

$$W_E = \tfrac{1}{2}\varepsilon E^2 \qquad (8.6\text{-}11)$$

$$W_M = \frac{1}{2} \frac{B^2}{\mu} \qquad (8.6\text{-}12)$$

$$P = \frac{EB}{\mu} \qquad (8.6\text{-}13)$$

$$P_G = JE \qquad (8.6\text{-}14)$$

where W_E = electric energy stored in space per unit volume

W_M = magnetic energy stored in space per unit volume

P = power (energy per unit time) of propagating energy per unit area

P_G = power volume density, which either is transformed to other types of energy (a loss from the point of view of electromagnetic energy) or is transformed from other types of energy into electromagnetic energy (a source of electromagnetic energy)

Rewriting (8.6-10) in terms of these quantities, we have

$$\frac{\partial P}{\partial z} + \frac{\partial}{\partial t} (W_E + W_M) + P_G = 0 \qquad (8.6\text{-}15)$$

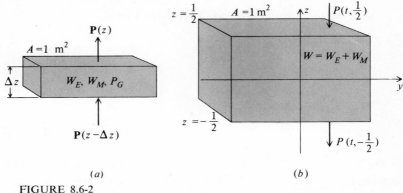

FIGURE 8.6-2
(a) $P(z - dz) - P(z) = (d/dt)(W_E + W_M) + P_G$. (b) Geometry of Example 8.6-1.

Equation (8.6-15) is the fundamental equation of electromagnetic energy propagation.

In words (refer to Fig. 8.6-2), Eq. (8.6-15) says that the amount of power entering an area encompassing a certain volume in space is equal to the rate of change of the electric and magnetic energy stored in that volume plus the amount of power gained or lost from or to other types of energy. In general, $\mathbf{P}$ is a vector whose direction is perpendicular to the plane formed by the vectors $\mathbf{E}$ and $\mathbf{B}$, and it gives the direction of propagation of electromagnetic energy. Thus

$$\mathbf{P} = \frac{1}{\mu} \mathbf{E} \times \mathbf{B} \quad (8.6\text{-}16a)$$

and it is used to find the power transmitted by a source of electromagnetic energy or received by a user of electromagnetic energy. Because of its importance it is called the *Poynting* vector after its discoverer.

EXAMPLE 8.6-1   In a certain region of space it is found that

$$E_x = E \cos \omega\left(t - \frac{z}{v_p}\right) \quad (8.6\text{-}16b)$$

$$B_y = \frac{E}{v_p} \cos \omega\left(t - \frac{z}{v_p}\right) \quad (8.6\text{-}16c)$$

and

$$J_x = 0 \quad (8.6\text{-}16d)$$

Find W_E, W_M, and P and verify (8.6-15) for a volume situated between $z = -\frac{1}{2}$ and $z = \frac{1}{2}$ and unit area in the xy plane (Fig. 8.6-2b).

SOLUTION   Using (8.6-11) to (8.6-14), we find that

$$W_E = \frac{\varepsilon E^2}{2} \cos^2 \omega\left(t - \frac{z}{v_p}\right) \qquad (8.6\text{-}17a)$$

$$W_M = \frac{E^2}{2\mu v_p{}^2} \cos^2\omega\left(t - \frac{z}{v_p}\right) \qquad (8.6\text{-}17b)$$

$$P = \frac{E^2}{\mu v_p} \cos^2\omega\left(t - \frac{z}{v_p}\right) \qquad (8.6\text{-}17c)$$

In words, (8.6-15) applied to the volume of Fig. 8.6-2b should verify that the power entering less the power leaving should equal the total power stored in the volume.

The power entering at $z = \frac{1}{2}$ less the power leaving at $z = -\frac{1}{2}$ is given, using (8.6-17c), by

$$P(t, \tfrac{1}{2}) - P(t, -\tfrac{1}{2}) = \frac{E^2}{\mu v_p}\left[\cos^2 \omega\left(t - \frac{1}{2v_p}\right) - \cos^2 \omega\left(t + \frac{1}{2v_p}\right)\right] \qquad (8.6\text{-}18)$$

The power per unit volume stored is equal to the sum of the time derivatives of (8.6-17a) and (8.6-17b).

$$\frac{\partial W_E}{\partial t} = -\frac{\varepsilon E^2 \omega}{2} \sin 2\omega\left(t - \frac{z}{v_p}\right) \qquad (8.6\text{-}19a)$$

$$\frac{\partial W_M}{\partial t} = -\frac{E^2 \omega}{2\mu v_p{}^2} \sin 2\omega\left(t - \frac{z}{v_p}\right) \qquad (8.6\text{-}19b)$$

The total power stored in this volume can be found by integrating (8.6-19a) and (8.6-19b) over the volume V.

Since the only variation is in the z direction, the total power stored will be

$$P_S = \int_{-1/2}^{1/2} \left(\frac{\partial W_E}{\partial t} + \frac{\partial W_M}{\partial t}\right) dz \qquad (8.6\text{-}19c)$$

where P_S is the total power stored. Using (8.6-19a) and (8.6-19b) in (8.6-19c), we get

$$P_S = \left(-\frac{\varepsilon E^2 \omega}{2} - \frac{E^2 \omega}{2\mu v_p{}^2}\right) \int_{-1/2}^{1/2} \sin\left(2\omega t - \frac{2\omega z}{v_p}\right) dz \qquad (8.6\text{-}19d)$$

Performing the required integration, we get

$$P_S = -\frac{E^2}{4}\left(\varepsilon v_p + \frac{1}{\mu v_p}\right)\left[\cos 2\omega\left(t - \frac{1}{2v_p}\right) - \cos 2\omega\left(t + \frac{1}{2v_p}\right)\right] \qquad (8.6\text{-}20)$$

The student is asked to verify in Prob. 8.6-5 that Eqs. (8.6-18) and (8.6-20) are identical. This verifies (8.6-15) for the volume under consideration.

////////

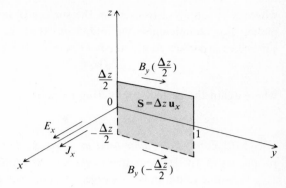

FIGURE 8.6-3
Geometry used to derive boundary conditions.

8.6-4 Boundary Conditions

In this section we use Eq. (8.6-5) to establish certain relations between the current considered as a source and the resulting electric and magnetic fields (refer to Fig. 8.6-3). The area S is a rectangle in the yz plane of unit length in the y direction and length Δz in the z direction. Integrating (8.6-5) over the area S and assuming E and J to be almost constant over Δz, we get

$$\int_{-\Delta z/2}^{\Delta z/2} \frac{\partial B}{\partial z}\, dz = \int_{-\Delta z/2}^{\Delta z/2} \left(-\mu J - \varepsilon\mu\, \frac{\partial E}{\partial t}\right) dz \approx -\Delta z\left(\mu J + \varepsilon\mu\, \frac{\partial E}{\partial t}\right)$$

$$B\!\left(\frac{\Delta z}{2}\right) - B\!\left(\frac{-\Delta z}{2}\right) = -\Delta z\left(\mu J + \varepsilon\mu\, \frac{\partial E}{\partial t}\right)$$

We further assume that as Δz approaches zero, J becomes very large, so that at all times the product

$$K_x = J\, \Delta z \qquad (8.6\text{-}21)$$

is finite. Note that **K** has the dimensions of amperes per meter. It is therefore called the *surface current*.

Letting Δz approach zero, we get

$$B(0^+) - B(0^-) = -\mu K_x \qquad (8.6\text{-}22)$$

regardless of the value of E_x. In cases where we know in advance, or decide from physical considerations, that $B_y(0^-) = 0$, (for example, $\mathbf{B} = 0$ within a perfectly conducting body) we get

$$B_y(0^+) = -\mu K_x \qquad (8.6\text{-}23a)$$

In a formal way (8.6-23a) is written

$$\mathbf{u}_z \times \mathbf{B} = \mu \mathbf{K} \qquad (8.6\text{-}23b)$$

where **K** is supposed to exist on the surface of a perfect conductor situated in the xy plane. For completeness we might add that the electric field parallel to and on the surface of a perfect conductor is also zero. We express this fact in the form

$$\mathbf{E} \times \mathbf{u}_z = 0 \qquad (8.6\text{-}24)$$

where again the perfect conducting plane is assumed parallel to the xy plane.

EXAMPLE 8.6-2 *A radar used as a range detector* We will use the propagation properties of an electromagnetic wave to determine the distance to a given target.

Assume that a pulse of current is generated on the surface of a perfect conductor situated in the xy plane at $z = 0$. Let the current be expressed by

$$K_x = P_T(t) \qquad (8.6\text{-}25)$$

where the pulse function $P_T(t)$ on the right-hand side of (8.6-25) is shown in Fig. 8.6-4a. At a distance $z = d$, there is a target made of a perfect conductor, as shown in Fig. 8.6-4b. Find the boundary conditions at the target and the time it takes the pulse to propagate in the z direction, reach the target, and return.

SOLUTION   Using (8.6-23a), we find that

$$B_y(0) = -\mu K_x = -\mu P_T(t) \qquad (8.6\text{-}26)$$

From (8.6-8) we know that

$$B_y(t, z) = -\mu P_T\!\left(t - \frac{z}{v_p}\right) \qquad (8.6\text{-}27)$$

Equation (8.6-27) tells us that the pulse will reach the target located at $z = d$ at a time $t' = d/v_p$. At $z = d$ the target is a perfect conductor, so that for $z > d$, B_y will be zero. Thus a surface current K'_x will appear in the x direction at the target. Also, from (8.6-8), we know that in the region

$$0 < z < d$$

an electric field must exist of value

$$E_x(t, z) = -v_p \mu P_T\!\left(t - \frac{z}{v_p}\right) \qquad (8.6\text{-}28)$$

But at $z = d$, we need to have zero electric field to satisfy the boundary condition (8.6-24). The only way this can be accomplished is by having another component of electric field at the point d. If we call this field E'_x, we get

$$E'_x(t, d) + E_x(t, d) = 0 \qquad (8.6\text{-}29)$$

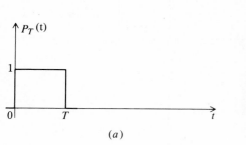

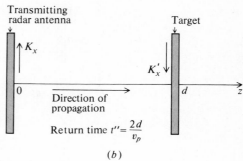

FIGURE 8.6-4

(a) Surface current of Example 8.6-2. (b) Geometry of Example 8.6-2.

Using (8.6-29), this yields

$$E_x'(t, d) = +\mu v_p P_T\left(t - \frac{d}{v_p}\right) \qquad (8.6\text{-}30)$$

This electric field will now propagate in the *negative z* direction.

Another way of saying the above is that the current K_x' on the target conductor at d will give rise to another electromagnetic field propagating in the only direction it can, i.e., the negative z direction.

It is easy to see that the *total* time taken by the pulse to reach the target, be reflected, and return to the position $z = 0$ is

$$t'' = \frac{2d}{v_p} \qquad (8.6\text{-}31)$$

Equation (8.6-31) is the fundamental relation of a radar ranging device, and the conducting sheet at $z = 0$ is called a *radar transmitting antenna*. Finally, since v_p is a known constant and t'' can be measured on an oscilloscope, the range d is readily calculated.

Figure 8.6-5 shows the electric field at $t = d/2v_p$ and $t = 3d/2v_p$ as a function of distance z. At $t = d/2v_p$,

$$E_x = -\mu v_p P_T\left(\frac{d}{2v_p} - \frac{z}{v_p}\right)$$

at $t = 3d/2v_p$,

$$E_x = +\mu v_p P_T\left(\frac{d}{2v_p} - \frac{z}{v_p}\right)$$

////////

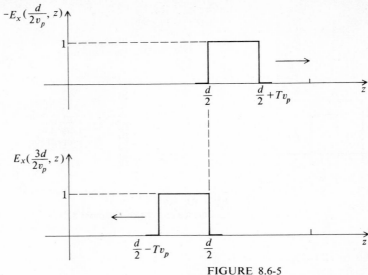

FIGURE 8.6-5
(*a*) Forward trip. (*b*) Return trip.

8.7 UNIFORM PLANE WAVES

In this section we study a particular type of electromagnetic wave called the *uniform plane wave*.

Consider a surface current in the xy plane at $z = 0$ of the form

$$K_x = K_0 \cos \omega t \qquad (8.7\text{-}1)$$

Using (8.6-23*a*), we find that

$$B_y(t, 0) = -\mu K_0 \cos \omega t \qquad (8.7\text{-}2)$$

Combining (8.7-2) with (8.6-8), we find that

$$B_y(t, z) = -\mu K_0 \cos \omega \left(t - \frac{z}{v_p} \right) \qquad (8.7\text{-}3a)$$

and

$$E_x(t, z) = -\mu v_p K_0 \cos \omega \left(t - \frac{z}{v_p} \right) \qquad (8.7\text{-}3b)$$

Equations (8.7-3) describe a uniform plane wave. Uniform plane waves are electromagnetic waves. Their characteristic features are (1) a constant-amplitude sine wave; and (2) the locus of all points having the same argument are *planes* perpendicular to the direction of propagation. Equations (8.7-3) represent uniform plane waves propagating in the z direction, and the planes of constant phase ($t - z/v_p = $ constant)

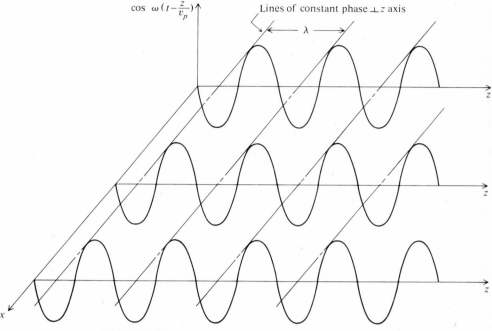

FIGURE 8.7-1
Planes of constant phase are separated by a distance λ. Note that plane waves
fill the entire space.

are planes perpendicular to the z axis. The plane waves have a characteristic radian
frequency ω and a characteristic *wave number k* defined as

$$k = \frac{\omega}{v_p} = \frac{2\pi f}{v_p} \qquad (8.7\text{-}4)$$

The ratio of the velocity v_p to the frequency f is called the *wavelength λ*. Thus

$$k = \frac{\omega}{v_p} = \frac{2\pi}{\lambda} \qquad (8.7\text{-}5)$$

In Fig. 8.7-1 it is shown that the wavelength is the distance between two constant
phase planes having equal phase. The importance of plane waves in electrical engineering applications is tremendous. It can be shown that any type of wave propagating
in space can be decomposed into a sum of plane waves; consequently, in our study of
radio receivers, antennas, microwaves, etc., we look for the response of the device due

to a plane wave and then find the total response by adding the responses to plane waves of different directions and frequencies.

8.7-1   An Engineering Application; AM Waves Radiated by an Infinite Planar Antenna

Consider a broadcast-band AM radio. The sounds we hear coming from our loud-speaker are the result of transmitting and then receiving electromagnetic waves formed by a current source proportional to the AM signal. At the transmitting antenna there is a surface current of the form

$$K_x = - [1 + f(t)]\cos \omega_c t \qquad (8.7\text{-}6)$$

If we assume the antenna to be in the xy plane, then at any distance z

$$\frac{B_y}{\mu} = \left[1 + f\left(t - \frac{z}{v_p}\right)\right]\cos \omega_c\left(t - \frac{z}{v_p}\right) \qquad (8.7\text{-}7a)$$

and
$$E_x = v_p B_y \qquad (8.7\text{-}7b)$$

Suppose we hear a single tone in our radio. A single tone corresponds to a single frequency ω_s. For this case $f(t) = A \cos \omega_s t$ and

$$\frac{B_y}{\mu} = \left[1 + A \cos \omega_s\left(t - \frac{z}{v_p}\right)\right]\cos \omega_c\left(t - \frac{z}{v_p}\right) \qquad (8.7\text{-}8)$$

Using the trigonometric identity

$$\cos a \cos b = \tfrac{1}{2}[\cos(a + b) + \cos(a - b)]$$

(8.7-8) can be written in the form

$$\frac{B_y}{\mu} = \cos \omega_c\left(t - \frac{z}{v_p}\right) + \frac{A}{2} \cos\left[(\omega_c - \omega_s)t - \frac{(\omega_c - \omega_s)z}{v_p}\right]$$

$$+ \frac{A}{2} \cos\left[(\omega_c + \omega_s)t - \frac{(\omega_c + \omega_s)z}{v_p}\right] \qquad (8.7\text{-}9)$$

Thus (8.7-8) represents the equation of three plane waves propagating in the same direction but with different frequencies, $\omega_c, \omega_c - \omega_s$ and $\omega_c + \omega_s$. In general, $f(t)$ can be represented by a fourier series

$$f(t) = \sum a_n \cos \omega_n t + \sum b_n \sin \omega_n t \qquad (8.7\text{-}10)$$

so that any AM propagating wave can be written as a sum of plane waves, all propagating in the same direction but with different frequencies.

EXAMPLE 8.7-1   An AM transmitter modulates two tones, 440 and 880 Hz, using a carrier frequency at 600 kHz. Find the frequencies and wavelengths of the component plane waves.

SOLUTION   Using (8.7-9) and (8.7-10), we recognize the existence of five frequencies and five wavelengths. With

$$f_c = 600 \text{ kHz}$$
$$f_{s1} = 440 \text{ Hz}$$
$$f_{s2} = 880 \text{ Hz}$$

we get

$$f_0 = f_c = 600,000 \text{ Hz} \qquad \lambda_0 = \frac{v_p}{f_0} = 500 \text{ m}$$

$$f_1 = f_c + f_{s1} = 600,440 \text{ Hz} \qquad \lambda_1 = \frac{v_p}{f_1} = 499.65 \text{ m}$$

$$f_2 = f_c - f_{s1} = 599,560 \text{ Hz} \qquad \lambda_2 = \frac{v_p}{f_2} = 500.35 \text{ m}$$

$$f_3 = f_c + f_{s2} = 600,880 \text{Hz} \qquad \lambda_3 = \frac{v_p}{f_3} = 499.3 \text{ m}$$

$$f_4 = f_c - f_{s2} = 599,120 \text{ Hz} \qquad \lambda_4 = \frac{v_p}{f_4} = 500.7 \text{ m}$$

Referring to Sec. (6.2), we see that both the transmitter and the receiver should be able to pass a band of at least

$$f_3 - f_4 = 1.76 \text{ kHz}$$

to accommodate all frequencies, and thus receive the signal without distortion.
////////

8.7-2 TEM Waveguides

In many cases we want to transmit electromagnetic waves in certain directions, either to avoid disturbing other transmissions or to ensure that only designated parties receive our message. One way to confine electromagnetic energy in a narrow region of space is to use *waveguides*. The simplest type of waveguide consists of two "infinite" parallel planes, usually assumed to be perfect conductors, separated by a distance a. For convenience we orient the *x axis* perpendicular to the planes, as shown in Fig. 8.7-2*a*.

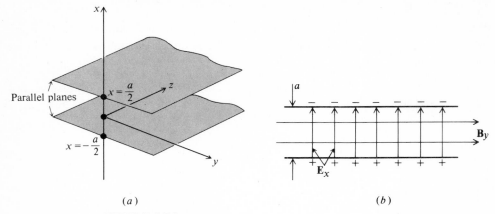

(a) (b)

FIGURE 8.7-2
(a) Geometry of TEM waveguides. (b) Cross section showing E and B fields at one instant of time.

When the electric field $\mathbf{E}$ is generated so as to be in the x direction and the magnetic flux density $\mathbf{B}$ in the y direction, the wave propagates in the z direction. Such waves are called *transverse electromagnetic waves*, often abbreviated TEM waves.

Since the differential equations (8.6-4) and (8.6-5) are valid between the plates, the electric and magnetic field vectors are

$$\mathbf{E} = Ef\left(t - \frac{z}{v_p}\right)\mathbf{u}_x \quad (8.7\text{-}11a)$$

and

$$\mathbf{B} = \frac{E}{v_p}f\left(-t\frac{z}{v_p}\right)\mathbf{u}_y \quad (8.7\text{-}11b)$$

similar to the case of electromagnetic waves in free space. The difference is that the waves represented by (8.7-11) are confined between the parallel planes. Note that since no variation in the y direction is assumed, the two planes must extend infinitely in the y direction. Otherwise our results are only approximately true; i.e., if the plates are finite in the y direction, there is a y variation on the boundary.

Figure 8.7-2b shows the electric and magnetic fields in the TEM waveguide. We know that the $\mathbf{E}$ field begins and ends on charges. In this example, the charges reside on the conducting surfaces. On the other hand, the $\mathbf{B}$ field must close on itself (there is no charge source for $\mathbf{B}$). In this example, the $\mathbf{B}$ field closes on itself at infinity.

One practical way to obtain a TEM waveguide is to *bend* the conductors on themselves, forming two concentric cylinders. Figure 8.7-3 shows such a TEM guide with the wave propagating in the z direction. Note that $\mathbf{E}$ is in the radial direction and $\mathbf{B}$ in the angular direction. Thus, the $\mathbf{E}$ field begins and ends on conducting surfaces and the $\mathbf{B}$ field closes on itself. This type of waveguide is called a *coaxial cable*.

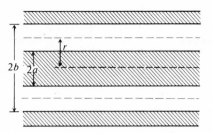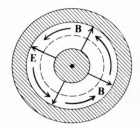

FIGURE 8.7-3
Electromagnetic fields in a coaxial cable.

8.8   TRANSMISSION LINES

As we mentioned earlier, most electrical measurements are made in terms of voltages and currents. It turns out that, in the case of TEM waveguides, the relationships between electric and magnetic fields can be transformed into relationships between voltages and currents. To do this we rewrite the field relationships

$$E_x = -E_0 f\left(t - \frac{z}{v_p}\right) \qquad (8.8\text{-}1a)$$

and

$$B_y = \frac{-E_0}{v_p} f\left(t - \frac{z}{v_p}\right) \qquad (8.8\text{-}1b)$$

We shall assume that the perfect conducting planes in Fig. 8.7-2 are separated by a distance a and are of width b in the y direction.

Because of the finite width of the plates we can not have ideal TEM waves, but let us assume that b is large compared with a wavelength, and our assumptions that we have TEM waves will then be approximately true.

To transform the field relations to voltage-current relations, we integrate E_x in the x direction. Using (8.4-7), we get

$$\phi(a) - \phi(0) = -\int_0^a E_x\,dx = aE_0 f\left(t - \frac{z}{v_p}\right) \qquad (8.8\text{-}2a)$$

Since we can measure only the difference of two potentials, we define

$$V = \phi(a) - \phi(0) \qquad (8.8\text{-}2b)$$

and thus find that the potential difference between the plates is

$$V = aE_0 f\left(t - \frac{z}{v_p}\right) \qquad \text{V} \qquad (8.8\text{-}3)$$

Due to boundary conditions at the perfect conductor, the surface current density will be [Eq. (8.6-23a)]

$$K_z = \frac{1}{\mu v_p} E_0 f\left(t - \frac{z}{v_p}\right) \qquad \text{A/m} \qquad (8.8\text{-}4)$$

The total current flowing on any of the plates is found by integrating over the width of the conductor.

$$i = \int_0^b K_z \, dy = \frac{b}{\mu v_p} E_0 f\left(t - \frac{z}{v_p}\right) \qquad \text{A} \qquad (8.8\text{-}5)$$

where use was made of (8.8-4). The characteristic resistance of this circuit is found by dividing the voltage by the current:

$$R_c = \frac{V}{i} = \frac{a\mu v_p}{b} = \frac{a}{b}\sqrt{\frac{\mu}{\varepsilon}} \qquad (8.8\text{-}6)$$

This result shows that this resistance is a constant which depends on geometry and material properties. We will call a device characterized by (8.8-3) and (8.8-5) a *transmission line*, with the *characteristic impedance* of the line given by (8.8-6).

Using this definition, we rewrite (8.8-3) and (8.8-5)

$$V = V_0 f\left(t - \frac{z}{v_p}\right) \qquad (8.8\text{-}7a)$$

$$i = \frac{V_0}{R_c} f\left(t - \frac{z}{v_p}\right) \qquad (8.8\text{-}7b)$$

where

$$V_0 = aE_0 \qquad (8.8\text{-}7c)$$

Equations (8.8-7) are the fundamental voltage-current relations of a transmission line.

8.8-1   An Engineering Application; The Matched Delay Line

In many engineering applications (Secs. 2.3 and 3.4-1) we need to delay a signal by a fixed amount of time. Consider the configuration represented in Fig. 8.8-1a. Here we see a voltage source $V(t)$ having an internal impedance R_g connected to the input of a transmission line. The output of the transmission line is terminated in a load resistor R_L equal to the characteristic impedance of the line R_c. When a transmission line is terminated in its characteristic impedance, it can be shown that the impedance seen looking into the line is also R_c. Such a transmission line is called a *matched delay line*.

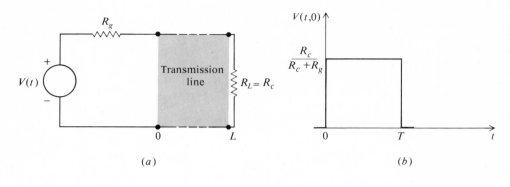

(a)   (b)

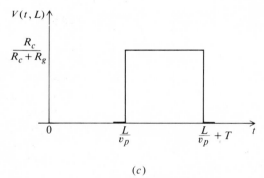

(c)

FIGURE 8.8-1
(a) Matched delay line. (b) Plot of $V(0, t)$ versus t. (c) Plot of $V(L, t)$ versus t.

Consider that $V(t)$ is a pulse of 1 V amplitude and duration T. The voltage pulse at $z = 0$ is shown in Fig. 8.8-1b. The pulse amplitude is calculated by replacing the transmission line by its characteristic impedance R_c. The pulse moves down the line with a velocity v_p, arriving at the load when $t = L/v_p$ (Fig. 8.8-1c). Thus the pulse is delayed by L/v_p.

To achieve practical time delays along with physically short lengths of cable, the delay line is constructed using materials with a high dielectric constant, i.e., low values of v_p. A typical delay line used in practice is, for example, a coaxial cable designated RG8U which has $R_c = 50\ \Omega$ and a propagation velocity of 2×10^8 m/s. It is used for delays on the order of 10^{-8} s.

At this point we mention, without going into details, that for certain applications we can use an *acoustic delay line* in which the transmitted wave is a sound (acoustic) wave instead of an electromagnetic wave. The sound wave is characterized by much lower velocities, so that shorter lengths of delay line are required. When acoustic delay lines are required by the engineering applications, we employ *piezoelectric transducers* which transform EMT waves into sound waves, and vice versa.

EXAMPLE 8.8-1 Design a matched delay line with a delay of 0.1 μs. Use a coaxial cable with $v_p = 5 \times 10^7$ m/s, and $R_c = 50\ \Omega$.

SOLUTION The delay time is

$$T_0 = \frac{L}{v_p} \qquad (8.8\text{-}8)$$

so that, to achieve $T_0 = 10^{-7}$ s, we require $L = T_0 v_p = 5 \times 10^7 \times 10^{-7} = 5.0$ m. For a matched line, we choose $R_L = R_c$. Referring to Fig. 8.8-1 and applying Eqs. (8.8-7), the voltage and current along the line are given analytically by

$$V(t, z) = \frac{R_c}{R_c + R_g} V\left(t - \frac{z}{v_p}\right) \qquad (8.8\text{-}9)$$

and

$$i(t, z) = \frac{V(t - z/v_p)}{R_c + R_g} \qquad (8.8\text{-}10)$$

where R_g is the internal resistance of the signal source. For example, if

$$V(t, 0) = P_T(t) \qquad (8.8\text{-}11a)$$

then at the output the voltage will be a pulse

$$V(t, L) = \frac{R_c}{R_c + R_g} P_T(t - T_0) \qquad (8.8\text{-}11b)$$

For the above case, see Fig. 8.8-1*b* and 8.8-1*c* for plots of $V(t, z)$ at $z = 0$ and $z = L$.
////////

8.9 RADIATION; ANTENNAS AND ANTENNA GAIN

The sources of electromagnetic waves in space are currents. The magnitude and distribution in space and time of these currents determine the magnitude and distribution of electromagnetic energy in space and time. The devices carrying these source currents are called *antennas*. If we know the antenna currents, we can calculate the electromagnetic energy everywhere in space by using Maxwell's equations and the boundary conditions between currents and electric and magnetic fields established in Sec. 8.6-4. We say that, due to the presence of these currents, the antenna *radiates* electromagnetic energy into space.

8.9-1   Antenna Characteristics

There are certain important characteristics which we associate with any antenna:

1   The spatial and temporal distribution of the average power density P_1 of electromagnetic waves radiated from an antenna.
2   The total average power W radiated by an antenna.
3   The equivalent load seen by an antenna radiating a total power W is the radiation resistance R_R defined by

$$R_R = \frac{W}{I_{RMS}^2} \qquad (8.9\text{-}1)$$

where I_{RMS} is the effective current circulating in the antenna.

4   The gain of the antenna, g, is defined as the ratio between the power density P_1 radiated by an antenna and the power density P_0 radiated by an *iso-tropic* antenna of equal total power W. An isotropic antenna is characterized by the fact that its radiated power density P_0 is uniformly distributed on the surface of a sphere of radius r at the antenna location. We have, then,

$$P_0 = \frac{W}{4\pi r^2} \qquad (8.9\text{-}2)$$

and

$$g = \frac{P_1}{P_0} = \frac{4\pi r^2 P_1}{W} \qquad (8.9\text{-}3)$$

8.9-2   The Herzian Dipole Antenna

Consider the configuration of Fig. 8.9-1. The antenna is a small rod of length $2a \ll \lambda = 2\pi v_p/\omega$ through which circulates a current

$$i = I_m \cos \omega t = \text{Re } I_m e^{j\omega t}$$

The antenna is positioned in the z direction at the center of the system of coordinates. Such an antenna is called a *herzian dipole antenna*. We will derive, using a heuristic argument, the temporal and spatial distribution of the magnetic and electric fields radiated by the antenna.

Fields and power transmitted by a herzian dipole   We first examine the reason why the small rod is called a dipole. In Sec. 8.5 we defined a dipole moment

$$p = 2aq \quad (8.5\text{-}5)$$

If the dipole changes with time, then

$$\frac{dp}{dt} = 2a \frac{dq}{dt} = 2ai \qquad (8.9\text{-}4)$$

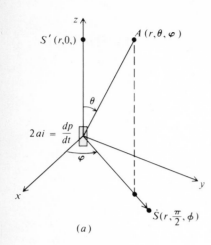

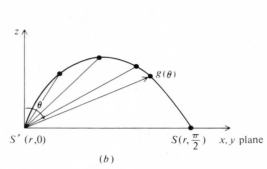

FIGURE 8.9-1
(a) A herzian dipole. (b) Gain versus θ for a herzian dipole.

Thus the effect of a current i in a small rod of length $2a$ is equivalent to the effect due to the time rate of change of a dipole. We make the following observations:

1 In Sec. 8.5 it was shown that the potential due to a dipole at a point $A(r, \theta)$ is a function of both the distance r from the dipole and the angle θ which the direction of r makes with that of the dipole moment.

2 Since we deal with time-varying fields, we expect that the fields at A should be of the form $\exp[j\omega(t - r/v_p)]$ (Sec. 8.6).

3 Since the length of the rod is very small compared with both the wavelength and the distance r at which the fields are measured, we will consider the dipole to be a point situated at the center of the coordinate axis. Consequently, the power at large distances will propagate mostly in the radial direction; i.e., the Poynting vector will be in the radial direction with **B** and **E** in a plane perpendicular to **P**.

Taking observations 1 to 3 into consideration, a rigorous mathematical analysis shows that the fields at $A(r, \theta)$ are given, using spherical coordinates, by

$$\mathbf{E} = \frac{\mu a I_m v_p}{r\lambda} \sin\theta \, \sin\left(\omega t - \frac{\omega r}{v_p}\right)\mathbf{u}_\theta \qquad (8.9\text{-}5)$$

$$\mathbf{B} = \frac{\mu a I_m}{r\lambda} \sin\theta \, \sin\left(\omega t - \frac{\omega r}{v_p}\right)\mathbf{u}_\varphi \qquad (8.9\text{-}6)$$

Using the relation $\mathbf{P} = \mathbf{E} \times \mathbf{B}/\mu$ and the concept of time average (Sec. 3.3-5), the student is asked to show (Prob. 8.9-1) that the time-average power density P_1 is given by

$$P_1 = \frac{\mu v_p}{2} \left(\frac{a I_m}{r\lambda} \sin \theta \right)^2 \qquad (8.9\text{-}7)$$

The herzian dipole is the basic element of any antenna. The average power propagated from any type of antenna can be calculated by assuming that the surface of the antenna is composed of a group of herzian dipoles. The total field at a point is then the resultant of all the fields due to all the dipoles.

Calculation of total power, radiation resistance, and gain of a herzian dipole antenna   The total power radiated by the antenna can be found by integrating P_1 over the surface of the sphere of radius r.

$$W = \int_s P_1 \, dS = \int_0^{2\pi} d\phi \int_0^{\pi} P_1 r^2 \sin \theta \, d\theta \qquad (8.9\text{-}8)$$

The student is asked to verify (Prob. 8.9-2) that the result is

$$W = \frac{\pi \mu v_p}{3} \left(\frac{2 a I_m}{\lambda} \right)^2 \qquad (8.9\text{-}9)$$

Since

$$I_{\text{rms}} = \frac{I_m}{\sqrt{2}}$$

we find using (8.9-1) that

$$R_R = \frac{W}{I_{\text{rms}}^2} = \frac{W}{I_m^2/2} = \frac{2\pi}{3} \mu v_p \left(\frac{2a}{\lambda} \right)^2 \qquad (8.9\text{-}10)$$

Finally, as can be easily verified,

$$g = \frac{4\pi r^2 P_1}{W} = \frac{3 \sin^2 \theta}{2} \qquad (8.9\text{-}11)$$

A plot of g versus θ is given in Fig. 8.9-1b. The gain is maximum on the xy plane and decreases to zero at a point on the z axis. The gain characteristic tells us that, in order to receive maximum power from the antenna, our receiver should be situated at point S. We therefore say that the dipole antenna is a *directional antenna* and has a maximum gain of 1.5.

EXAMPLE 8.9-1 *The half-wave dipole*   A very common directional antenna used in FM radio receivers is the half-wave dipole. It is formed by using two transmission lines, each of length $d/2 = \lambda/4$, open-ended and fed at the center (Fig. 8.9-2).

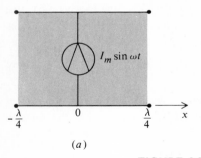

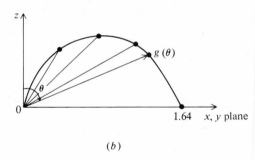

(a)   (b)

FIGURE 8.9-2
(a) A half-wave dipole antenna. (b) Gain versus θ for a half-wave dipole.

Since $d = \lambda/2$, the variation of average power with θ is more involved than for the simple dipole moment. Calculations beyond the scope of this text show that

$$P_1 = \frac{15I_m^2}{\pi r^2} \left[\frac{\cos(\pi/2 \cos \theta)}{\sin \theta} \right]^2 \quad \text{W/m}^2 \qquad (8.9\text{-}12)$$

and
$$W = 36.5I_m^2 \quad \text{W} \qquad (8.9\text{-}13)$$

Calculate the radiation resistance and the antenna gain.

SOLUTION   Combining (8.9-12) and (8.9-13) with (8.9-1) and (8.9-3), we find

$$R_R = 73 \ \Omega \qquad (8.9\text{-}14)$$

and
$$g = 1.64 \frac{\cos^2(\pi/2 \cos \theta)}{\sin^2 \theta} \qquad (8.9\text{-}15)$$

A plot of this gain is shown in Fig. 8.9-2b. We see that the gain is a maximum at $\theta = \pi/2$ and its value is 1.64.
////////

A comparison between the half-wave dipole and the herzian dipole shows that the maximum gains are not very different (1.64 versus 1.5), but the radiation resistance of a herzian dipole is much smaller than that of a half-wave dipole. For example, if $2a/\lambda = 0.2$, using the values of μ and v_p for vacuum,

$$\mu = 4\pi \times 10^{-7} \quad \text{H/m}$$

and
$$v_p = 3 \times 10^8 \quad \text{m/s}$$

we find for the herzian dipole, using (8.9-10), that

$$R_R = \frac{2\pi}{3} \ 120\pi \times (0.2)^2 = 31.5 \ \Omega$$

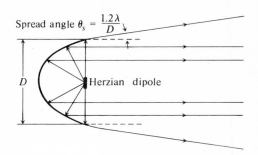

FIGURE 8.9-3
A parabolic reflector.

as compared with $R_R = 73\ \Omega$ for the half-wave dipole. This means that, in order to have the same output power, the maximum current in a herzian dipole has to be about 1.5 times larger (Prob. 8.9-5). That is why the half-wave dipole is generally used in practice, the role of the herzian dipole being that of an elementary component, from which the value of the fields at far distances can be calculated by superposition.

8.9-3 Other Types of Antenna

For most home FM radio and TV receivers a half-dipole antenna is usually sufficient. By directing the antenna toward the transmitting station so as to receive the maximum power, good reception is assured, if the station is not too far. On the other hand, for navigational and military purposes, a higher gain and directivity are required. This results in a need for special geometries. Although many types of antennas are in use, we will discuss three: the *parabolic reflector*, the *horn* and the *phased array*.

The parabolic reflector   Consider the paraboloid of revolution in Fig. 8.9-3. A herzian dipole is situated at its focal point. The waves radiated by the dipole are reflected by the paraboloid and come out such that their direction of propagation is almost parallel to the axis of revolution of the paraboloid. If the paraboloid were infinite in length, this would indeed be the case. Unfortunately, the finite dimensions of the antenna create problems at the exit, and the beam spreads out in a conical shape. A calculation of the average power distribution is beyond the scope of our text. We will give some results valid for $\pi D/\lambda \gg 1$, where D is the diameter of the exit face. For the above case we find the spread angle and the gain to be

$$\theta_s = \frac{1.2\lambda}{D} \qquad (8.9\text{-}16)$$

$$g = \left(\frac{\pi D}{\lambda}\right)^2 \qquad (8.9\text{-}17)$$

Typical values are found in Prob. 8.9-6.

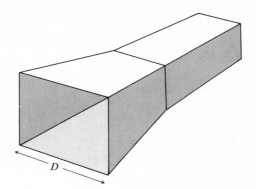

FIGURE 8.9-4
The electromagnetic horn.

Electromagnetic horn   An electromagnetic horn (Fig. 8.9-4) is a radiator designed to match waves coming from a waveguide to a large radiating aperture. The large aperture is necessary in order to have better directivity, and its shape is designed so as to give a better match between space and the waveguide system (e.g., maximum output power). Equations (8.9-16) and (8.9-17) usually hold for the horn, although they represent an upper limit rarely reached.

Phased arrays   Another arrangement which produces high directivity is that of an array of dipoles, linear or planar. The advantage of this arrangement is that it can produce a very directive radiator of electromagnetic energy whose directivity can be changed at will. That is, it produces a beam which can be scanned electronically over the horizon. The reason is that at every point in space we get electric and magnetic fields due to each dipole. Since these fields are time phasors and space vectors, at some points in space they will add so as to reinforce each other, whereas at other points in space they cancel each other, so that the average power radiated is very strong in certain directions and decays to zero at others.

EXAMPLE 8.9-2   Figure 8.9-5a represents two identical dipoles directed along the z axis and situated on the y axis at a distance $2L$ from each other. The normalized gain in the xy plane as a function of φ is found to be

$$g = \cos^2 \frac{2\pi L}{\lambda} \sin \varphi \qquad (8.9\text{-}18)$$

Plot g as a function of φ

SOLUTION   The gain is plotted in Fig. 8.9-5b for two values of L. Note that, for $L = \lambda/4$, there is only one maximum, whereas for $L = \lambda/2$, we obtain two directions of maximum. Since, in general, we prefer a directional antenna with a directivity in one direction only, $L = \lambda/4$ is more frequently used in practice.
/////////

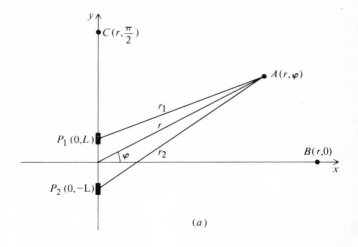

(a)

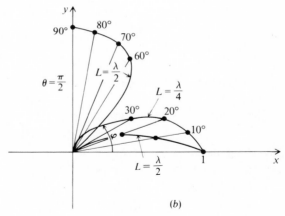

(b)

FIGURE 8.9-5
(*a*) Array of two dipoles. (*b*) Normalized gain versus φ for a two-dipole array.

If a much narrower beam is required, this can be accomplished by increasing the number of dipoles in the array. It can be shown that the angular spread of the beam is given approximately by

$$\Delta \approx \frac{\lambda}{NL} \qquad (8.9\text{-}19)$$

where N is the number of dipoles in the array. The interested student is referred to specialized texts for a more thorough analysis.

PROBLEMS

8.3-1 Show that the magnitude of $\mathbf{u}_F$ as defined by Eq. (8.3-5) is 1 and its direction is α.

8.3-2 Given $\mathbf{A} = 5 \angle 60°$ and $\mathbf{B} = 8 \angle 30°$, find $\mathbf{C} = \mathbf{A} + \mathbf{B}$.

8.3-3 Find the dot product $D = \mathbf{A} \cdot \mathbf{B}$, where $\mathbf{A}$ and $\mathbf{B}$ have the value given in Prob. 8.3-2.

8.3-4 An integration is often considered a summation of dot products.

Let
$$I = \int \mathbf{F} \cdot d\mathbf{s}$$

Assuming $\mathbf{F} = 2\mathbf{u}_x + 4\mathbf{u}_y$, integrate F from $A(0, 0)$ to $B(1, 1)$ along the lines shown in Fig. P8.3-4.

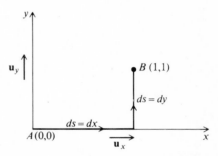

FIGURE P8.3-4

8.3-5 Integrate $\mathbf{F}$ along the straight line from A to B. Compare your answer with that of Prob. 8.3-4.

8.3-6 Given $\mathbf{C} = \mathbf{A} + \mathbf{B}$, verify the law of cosines
$$C^2 = A^2 + B^2 - 2AB \cos \theta$$
by taking the dot product $\mathbf{C} \cdot \mathbf{C}$.

8.3-7 Using the definition of vector product, show that
$$\mathbf{u}_x \times \mathbf{u}_x = 0$$

8.3-8 Find the area of the parallelogram with sides
$$\mathbf{A} = 3\mathbf{u}_x + 4\mathbf{u}_y \qquad \text{and} \qquad \mathbf{B} = 2\mathbf{u}_x + 6\mathbf{u}_y$$

8.3-9 Using the concept of area for a triangle, verify the law of sines.
$$\frac{A}{\sin \alpha} = \frac{B}{\sin \beta} = \frac{C}{\sin \gamma}$$

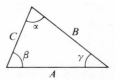

FIGURE P8.3-9.

8.4-1 An electron enters an electric field with a velocity 10^5 m/s parallel to the field direction. If it stops after 5 μs, how large is the field?

8.4-2 The field in an accelerator is given by

$$E = 2 \times 10^6 \text{ V/m}$$

How large is the potential difference between the ends of the accelerator if the accelerator is 1 cm long?

8.4-3 The number of electrons in a conductor is 10^{29} per cubic meter. If the velocity of one electron is 0.01 m/s, find the magnitude of the current density J.

8.4-4 If the area of the conductor in Prob. 8.4-3 is 1 cm², what is the value of the current i?

8.5-1 Two charged spheres have equal charges of 10^{-6} C and are kept from flying apart by two walls. What is the force the wall must withstand if the distance between them is $r = 10$ m. Note $\epsilon = 10^{-9}/36\pi$ F/m.

8.5-2 Plot the potential due to a dipole of 10^{-6} C·m as a function of θ. Assume $r = 100$ m.

8.5-3 To calculate the concentration of poles carrying two electric distribution lines, we must know the magnetic force between the two lines. It is known that the distance between the lines is 25 cm, the average current per line is 100 A, and $\mu = 4\pi \times 10^{-7}$ H/m. Find the force per unit length. If no more than 0.5 N is allowed between free-standing wires, what is the maximum distance between two adjacent poles?

8.5-4 Find the magnetic flux density due to the currents in the wires of Prob. 8.5-3 as a function of r. Plot your result.

8.6-1 Verify Eq. (8.6-7).

8.6-2 Verify Eqs. (8.6-8) by substitution in (8.6-4) and (8.6-5) with $J = 0$.

8.6-3 Verify Eq. (8.6-10).

8.6-4 Find the dimensions of W_E, W_M, P, and P_G.

8.6-5 Verify that (8.6-18) and (8.6-20) are identical.

8.6-6 The surface current in a plane at $z = 0$ is 2 A/m, and it lasts for 1 ms. Find and plot the electric fields at $z = 1$ km and $z = -1$ km. Note that the electric field at $z = 0^-$ is equal to the field at $z = 0^+$.

8.6-7 A radar receiver is situated at 10 km from the surface current of Prob. 8.6-6. How long will the pulse take to reach the receiver? Assume that the velocity of the radar wave is 3×10^8 m/s.

8.7-1 The frequency of a plane wave is 10^8 Hz. Find its period, wavelength, and wave number.

8.7-2 A radio station is amplitude modulating, on a carrier frequency of 1,500 kHz, two tones, of 3,000 Hz and 6,000 Hz. Write $E(t, z)$ as a sum of plane waves. What is the bandwidth required of the receiver?

8.7-3 A perfect conductor is used to shield a room from the radiation transmitted in Prob. 8.7-2. If the maximum value of the electric field is 100 V/m, what is the maximum value of the current induced on the conductor?

8.7-4 Why is it impossible that

$$\mathbf{E} = E_0 \cos\left(\omega t - \frac{\omega z}{v_p}\right)\mathbf{u}_y$$

be a TEM wave for the geometry of Fig. 8.7-2?

8.7-5   The electric and magnetic fields in the coaxial cable of Fig. 8.7-3 are given by

$$\mathbf{E} = \frac{E_0}{2\pi r} f\left(t - \frac{z}{v_p}\right)\mathbf{u}_r$$

$$\mathbf{B} = \frac{E_0}{2\pi r v_p} f\left(t - \frac{z}{v_p}\right)\mathbf{u}_\theta$$

(a)   Using Eq. (8.4-7), show that the potential difference between the two conductors of the cable is

$$V = \frac{E_0}{2\pi}\left(\ln\frac{a}{b}\right)f\left(t - \frac{z}{v_p}\right)$$

(b)   Find the surface current density on both conductors.

(c)   Find the total current in each conductor.

(d)   Find the characteristic impedance of the coaxial cable.

8.8-1   One element of a shift register is a 10-μs delay line. The width of the pulse is 10^{-7} s, and its height 1 V. A coaxial cable with $v_p = 2 \times 10^7$ m/s and $R_c = 50\ \Omega$ is used. The pulse generator has an output impedance of 300 Ω.

(a)   Find the length of the cable.

(b)   Find the height and width of the pulse delivered by the generator.

(c)   What should have been the output impedance of the generator for maximum power transfer?

8.9-1   Verify Eq. (8.9-7).

8.9-2   Verify Eq. (8.9-9)

8.9-3   The current in a herzian dipole $\lambda/10$ long is

$$i = 10\cos 10^8 t$$

(a)   Find and plot $\mathbf{E}$, $\mathbf{B}$, and P_1 at $r = 1,000\ \lambda$.

(b)   Find the total power W and R_R, the radiation resistance.

(c)   A transmission line feeds the dipole at maximum power. What is its characteristic impedance?

(d)   Find the magnitude of the generating voltage at the source end of the line.

8.9-4   By graphical methods find the angle of the half-wave dipole at half-power. Compare it with that of a herzian dipole.

8.9-5   A half-wave dipole and a herzian dipole $\lambda/10$ long radiate the same total power W. Find the ratio of the maximum currents in the two dipoles.

8.9-6   Design a parabolic antenna which transmits a wave at a frequency of 3×10^8 Hz with a diffraction angle of $1°$. Assume the feed is in the plane of the aperture. What will its gain be?

8.9-7   Find the values of $\mathbf{E}$, $\mathbf{B}$, and P_1 for the array of Example 8.9-2 at a point on the x axis. Assume $L = \lambda/4$.

8.9-8 It is desired to construct a beam 20° wide using a phased array. The separation of the dipoles is $L = \lambda/4$.

(a) Find N, the number of dipoles, in the array.

(b) It is known that the angular gain distribution of an array with N dipoles is

$$F(\varphi) = \frac{\sin^2(2\pi LN/\lambda)\sin\varphi}{\sin^2(2\pi L/\lambda)\sin\varphi}$$

Plot $F(\varphi)$ versus φ using N from part a.

(c) What is the ratio of $F(\varphi)$ at $\varphi = 0$ to the maximum of the next lobe?

(d) Find graphically the angle of the beam and compare it with the desired result.

REFERENCES

DURNEY, C., and C. JOHNSON: "Introduction to Modern Electromagnetics," McGraw-Hill Book Company, New York, 1969.

HAYT, JR., W. H., and G. W. HUGHES: "Introduction to Electrical Engineering," McGraw-Hill Book Company, New York, 1968.

MOORE, R. K.: "Traveling Wave Engineering," McGraw-Hill Book Company, New York, 1960.

RAMO, S., J. R. WHINNERY, and T. VANDUZER: "Fields and Waves in Communication Electronics," John Wiley & Sons, Inc., New York, 1967.

9

MATERIAL SCIENCE

INTRODUCTION

In this chapter we consider the subject of *material science*, which deals with the physical properties of solids. We shall be concerned with the transport of electromagnetic energy within a solid and its relation to the properties of that particular solid. This study will lead us to a quantitative picture of current conduction in metals and semi-conductors, which will help us to understand and predict the behavior of junction diodes, transistors, and integrated circuits.

The transport of electromagnetic energy in solids takes place principally due to two mechanisms, drift and diffusion. Before attempting to show the relation between the amount of transport and the nature of the materials in which this transport occurs, let us define what we mean by the terms drift and diffusion.

9.1 BASIC CONCEPTS; DRIFT AND DIFFUSION

A *drift* current represents a movement of charges in a certain direction due to the presence of an electric field. This is analogous to the transport of heat by convection.

To explain diffusion in a crude way, consider two cylindrical tubes having the

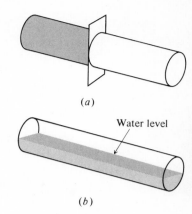

(a)

Water level

(b)

FIGURE 9.1-1
(a) Water distribution before cardboard
is removed. (b) Water distribution after
cardboard is removed.

same diameter. They are placed together, separated by a thin cardboard divider, as
shown in Fig. 9.1-1. Water is placed in the left-hand cylinder, and the center divider
is removed. Water then flows to the right-hand cylinder. The water flow ceases when
the level in both cylinders is the same; i.e., the water pressure is equalized.

In a solid-state material, electric energy *diffusion* is a process in which a large
number of charged particles are moving at random in a given volume, as shown in
Fig. 9.1-2. We assume that the probability of a particle having a velocity v_T is equal
to the probability of its having a velocity $-v_T$. Then, if we set up an arbitrary surface
in this volume, as many particles will cross this surface from the right as from the left,

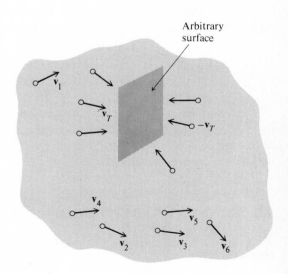

Arbitrary
surface

FIGURE 9.1-2
Particles with random velocities
average velocity across any arbitrary surface is zero.

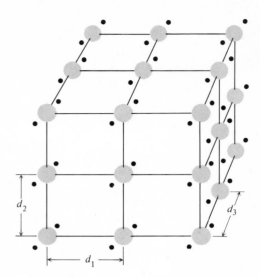

FIGURE 9.2-1
Periodic arrangement of molecules in a
crystal.

so that the net number of particles crossing the surface per unit time will be zero. On
the other hand, if by some chance there are more particles on the left side than on the
right side, more particles on the average will cross from left to right and a net amount
of electric energy will be transferred across the surface. This method of transporting
energy is called diffusion.

Diffusion is a statistical process because the velocities of the charged particles
are a random quantity. The net flow of particles across a surface is due to the existence of a net average value of velocity in that direction; i.e., if there are N particles,
each with a velocity v_i, then the average velocity is

$$v_{avg} = \frac{1}{N} \sum_{i=1}^{N} v_i$$

To find the amount of electromagnetic energy transported by drift and diffusion,
we must determine the relation between the electromagnetic forces present, the number
of charged particles, their distribution in time and space, and the nature of the materials
with which we are concerned.

9.2   CRYSTAL STRUCTURE

Most solid-state electronic devices are made from silicon, which is classified as a
crystalline solid.

A crystalline solid is characterized by the fact that it is formed of molecules arranged in a regular three-dimensional periodic structure. That is, if we connect the position of one molecule in space with the positions of its neighboring molecules, a prism will be formed with molecules at every corner. Connecting all these prisms (called *primitive cells*), we obtain the whole crystal (Fig. 9.2-1). It can be shown that the energy and concentration of electrons in a crystal is directly related to the periodicity of the crystal, the arrangement of molecules in a primitive cell, and the dimensions of the cell.

9.3 ENERGY RELATIONS IN A CRYSTAL

In this section we will derive the energy distribution of electrons due to the periodic structure of crystals. Using this distribution as a starting point, we will define three types of crystalline structure, and will end by applying Ohm's law to a solid-state material.

9.3-1 Basic Formulas

We conceive of a molecule as being composed of one or more atoms. An atom consists of a heavy, positively charged nucleus surrounded by lighter, negatively charged electrons. The forces between the nucleus and electrons are conceived as similar to those existing between the planets and the sun; i.e., the nearer an electron is to the nucleus, the greater is the force of attraction between the nucleus and the electron. As a corollary, the greater the force of attraction, the more work we have to expend to remove an electron from the neighborhood of a nucleus. We express the above in mathematical form by defining the energy of an electron as

$$W = -\frac{A}{r} \qquad (9.3\text{-}1)$$

where A = a constant depending on the charge of the nucleus

r = distance from the nucleus to the electron

Note that as the radius increases, the total energy of an electron becomes more positive, the energy being zero at infinity. Also, the more positive its energy, the farther will an electron be from the nucleus and the less will its movements depend on the nucleus. That is, at infinity the influence of the nucleus will be nil and the electron will act as if it were a free body. This means that it will move with a constant velocity in whichever direction it happens to be caused to move by an initial impulse.

In a crystal there are a large number of atoms arranged in a periodic structure. The total potential energy of an electron is the sum of the potential energies due to

FIGURE 9.3-1
Positions of electrons between two
nuclei.

all atoms. Thus an electron in a crystal will be under the influence of more than one nucleus. Referring to Fig. 9.3-1, we see that electron 1 being nearer to nucleus a, will be more attracted by it and will spend most of its time near nucleus a. The same comment holds for electron 3 and nucleus b. Electron 2, on the other hand, being equidistant from a and b, will be equally attracted by both of them and will have a hard time deciding whether it belongs to a or to b.

Now, if instead of two nuclei there were a large number of nuclei, some electrons would spend their time near a particular nucleus; other electrons would be equally attracted by two nuclei; and finally, there might be some electrons equally attracted to all the nuclei in the crystal. Clearly, the more positive their energy, the more likely it is that they will be in the last category.

9.3-2   Electron Energy Levels

We divide crystalline solids into three categories according to where the electrons of *highest positive energy* spend most of their time.

If there are a large number of electrons equally attracted to all nuclei, we call the crystalline solid a *conductor*. If there are many electrons which seem to spend their time mostly in the neighborhood of a small cluster of atoms, we call the crystal a *semiconductor*. Finally, if all electrons belonging to an atom are strongly bound to that particular atom, the crystal is an *insulator*.

From the above definitions it can be inferred that the highest-energy electrons (least negative energy) play an important role in determining the properties of a crystal. These electrons are called the *valence* electrons.

To establish more quantitative criteria, we must calculate the energies of all the electrons in a crystal. Because of the large number of electrons involved, and the fact that we cannot distinguish one electron from another, the approach will, of necessity, be statistical; i.e., we will compute the average energy.

It can be demonstrated that, due to the periodicity of the crystal, the electrons can have only a discrete range of energies, and a typical energy-band diagram is shown in Fig. 9.3-2. We call the range of possible energies which electrons can have *allowed bands*, and the range of energies which cannot occur *forbidden bands*. We will be most interested in the two highest ranges of allowed energy bands.

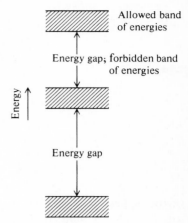

FIGURE 9.3-2
Energy-band diagram of a crystal.

The highest energy band is called the *conduction band*, and the next highest the *valence band*. The reason for these names will become obvious as we proceed. The value of the energy difference between the conduction and valence bands is called the *energy gap* W_g. Its value depends on the physical nature of a crystal and is usually given in units of *electron volts* (eV), the relation between electron volts and joules being

$$1 \text{ eV} = 1.6 \times 10^{-19} \text{J} \qquad (9.3\text{-}2)$$

It can be shown that the number of electrons per unit volume having a certain energy W is a function both of the energy of the electrons and of the temperature of the crystal. A curve showing this dependence at $0°K$ is plotted in Fig. 9.3-3. The equation of the curve is

$$n(W) = \frac{3n}{2} \sqrt{\frac{W}{W_{F0}{}^3}} \qquad (9.3\text{-}3)$$

where $n(W)$ = number of electrons per unit volume at the energy, W

n = total number of electrons per unit volume of crystal

W_{F0} = highest energy an electron can have at $0°K$

The position of W_{F0} in the energy-band diagram depends on the nature of the crystalline body. The electrons usually fill the low-energy band first, leaving the highest one empty or partially empty.

We will now show the energy-band diagrams for conductors, semiconductors, and insulators. We show in Fig. 9.3-4a the energy-band diagram of a perfect *conductor*. Note that the highest band is half empty and that W_{F0} is situated in the middle

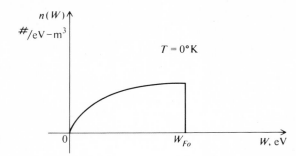

FIGURE 9.3-3
Distribution of electrons with energy at
0°K.

of the highest band. Accordingly, we say that for a conductor the conduction band
and the valence band coincide.

In a semiconductor or insulator, the conduction band is empty and the valence
band is full of electrons. W_{Fo} is situated on the top of the valence band (Fig. 9.3-4b).
The difference between a semiconductor and an insulator lies in the value of the energy
gap W_g.

For a semiconductor, W_g typically ranges from 0.5 to 1.5 eV. For an insulator,
W_g is much higher, reaching 7 to 8 eV.

It is interesting to note that Fig. 9.3-4a and b represents energy-band diagrams
for electrons at 0°K. Since the energy of electrons increases with temperature, some
electrons will appear in the conduction band of semiconductors, and even of insulators.
That is the reason why, as we shall see later, the conductivity of semiconductors and
insulators increases with temperature.

9.3-3   Conduction-band Electrons

We will now examine the characteristics of the electrons in the conduction band. As
mentioned before, these electrons behave as if they belong equally to all nuclei; i.e.,
they are equally attracted to all nuclei, and as such, they will see a constant potential
everywhere. The magnitude of the constant potential energy is W_c, which is the magnitude of the lowest energy level in the conduction band. Any additional energy pos-
sessed by an electron is then its kinetic energy. In other words, for electrons in the
conduction band, we have

$$W = W_c + \frac{mv^2}{2} \qquad (9.3\text{-}4)$$

Since the potential energy is constant, no internal forces are applied to the electrons.
Consequently, the electrons are characterized by their velocity only, and they behave

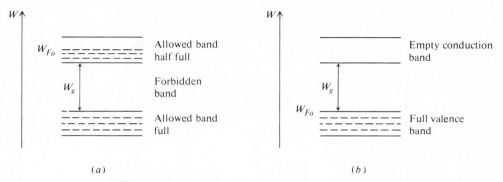

(a)   (b)

FIGURE 9.3-4
(a) Energy-band diagram for a conductor at 0°K. (b) Energy-band diagram for a semiconductor or insulator at 0°K.

as if they do not see either each other or any other material particle; i.e., they are "free electrons" (no forces act to change their path or accelerate them).

In reality, this is not completely true, since slight internal forces do exist. But to a first order of approximation, we can treat them as if they were free, and we call them *quasi-free electrons*.

If the electrons were completely free, having once acquired a certain velocity they would continue in the same direction and with the same velocity for all time. But there are certain forces which interfere with their motion. First of all, the crystal has finite dimensions, which means that near the surface periodicity does not hold, and the laws based on periodicity are no longer valid. Thus there will be forces which must cause the electrons to move back into the crystal; otherwise all electrons would have left the crystal a long time ago. Furthermore, inside the crystal the potential is not really a constant. As shown in Fig. 9.3-5a, a slight change in potential exists in the neighborhood of a nucleus. The reason for this change in potential is that, when the electron is near a nucleus, the influence of this particular nucleus is stronger than that of the other nuclei.

An analogy can be made to a rocket fired from the earth. As shown in Fig. 9.3-5b, if space were completely empty, the rocket would travel in a straight path away from the earth with a velocity v_1. However, as it moves, if it happens to pass Mars, the force of attraction due to this planet will tend to change the direction and velocity of the rocket, so that it will leave the neighborhood of Mars with a different velocity, v_2. Next, passing Jupiter, another change occurs, etc. For an observer who does not know the position and force of attraction of these planets as well as the initial velocity

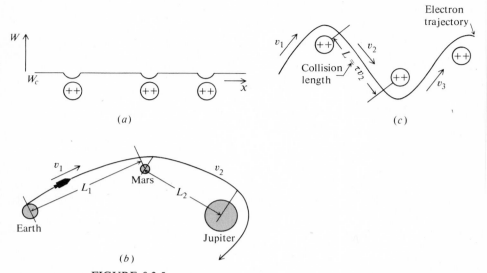

FIGURE 9.3-5
Effect of collisions on path of electrons (electron scattering). (*a*) Slight dip in potential curve near nuclei causes scattering of electrons; (*b*) effect of collisions on path of space rockets; (*c*) path of electron in crystal.

of the rocket, these changes appear to be completely erratic. Now, if instead of one rocket, we picture millions of rockets wandering in free space, all the observer sees are rockets wandering all over, suddenly changing the direction and magnitude of their velocity, without the observer being able to discern any clear pattern of their motion.

In a crystal there are about 10^{30} free electrons per cubic meter which wander freely in the "vast empty spaces" which exist (for them) between the fixed position of the atoms. In the same way, as the rockets wander in the empty vast spaces of the universe, either remaining in the vicinity of a planet if they do not have enough energy, or in the solar system if they have more energy, finally escaping into the vast interstellar or intergalactic space if they have enough energy to escape the solar system, so do the electrons wander in a crystal, being either trapped in the orbit of an atom if they do not have enough energy, or having only their velocity changed if they have higher energy, or finally leaving the crystal if they possess a very high energy. In summary, then, as shown in Fig. 9.3-5*a* and *c*, this slight change in potential causes the electrons suddenly to change their momentum (direction and magnitude of velocity). This phenomenon of sudden change in momentum is analogous to a series of collisions between electrons and atoms. This process is commonly called *scattering*.

If we were able to see an electron, we would be able to follow it in its peregrination and thus trace a path of its trajectory in space. Since there are so many of them and we cannot distinguish one electron from another, we are obliged to apply an averaging approach to their behavior. We do that by defining a parameter which will characterize this collision process. The parameter is the *collision time* τ, and it represents the average time between *two collisions* of an electron. It is obvious that τ is a parameter which will depend on the energy of the electron and the geometry and physical characteristics of the crystal.

It turns out that it is sometimes better to characterize a *collision length L* as the average distance the electron travels between two collisions. The collision length and collision time are related by

$$L = v\tau \qquad (9.3\text{-}5)$$

because we assume that between two collisions no force is applied to the electron, so that its velocity is a constant.

9.3-4   Ohm's Law; Conductivity

When we study the properties of solids, we are interested in parameters which are immediately useful for our needs and also easily measurable. One of these parameters, which is of tremendous value, both in application and in understanding the characteristics of crystalline solids, is the *conductivity*. This is a parameter which relates the electric field applied to a solid to the current density which results. The relation is called *Ohm's law*, and is given by

$$J = \sigma E \qquad (9.3\text{-}6)$$

where J = current density, A/m^2
E = electric field, V/m
σ = conductivity, $\mho$/m
In Sec. 8.4 we defined current density as

$$J = qnv \qquad (8.4\text{-}13)$$

where qn represents the number of charges per unit volume and v is their average velocity. Experimentally, we find that, in the absence of an electric field, the current is zero. This implies that with no electric field present, the average velocity of the charges is zero. Since we have to apply an electric field to observe a current flow, it is obvious that the average velocity of charges in a solid depends on the field. The reason for this behavior is as follows:

In Fig. 9.3-6a we plot the variation of velocity of an electron in a collision-free region. Due to the presence of the electric field, the velocity tends to increase without limit.

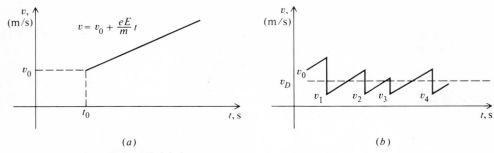

(a)   (b)

FIGURE 9.3-6
(a) Electron velocity in a collisionless region. (b) Electron velocity changes suddenly because of collisions. An average velocity V_D exists in the steady state. Note that the average velocity depends on the average time between collisions and on the magnitude of the electric field.

In Fig. 9.3-6b we plot the variation of velocity of an electron in a crystalline solid. Because of the presence of the electric field, it will tend to grow in the direction of the field. However, because of collisions, its velocity will suffer sudden changes in magnitude and direction so that in the steady state an average velocity in that direction will exist.

We call this average velocity the *drift velocity* v_D. Note that in the absence of the field, there is no bias in the behavior of the electron and the drift velocity is zero.

The magnitude of the drift velocity, as expected, is proportional to the magnitude of the applied electric field:

$$v_D = \mu E \qquad (9.3\text{-}7)$$

where μ is a constant of proportionality called the *mobility*. The mobility of a conducting material is a function of the collision time τ and the internal forces in the crystal. Its dimensions are $m^2/V\cdot s$.

If we combine (8.4-13) with (9.3-6) and (9.3-7), replacing q by e since we deal exclusively with electron charges, we find that

$$\sigma = en\mu \qquad (9.3\text{-}8)$$

Thus conductivity is a function of the concentration of quasi-free electrons in a conductor, the geometric structure of the crystal, and the nature of its molecules.

Table 9.3-1 gives some typical values for metal conductors at room temperature ($300°K$).

Table 9.3-1

Metal	Conductivity σ, $\mho/m$
Aluminum	3.5×10^7
Copper	5.9×10^7
Iron	10^7

Before ending this section, it is interesting to mention that *resistivity*, which is defined by

$$\rho = \frac{1}{\sigma} \qquad \Omega \cdot m$$

is a parameter as important as *conductivity*. Both parameters are used indiscriminately in engineering problems.

9.4 SEMICONDUCTORS

The preceding analysis holds true for any crystal. In this section we extend our discussion to the case of semiconductors, which are the basic elements of most devices used in electronic technology.

9.4-1 Intrinsic Semiconductors

As mentioned in Sec. 9.3, the difference between a conductor and a semiconductor lies in the fact that at temperatures other than $0°K$, the valence and conduction bands coincide for a conductor, and almost all valence electrons contribute to the drift current, whereas in a semiconductor, because of the energy gap between valence and conduction bands, only some very high-energy electrons will be in the conduction band, the rest being strongly bound to the neighboring atoms. Due to this disparity between the valence electrons, local disturbances appear in semiconductors which create a movement of electrons in the valence band.

Let us be somewhat more explicit. Consider silicon, often used as a semiconductor. Silicon has a valence of 4 (that is, every atom of silicon contributes four electrons to the valence band), and the valence electrons are strongly bound to their atoms, so that they spend most of their time between neighboring atoms.

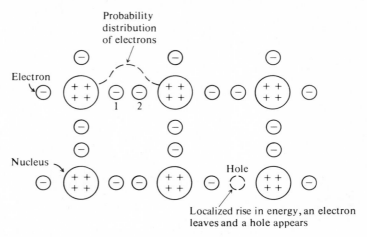

Two-dimensional arrangement of silicon atoms

FIGURE 9.4-1
An intrinsic semiconductor.

Figure 9.4-1 is a diagram showing the relative position of atoms and valence electrons in a silicon crystal. The probability of electron 1 or 2 being any place between the two atoms is given by the dotted curve in Fig. 9.4-1. If by chance an electron gains some energy and moves into the conduction band, i.e., it moves far enough away from the nucleus holding it so that it can be anywhere with equal likelihood, a localized change in potential occurs which creates a local force capable of attracting a neighboring electron. This, in turn, creates a disturbance in the region where the electron came from, which might attract another electron, etc. In this way, a new type of electron motion is created in the valence region. To differentiate it from the movement of high-energy electrons in the conduction band, we say that it is a movement of the lack of electrons, i.e., of *holes*. If the electrons move from left to right, this is the same as if the holes move from right to left. It turns out that in a formal way we can assign to the holes an *effective mass* and *mobility* and treat them as if they were real particles of positive mass and positive charge. We therefore say that the current in a semiconductor is *bipolar*; i.e., *the total current is composed of two currrents, one consisting of electrons in the conduction band, and one consisting of holes in the valence band.* Of course, because of different conditions, both the effective mass and the mobility will be different for holes and electrons, although the charge will be the same. We then write for the conductivity of a semiconductor

$$\sigma = e(\mu_e n + \mu_h p) \qquad (9.4\text{-}1)$$

where μ_e = mobility of an electron, m²/V·s

μ_h = mobility of a hole, m²/V·s

n = number of electrons in conduction band per cubic meter

p = number of holes in valence band per cubic meter

Since for every electron in the conduction band a hole remains in the valence band, and since charge neutrality is a characteristic of any material body, the number of holes and electrons will be equal. We call a semiconductor with $n = p = n_i$ an *intrinsic semiconductor*.

Typical mobilities and effective masses for some semiconductor materials are given in Table 9.4-1.

EXAMPLE 9.4-1 Find the conductivity of an intrinsic silicon semiconductor.

SOLUTION From Table 9.4-1 we have

$$\mu_e = 0.135 \text{ m}^2/\text{V·s}$$
$$\mu_h = 0.048 \text{ m}^2/\text{V·s}$$

The concentration of free electrons in an intrinsic semiconductor is a function of temperature and energy gap, and is given approximately by

$$n_i = 10^{21.7} T^{3/2} \times 10^{-2,500 W_g/T} \qquad \text{per cubic meter} \qquad (9.4\text{-}2)$$

where T = temperature, °K

W_g = energy gap, eV

For silicon at room temperature,

$$T = 300°\text{K}$$
$$W_g = 1.2 \text{ eV}$$

so that

$$n_i = 10^{15.5} \text{ per cubic meter}$$

Using (9.4-1), with $n = p = n_i$

$$\sigma = n_i e(\mu_e + \mu_h)$$

Table 9.4-1

	μ_e, m²/V·s	μ_h, m²/V·s	m_e, kg	m_h, kg
Si	0.135	0.048	9×10^{-31}	4.5×10^{-31}
Ge	0.39	0.19	15×10^{-31}	2.6×10^{-31}
InSb	7.8	0.075	0.12×10^{-31}	5.5×10^{-31}
GaAs	0.85	0.04	0.70×10^{-31}	4.6×10^{-31}

Substituting numerical values, we find that

$$\sigma = 10^{15.5} \times 1.6 \times 10^{-19} \times 0.183 \approx 10^{-4}\ \mho/m$$

////////

9.4-2 Impurity Doping; Donors

We saw in Example 9.4-1 that the conductivity of a typical semiconductor like silicon is about $10^{-4}\ \mho/m$. A comparison with a typical conductor like copper will show a ratio of conductivities on the order of 10^{-11} (Table 9.3-1). One way to improve this ratio would be to increase the number of free electrons or holes present. The method used is called *impurity doping*.

Let us consider a typical arrangement of valence electrons in a four-valence semiconductor (Fig. 9.4-1). As we mentioned previously, the electrons are strongly bound to the atoms, and their freedom of movement is limited to a region in the neighborhood of a group of atoms. Occasionally, an electron receives an extra amount of energy which enables it to escape the attraction of a particular group of atoms. In this case its field of motion is expanded to include the entire crystal. We called such an electron a *quasi-free electron*. In terms of energy bands we say that the electron passed from the valence band into the conduction band, leaving behind a hole in the valence band. This process depends on temperature: the higher the temperature of the crystal, the more free electrons will exist in a given volume. However, as seen from Example 9.4-1, their number is very small, and this results in a low conductivity.

Suppose now that we replace one of the four-valence atoms by a five-valence atom. As seen in Fig. 9.4-2, there will be one electron which is less bound to the atom. By this we mean that the forces of attraction on this particular electron will be less localized than for the other electrons. An analogy could be made to the position of a spaceship equally and weakly attracted to a group of planets in the solar system. The slightest boost, depending on its direction, might bring it into the orbit of one of the planets or let it escape completely into outer space. The reason for the peculiar behavior of the fifth electron can be found by studying the electrostatic forces at work in the crystal.

In the doping process, the number of *impurity atoms* introduced is much smaller than that of the host medium. For example, the number of silicon atoms is about 10^{29} per cubic meter, and those of the often used five-valence phosphorus about 10^{24} per cubic meter. On the average, then, the phosphorus atoms, being so few, are at a great distance from each other. Let us call the combination of a phosphorus nucleus and four of its electrons an *ion*. Each phosphorus ion will have a positive charge and will be situated far from any other ion in a "sea" of neutral silicon atoms.

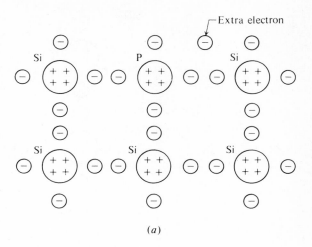

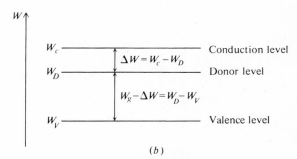

FIGURE 9.4-2
Crystal structure and energy-band diagram of extrinsic semiconductor with donor impurity. (*a*) Crystal structure; (*b*) energy-band diagram.

Consequently, we can consider the extra electron as being situated in a space where the only forces of attraction come from these far-distanced ions. Moreover, these forces are applied in a material medium, silicon, which further diminishes their strength.

Summarizing, then, since the electric forces are inversely proportional to the square of the distance and to the dielectric constant of the medium (Sec. 8.4), the internal forces applied to the extra electron will be very weak. Consequently, the slightest addition of energy, an increase in temperature for example, will suffice to make them free electrons.

We express the above situation symbolically by putting an extra level of energy in our energy diagram as shown in Fig. 9.4-2*b*, and call this level a *donor level*, because electrons will be *donated* from this level to the conduction level.

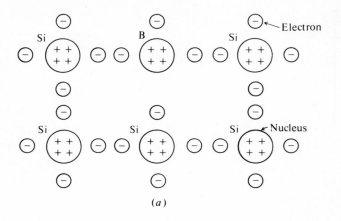

(a)

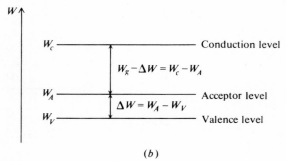

(b)

FIGURE 9.4-3
Crystal structure and energy-band diagram of extrinsic semiconductor with acceptor impurity. (a) Crystal structure; (b) energy-band diagram.

9.4-3 Impurity Doping; Acceptors

There is another way by which we can increase the conductivity of a semiconductor.

This method consists in doping a semiconductor with three valence atoms, as shown in Fig. 9.4-3. (Boron is a commonly used three-valence material.) Due to doping, the original potential distribution in the crystal is disturbed, because additional holes are created in the vicinity of the boron atoms. That is, since one electron is missing in the bond between the boron atom and the neighboring silicon atoms, the attractive forces will be stronger at the hole position (missing electron position), thereby increasing the likelihood of attracting an electron to that particular location. There will then be two kinds of holes. The first kind is due to the creation of free electrons, and the second kind is due to impurity doping. The number of holes will thus increase, and hence, the conductivity.

Because the neighborhood of the boron atom is a region more likely to attract an electron, we call the boron atom an *acceptor*. Because of neutrality conditions, since we consider the hole a positive-charged particle, we will consider the rest of the boron atom, the acceptor, to be negatively charged. It is as if we took the empty space in Fig. 9.4-3a and created from it two particles, one positive (the *hole*) and one negative (the *electron*). We put the electron in this space, thereby creating a four-valence negatively charged element, called an *acceptor ion*, and we let the hole wander around as if it were a free particle. As shown in Fig. 9.4-3b, we represent symbolically this new source of holes by introducing a new level in the energy-gap region, called the *acceptor level*. This level is slightly above the valence level to signify that only a slight amount of energy is required to bring electrons from the valence level into the acceptor level, thus creating more holes in the valence band.

9.4-4 Hole-Electron Relations; Extrinsic Semiconductors

Semiconductors with an excess of electrons or holes are called *extrinsic semiconductors*. The number of free electrons increases with the number of donors, and the number of holes with the number of acceptors. It can be shown by statistical analysis that no matter what the number n of electrons is, or the number p of holes, their product is always a *constant* equal to the square of the number of electrons or holes in an intrinsic semiconductor. We will have, then,

$$np = n_i{}^2 \qquad (9.4\text{-}3)$$

where n_i represents the number of free electrons in the intrinsic semiconductor. Equation (9.4-3) holds for both donor and acceptor extrinsic semiconductors, the difference being that in the donor case there are more electrons, and in the acceptor case more holes.

A semiconductor crystal is a neutral body. As such, the number of positive and negative charges should be the same. If we call the number of positive donor ions N_D, the number of free electrons n_D, and that of holes p_D, then charge neutrality for a donor semiconductor requires that

$$n_D = p_D + N_D \qquad (9.4\text{-}4)$$

Similarly, with N_A the number of negative acceptor ions and p_A and n_A that of holes and electrons, respectively, charge neutrality in an acceptor semiconductor requires that

$$p_A = n_A + N_A \qquad (9.4\text{-}5)$$

Since at room temperature the number of electrons in a donor impurity semiconductor exceeds by far the number of holes (about 10^4 electrons to one hole), we will call the electrons *majority carriers* and the holes *minority carriers*. Then, since $n_D \gg p_D$, (9.4-4) becomes

$$n_D \approx N_D \qquad (9.4\text{-}6a)$$

$$p_D \approx \frac{n_i^2}{N_D} \qquad (9.4\text{-}6b)$$

For an acceptor impurity semiconductor, the reverse is true, with

$$p_A \approx N_A \qquad (9.4\text{-}7a)$$

$$n_A \approx \frac{n_i^2}{N_A} \qquad (9.4\text{-}7b)$$

We conclude this section by mentioning that a donor impurity semiconductor is called an *n-type* semiconductor, and an acceptor impurity semiconductor is called a *p-type* semiconductor.

9.4-5   Diffusion Current

The average number of holes and electrons in a semiconductor depends only on temperature. Thus the holes and electrons are equally distributed in space, and in the absence of an electric field, their average velocity is zero and no current flows. We say that they are in *thermal equilibrium.*

Suppose that something happens which destroys this equilibrium, e.g., a sudden rise in temperature, a high localized electric field, etc., that is, any process which might create additional electron-hole pairs in a particular region of the crystal, or possibly in the entire crystal.

In this case the thermal equilibrium, as represented by Eqs. (9.4-3) to (9.4-7), is disturbed, and a *diffusion current* will result which attempts to restore this equilibrium, i.e., cause the additional hole-electron pairs to disappear. Physically, what happens is that an electron is trapped by a positive ion, thus forming a neutral atom. We call this phenomenon a hole-electron *recombination.*

This current will flow from a region of high carrier concentration to one of low carrier concentration and will be proportional to the rate of change of carrier concentration per unit length (*gradient*). It is common to assume that the concentration of holes and electrons varies linearly across the crystal, as shown in Fig. 9.4-4. Under this assumption the hole and electron current densities are

$$J_p(x) = e D_p \frac{p(0) - p_0}{L_p} \qquad (9.4\text{-}8a)$$

and

$$J_n(x) = e D_n \frac{n(0) - n_0}{L_n} \qquad (9.4\text{-}8b)$$

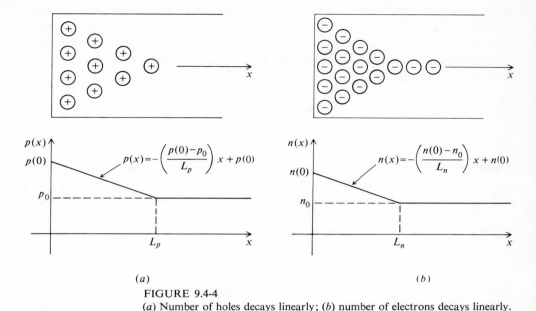

FIGURE 9.4-4

(a) Number of holes decays linearly; (b) number of electrons decays linearly.

where $J_p(x)$, $J_n(x)$ = current densities of holes and electrons

D_p, D_n = proportionality constants, called *diffusion constants*

p_0, n_0 = equilibrium concentration of holes and electrons

L_p, L_n = *diffusion lengths* of holes and electrons

Physically, L_p represents the average distance a hole travels before recombining with an electron, whereas L_n is the average distance traveled by an electron before it recombines with a hole. L_p, L_n, D_p, and D_n depend on the geometry of the crystal and the nature of its molecules, as well as the nature and concentration of the doping material.

Combining (9.4-8a) and (9.4-8b), we find the total diffusion current.

$$J(x) = e\left[D_p \frac{p(0) - p_0}{L_p} + D_n \frac{n(0) - n_0}{L_n} \right] \qquad (9.4-9)$$

Diffusion current; a minority-carrier current   In this section we will show that the diffusion current is due mostly to the change in equilibrium of the minority carriers. Let us assume an *n*-type semiconductor with $n_0 = 10^{23}$ per cubic meter and $p_0 = 10^{16}$ per cubic meter. Next, assume that, due to a sudden local rise in temperature, 10^{16} per cubic meter additional electron-hole pairs are created. The number of holes is doubled, but there is very little change in the number of electrons, about 1 in 10^7 $\{p(0) = 2 \times 10^{16}, n(0) = 10^{23} + 10^{16}\}$. Since the equilibrium will be restored by electron-hole combination, a larger percentage of holes will disappear per unit length than electrons and, therefore, the hole current $J_p(x)$ will greatly exceed the electron current $J_n(x)$.

Hence,

$$J(x) \approx J_p(x) = +e\,\frac{D_p}{L_p}\,[p(0) - p_0] \qquad (9.4\text{-}10)$$

Parameters in diffusion processes   The parameters D and L defined previously are a function of the nature and geometry of the semiconductor crystal. We now define certain relations from which we can find these parameters experimentally.

There is a relation between the diffusion constant D and the mobility μ called *Einstein's relation*. It is given by (Sec. 5.1)

$$V_T = \frac{kT}{q} = \frac{D}{\mu} \qquad (9.4\text{-}11)$$

where V_T is called the *thermal voltage*, with a value at room temperature of about 0.025 V. The mobility of a material is relatively easy to measure in the laboratory. Knowing V_T, the diffusion constant can thus be found from Einstein's relation and the measured value of mobility.

Next, since motion is related to time, we will define the *relaxation times* τ_p and τ_n as the average time that a hole or an electron travels before it recombines with an electron or hole. Since all three, diffusion constant, diffusion length, and relaxation time, are connected with the diffusion current in a semiconductor, we might suspect that a relation must exist between them. Indeed, it can be shown that such a relation exists, and it is given by

$$L_p = \sqrt{D_p \tau_p} \qquad (9.4\text{-}12a)$$

$$L_n = \sqrt{D_n \tau_n} \qquad (9.4\text{-}12b)$$

for the hole and electron parameters, respectively. Since μ and τ are much easier to measure in practice, the usual procedure is to determine μ and τ experimentally and then find D and L using (9.4-11) and (9.4-12).

9.5   *pn* JUNCTIONS

One of the most useful engineering applications of semiconductors is that of diode rectifiers and transistor amplifiers. The basic mechanism of these devices is the *pn junction*.

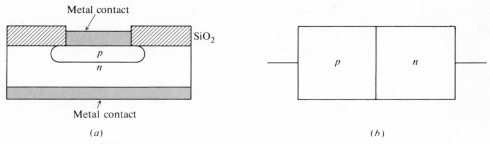

(a)   (b)

FIGURE 9.5-1
Semiconductor sample forming a *pn* junction. (*a*) *pn* junction; (*b*) schematic one-dimensional representation.

As shown in Fig. 9.5-1, *pn* junctions are samples of semiconductor material which, by selective doping, can carry both *p* and *n* majority carriers in adjacent areas. This type of device is called a *diode*.

In the following sections we will present the basic theory of such devices.

9.5-1   Potential Barrier and Depletion Width

An important characteristic of *pn* junctions which determines their behavior as rectifiers is the appearance of a voltage at the junction between the *p* and *n* regions. This voltage is called the *potential barrier*. The reason for the appearance of a potential barrier is as follows: As shown in Fig. 9.5-2*a*, at the junction, on the *p* side, there is a high concentration of holes, p_{p0}. On the other hand, on the *n* side, there is a low concentration of holes, p_{n0}. Consequently, a diffusion current will flow from the *p* side to the *n* side. For the same reason electrons will flow from the *n* side of the junction to the *p* side. These holes and electrons will recombine, leaving a distribution of fixed negative ions N_A on the *p* side of the junction and a distribution of fixed positive ions N_D on the *n* side of the junction. This distribution is called a *depleted layer of fixed charges*.

As shown in Fig. 9.5-2*a* and *b*, these fixed charges will give rise to an electric field which will oppose the carrier flow by creating a drift current in the opposite direction. At equilibrium the two currents will be equal and the total current is zero. Since potential is the integral of electric field, a voltage will appear across the junction, as shown in Fig. 9.5-2*b*. This voltage is called the *potential barrier*, and its value is

$$V_B = V_T \ln \frac{p_{p0}}{p_{n0}} = V_T \ln \frac{N_A N_D}{n_i^{\,2}} \qquad (9.5\text{-}1)$$

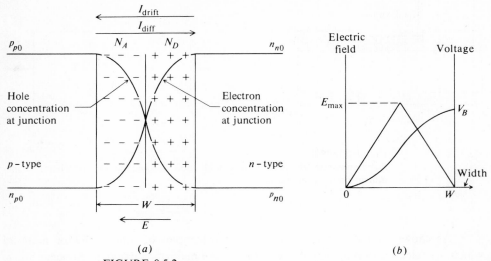

(a) (b)

FIGURE 9.5-2
Distribution of charges, electric field, and potential at a *pn* junction. (*a*) Charge distribution; (*b*) electric field and potential across junction.

where V_T = thermal potential

$N_A = p_{p0}$, the equilibrium concentration of holes on the *p* side

$\dfrac{n_i^2}{N_D} = p_{n0}$, the equilibrium concentration of holes on the *n* side

The width of the depletion layer depends on the potential barrier and on the carrier concentration. It is important because it determines the characteristics of the junction as a diode rectifier. Its value for a constant charge distribution is

$$W = \sqrt{\frac{2\varepsilon V_B}{e}\left(\frac{1}{N_A}+\frac{1}{N_D}\right)} \qquad (9.5\text{-}2)$$

where ε is the dielectric constant of the medium.

9.5-2   *pn* Junctions with Reverse Bias

Assume that, as shown in Fig. 9.5-3*a*, we apply a voltage V across the device. If we neglect the resistance of the semiconductor material, we find that the voltage V appears across the junction. Referring to Fig. 9.5-2*b*, we see that, with no voltage applied, the potential across the junction is V_B. In Fig. 9.5-3*b* we note that the voltage V increases

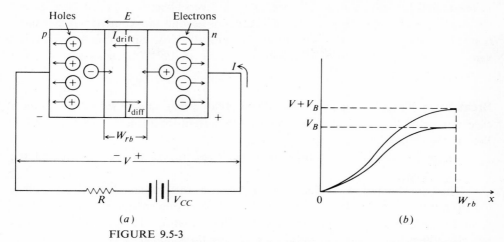

FIGURE 9.5-3
(*a*) Reverse-bias diagram. Holes and electrons move farther away from junction, thus increasing depletion layer from W to W_{rb}. I_{drift} increases, and I_{diff} decreases. (*b*) Potential distribution with reverse bias.

the junction potential from V_B to $V + V_B$. We call the voltage V which increases the barrier potential a *reverse-bias voltage*.

The voltage V will cause a current I to flow in the direction shown in Fig. 9.5-3*a*. Our objective in this section is to find the relation between V and I.

As mentioned before, two kinds of currents will flow through the junction, a drift current and a diffusion current. In our analysis we will consider only the hole flow. The electron flow is similar, but in the reverse direction.

The drift current is due to the presence of an electric field which forces positive charges to flow in the direction of the field. Referring to Fig. 9.5-3*a*, the drift current is represented by a flow of holes from the n to the p side across the junction; i.e., it is a flow of *minority carriers*. The resulting increase in the potential barrier results in an increase in the electric field across the junction. Thus the drift current increases. However, since the number of charges is small (holes are a minority in the n-type material), the drift currents, although larger, will remain relatively small.

The diffusion current is due to the presence of a gradient in the distribution of charges. Since there are more positive charges in the p side than in the n side, it will always represent a flow of *majority carriers*; holes flow from the p side to the n side, and electrons flow from the n side to the p side. As the potential barrier is increased, so will the width of the depletion layer from W to W_{rb} [Eq. (9.5-2) and Fig. 9.5-3]. An increase in the width of the depletion layer will result in a decrease in the gradient, and with it a decrease in the value of the diffusion current. Since the drift current increases and the diffusion current decreases, a reverse-bias current will flow across the junction, as shown in Fig. 9.5-3*a*. Calculations beyond the scope of this text show that the value of the reverse-biased current is about 10^{-12} A. Since this is a very small value, we usually consider a reverse-biased diode to be an *open circuit*; i.e., the impedance is infinite.

Breakdown voltage   Figure 9.5-4 shows that when the reverse-bias voltage exceeds a value V_{BR}, there is a large increase in current for a small change in voltage. We call the voltage V_{BR} the *breakdown voltage*.

There are two kinds of breakdown voltages, the zener breakdown and the avalanche breakdown.

The zener breakdown is due to the fact that as the voltage V increases, so does the electric field. When the force due to this field is strong enough to bring electrons from the valence to the conduction band, thus creating electron-hole pairs, this increases the drift current tremendously with very little change in voltage. The value of the zener voltage is usually less than about 7 V.

The avalanche breakdown occurs with diodes designed to sustain much larger reverse-bias voltages: the value of the avalanche breakdown voltage can reach as high as 2,000 V. The cause of the breakdown is as follows: As the voltage increases, the velocity, and with it the energy of the drift electrons, increases. As an electron traverses the diode, it collides with the atoms therein. If its energy is very high, it might succeed in raising the energy of another electron from the valence to the conduction band. As these two electrons travel they might raise other electrons, and so forth, creating an *avalanche*. The value of the avalanche-breakdown voltage depends on the doping on both sides of the junction. For very high breakdown voltages one side is usually much more lightly doped than the other.

9.5-3   *pn* Junctions with Forward Bias

Some useful relations   We now consider the case where the positive terminal of the voltage source is connected to the *p* side of the *pn* junction (Fig. 9.5-5*a*). This produces a voltage V which lowers the potential barrier to $V_B - V$ (Fig. 9.5-5*b*). Thus electrons and holes with energy lower than V_B can more easily diffuse across the junction, increasing the diffusion current, while the drift current changes by only a small amount. Consequently, I_{diff} becomes relatively large, so that the total current $I = I_{\text{diff}} - I_{\text{drift}}$ is mainly a diffusion current. Since the supply of electrons from the *n* side and of holes from the *p* side is very large (they are majority carriers there), the total current will be much larger than in the previous case of a reverse-biased diode.

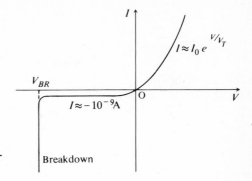

FIGURE 9.5-4
Graph of the vi relation of a semiconductor diode. (Not to scale.)

Let us attempt a quantitative evaluation of this current. We will consider only the diffusion of holes; the diffusion of electrons is similar, but in the opposite direction. Refer to Fig. 9.5-5c. The voltage across the depletion layer is $V_B - V$. Since a large quantity of holes will now diffuse into the n region, the concentration of holes in the n side of the depletion layer near the junction will be much larger than p_{no}, the thermal equilibrium concentration. If we call the concentration of holes in the n region near the junction $p_n(0)$ and assume a relation similar to (9.5-1), we find that

$$V_B - V = V_T \ln \frac{p_{po}}{p_n(0)} \qquad (9.5\text{-}3a)$$

Eliminating V_B by substituting (9.5-1) into (9.5-3a) yields

$$V = V_T \ln \frac{p_{po}}{p_{no}} - V_T \ln \frac{p_{po}}{p_n(0)} = V_T \ln \frac{p_n(0)}{p_{no}} \qquad (9.5\text{-}3b)$$

Solving for $p_n(0)$ yields

$$p_n(0) = p_{no} \, e^{V/V_T} \qquad (9.5\text{-}4)$$

As can be seen from (9.5-4) and Fig. 9.5-5c, the number of holes in the n side of the junction $p_n(0)$ will be much larger than the number of holes deep in the body of the sample where it is p_{no}. This departure from equilibrium will give rise to a diffusion current as holes try to reach a new state of equilibrium. As the holes spread toward the region of less concentration, they combine with electrons and disappear, so that in the end, if the supply were limited, the concentration of holes would be that at thermal equilibrium, p_{no}. However, as the holes from the boundary diffuse, new holes are continuously supplied from the p side. Thus thermal equilibrium is never reached, and a continuous diffusion current is maintained. To complete the cycle, we note that the depletion of holes from the p region is compensated by holes supplied by the

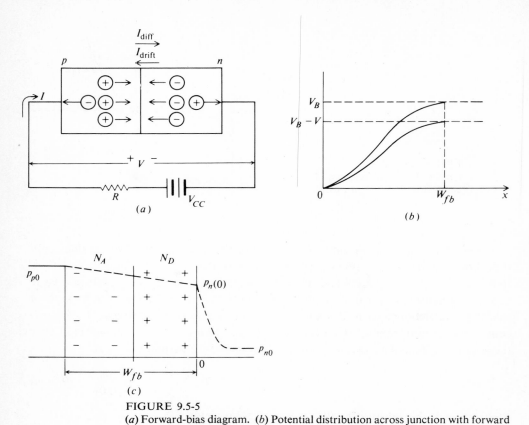

FIGURE 9.5-5

(*a*) Forward-bias diagram. (*b*) Potential distribution across junction with forward bias. (*c*) Hole concentration in a *pn* junction with forward bias.

battery. Actually, the positive side of the battery attracts electrons, and thus increases the hole concentration in the *p* region.

Quantitative evaluation of total current in a forward-biased *pn* junction   As mentioned before, the current in a forward-biased *pn* junction is mainly a diffusion current.   In the *n* region the current density will be [Eq. (9.4-11)]

$$J_{pn}(x) = +eD_{pn}\frac{p_n(0) - p_{n0}}{L_{pn}} \qquad (9.5\text{-}5)$$

where L_{pn} = average distance a hole travels before it recombines with an electron
   D_{pn} = diffusion constant of holes in an *n*-type semiconductor

Combining (9.5-4) and (9.5-5), we get

$$J_{pn,\text{avg}} = \frac{eD_{pn}}{L_{pn}} p_{no}(e^{V/V_T} - 1) = J_0(e^{V/V_T} - 1) \qquad (9.5\text{-}6)$$

where $J_0 = eD_{pn}p_{no}/L_{pn}$.

Of course, a similar relation can be established for the electron diffusion current density in the p region.

Since the drift current is usually much smaller than the diffusion current, the total current in a forward-biased pn junction is given by an equation similar to (9.5-6). That is,

$$I = I_0(e^{V/V_T} - 1) \qquad (9.5\text{-}7a)$$

If we extend (9.5-7a) by continuity to the reverse-biased case, we will have

$$I = I_0(e^{-V/V_T} - 1) \qquad (9.5\text{-}7b)$$

which is obtained by merely changing the sign of the voltage. Since the theoretical value of I_0 turns out to be about 10^{-12} A and the measured reverse-bias current is about 10^{-9} A, we account for the extra current by adding to Eqs. (9.5-7) the current $V/R_L(V)$:

$$I = I_0(e^{V/V_T} - 1) + \frac{V}{R_L(V)} \qquad (9.5\text{-}8)$$

where $R_L(V)$ represents the equivalent *leakage resistance* across the surface of the junction. Note that the resistance is not a constant, but depends on the voltage applied. A graph of the measured vi relationship for a typical diode is shown in Fig. 9.5-6. Note that Eq. (9.5-8) is valid only in the region $V > V_{BR}$.

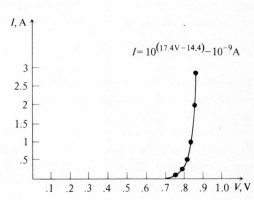

FIGURE 9.5-6
Measured and calculated values of the vi
relation of a semiconductor diode.

9.6 TRANSISTORS

9.6-1 Bipolar Junction Transistors, BJT

A configuration of great interest in electrical engineering is shown schematically in Fig. 9.6-1. It is called a *bipolar transistor*. It consists of two diodes arranged back to back, the first one forward-biased, the second one reverse-biased. The letters E, B, C attached to the three terminals are symbols for the *emitter, base,* and *collector.* The emitter acts as the source of current in the transistor, whereas the collector acts as the sink of current. The name base is applied to the center region because the process which makes the transistor a useful device takes place in the base.

The fundamental current relations of a transistor are (Fig. 9.6-1)

$$i_E = i_C + i_B \qquad (9.6\text{-}1)$$

and

$$i_C = \beta i_B \qquad (9.6\text{-}2)$$

Equation (9.6-1) is a direct consequence of Kirchhoff's current law. Equation (9.6-2) is a characteristic of the transistor and is the basis for the use of the transistor as an amplifier.

Calculation of i_C, i_B, i_E, and β In this section we derive a relation between the value of β and the parameters of the transistor. In this derivation, use will be made of Fig. 9.6-2, which describes the carrier concentration along the transistor. Figure 9.6-2 represents an *npn* transistor with the emitter-base (EB) junction forward-biased and the base-collector (BC) junction reverse-biased. The electron and hole concentration in the emitter far from the junction will be n_{n0} and p_{n0} where [Eq. (9.4-3)]

$$n_{n0} p_{n0} = n_i^2 \qquad (9.6\text{-}3)$$

Near the junction, due to the forward bias V_{BE}, an excess of minority carriers $p_n(0)$ and $n_p(0)$ will appear on both sides of the EB junction. This excess will start diffusing into the n and p sides as expected. The charge $p_n(0)$ will diffuse into the emitter region and recombine with the electrons which are there, thereby giving rise to the usual hole current of a forward-biased junction. Its value [Eq. 9.5-6)] is

$$i_{pBE} = \frac{eD_{pE}p_{n0}}{L_{pE}} A(e^{V_{BE}/V_T} - 1) \qquad (9.6\text{-}4)$$

where D_{pE} and L_{pE} represent the hole diffusion constant and hole diffusion length, respectively, in the emitter, and A is the area of the junction perpendicular to the current flow.

The current due to excess electrons in the base follows another law. To determine this law we note the following: We choose the value of the base width W to be much smaller than L_{nB}, the diffusion length of electrons in the base. This means that the

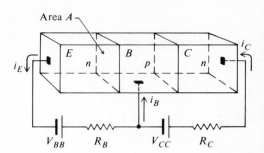

FIGURE 9.6-1
Transistor configuration.

electrons will traverse the base in a time much shorter than τ_{nB}, the average time an electron moves in the base before it recombines with a hole. Since τ_{nB} and L_{nB} are average values, some electrons will still recombine with holes in the base, whereas most of them will succeed in evading this "trap" and reach the base-collector junction safely. The average number of electrons which will recombine with holes can be shown to be approximately,

$$n_{pB,\,avg} \approx \frac{W}{2L_{nB}} n_p(0) \qquad (9.6\text{-}5)$$

There exists a wide depletion layer at the BC junction because V_{BC} is a reverse-bias voltage. This creates (Sec. 9.5-2) a strong electric field from C to B, as shown in Fig. 9.6-2. The electrons reaching the base-collector junction receive an acceleration from the electric field which increases their velocity. The electrons are therefore swiftly swept into the collector region, forming a current in the collector. We shall call this current i_C. Let us find the value of this current as well as the value of the base current i_B.

Since the electrons decay in the base region from $n_p(0)$ to n_{p0} over width W instead of L_{nB} (Fig. 9.6-2), the collector current i_C will be [Eqs. (9.5-5) and (9.5-6)]

$$i_C = en_{p0} \frac{D_{nB}}{W} A(e^{V_{BE}/V_T} - 1) \qquad (9.6\text{-}6)$$

A similar analysis yields

$$i_{nB} = Aen_{p0} \frac{D_{nB}}{L_{nB}} \frac{W}{2L_{nB}} (e^{V_{BE}/V_T} - 1) \qquad (9.6\text{-}7)$$

Figure 9.6-2b shows the above currents and their directions.

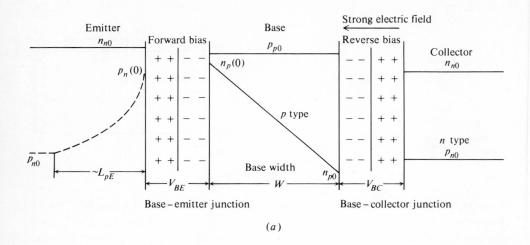

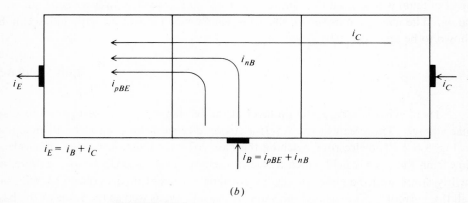

FIGURE 9.6-2
(a) Charge distribution in a transistor. (b) Flow of currents in a transistor.

The total current leaving the emitter will be the sum of all currents. Combining (9.6-4) with (9.6-6) and (9.6-7), we get

$$i_E = i_{pBE} + i_{nB} + i_C = i_B + i_C \qquad (9.6\text{-}8)$$

Current amplification factor   The student is asked to verify (Prob. 9.6-2) that the value of β is given by

$$\frac{1}{\beta} = \frac{i_B}{i_C} = \frac{i_{pBE}}{i_C} + \frac{i_{nB}}{i_C} = \frac{p_{n0}}{n_{p0}} \frac{D_{pE}W}{D_{nB}L_{pE}} + \frac{W^2}{2L_{nB}^2} \qquad (9.6\text{-}9)$$

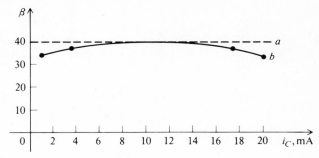

FIGURE 9.6-3
Curve a is the expected value of β. Curve b is measured values of β as a function of collector current.

We would like to express (9.6-9) in terms of easily measurable quantities. It is easy to show (Prob. 9.6-7) that

$$\frac{p_{n0}}{n_{p0}} \frac{D_{pE}}{D_{nB}} = \frac{\sigma_B}{\sigma_E} \qquad (9.6\text{-}10)$$

where σ_B is the conductivity of the base and σ_E that of the emitter. Combining (9.6-9) and (9.6-10), we get

$$\frac{1}{\beta} = \frac{W}{L_{pE}}\left(\frac{\sigma_B}{\sigma_E}\right) + \frac{1}{2}\left(\frac{W}{L_{nB}}\right)^2 \qquad (9.6\text{-}11)$$

Note that β is a function of the parameters of a transistor. One main use of the transistor is as an amplifier. In that case we want to have a value of β as large as possible. An analysis of (9.6-11) shows that we should make the base width W as small as possible and the base conductivity σ_B much less than the emitter conductivity σ_E. Once the transistor is built, we would then expect that β should be a constant independent of the value of the current.

An actual measured plot of β versus i_C is shown in Fig. 9.6-3. Note that at both high and low currents, β is smaller than the value given in (9.6-11). The reason for this discrepancy at low currents is that the recombination of electrons with holes represents a larger percentage of the total electrons present; i.e., at low currents p_{p0} is a constant but n_p decreases. Since the total number of recombinations is about the same, i_{nB} is the same but i_C decreases, and with it β. At high currents, because of the high concentration of electrons at the emitter-base junction, charge neutrality requires a hole concentration larger than the equilibrium condition. This distribution of charges creates an electric field which opposes the flow of electrons, so that the effective velocity D_{nB}/W is reduced, i_C is thus reduced, and with it β.

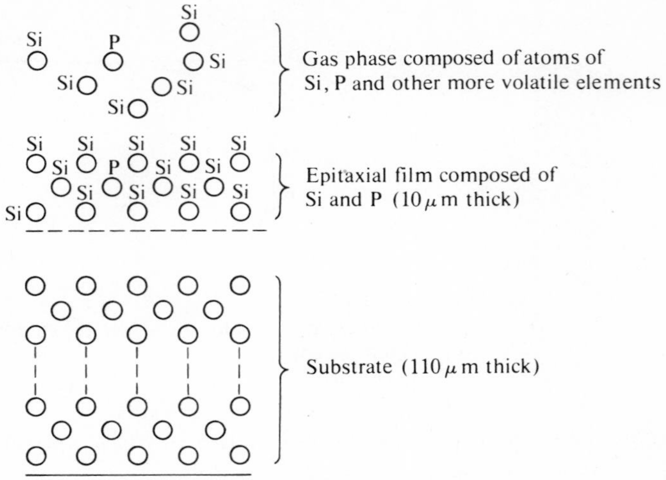

FIGURE 9.6-4
Epitaxial growth. (NOTE: 1 μm $= 10^{-6}$ m.)

9.6-2   Technology of Bipolar Transistors

The fabrication of transistors begins with the introduction of *impurities* into a semi-conductor sample. There are two ways by which these impurities are introduced, *epitaxial growth* and *diffusion*.

Epitaxial growth   Assume that we want to deposit an *n*-type impurity. To do this we put a sample into an oven into which we introduce a gas, as shown in Fig. 9.6-4. A chemical reaction in the gas liberates atoms of silicon and phosphorus in a previously prescribed ratio. These atoms settle on the surface of the sample, which is called a *substrate*, creating a thin layer of *n*-type impurity. This is a slow process, and it takes place as if the crystal were growing naturally; i.e., the natural crystal arrangement of the substrate is not disturbed, and the impurities are uniformly distributed in the layer according to their previously prescribed ratio. The thin layer thus produced is called an *epitaxial film* because its thickness is much smaller than that of the substrate. The arrangement is shown in Fig. 9.6-4.

Impurity diffusion in a semiconductor sample   In diffusion processes we deposit a high concentration of impurity atoms on the surface of the sample and then heat the assembly in an oven. This causes the impurities to *diffuse* into the body of the sample. With this method the impurities are not evenly distributed since the concentration is

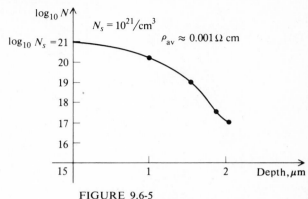

FIGURE 9.6-5
Impurity concentration distribution with depth.

higher near the surface than inside the material. A typical impurity-concentration distribution with depth is shown in Fig. 9.6-5.

9.6-3 Bipolar-transistor Fabrication

We will now describe the steps in the fabrication of a transistor with pertinent numerical values. We start with a sample of an n^+ (high-conductivity) type of semiconductor, as shown in Fig. 9.6-6a, on which we grow epitaxially an n-type (low-conductivity) semiconductor. A cross section of the sample is shown in Fig. 9.6-6a, and the concentration of impurities with depth is plotted in Fig. 9.6-6b. The n-type layer will form the collector part of the transistor. On top of the n-type epitaxial layer, a thin film of insulation SiO_2 forms, due to oxidation in the air. Next, the insulator film is coated with a photographic emulsion. On top of the emulsion we place a mask, as shown in Fig. 9.6-7. The coated surface is subjected to a strong ultraviolet light which hardens the crosshatched area of Fig. 9.6-7 after developing.

The next step consists of removing the emulsion and insulator from the noncrosshatched part, thus uncovering the n-type material under it. A high concentration of boron (about 10^{19} per cubic centimeter) is deposited on the uncovered n surface, and the boron is diffused into the sample by heating in an oven at a temperature (about 1100°C) such that the boron diffuses in a given prescribed concentration (for example, 10^{16} per cubic centimeter at 3 μm). The resulting impurity distribution and a cross section of the pn junction formed is shown in Fig. 9.6-8a and b. This section will form the base of the transistor. Note that since the diffusion is *isotropic*, the result looks more like a trapezoid than a rectangular section; in fact, the section is a

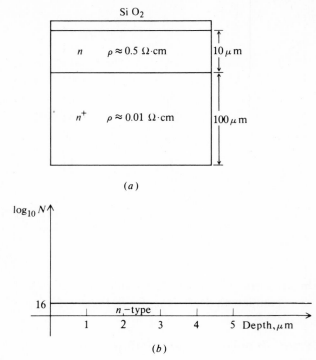

(a)

(b)

FIGURE 9.6-6
Step 1 in transistor fabrication. Epitaxial growth of collector region.
(a) Transistor-layer cross section for step 1; (b) impurity concentration with depth.

rectangle with two quarters of a circle on its side. We might add that we have to take this particular geometry into consideration when designing the transistor. Once the boron diffusion is finished, the surface is oxidized, so that a new film of SiO_2 covers it.

The previous steps, pattern forming, emulsion hardening, and removing, are repeated, and a high concentration (about 10^{21} per cubic centimeter) of phosphorus is diffused to form an n^+-type layer. The new distribution and cross section are shown

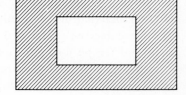

FIGURE 9.6-7
First mask for base layout.

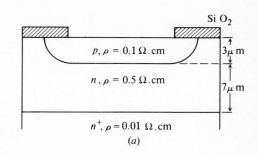

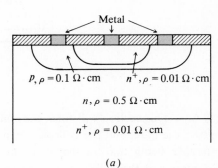

FIGURE 9.6-8
Step 2 in transistor fabrication: base diffusion. (*a*) Cross section of transistor layout for step 2; (*b*) impurity concentration with depth.

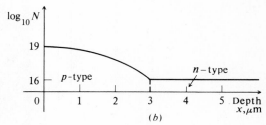

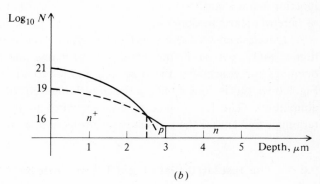

FIGURE 9.6-9
Step 3 in transistor fabrication: emitter diffusion. (*a*) Transistor cross section for step 3; (*b*) impurity concentration distribution with depth.

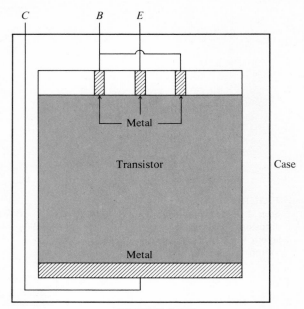

FIGURE 9.6-10
Transistor packaging. (Not to scale.)

in Fig. 9.6-9. This section will form the emitter of the transistor. Note that all three, the emitter, the base, and the collector, contain donor as well as acceptor impurities, the difference being that in the base, the acceptor impurities dominate, whereas in the emitter and the collector, the donor impurities are in the majority. Also, the junction is not sharply defined and is taken arbitrarily as the depth at which one type of impurity starts to dominate.

Once the emitter section is formed, a new cycle begins: oxidation to form a new film of SiO_2, pattern laying, emulsion hardening and removing, ending finally with openings for connecting the base and emitter to the outside world. As shown in Fig. 9.6-9a, this is done by filling the connecting wells (dark shade) with metal (usually aluminum). The last step is to connect wires to the emitter, base, and collector terminals and encase the transistor for protection, as shown in Fig. 9.6-10.

9.6-4 The Insulated Gate Field Effect Transistor (IGFET)

A device used widely today in digital circuits is the insulated gate field effect transistor (IGFET). The difference between the IGFET and the BJT is the following: In the IGFET the current is mainly a drift current, whereas in the BJT it is a diffusion current.

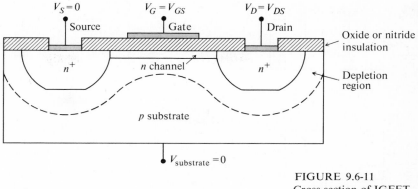

FIGURE 9.6-11
Cross section of IGFET.

The equivalent circuit model for the IGFET is a voltage-dependent current source, whereas that of the BJT is a current-dependent current source. In the BJT, the input current i_B varies and the input voltage v_{BE} is almost a constant. In the IGFET, the input voltage v_G (we will explain its significance later) varies, whereas the input current i_G is almost a constant (considered zero most of the time).

The device as shown in Fig. 9.6-11 consists of a p substrate in which are embedded two highly doped n^+ regions connected by a lightly doped narrow channel of n-type impurities. With a voltage V_{DS} present, current will flow from terminal D to S; that is, electrons will flow from S to D. This is the origin of the names *source* and *drain*. The flow of current is controlled by the voltage V_{GS} from gate to source. The gate is formed by depositing an insulator layer above the semiconductor, and then a metal layer on top of the insulator. To complete the description, the p substrate is connected to the source to eliminate from the input circuit the capacitance which might exist because of the pn^+ junction.

The device can be operated in two modes, called the *depletion mode* and the *enhancement mode*. In the depletion mode the gate-to-source voltage is negative; in the enhancement mode we operate with a positive gate-to-source voltage.

To understand how the n channel is formed in the enhancement mode, consider the one-dimensional structure of Fig. 9.6-12. This is a much simplified version of Fig. 9.6-11, with both drain and source grounded. As shown in Fig. 9.6-12a, as V_{GS} is made positive, a hole current will flow to ground, depleting the p region and leaving a region of negative acceptors. At a certain voltage $V_{GS} = V_p$, the entire region between S and G is depleted, as shown in Fig. 9.6-12b. Due to the appearance of these negative fixed charges, an electric field will appear. As V_{GS} increases, the electric field will become so strong that it will attract electrons from the ground side and accelerate them toward the positive terminal of the battery. Because of the high

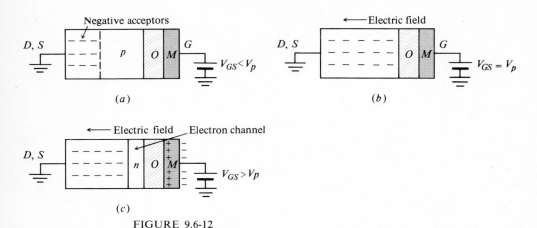

FIGURE 9.6-12
Schematic of channel formation for enhancement mode IGFET. Both source and drain are grounded. (a) Depletion layer for $V_{GS} < V_p$; (b) depletion layer at $V_{GS} = V_p$; (c) channel formation for $V_{GS} > V_p$.

resistivity of the oxide, they will suddenly be stopped at the insulator-semiconductor junction, and thus create a negative-charge accumulation of electrons near this junction. This accumulation of electrons will form an n-type channel, as shown in Fig. 9.6-12c. Simultaneously, positive charges will accumulate on the metal side of the oxide, and eventually an equilibrium will be reached; i.e., the equivalent capacitor will be charged. As in any capacitor the total charge accumulated, and consequently the width of the n channel, will depend on $V_{GS} - V_p$.

Since a channel of free-electron carriers exists in the region between D and S (Fig. 9.6-13), if we connect a battery from drain to source, a current i_D will flow. For a fixed V_{GS}, the current i_D will increase with V_{DS} until V_{DS} equals $V_{GS} - V_p$. Thereafter the current remains a constant, independent of any increase in V_{DS}. The reason for this behavior is thought to be as follows. As V_{DS} increases there is an asymmetry at the S and D ends of the channel; V_{GS} is a constant whereas V_{GD} decreases. Consequently, as shown in Fig. 9.6-13a, the charge is not uniformly distributed in the channel. When V_{DS} becomes equal to $V_{GS} - V_p$, the region near the drain is completely depleted, and any further increase in V_{DS} serves only to increase the depletion near the drain (Fig. 9.6-13b and c). A typical plot of i_D versus V_{DS} with V_{GS} as a parameter is shown in Fig. 9.6-14. Note that at $V_{DS} = V_{GS} - V_p$, a drastic change in slope occurs and the current remains almost constant as V_{DS} increases. An approximate calculation, verified experimentally, shows that in the region $V_{DS} > V_{GS} - V_p > 0$, the vi relation is given by

$$i_D = K(V_{GS} - V_p)^2 \qquad (9.6\text{-}12)$$

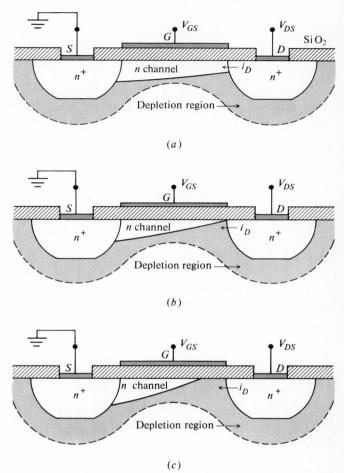

FIGURE 9.6-13
Channel narrowing with increase in V_{DS} for an IGFET. (a) Channel thickness at $V_{GS} - V_{DS} < V_p$; (b) channel thickness at $V_{GS} - V_{DS} = V_p$; (c) channel thickness at $V_{GS} - V_{DS} > V_p$.

where K is a constant dependent on the geometry of the transistor and the nature of its material. The value of K usually varies between 10^{-4} and 10^{-3} A/V^2.

Use of the IGFET as an amplifier   The IGFET is used as an amplifier in the region

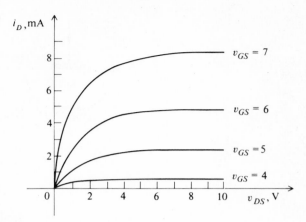

FIGURE 9.6-14
vi characteristic of an IGFET transistor in the enhancement mode.

$V_{DS} > V_{GS} - V_p$. In this region the variation of the current i_D depends exclusively on the variation of v_{GS}. We will define a transconductance g_m:

$$g_m = \frac{di_D}{dv_{GS}}\bigg|_{v_{GS}=V_{GS}} = 2K(V_{GS} - V_p) \qquad (9.6\text{-}13)$$

which plays the same role in IGFET operation as β does in the case of BJTs where a variation i_B in the input causes a variation $i_C = \beta i_B$ in the output. For an IGFET, a variation v_{gs} in the input will cause a variation $i_d = g_m v_{GS}$ in the output. Since i_d is a function of the gate-source voltage, an IGFET acts like a voltage-dependent current source.

We end this section by mentioning that since the gate input to the IGFET looks like a capacitor, it represents a very high input impedance, so that i_G is approximately zero at low to medium frequencies.

9.7 INTEGRATED CIRCUITS

The useful area of a transistor is only about 0.04 mm². The additional space is used to give body to the transistor, to help prevent physical breakage, and to provide space for connections to other elements.

As electronic circuits became more and more complicated, the need for smaller and smaller devices increased. This led to the development of a special technology of miniaturized circuits known today as integrated circuits (ICs).

Integrated circuits are different from discrete circuits in that an entire system is built in one body. The components are not transistors or diodes or resistors, but rather, complex functional devices, i.e., amplifiers, flip-flops, etc. Each device is a complete unit enclosed in a case which is often no larger than the case of a discrete transistor, the difference being only that, whereas the transistor always had three terminals, the number of terminals in an integrated circuit is dependent upon its function and most of the time is greater than three. To explain the technology and design specifics, we will discuss an example in all its details.

9.7-1 Design of a Differential Amplifier

The schematic circuit of a differential amplifier is shown in Fig. 9.7-1. We are going to implement this circuit in the form of a *monolithic integrated circuit*. In such a circuit the transistors and resistors are all fabricated in the same piece of silicon. Also, since this is an industrial process, the manufacturing method has to be such as to result in a large quantity of standardized devices of reliable performance. To accomplish this we have to manufacture all our devices under similar conditions of temperature, time of diffusion, and impurity concentration. For our design the amplifier will be fabricated by epitaxy of the collector region, followed by impurity diffusion of the base and emitter regions. The resistors will be fabricated during the base stage of diffusion from the same material as the base. For every diffusion stage a mask will be constructed, so that the final result will be our amplifier.

We will describe the fabrication and mask design, giving the reason behind each step as we go along.

Chip design We start with a *wafer* of p-type semiconductor of about 1 in diameter (25,000 μm) and 200 μm thick. This will serve both as a substrate and an insulating material for the different elements of the device; as such, it has to be thick enough to prevent breakage and of a high enough resistivity to be an insulator. A resistivity of about 10 $\Omega \cdot$cm is usually chosen. The wafer is divided into squares called *chips*, each chip containing a complete differential amplifier like the one in Fig. 9.7-1. Since, as we shall see later, we require an area of about 10^6 μm^2 for each chip, the 1-in-diameter wafer will contain

$$\frac{25^2 \times 10^6}{10^6} = 625 \text{ differential amplifiers}$$

Epitaxial layout The first stage in the manufacturing process is to grow an n-type epitaxial layer about 25 μm thick. This will serve as the collector for transistors and as an insulating bed for the resistors. Above this layer a film of SiO_2 about 0.5 μm

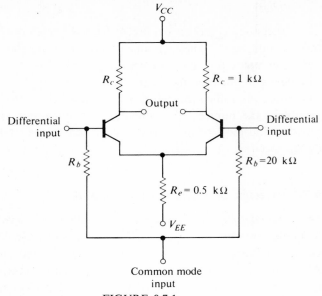

FIGURE 9.7-1
Schematic diagram of a differential amplifier.

thick is grown. Next, we put on top of the oxide a photosensitive emulsion, and on top of this an isolation mask.

First-mask design   The first mask is designed to separate the different regions of *n*-type material, which are supposed to be at different potentials. An examination of Fig. 9.7-1 shows that we need three separate *n* regions. Two will serve as collectors for the two transistors, and the third will be a bed for the resistors in the circuit. The area of these regions will depend on the ohmic value of the resistors and the current-carrying capacity of the transistors. We will see later how the above values are calculated. For the moment we shall give the results.

We need an isolation area of about $1,200 \times 800$ μm for the resistance setting and two isolation areas of 160×280 μm each for the setting of the two transistors. Detailed masks are drawn and then reduced to the required size of the chips by photographic processes. The reduced masks are then placed over the wafer (Fig. 9.7-2a). Next the photosensitive material is illuminated with ultraviolet light. The emulsion is hardened by light in the places not covered by the mask. The part covered remains soft and is easily etched out with hydrofluoric acid, which also removes the SiO_2 under it, leaving the rest untouched. Sketches illustrating the result are shown in Figs. 9.7-2a, b, and c. Through the etched layers, we diffuse boron, the time of diffusion being such that it will reach the substrate. This creates isolated islands of

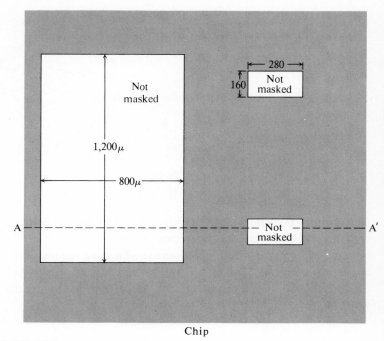

FIGURE 9.7-2*a*
The first mask for fabrication of the differential amplifier: *n*-island formation.

n-type regions separated by *p*-type regions, as shown in Fig. 9.7-2*b*. To isolate the *n* islands electrically, we will always connect the *p* substrate to the most negative potential in the amplifier. Thus, between two *n* regions, there will always exist two reverse-biased diodes, as shown symbolically in Fig. 9.7-2*b*. Note that during the diffusion cycle, a new layer of SiO_2 forms over the surface.

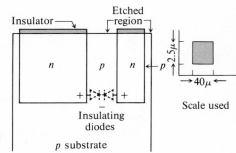

FIGURE 9.7-2*b*
AA' cross section of die for creating *n*-type islands.

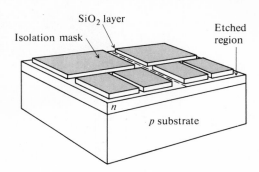

FIGURE 9.7-2c
Pictorial representation of mask used to
create *n*-type islands.

Base-region layout   In the next step a second pattern is prepared which will result
in formation of the transistor base region and resistors for our device.   After illumina-
tion and etching, we diffuse boron so as to have a *p* region about 3 μm thick.   Finally,
a SiO$_2$ layer is grown over the surface.   The layout in Figs. 9.7-3*a* and *b* shows the
device at the end of this stage.   The reasons for the numerical values used will be
given later.

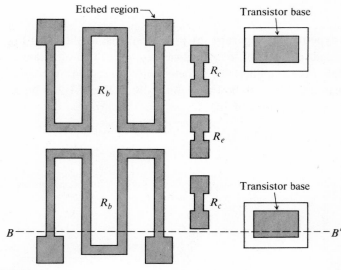

FIGURE 9.7-3a
Mask layout for diffusion of *p*-type impurity to form resistors and base of
transistors.

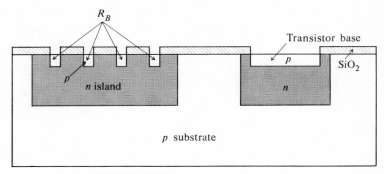

FIGURE 9.7-3*b*
Cross section *BB'* of Fig. 9.7-3*a*. *p*-type impurity diffusion.

Emitter-region layout   The oxide coating is again selectively etched to open windows in the base region to permit phosphorus diffusion for emitter formation. At the same time windows are etched over the *n*-collector region so that contacts can be established between the collector and the surface. A high surface concentration of phosphorus is then diffused to form the transistor emitter area and the contacts to the collector. The contacts to the collector are made with a higher concentration of donors to counteract the influence of the aluminum, which is used as a metallic connection with the rest of the circuit. It turns out that aluminum acts like an acceptor impurity in relation to silicon, and it has a solubility of about 2×10^{19} aluminum atoms per cubic centimeter of silicon. Experience has shown that in order to ensure an ohmic contact, i.e., avoid a *pn* junction, the concentration of phosphorus near the surface should be about 2×10^{20} per cubic centimeter.

Once the phosphorus is diffused, a new oxide layer is grown and the device is ready for metalization. The results are shown in Figs. 9.7-4*a* and *b*.

Metalization   To provide interconnection between the various components of the differential amplifier, a fourth set of windows is etched into the silicon dioxide layer at the points where contact is to be made. A thin, even coating of aluminum is vacuum-deposited over the entire surface of the wafer. The interconnection pattern between components is then formed by photoresist techniques with strips about 125 μm wide. The undesired aluminum areas are etched away, leaving a pattern of interconnections between transistors, resistors, and outside terminals. The completed connections are shown in Fig. 9.7-5.

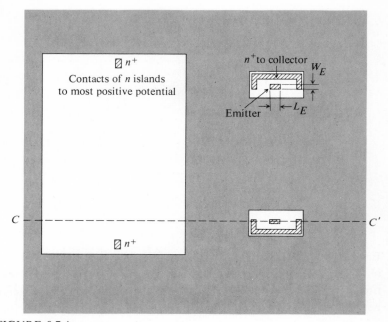

FIGURE 9.7-4*a*
Mask for diffusion of highly doped donor impurity to form emitters and connections to the collector and the bed of the resistors.

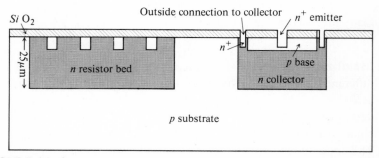

FIGURE 9.7-4*b*
Cross section *CC'* of Fig. 9.7-4*a*. Depth of penetration of donor and acceptor impurities is shown.

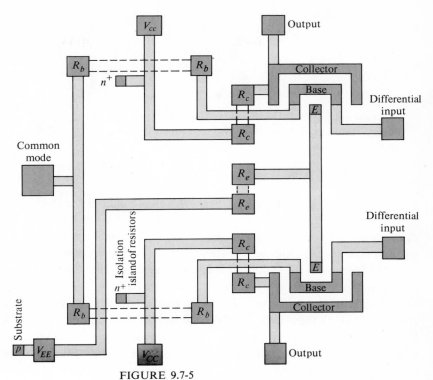

FIGURE 9.7-5
Metalization layout for integrated circuit differential amplifier.

Packaging   The wafer is separated into individual chips, each of which contains one amplifier. The chips are then mounted in an all-ceramic flat package. Wires about 25 μm in diameter are bonded from the circuit to the package terminals. The finished package is shown in Fig. 9.7-6.

9.7-2   Transistor and Resistor Layout

We will now present the reasoning behind the choice of geometries shown in Figs. 9.7-2 to 9.7-5.

Transistor layout   In designing a transistor the most important specifications are its gain β and its dc current capability. As shown in Sec. 9.6-4, the value of β depends on the resistivity of the base and emitter material and on the depth of the base. To

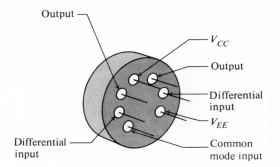

FIGURE 9.7-6
Package containing differential amplifier
with outside connections.

ensure a value of β of about 100 (Prob. 9.7-1), we choose for the transistors of Fig. 9.7-1 a base resistivity of 0.1 Ω·cm, an emitter resistivity of 0.01 Ω·cm, a penetration depth of the base of 3 μm, and a penetration depth of the emitter of 2.5 μm. What we need now are the required surface areas for the emitter, base, and collector.

We begin with the emitter. Experience has shown that this area should be chosen so as not to exceed an average current density of about 1,000 A/cm^2. Also (refer to Fig. 9.7-4a) the current density will tend to vary across the surface of the emitter, being more dense along the length L_E. What we would like to have is an emitter which is all length and no width, i.e., a long rectangle with minimal width. Practical consideration (metalization, etc.) limits the minimum width to about 25 μm. If we require an emitter current of about 10 mA, this will give us an emitter area of about 40 × 25 μm (Prob. 9.7-2). The size of the base is next chosen such as to permit outside connections and also take into account lateral diffusion. Assuming about 50 μm as a guard band around the emitter gives a base area of about 75 × 100 μm. Using similar considerations, an area of 150 × 200 μm was chosen for the collector.

Resistor layout As mentioned in Sec. 9-7.1, the resistors are formed at the same time as the base region. In making resistors we stop the diffusion with the base. The value of a resistor is (Fig. 9.7-7)

$$R_{AB} = \frac{\rho L}{TW} \qquad (9.7-1)$$

In integrated circuits, for obvious reasons, the thickness T will always be a constant. We can define, then, a new type of resistivity

$$R_s = \frac{\rho}{T} \qquad (9.7-2)$$

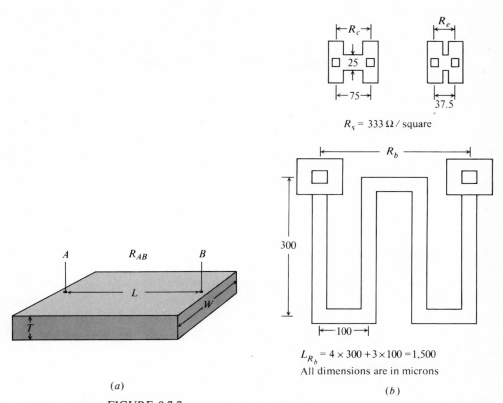

FIGURE 9.7-7
(a) Geometry used in calculating resistor value. (b) Layout of calculated resistors.

where R_S is a resistance per square, often called *sheet resistance*. Combining (9.7-1) and (9.7-2), we get

$$R_{AB} = R_S \frac{L}{W} \qquad (9.7\text{-}3)$$

Equation (9.7-3) shows that in the case of integrated circuits, the resistance can be simply determined from the ratio of length to width.

For our case, $\rho_B = 0.1$ Ω·cm and $T = 3$ μm, so that

$$R_S = \frac{\rho_B}{T} = \frac{0.1}{3 \times 10^{-4}} = 333 \ \Omega/\text{square} \qquad (9.7\text{-}4)$$

Figure 9.7-1 shows that we need three values of resistances,

$$R_c = 1 \ \text{k}\Omega \qquad R_e = 0.5 \ \text{k}\Omega \qquad R_b = 20 \ \text{k}\Omega$$

Combining these values with (9.7-3) and (9.7-4) and assuming that the width W is equal to 25 μm, we get $L_c = 75$ μm for R_c, $L_e = 37.5$ μm for R_e, $L_b = 1,500$ μm for R_b. The layout is shown in Fig. 9.7-7b. Note that, in order to conserve space, R_b was constructed in a zigzag pattern. Finally, we might mention that the n-type bed in which the resistors lie is connected to the most positive potential of the circuit in order to eliminate current leakage from the resistor. Note the p-type resistor and the n-type bed form a pn junction. A positive voltage makes this junction back-biased. This provides isolation, since a back-biased diode acts as an open circuit. Once the layouts of individual transistors and resistors is completed, they are arranged in a pattern similar to Figs. 9.7-2 to 9.7-5 so as to minimize space and allow for guard bands at the ends, for diffusion spreading (Sec. 9.6), and metalization needs.

9.8   CONCLUSION

In this chapter we have presented in a simplified form the basic principles of material science. Through simple examples we have tried to show some of its applications in electrical engineering. The electronics engineer continually uses transistors as amplifiers and as switches in electronic circuits. Research in the domain of material science will help improve the gain β and other characteristics of transistors, such as speed of response and bandwidth. This will extend its range of applicability and help to further miniaturize electronic circuits. This latest factor is of paramount importance for communications in outer space.

Transistors and diodes are basic ingredients in computerized circuits. Research leading to materials with a fast response and large storage capacity is essential in a field where the amount of data and the necessary speed of information increases by leaps and bounds.

Associated with miniaturized active elements is the search for materials to give us a wide range of values of miniaturized resistances, capacitances, and inductances.

PROBLEMS

9.3-1   The highest energy of an electron at $0°$K is found to be 1 eV.
    (a)   Plot $[n(W)]/n$ versus W for $0 < W < W_{FO}$.
    (b)   Show that the area under the curve is 1.
    (c)   If $n = 10^{29}$ per cubic meter, what is the value of $n(W_{FO})$?
9.3-2   Sketch the energy diagram of a conductor showing clearly W_g, W_c, W_{FO}.

9.3-3 The atomic distance in a crystal is about 2×10^{-10} m. Assuming that this represents the collision length and the average velocity is given by

$$v \approx \sqrt{3 \frac{e}{m} V_T}$$

where e/m is the ratio of charge to mass for an electron and V_T is the thermal voltage (25 mV at 300°K), find the collision time τ.

9.3-4 An electron after a collision has a velocity 10^5 m/s in the x direction. An electric field of 100 V/m is applied in the x direction. If the collision length is 2×10^{-10} m, find the electron velocity at the time of the next collision. What is the time between the two collisions?

9.3-5 If the electron in Prob. 9.3-4 loses half its energy in the collision process, what is its velocity after collision?

9.3-6 One V is applied across a prism 1 m long which has a base 10^{-6} m² (Fig. P9.3-6). A current of 10 A is measured.

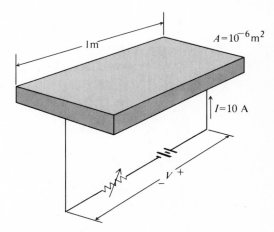

FIGURE P9.3-6

(a) Find the conductivity and determine the nature of the material.

(b) An independent measurement shows that the concentration of electrons is 10^{26} per cubic meter. Find the mobility of the material.

9.4-1 Repeat Example 9.4-1 for silicon at temperatures of 10°K and 550°K, the range of temperatures on the moon.

9.4-2 Repeat Prob. 9.4-1 for a GaAs semiconductor, assuming that

$$\frac{n_i(\text{Si})}{n_i(\text{GaAs})} = \left(\frac{m_e m_h \text{ of Si}}{m_e m_h \text{ of GaAs}} \right)^{3/2}$$

and that W_g for GaAs is 1 eV.

9.4-3 The distance between two silicon atoms is 2×10^{-10} m. If there are 10^{29} silicon atoms per cubic meter and 10^{24} phosphorus atoms per cubic meter, what is the average distance between two phosphorus atoms?

9.4-4 What is the conductivity of the extrinsic semiconductor of Prob. 9.4-3?

9.4-5 It is desired to increase the conductivity of silicon by adding phosphorus impurities. It is known that $n_i = 10^{16}$ per cubic meter. Find the concentration of phosphorus donors necessary to increase the conductivity by a factor of 10^3. What is the hole concentration for the extrinsic material?

9.4-6 Repeat Prob. 9.4-5 if boron atoms are diffused instead of phosphorus atoms.

9.4-7 An extrinsic n-type material is shown in Fig. P9.4-7. A beam of light at A creates an additional 10^{16} hole-electron pairs per cubic meter. The current density is found to be 10 mA/m^2. $D_p = 1.35 \times 10^{-3} \text{ m}^2/\text{s}$. Find the diffusion length of holes in the material.

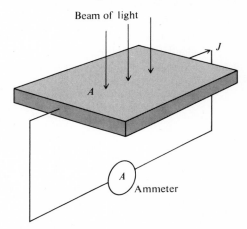

Beam of light

J

A

A Ammeter

FIGURE P9.4-7

9.4-8 Find the hole-diffusion time and mobility for the material in Prob. 9.4-7.

9.5-1 The potential barrier of a certain material is 0.2 V. If $N_A = N_D = 10^{21}$ per cubic meter find the intrinsic concentration n_i.

9.5-2 What is the width of the depletion layer of the junction in Prob. 9.5-1 if the dielectric constant of the material is 10^{-11} F/m?

9.5-3 What is the average electric field across the material of Prob. 9.5-1?

9.5-4 Find I_0 across a junction 0.1×0.1 mm area.

$$D_{pn} = 12.5 \text{ cm}^2/\text{s}$$
$$L_{pn} = 300 \ \mu\text{m}$$
$$p_{no} = 10^{14} \text{ per cubic meter}$$

9.6-1 Verify (9.6-9).

9.6-2 Find the emitter hole current [Eq. (9.6-4)] as a function of V_{BE}. Assume an npn bipolar transistor with $n_i = 10^{16}$ per cubic meter, $N_D = 10^{22}$ per cubic meter, $D_{pE} = 12.5 \text{ cm}^2/\text{s}$, $L_{pE} = 3 \times 10^{-5}$ m, and $A = 4 \times 10^{-8} \text{ m}^2$.

9.6-3 For the transistor of Prob. 9.6-1 find i_C. Assume $N_A = 10^{16}$ per cubic meter, $D_{nB} = 35 \text{ cm}^2/\text{s}$, $W = 3 \times 10^{-6}$ m.

9.6-4 For the transistor of Prob. 9.6-1 find i_{nB}. Assume $L_{nB} = 10^{-3}$ cm.

9.6-5 For the transistor of Prob. 9.6-1 find the value of β.

9.6-6 Verify (9.6-10).

9.6-7   Plot i_D and g_m for an IGFET with $K = 10^{-3}$ A/V^2 and $V_p = 3$ V.

9.7-1   Find β for the transistors of Sec. 9.7-2. Use Eq. (9.6-11). Assume $L_{pE} = 10^{-3}$ cm and $L_{nB} = 10^{-3}$ cm.

9.7-2   Calculate the area of the emitter in Sec. 9.7-2.

9.7-3   Using (9.7-4), verify the geometry of R_c, R_e, and R_b in Sec. 9.7-2.

REFERENCES

GIBBONS, J. F.: "Semiconductor Electronics," McGraw-Hill Book Company, New York, 1966.

PEDERSON, D. O., J. J. STUDER, and J. R. WHINNERY: "Introduction to Electronic Systems, Circuits and Devices," McGraw-Hill Book Company, New York, 1966.

WANG, S.: "Solid-state Electronics," McGraw-Hill Book Company, New York, 1966.

WARNER, R. M., and J. N. FORDEMWALT: "Integrated Circuits, Design Principles and Fabrication," McGraw-Hill Book Company, New York, 1965.

10

POWER CONVERSION

INTRODUCTION

In this chapter we study a series of devices used in power conversion. To explain the meaning of power conversion we begin by defining the concepts of power and energy.

Our fundamental experience is that of *bodily motion*, i.e., bodies which move in different directions with different velocities. To put this experience on a quantitative basis, we attach to bodily motion two concepts, *energy* and *momentum*, and we say that all bodies possess energy and momentum. The motion of these bodies changes continuously due to their interaction with other bodies. We then say that a continuous exchange of energy and momentum occurs between bodies or systems of bodies. Depending on the type of bodies we are concerned with, we give different names to their energy. Some examples are:

Thermal energy Molecules in air, or atoms in a solid body, are in continuous random motion with varying velocity and direction. This is a bodily motion which we perceive on the average as a fixed temperature of the body or of the system of bodies under observation. We then associate with this type of motion the concept of thermal energy.

Electric energy We associate the concept of electric energy with the flow of electrons in a given direction (again a bodily motion). Electrons moving through a conductor encounter atoms with which they collide. Due to this collision the electrons exchange energy and momentum with the atoms; i.e., both atoms and electrons gain or lose velocity by colliding with each other. As a result, electric energy changes into thermal energy, and vice versa.

Mechanical energy We associate the concept of mechanical energy with the motion of macroscopic bodies. These bodies lose or gain energy by collision with other bodies. This exchange of energy results either in a change in the state of motion of the entire body (gain or loss of mechanical energy) or in a change in the internal energy of the body (e.g., a change in its temperature, such as gain or loss of thermal energy).

The above examples represent only a limited enumeration of the type of energy conversions existing in nature.

In the sections to follow we will study devices which convert mechanical energy into electric energy, electric energy into mechanical energy, electric energy into optical energy, optical energy into electric energy, etc.

In each case we will discuss the basic principles associated with the particular type of conversion, followed by a description of some well-known devices.

10.1 ELECTROMECHANICAL ENERGY CONVERSION

10.1-1 Fundamental Relations

The fundamental relation of electromechanical energy conversion is *Lorentz' law*

$$m \frac{d\mathbf{v}}{dt} = q(\mathbf{E} + \mathbf{v} \times \mathbf{B}) + \mathbf{f} \qquad (10.1\text{-}1)$$

This law states that the acceleration of a body is equal to the sum of the electrical and mechanical forces. Here, $\mathbf{f}$ is the mechanical force.

Starting with (10.1-1), we will derive the laws of electromechanical energy conversion in terms of practical measurable quantities, such as voltage, current, mechanical force, and torque.

A device which is used to transform mechanical energy into electric energy is called a *generator*, and its action is called *generating*.

A device which is used to transform electric energy into mechanical energy is called a *motor*, and its action is called *motoring*.

In the following sections we will derive, using Lorentz' law, the relations governing *generating* and *motoring*.

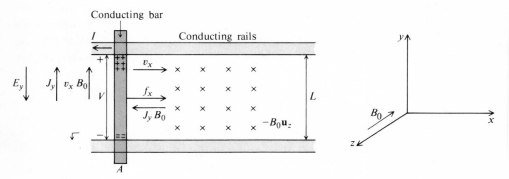

FIGURE 10.1-1
Configuration used to derive the generating laws.

10.1-2   The Generating Laws

Consider the configuration of Fig. 10.1-1. A conducting bar of cross section A and conductivity σ is sliding on a pair of conducting rails separated by a distance L. We apply to the bar a force density in the x direction

$$\mathbf{f} = f_x \mathbf{u}_x \qquad \text{N/m}^3 \qquad (10.1\text{-}2)$$

In the presence of a magnetic flux density

$$\mathbf{B} = -B_0 \mathbf{u}_z \qquad \text{Wb/m}^2 \qquad (10.1\text{-}3)$$

the following chain of events occurs: The force f_x accelerates the bar in the x direction; consequently, the bar gains a velocity v_x in the x direction. Since the bar has this velocity, the electrons and ions composing the bar have this velocity. Moving charges in the presence of a magnetic field give rise to a force perpendicular to their plane. Since v_x is in the x direction and B_0 is in the negative z direction, the force per unit charge $v_x B_0$ will be in the positive y direction.

Force $v_x B_0$ will tend to push the electrons in the negative y direction and the ions in the positive y direction. This charge separation gives rise to an electric field in the negative y direction. Since motion of charges is by definition current and since electrons move in the negative y direction, a current density $J_y = q v_y$ will exist in the positive y direction.

The electrons moving in the negative y direction will react with the magnetic field in the negative z direction, giving rise to a force $q v_y B_0 = J_y B_0$ in the negative x direction. This force will tend to oppose the action of the force f_x. We now translate the above observations based on (10.1-1) to mathematical form.

In the x direction:

$$m \frac{dv_x}{dt} = -J_y B_0 + f_x \quad (10.1\text{-}4a)$$

In the y direction, since $f_y = 0$,

$$m \frac{dv_y}{dt} = q(E_y - v_x B_0)$$

Since $v_x B_0$ behaves like an electric field (note that it "pushes" the electrons in the negative y direction) the difference $E_y - v_x B_0$ can be represented as an equivalent electric field E_y' acting across the bar. This gives rise to the current density

$$-J_y = \sigma E_y' = \sigma(E_y - v_x B_0) \quad (10.1\text{-}4b)$$

where σ is the conductivity of the bar. Note that J_y/σ is equivalent to $(m/q) \, dv_y/dt$.

Since our measurements are usually made in terms of voltages, currents, and total forces, we transform (10.1-4) by multiplying (10.1-4a) by AL, the volume of the bar, and (10.1-4b) by L, the useful length of the bar. The student is asked to show (Prob. 10.1-1) that if we call:

$$M = mAL \quad \text{total mass of the bar}$$
$$F_x = f_x AL \quad \text{total force on the bar}$$
$$I = J_y A \quad \text{current through the bar}$$
$$V = -E_y L \quad \text{voltage across the bar}$$

and

$$R = \frac{L}{\sigma A} \quad \text{resistance of the bar}$$

Equations (10.1-4) become, after some manipulation,

$$M \frac{dv_x}{dt} = F_x - IB_0 L \quad (10.1\text{-}5a)$$

and

$$v_x B_0 L = V + IR \quad (10.1\text{-}5b)$$

It is important to mention that $v_x B_0 L$ is called the *electromotive force* (emf), and it represents the electric potential equivalent to the absorbed mechanical energy. As any electric potential, it is defined by

$$\text{emf} = -\int_0^L v_x B_0 \, dy \quad (10.1\text{-}6)$$

$IB_0 L$ is called the *equivalent electromechanical force* F_{em} and is defined by

$$F_{em} = \int_V J_y B_0 \, dx \, dy \, dz \quad (10.1\text{-}7)$$

where $V = AL$ is the volume of the bar. Equations (10.1-5) are the fundamental relations of a generator, and we will use them in the following example.

EXAMPLE 10.1-1   Assume that the bar in Fig. 10.1-1 has a cross section $A = 10^{-4}$ m^2 and a length $L = 1$ m and is made of iron which has a conductivity of 10^7 ℧/m and a specific density of 7.5×10^3 kg/m^3. A voltage $V = 9.9$ V is generated across the bar when a load current $I = 100$ A passes through the bar. The bar moves with a constant velocity $v_x = 100$ m/s.

(a) Find the applied magnetic flux density B_0.
(b) Find the applied mechanical force F_x.

SOLUTION   (a) Using the data given, we find

$$R = \frac{L}{\sigma A} = \frac{1}{10^7 \times 10^{-4}} = 10^{-3}\,\Omega$$

Substituting in (10.1-5b), we find

$$v_x B_0 L = V + IR = 9.9 + 100 \times 10^{-3} = 10\,\text{V}$$

Hence,

$$B_0 = \frac{10}{100 \times 1} = 0.1\ \text{Wb/m}^2$$

(b) Since v_x is a constant, $dv_x/dt = 0$, so that

$$F_x = IB_0 L = 100 \times 0.1 \times 1 = 10\,\text{N}$$

////////

10.1-3   Motoring Action

The laws of motoring are similar to the laws of generating. Using a similar analysis we will derive these laws directly in terms of voltages and currents. Consider the configuration of Fig. 10.1-2. A voltage source V is applied across the perfect conducting rails. The voltage source will cause a current density $-J_y$ in the bar. J_y will react with the magnetic flux B_0, giving rise to an electromechanical force $J_y B_0$ in the positive x direction. This force tends to accelerate the bar in the positive x direction. Thus the bar acquires a velocity v_x in the positive x direction. The charges in the bar having acquired this velocity react with the magnetic flux B_0, giving rise to a force $v_x B_0$ in the positive y direction. We note that since $v_x B_0$ behaves like an electric field in the positive y direction it opposes the action of the voltage source.

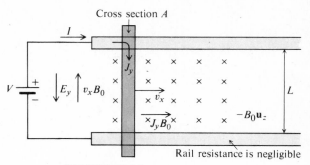

Cross section A

FIGURE 10.1-2
Geometry used in deriving motoring action laws.

Translating the above observations to mathematical terms yields
In the x direction, since $f_x = 0$:

$$m \frac{dv_x}{dt} = J_y B_0 \quad (10.1\text{-}8a)$$

In the y direction [following (10.1-4b)]:

$$-J_y = \sigma(-E_y + v_x B_0) \quad (10.1\text{-}8b)$$

As before, we now express these equations in terms of voltages and currents:

$$M \frac{dv_x}{dt} = ILB_0 - F_x \quad (10.1\text{-}8c)$$

$$v_x B_0 L = V - IR \quad (10.1\text{-}8d)$$

Note that in (10.1-8c) we introduced a force F_x which opposes the action of the electro-mechanical force ILB_0. The force F_x represents any mechanical load or a restraining force on the bar.

EXAMPLE 10.1-2 *An electromechanical slider* As an example of motoring action, consider the configuration shown in Fig. 10.1-3. The iron bar has a cross section $A = 1 \text{ cm}^2$ and is 50 cm long. The perfect conducting rails are fixed to a 45° inclined plane. The coefficient of friction between the rails and the bar is $\gamma = 0.1$. The magnetic flux B_0 is equal to 0.1 W/m². The bar is to climb the ramp with a constant velocity v_x. Find and sketch the required voltage V versus the velocity v_x.

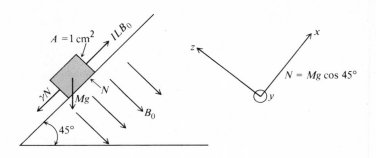

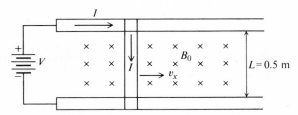

FIGURE 10.1-3
Figure for Example 10.1-2. (a) Side view; (b) horizontal view.

SOLUTION   Using the data given in Example 10.1-1, namely,

$$\sigma = 10^7 \ \mho/m \qquad \text{and} \qquad m = 7.5 \times 10^3 \ kg/m^3$$

we find

$$M = mAL = 7.5 \times 10^3 \times 10^{-4} \times 0.5 = 0.375 \ kg$$

$$R = \frac{L}{\sigma A} = \frac{0.5}{10^7 \times 10^{-4}} = 0.5 \times 10^{-3} \ \Omega$$

The forces opposing the electromechanical force are the weight of the bar and the friction force. An examination of Fig. 10.1-3 shows that

$$F_x = \gamma N + Mg \sin 45° = Mg(\gamma \cos 45° + \sin 45°)$$

Since we require the bar to climb with a constant velocity, (10.1-8a) reduces to

$$ILB_0 = F_x = Mg(\gamma \cos 45° + \sin 45°) \qquad (10.1-9)$$

Substituting numerical values in (10.1-9) yields

$$I = \frac{(0.375)(9.8)[(0.1)(0.707) + (0.707)]}{(0.5)(0.1)} = 56.5 \ A$$

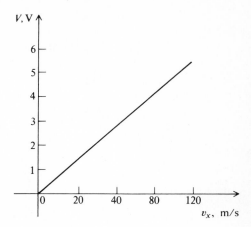

FIGURE 10.1-4
Graph of Eq. (10.1-10).

Substituting this value of I in (10.1-8b) yields

$$V = (56.5)(0.5 \times 10^{-3}) + (0.1)(0.5)v_x$$

Thus

$$V = 0.028 + 0.05v_x \quad (10.1\text{-}10)$$

Note that the velocity of the bar is directly proportional to the applied voltage. A plot of (10.1-10) is shown in Fig. 10.1-4.
////////

10.1-4 Comparison of Motoring Laws with Generating Laws

A comparison of (10.1-8) with (10.1-5) shows that the only difference between a device acting as a motor and a device acting as a generator is that, in the case of a motor, current is supplied *to* the device, whereas in the case of a generator, current is supplied *by* the device. Summarizing, for a motor the voltage source is larger than the electromotive force, whereas for a generator the electromotive force is larger than the output voltage. We end this section with the following example.

EXAMPLE 10.1-3 It is desired to design a system to carry a load for a distance d equal to 10 m up an inclined plane to a variable-height platform, as shown in Fig. 10.1-5. We have available a circular electromagnet of area 0.4 m², capable of delivering 1 Wb/m² and a current source capable of delivering up to 100 A. Design the

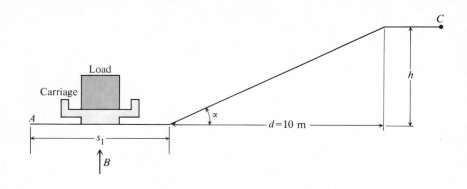

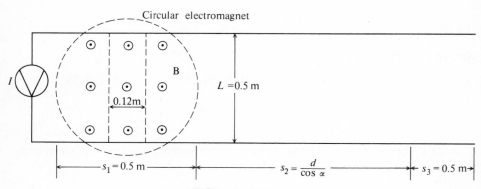

FIGURE 10.1-5
Geometry for Example 10.1-3. (*a*) Side view; (*b*) top view.

system in terms of h, the height of the movable platform, and M, the total mass of the carriage and load. The carriage starts at point A with zero velocity and is to stop on the platform at point C. Assume that the coefficient of friction γ of the rails is 0.01.

SOLUTION   As shown in Fig. 10.1-5, the system will consist of a sliding carriage carrying the load, accelerated for a short distance s_1, before the ramp by the electromagnetic field force. The kinetic energy thus acquired is used by the carriage to overcome friction and gravitational forces going up the ramp and enable the loaded carriage to come to a stop after a distance s_3 on the discharging platform.

Referring to (10.1-8) and Fig. 10.1-5, the equations of motion in the three regions s_1, s_2, and s_3 are

In the acceleration region s_1:

$$\frac{dv_x}{dt} = -\gamma g + \frac{ILB_0}{M} \qquad (10.1\text{-}11a)$$

On the ramp s_2:

$$\frac{dv_x}{dt} = -g(\gamma \cos \alpha + \sin \alpha) \qquad (10.1\text{-}11b)$$

On the platform s_3:

$$\frac{dv_x}{dt} = -g\gamma \qquad (10.1\text{-}11c)$$

It can be shown (Prob. 10.1-7) that the relation between initial and final velocities for the three regions are

$$v_1{}^2 = 2\left(-\gamma g + \frac{ILB_0}{M}\right)s_1 \qquad (10.1\text{-}12a)$$

$$v_2{}^2 - v_1{}^2 = -2gs_2(\gamma \cos \alpha + \sin \alpha) \qquad (10.1\text{-}12b)$$

$$v_2{}^2 = 2s_3\,\gamma g \qquad (10.1\text{-}12c)$$

where v_1 is the carriage velocity when it starts climbing the ramp, and v_2 its velocity on reaching the platform. Now, since the area of the electromagnet is 0.4 m², its diameter will be

$$D = \sqrt{\frac{4}{\pi}\,A} = \sqrt{\frac{4 \times 0.4}{\pi}} = 0.71 \text{ m}$$

Referring to Fig. 10.1-5, we will choose for the rails a separation $L = 0.5$ m and an accelerating distance $s_1 \approx 0.5$ m. Note that these values are chosen to be less than the diameter D of the electromagnet, so that the magnetic field covers the region of acceleration. Substituting (10.1-12a) and (10.1-12c) into (10.1-12b), we obtain

$$\left(\frac{ILB_0}{M\gamma g} - 1\right)s_1 = s_2\left(\cos \alpha + \frac{\sin \alpha}{\gamma}\right) + s_3 \qquad (10.1\text{-}13)$$

From Fig. 10.1-5 we see that

$$s_2 = \frac{d}{\cos \alpha} \qquad (10.1\text{-}14a)$$

$$\frac{h}{d} = \tan \alpha \qquad (10.1\text{-}14b)$$

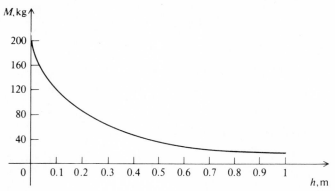

FIGURE 10.1-6
Variation of mass of carriage and load with platform height h for Example 10.1-3.

Combining (10.1-13) and (10.1-14) and using $ILB_0/M\gamma g$ as a parameter, we get

$$\frac{ILB_0}{M\gamma g} = \frac{d}{s_1} + \frac{s_3}{s_1} + 1 + \frac{h}{\gamma s_1} \quad (10.1\text{-}15)$$

Substituting the values given into (10.1-15), we find

$$M = \frac{(100)(0.5)(1)}{(0.01)(9.8)(20 + 1 + 1 + 200h)} = \frac{2,550}{11 + 100h} \quad \text{kg} \quad (10.1\text{-}16)$$

A plot of Eq. (10.1-16) is shown in Fig. 10.1-6. As expected, the higher the platform, the smaller the load that can be transported. For example, if $h = 1$ m, then $M \approx 23$ kg, but for $h = 0.1$ m, $M = 121$ kg.
////////

Note that in Example 10.1-3 we assumed a constant current, thus "decoupling" (10.1-8a) from (10.1-8b). If we use a voltage supply to provide the constant current I, then V must vary with time. Referring to (10.1-11a), since

$$v_x = \left(\frac{ILB_0}{M} - \gamma g\right)t \quad (10.1\text{-}17)$$

we find, by combining (10.1-17) with (10.1-8b), that

$$V = IR + \left(\frac{ILB_0}{M} - \gamma g\right)B_0 Lt \quad (10.1\text{-}18)$$

In a practical system, a constant current source can be constructed using a transistor or a constant voltage source with a very large output resistance R_0 (Prob. 10.1-8). In this case the IR term of (10.1-18) is much larger than the time-varying term and

$$I \approx \frac{V}{R} \quad (10.1\text{-}19)$$

Note also that R in (10.1-19) represents the series combination of the output resistance of the voltage source with the resistance of the rails and carriage. To complete the cycle, the student is asked to show (Prob. 10.1-9) that the electromechanical force ILB_0 will act as a brake for the descending carriage.

10.1-5 A DC Motor-Generator

In this section we shall discuss a device commonly used in electromechanical power conversion. In analyzing the performance of this machine, we will make a series of simplifying assumptions which will reduce the complicated equations involved to several simpler relations. Refer to Fig. 10.1-7. The actual device is more complicated, but its main features are similar to those shown in Fig. 10.1-7. The device is composed of a cylindrical block made of iron with a cylindrical shell cut out of the inside, called the *air gap*. Situated within the air gap there are current-carrying coils which give rise to a magnetic flux B_0 in the direction shown. A thin copper cup rotates in the air gap with angular velocity ω. The copper cup is in contact with two rings, called *brushes*, spaced a distance L apart. The voltage between the brushes is V. Before deriving the relations between the voltage V and the angular velocity ω of the copper cup, we will make some simplifying assumptions. We assume first that near the cup the flux is only in the radial direction as shown. Second, since the cup is thin, we assume that each point in the cup has the same velocity $v = \omega r_c$, where r_c is the radius of the cup. At $r = r_c$ we construct a cartesian system of coordinates as shown in Fig. 10.1-8: the radial direction becomes the z axis, the tangential direction becomes the x axis, and the axial direction becomes the y axis.

We now apply (10.1-5) or (10.1-8), which we repeat for convenience, to our system.

$$M \frac{dv_x}{dt} = F_x - ILB_0 \quad (10.1\text{-}5a)$$

$$v_x B_0 L = V + IR \quad (10.1\text{-}5b)$$

$$M \frac{dv_x}{dt} = ILB_0 - F_x \quad (10.1\text{-}8a)$$

$$v_x B_0 L = V - IR \quad (10.1\text{-}8b)$$

To identify the various terms in these equations, we make the following observations:

1   The mass M is that of the copper cup and associated shaft.
2   This is a rotating body, so that the angular velocity ω is a more significant parameter than the linear velocity v.

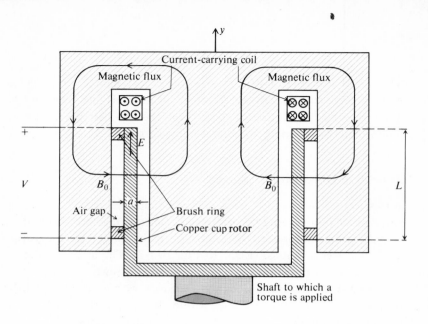

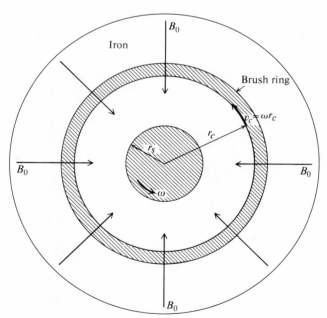

FIGURE 10.1-7
A dc motor-generator. (*a*) Side view; (*b*) bottom view.

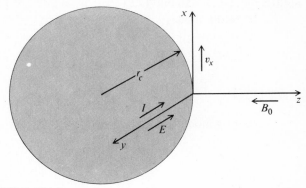

FIGURE 10.1-8
Coordinate axis used in deriving the dc motor-generator relations.

3   The load on the shaft exerts a torque on the rotating mass equal to $F_x r_s$ (Fig. 10.1-7).

4   It is usual to express the device relations in terms of the total magnetic flux ψ. Since **B** is radial, the area perpendicular to **B** is represented by the lateral area of the cylindrical cup located between the brushes. This gives us a magnetic flux

$$\psi = 2\pi r_c L B_0$$

5   R is the resistance of the cup measured between the brushes.

Taking into account points 1 to 5, (10.1-5) and (10.1-8) become
    Generating mode:

$$M r_c^2 \frac{d\omega}{dt} = T - \frac{I\psi}{2\pi} \quad (10.1\text{-}20a)$$

$$\frac{\omega\psi}{2\pi} = V + IR \quad (10.1\text{-}20b)$$

    Motoring mode:

$$M r_c^2 \frac{d\omega}{dt} = \frac{I\psi}{2\pi} - T \quad (10.1\text{-}21a)$$

$$\frac{\omega\psi}{2\pi} = V - IR \quad (10.1\text{-}21b)$$

We are interested in the electromechanical power conversion in the steady state. Thus we assume that the angular velocity ω is a constant, that is, $d\omega/dt = 0$. Now

multiplying (10.1-20a) and (10.1-21a) by ω and (10.1-20b) and (10.1-21b) by I, we get
Generating mode:

$$\omega T = \frac{\omega I \psi}{2\pi} \qquad (10.1\text{-}22a)$$

$$\frac{\omega I \psi}{2\pi} = VI + I^2 R \qquad (10.1\text{-}22b)$$

Motoring mode:

$$\omega T = \frac{\omega I \psi}{2\pi} \qquad (10.1\text{-}23a)$$

$$\frac{\omega I \psi}{2\pi} = VI - I^2 R \qquad (10.1\text{-}23b)$$

We make the following observations: (1) $P_m = \omega T$ represents the mechanical power at the shaft either absorbed by the device when it acts as a generator or delivered by the device when it acts as a motor. (2) $P_c = \omega I \psi / 2\pi$ is the power converted either from mechanical power to electric power or from electric power to mechanical power. (3) $P_d = RI^2$ is the power dissipated in the copper cup. It represents a loss from the point of view of electromechanical power conversion, since all it does is heat the copper cup. (4) $P_e = VI$ is the electric power either absorbed by the device acting as a motor or supplied by the device acting as a generator.
Summarizing,

$$P_e = P_d + P_m \qquad (10.1\text{-}24)$$

for a motor, and

$$P_e = P_m - P_d \qquad (10.1\text{-}25)$$

for a generator.
This type of motor-generator usually operates at low voltages and high currents. A typical example would be a General Electric generator rated at $V = 67$ V which delivers an electric power of 10,000 kW at $\omega = 377$ rad/s.

Brushes, efficiency, regulation   Since the electric power is produced by the rotating cup (armature), the connections to the outside voltage supply in the case of a motor, or user in the case of a generator, cannot be made by simply attaching wires. The method employed is to use two rings, called *brushes*, which slide over the ends of the rotor (Fig. 10.1-7), collect the current, and transmit it to the outside. To minimize the contact resistance, these brushes are often made from liquid metal. This method smooths the contacts and reduces the total resistance, and therefore reduces the total power losses. Finally, since the area of the brush is much smaller than that of the motor, it is this area which determines the maximum allowable current into or out of the machine.

The *efficiency* of the device is given by the ratio of electric output power to mechanical input power for a generator, and by the ratio of output mechanical power to input electric power for a motor.

The *regulation* of the device is defined as the variation of output voltage with output current for a generator or output speed with output torque for a motor. The regulation is an important parameter, especially in cases where a constant output voltage or output speed is desired. Mathematically, we have

Efficiency of a generator:

$$\eta_g = \frac{P_e}{P_m} \quad (10.1\text{-}26)$$

Efficiency of a motor:

$$\eta_m = \frac{P_m}{P_e} \quad (10.1\text{-}27)$$

Percent regulation of a generator:

$$\% \text{ regulation} = \frac{V_{NL} - V_L}{V_L} \times 100 \quad (10.1\text{-}28)$$

Percent regulation of a motor:

$$\% \text{ regulation} = \frac{\omega_{NL} - \omega_L}{\omega_L} \times 100 \quad (10.1\text{-}29)$$

where V_{NL} and ω_{NL} represent the no-load voltage and no-load angular velocity, respectively, and V_L and ω_L represent the voltage and angular velocity under load.

Equivalent circuit of a motor-generator   Electrical engineers often find it conceptually useful to represent electromechanical systems such as the motor-generator in terms of all-electric *equivalent circuits*. These equivalent circuits can be drawn by considering the equations describing the dynamic behavior of the device. For the motor-generator the pertinent relations are Eqs. (10.1-20) and (10.1-21). The equivalent circuit is shown in Fig. 10.1-9a for operation as a motor and in Fig. 10.1-9b for operation as a generator.

For both modes of operation, the left (electrical) side of each circuit is a model for (10.1-20b) and (10.1-21b), and contains a voltage source whose value is proportional to the angular velocity of the rotor. This represents the electromechanical coupling, and as we mentioned before [Eq. (10.1-6)], it is called the electromotive force.

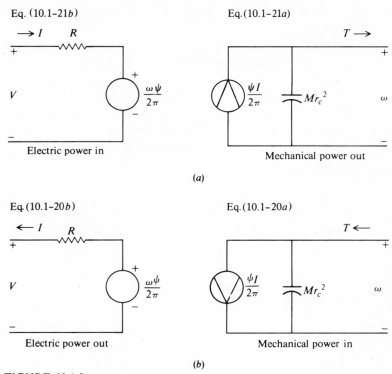

Eq. (10.1-21b)   Eq. (10.1-21a)

Electric power in   Mechanical power out

(a)

Eq. (10.1-20b)   Eq. (10.1-20a)

Electric power out   Mechanical power in

(b)

FIGURE 10.1-9
All-electric analog equivalent circuits of dc motor-generator. (*a*) Motor; (*b*) generator.

The right (mechanical) side which models (10.1-20*a*) and (10.1-21*a*) contains a current-dependent current source and a capacitance representing the moment of inertia of the rotor. In this electromechanical analog, angular velocity is analogous to voltage, and torque is analogous to current. Similar analogies are often encountered in the study of acoustical and thermal devices. They provide engineers with means to perform "simulation tests"; i.e., they study the importance of different parameters by simply changing values of resistances and capacitances in the all-electrical analog. This is easier than replacing heavy and hard-to-construct mechanical devices. Devices which perform this type of tests are called *analog computers*.

EXAMPLE 10.1-4 A generator is designed to deliver 500 kW. When its speed is

60 revolutions per second (rps), the generated voltage is 50 V. The dimensions of the copper-cup rotor are

$$L = 0.3 \text{ m}$$
$$r_c = 0.3 \text{ m}$$
$$a = 0.5 \text{ mm}$$
$$\sigma = 5 \times 10^7 \text{ ℧/m}$$

(a) Find the resistance of the copper cup.

(b) Find the required magnetic flux density.

(c) Find the torque and the mechanical power necessary to generate 500 kW of electric power.

(d) Assuming mechanical power losses of about 5 kW, find the efficiency of the generator.

SOLUTION   (a) The resistance of the cup is given by (Fig. 10.1-7)

$$R = \frac{L}{\sigma A_R} = \frac{1}{\sigma} \frac{L}{2\pi r_c a} = \frac{0.3}{5 \times 10^7 \times 2 \times 0.3 \times 0.5 \times 10^{-3}} = 6.36 \times 10^{-6} \ \Omega$$

$$I = \frac{P_e}{V} = \frac{500 \times 10^3}{50} = 10,000 \ A$$

(b) To find B_0, we use the equivalent circuit of Fig. 10.1-9b. For the electrical side, KVL yields

$$\frac{\omega \psi}{2\pi} = V + IR = 50 + 10^4 \times 6.36 \times 10^{-6} \approx 50.06 \text{ V}$$

or

$$\psi = \frac{2\pi \times 50.06}{2\pi \times 60} = 0.835 \text{ Wb}$$

Next we find the flux density B_0 from

$$B_0 = \frac{\psi}{A} = \frac{\psi}{2\pi r_c L} = \frac{0.835}{2\pi \times 0.3 \times 0.3} = 1.48 \text{ Wb/m}^2$$

(c) From Fig. 10.1-9b we see that in the steady state (constant angular velocity)

$$T = \frac{I\psi}{2\pi} = \frac{10^4 \times 0.835}{6.28} = 1,330 \text{ N·m}$$

and, as noted previously

$$P_m = \omega T = \frac{2\pi \times 60 \times 10^4 \times 0.835}{2\pi} = 50.06 \times 10^4 \text{ W}$$

(d) The efficiency of a generator with mechanical power losses is

$$\eta_g = \frac{P_e}{P_m + P_{loss}} = \frac{500 \times 10^3}{500.6 \times 10^3 + 5 \times 10^3} = 98.9\%$$

EXAMPLE 10.1-5   The generator of Example 10.1-4 is to be used as a motor. If the input voltage and electric power are as above, find the mechanical power delivered at the shaft and the efficiency of the motor.

SOLUTION   Since power delivered and the voltage remain the same, the motor current does not change. The dissipated power will be, then,

$$P_d = I^2 R = (10,000)^2 \times 6.36 \times 10^{-6} = 636 \text{ W}$$

The mechanical power at the shaft will then be

$$P_m = P_e - P_d - P_{\text{mechanical losses}} = 5 \times 10^5 - 636 - 5,000 = 494,364 \text{ W}$$

The efficiency of the motor is then

$$\eta_m = \frac{P_m}{P_e} = \frac{494,364}{500,000} = 98.8\%$$

The above efficiencies, although a little high, are typical for this type of motor-generator. Measured efficiencies of 95 percent are quite common.
///////

10.2   ELECTROOPTICAL POWER CONVERSION; THE LASER

Optical waves are electromagnetic waves in the frequency range from 10^{13} to 10^{15} Hz. The optical waves in the region from 4×10^{14} to 7.5×10^{14} Hz are perceived by us as visible light. In this section we investigate some recent developments in this area.

10.2-1   Sources of Light

Light is a radiation phenomenon; as in any radiation process, the source of the radiation is a current. The current producing this radiation is formed by an electron which is bound to a nucleus. From Sec. 9.1 we know that one can relate the energy of the electron to its distance from the nucleus. We also know that the electron can have only certain allowable energies with which we can associate certain fixed distances from the nucleus. For a body in thermal equilibrium, the number of electrons at every energy level is a function of the energy level, the temperature, and the nature of

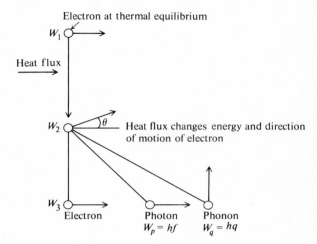

FIGURE 10.2-1
The electron absorbs energy from the heat flux and later goes to a new thermal equilibrium, emitting a photon and a phonon.

the body. If an electron rises from a lower to a higher energy level, it will absorb energy, and if it drops from a higher to a lower energy level, it will deliver energy.

The rise in energy is due to collisions with free electrons, ions, or photons (incoming external radiation). When an electron loses energy, the amount lost is transformed either into a vibration of the atom (rise in temperature of the body) or into radiation of electromagnetic waves, or both.

For example, consider the heating of iron for forging. As the temperature of the iron increases, we observe a red glow at about 600°C which turns into yellow as the temperature increases further. Ultimately, it becomes a bright white glow at extremely high temperatures. What happens is that the heat energy absorbed by the iron is transformed partly into a vibration of its atoms, thus raising its temperature, and partly into electromagnetic radiation which we observe as a visible glow. A diagram of the process is shown in Fig. 10.2-1. The electron at W_1 absorbs energy from the heat flux, thus changing its energy from W_1 to W_2 and its direction of motion from an angle 0 to an angle θ. In trying to reach a new thermal equilibrium, it releases the energy $W_2 - W_3$, which partly is transformed into electromagnetic radiation and partly serves to increase the vibrations of the atoms. A useful way to represent radiation is as a flow of particles called *photons*, each having an energy hf, where f is the frequency of the radiation, and $h = 6.6 \times 10^{-34}$ J·s is a constant of proportionality called *Planck's constant*.

Similarly, the vibrations of atoms (acoustical energy) can be represented as a flow of particles called *phonons*, each of energy hq, where q is the frequency with which the atoms vibrate. The law of conservation of energy then gives

$$W_2 - W_3 = hf + hq \qquad (10.2\text{-}1)$$

The law of conservation of momentum gives (Fig. 10.2-1)

$$mv \sin \theta = \frac{hq}{C_q} \qquad (10.2\text{-}2a)$$

where C_q = velocity of propagation of acoustic waves
  hq/C_q = moment of a phonon
    mv = moment of the electron with energy W_2
Assuming that most of the electron energy was kinetic, it is easy to show that (Prob. 10.2-1)

$$\sqrt{2mW_2} \sin \theta \approx \frac{hq}{C_q} \qquad (10.2\text{-}2b)$$

We see from Fig. 10.2-1 that the directions of propagation of acoustic and electromagnetic waves are perpendicular to each other. We will concentrate on the propagation of the electromagnetic wave.

10.2-2   Coherent and Incoherent Sources

Since electrons have mass, the transition from one energy level to another takes time. Due to the way we measure the transition time and the frequency of the resulting radiation, it turns out that the faster the transition, the less precisely we know the exact frequency of the emitted radiation. This means that we can associate with the radiation a *band spread*; i.e., the photon can have any one of a number of energies. A body contains many atoms, and due to heating, it will emit a large number of photons. The intensity distribution of this radiation is shown in Fig. 10.2-2 as a function of normalized frequency. The maximum value of the intensity depends on temperature and occurs at higher and higher frequencies as the temperature increases. Because of the large bandwidth, the radiation will consist of a large number of frequencies, so that the intensity over a narrow band will be very small. Also, since large bandwidth means a small time constant, the electrons will be excited and lose their energy so fast that they are not able to influence each other. This means that the photons will be launched at random times, or what is the same thing, the phase of the plane waves (Chap. 8) representing the radiation components will be random. We call such a radiation an *incoherent temporal radiation*. Also, since the electrons do not "see" each other, the direction of this radiation varies at random, thus reducing the average intensity in any given direction even more. We call this a *spatially incoherent radiation*. In summary, then, the radiation from a heated source is spatially

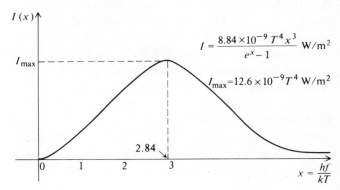

FIGURE 10.2-2
Radiation intensity versus normalized frequency for an incoherent source.

and temporally incoherent, and this results in a low average energy per unit area and time, i.e., a low brightness. (*Brightness* is defined as the average energy per unit time and area emitted by a source of light.)

The brightness of an ordinary source is found by integrating the area under the curve of Fig. 10.2-2:

$$B = 5.67 \times 10^4 \left(\frac{T}{1,000}\right)^4 \quad \text{W/m}^2 \quad (10.2\text{-}3)$$

with T the temperature in degrees Kelvin. Equation (10.2-3) is called *Stefan's law*. As an example, the light from a tungsten incandescent bulb at 2000°K has a brightness of 9×10^5 W/m^2, which is very small indeed as compared with that of the laser, which is about 10^{13} W/m^2. To achieve a high brightness, we require a process with a very slow deexcitation rate of electrons, one in which the electrons will stay in the excited level for a long time, "get to know each other," and then jump together, so that the emitted radiation will be unidirectional and almost monochromatic; that is, it will be *coherent in space and time*.

Such a process was found with the discovery of the laser.

10.2-3 Characteristics of Laser Light

Before describing the process by which *laser* light is produced, let us make a comparison between the radiation characteristics of a helium-neon laser and an ordinary source such as a tungsten bulb.

Bandwidth A helium-neon laser has a center frequency of 4.75×10^{14} Hz with a bandwidth of 10^8 Hz, while a tungsten lamp has for the same center frequency a bandwidth of about 6×10^{14} Hz. A bulb would have to deliver 6×10^6 greater power than a helium-neon (He-Ne) laser to produce equivalent power in the same range of frequencies. For example, if the laser power were 1 mW, the bulb would have to deliver 6,000 kW to achieve the same power over the 10^8 Hz range.

Directivity The angular spread of a laser light is about 1.5 minutes of arc. To achieve the same intensity in a given direction, since the light from a bulb is isotropic, (i.e., uniform in all directions), the ratio of bulb to laser power would have to be (there are 60 minutes per degree)

$$\frac{P_B}{P_L} = \frac{360° \times 60'}{1.5'} = 144,000$$

Brightness The brightness of a laser source is, approximately,

$$B = \left(\frac{10}{\lambda}\right)^2 P \qquad \text{W/m}^2 \qquad (10.2\text{-}4)$$

where λ = wavelength of the laser radiation
  P = power radiated by the laser
For a 100-mW He-Ne laser with a wavelength of 0.6328×10^{-6} m, this comes to about 2.5×10^{13} W/m^2. Using Stefan's law, we observe that a bulb would have to be raised to a temperature

$$T = \left(\frac{2.5 \times 10^{13} \times 10^{12}}{5.67 \times 10^{-2}}\right)^{1/4} = (4.4 \times 10^{26})^{1/4} = 4.6 \times 10^6 \text{ °K}$$

to achieve the same brightness. Note that the normal operating temperature of a tungsten bulb is ≈ 2000°K.

The above figures show succinctly why the scientists were so excited about the discovery of the laser and why its discoverers received the Nobel prize.

10.2-4 Laser Devices; How Laser Action Is Achieved

In this section we shall describe the action of a gas laser. To this end we introduce the concept of a *resonant cavity* and study its basic characteristics.

The helium-neon laser A typical gas laser is shown in Fig. 10.2-3a. It is composed of a hermetically sealed tube in which a gas or a mixture of gases exists. The tube is sealed at its ends by two inclined windows, called the *Brewster windows*. The tube is

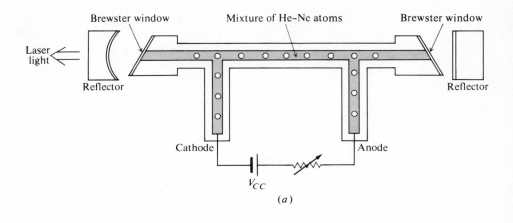

Brewster window · Mixture of He-Ne atoms · Brewster window

Laser light

Reflector · Cathode · Anode · Reflector

V_{CC}

(a)

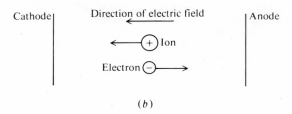

Cathode · Direction of electric field · Anode

(+) Ion

Electron (−)

(b)

FIGURE 10.2-3
(a) A He-Ne laser. (b) Direction of electric field and of flow of charges in the He-Ne tube.

supplied with energy from a dc voltage source which creates a strong electric field between the two terminals, called the *anode* and the *cathode*. Finally, on the same axis as the tube are two reflectors which are coated with a dielectric material. We will describe the function of each element as we proceed.

Before continuing we should note that the arrangement in Fig. 10.2-3a is typical, although not unique.

To proceed in a logical way, we divide the analysis of the laser action into two parts. First we describe the light amplification occurring in the tube, and second, the role of the device as an oscillator.

The electric field produced by the voltage V_{CC} ionizes some of the atoms in the He-Ne mixture, thus creating free electrons, ions, and neutral atoms. This mixture is called a plasma. Due to the electric field, the electrons and ions will be accelerated toward the anode and cathode, as shown in Fig. 10.2-3b. Since the electrons have a smaller mass, they acquire a higher velocity. While in motion, the electrons will

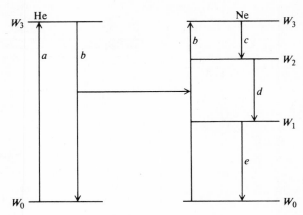

FIGURE 10.2-4
(*a*) He is excited to level W_3 by electron collision. (*b*) He collides with Ne, thus exciting a Ne atom to level W_3. (*c*) Ne collides with an outside photon of energy $W_3 - W_2$. Ne drops to level W_2, emitting a photon of energy $W_3 - W_2$. (*d*) Ne drops to level W_1, emitting incoherent radiation at $W_2 - W_1$. (*e*) Ne drops by collision with the walls of the tube.

collide with ions and atoms of both He and Ne and transfer part of their energy to these ions and atoms. Because He atoms are lighter, they will be more affected by these collisions, and their electrons will rise to a higher energy level. We say that the atoms of He are excited to a higher level.

In Fig. 10.2-4 we represent this by an arrow *a*. The helium atom or ion in turn collides with a neon atom, thereby losing its energy to it. The remarkable fact here is that for this type of energy exchange to be efficient, the two gases must have *equal energy levels*, which is indeed the case for He and Ne. If the two levels W_3 of Ne and He were not equal, the energy exchange would not occur and the story would stop here. An analogy could be made with two billiard balls. To have a strong collision with one ball stopping and the other taking over all the energy, a head-on collision is necessary. Due to this collision, the helium electron returns to energy W_0 and the Ne electron is excited to level W_3. This is a level in which the Ne electron can stay excited for a relatively long time. We then have a situation where we get many neon atoms excited at the W_3 level. If now a photon of energy $W_3 - W_2$ strikes the Ne atom, the atom drops to energy W_2, emitting a photon of energy $W_3 - W_2$ in phase with the striking photon. Thus we get two photons traveling together and "knowing about each other" so that the distance between them and their direction with respect to each other are fixed. As these photons meet other excited Ne atoms in their paths, more and more photons of the same energy and direction are created, giving rise to a spatially and temporally coherent light wave. Of course, if we send a beam of light containing many photons having energy $W_3 - W_2$, not all of them will collide with the neon atoms, so that the gain turns out to be only about 10 percent per meter of tube.

For completeness we note that from level W_2 the electron drops quickly to level W_1, emitting a photon which, because of the speed of the decay, gives rise to an incoherent light beam (Sec. 10.2-2). Finally, the neon atom drifts toward the wall and collides with it, giving up the energy $W_1 - W_0$. This heats the wall and returns the neon atom to its W_0 level.

Laser oscillation   If no external beam of photons exists, we might expect that no light will come from the laser. This is not quite so. First, the electrons in level W_3, although they stay there for a long time, eventually drop down to level W_2, thereby creating photons of energy $W_3 - W_2$. Also, light from the surroundings contains all kinds of photons of different energies, among them the energy $W_3 - W_2$, and a photon of this type might also start a chain reaction. In general, then, corresponding to a certain dc energy input, there will always be a certain amount of photons of energy $W_3 - W_2$ emitted by the tube; but since this energy is lost to the surroundings upon reaching the walls of the tube, its power will be very small.

Suppose now (Fig. 10.2-3) that we attach two reflectors coated so as to reflect back all photons of energy $W_3 - W_2$ and be transparent to photons of other energies. Then a photon of energy $W_3 - W_2$ moving in the direction of the reflector will be turned back and thus pass through the tube again. This will enable it to increase the stimulated emission of photons at this energy, thus creating more photons, which are also reflected back and forth, until a state of equilibrium between the number of excited helium and neon atoms and the number of photons of energy $W_3 - W_2$ is created, thus producing a steady flow of photons bouncing between the two reflectors.

If we now make the reflectors less than perfect (say, 99 percent reflection), a beam of photons will trickle out, and thus we obtain a source of coherent light. This light is coherent because, as we mentioned before, the photons are emitted in phase and in the same direction. Thus each photon keeps in touch with each other photon for a long time. To improve this coherence further, we attach the Brewster windows to the ends of the tube. The Brewster windows have the property that they pass electromagnetic waves with an electric field in a fixed direction, totally reflecting waves with an electric field in the perpendicular direction, so that the light coming out is *linearly polarized*, a fact which helps keep the beam coherent for a longer time, and it is also useful in certain applications, such as *light modulation*.

The reflectors, by virtue of their characteristics, also help improve the coherence of the laser beam. To show this, consider that we transmit a light beam as in Fig.

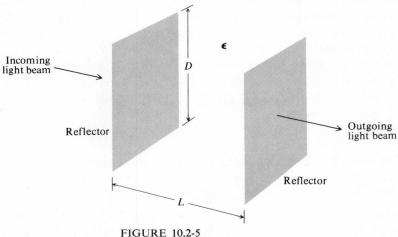

FIGURE 10.2-5
A Fabry-Perot interferometer used as a resonating cavity.

10.2-5. Then resonance conditions (Prob. 10.2-5) require that maximum transmission occurs at values of frequency given by

$$f = \frac{N v_p}{2L} \quad (10.2\text{-}5)$$

where v_p = velocity of light in the host medium
     L = distance between the two reflectors
     N = an integer

The device shown in Fig. 10.2-5 is called a *Fabry-Perot interferometer*. If the dimensions of the reflectors were infinite and their thickness zero, the transmission would drop to zero at all other frequencies. Since their dimensions are by necessity finite, and some losses occur as light bounces between them, transmission will occur in a narrow range of frequencies around the center frequency given by (10.2-5). It can also be shown that the reflectors will favor the transmission of a light beam with a direction of propagation perpendicular to their plane.

Returning to the He-Ne laser, we see that the presence of the Fabry-Perot resonator will facilitate the appearance of light of frequencies given by (10.2-5). This light wave will have a very narrow bandwidth and will be of fixed directivity as determined by the axial direction of the tube which is perpendicular to the plane of the reflectors.

EXAMPLE 10.2-1   Assume a Fabry-Perot resonator as shown in Fig. 10.2-5. The host medium is He-Ne, and the velocity of light in this medium $v_P = 3 \times 10^8$ m/s. A photon is generated spontaneously at time $t = 0$. Find the time it takes for a steady-state output of 50 mW to occur. Assume all other photons are created by stimulated emission and the one-trip gain is 4 percent. Assume a 1 percent power transmission and an axial length of 1 m.

SOLUTION   Since the host medium is He-Ne,

$$f = 4.75 \times 10^{14} \text{ Hz}$$

and the energy of a photon is

$$W_p = hf = 6.62 \times 10^{-34} \times 4.75 \times 10^{14} = 31.5 \times 10^{-20} \text{ J}$$

The average energy of a sine wave of frequency f and power P is

$$W_{\text{avg}} = \frac{P}{f}$$

The power of the laser is 50 mW. Since the transmission power is 1 percent, the internal power is 5 W and its average energy is

$$W_{\text{avg}} = \frac{5}{4.75 \times 10^{14}} = 1.05 \times 10^{-14} \text{ J}$$

The number of photons in a period is then

$$n = \frac{W_{\text{avg}}}{W_p} = \frac{1.05 \times 10^{-14}}{31.5 \times 10^{-20}} = 3.33 \times 10^4 \text{ photons}$$

Assuming one photon starts at $t = 0$ and the gain is 4 percent per trip, we will have, after p trips, a number of photons

$$n = (1.04)^p \qquad (10.2\text{-}6)$$

Substituting numerical values, we get

$$p = \frac{\log n}{\log 1.04} = \frac{\log 3.33 \times 10^4}{\log 1.04} \approx 260$$

The time for one trip is

$$t_0 = \frac{L}{v_p} = \frac{1}{3 \times 10^8} = 0.333 \times 10^{-8} \text{ s}$$

The time for 260 trips is then

$$T = pt_0 = 0.333 \times 10^{-8} \times 260 = 8.67 \times 10^{-7} \text{ s}$$

T represents approximately the transient time necessary for steady state to be reached. From Sec. 4.2-4 the transient time is approximately the inverse of bandwidth. The bandwidth will then be

$$B \approx \frac{1}{T} = \frac{1}{8.67 \times 10^{-7}} \approx 1.15 \times 10^6 \text{ Hz} = 1.15 \text{ MHz} \qquad (10.2\text{-}7)$$

Note that this represents the bandwidth of the Fabry-Perot interferometer, not of the He-Ne mixture, which is much higher.

EXAMPLE 10.2-2   The natural bandwidth of a He-Ne mixture is 1,500 MHz. For the laser in Example 10.2-1 find and sketch the number of center frequencies present in the output. These center frequencies are called *axial modes*.

SOLUTION   According to Eq. (10.2-5) (see also Prob. 10.2-6), the distance between two axial modes is

$$\Delta f = \frac{v_P}{2L} = \frac{3 \times 10^8}{2} \text{ Hz} \qquad (10.2\text{-}8)$$

The number of modes will be

$$m = \frac{1,500}{150} = 10$$

A sketch is shown in Fig. 10.2-6.

////////

From Examples 10.2-1 and 10.2-2 we see that the laser beam will consist of electromagnetic waves of different frequencies, each having a bandwidth as given by Eq. (10.2-7). The number of waves m will depend on the natural bandwidth of the host medium and the axial length of the laser. The bandwidth of these waves, on the other hand, will depend on the time it takes the beam to reach steady state.

10.2-5   Other Laser Devices

A detailed description of laser action was given in Sec. 10.2-4 for the He-Ne laser. A He-Ne mixture is only one of many types of host media. There are lasers with host media consisting of other gases, solid-state lasers, liquid lasers, chemical lasers, etc. The external energy supply instead of a dc field could be an RF (radio-frequency) field, light, or a chemical reaction. In all these devices the laser action is due to an accumulation of electrons or atoms or molecules in an excited state, from which they drop to thermal equilibrium by stimulated emission due to a passing photon. The

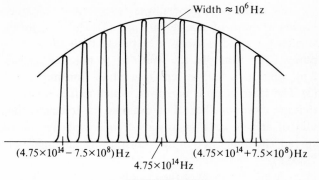

FIGURE 10.2-6
Axial modes of a 1-m-long He-Ne laser.

stimulated emission generates photons which are coherent in time and space, as described above. Different types of lasers, their frequency, and *lasing* action are given in Table 10.2-1.

10.2-6   Laser Applications

The laser as a ranging device; laser radar   In Chap. 8 we discussed the use of microwave frequencies in ranging devices. In a similar fashion we can use a laser pulse. The advantages are: (1) The laser pulses are shorter, so that the ranging accuracy is improved. Pulses of the order of picoseconds to nanoseconds are within

Table 10.2-1

Type of laser	Frequency, Hz	Power	Type of excitation	Laser action
GaAs *pn* junction	4×10^{14} to 5×10^{14}	1 mW	dc	Electron-hole re-combination at junction
CO_2 gas laser	2.83×10^{14} and 3.12×10^{14}	mW to kW	dc	Molecular vibra-tion or rotation
Ruby (aluminum oxide $+0.05\%$ chromium)	4.32×10^{14}	Giant pulses up to 50 MW in 10^{-8} s	Light	Deexcitation of chromium atom
Nd-YAG ($Y_3Al_5O_{12} + $ Nd)	2.83×10^{14}	Giant pulses up to 50 MW in 10^{-8} s	Light	Deexcitation of neodymium ion

the state of the art for lasers, whereas microwave-frequency radars operate with pulses having a width of about 0.01 μs. (2) The dimensions of the sending antenna are smaller for a radar using laser pulses than for a radar using microwave-frequency pulses. For example, the width of an antenna transmitting at 4×10^9 Hz is about 3 m, whereas a 0.05-m lens is used to transmit a laser frequency of 5×10^{14} Hz. (3) The laser beam is narrower, which makes it easier to distinguish between targets that are close together. For example, laser beams have a spread of about 1.5 minutes of arc; to get a microwave-frequency beam of 10^9 Hz, say, to have a similar spread, the dimension of the transmitting antenna would have to be in the order of 7,200 m.

A disadvantage of the laser beam is that, in the atmosphere, the higher frequencies are more quickly dispersed (made less directional). That is why laser radar is used mostly either in outer-space ranging or over very short ranges. A laser radar was used to measure the distance to the moon with the help of a mirror left there by the astronauts. This measurement has led to corrections to previous measurements of the distance to the moon, its orbit, and shape.

EXAMPLE 10.2-3   Compare the range accuracy and power spread of a microwave-frequency radar with that of a laser-beam radar. The microwave radar has a horn antenna 3 m in diameter. Its frequency is 4×10^9 Hz, and the width of the pulse is 5×10^{-8} s. The laser-beam antenna is a lens 5×10^{-2} m in diameter, its frequency is 5×10^{14} Hz, and the width of the pulse is 100×10^{-12} s. It is assumed that the arrival time of the received pulse is known within half its width. The reason for this is that the pulse gets distorted (Fig. 10.2-7) in its travel to the target and back. Next, it is assumed that the angular spread is given by λ/D, where λ is the wavelength, and D is the diameter of the antenna. Consequently, the area of the beam at the target will be, approximately,

$$A_R = \frac{\lambda^2}{A_T} R^2 \qquad (10.2\text{-}9)$$

where A_T = area of beam transmitted
   A_R = area of beam at the target
   R = distance to target

   SOLUTION   Since the range accuracy is known within $T/2$, the ratio of the two errors will be proportional to the ratio of their respective pulse widths.

$$\frac{\Delta R_M}{\Delta R_L} = \frac{T_M}{T_L} = \frac{5 \times 10^{-8}}{10^{-10}} = 500$$

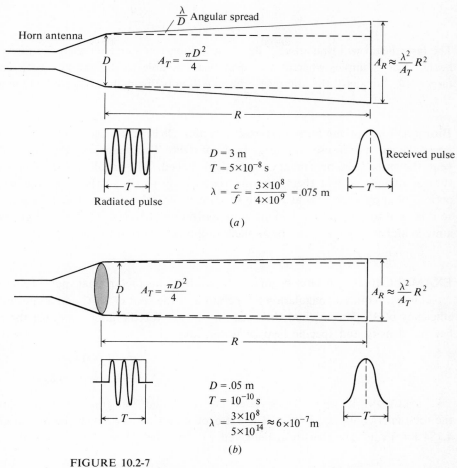

FIGURE 10.2-7
(*a*) Geometries associated with the microwave-frequency radar. (*b*) Geometries associated with the laser radar.

That is, the laser beam will determine the range 500 times more accurately than the microwave beam. The resolution of the radar depends on the area covered by the beam. The larger the area, the less fine the detail that can be discerned. The ratio of the two areas is [Eq. (10.2-9)]

$$\frac{A_{RM}}{A_{RL}} = \frac{\lambda_M^2 D_L^2}{\lambda_L^2 D_M^2}$$

Substituting numerical values, the student is asked to show that

$$\frac{A_{RM}}{A_{RL}} = 4.34 \times 10^6$$

The laser beam will thus discern details a million times smaller than the microwave beam. For example, whereas the laser beam is able to differentiate between two targets 10^{-3} m apart, the microwave beam will only distinguish targets 4.34 km apart. ////////

Biological use of the laser: eye-retina repair   When the retina of an eye is torn, one way to repair it is to use an intense beam of light. This coagulates the spot and prevents the retina from becoming completely detached. The problem with using regular sources of light is that their intensity is relatively small, so that they require long periods of application (about $\frac{1}{2}$ s). In such long intervals, the eye usually moves, and so it is hard to fix the spot, and eye immobilization is necessary. A laser light having a much higher brightness can be applied for a much shorter time.

EXAMPLE 10.2-4   A laser beam is focussed for 1 ms on a retinal spot 0.1 mm wide. Assuming a required coagulation temperature of the spot of 80°C and a laser heating efficiency of 10 percent, find the necessary power for the laser. Assume the retina has the density and specific heat of water, i.e.,

$$m = 1,000 \text{ kg/m}^3$$
$$c = 1 \text{ cal/(°C)(kg)}$$

SOLUTION   If we call the laser power P and the time of application t_0, the total energy applied is Pt_0. The ratio of joules to calories in the mks system is 4,184 J = 1 cal. The total heat delivered will then be

$$Q = \frac{Pt_0}{4,184} \qquad (10.2\text{-}10)$$

Part of this heat will raise the temperature of the spot, and the rest will either be radiated to the surroundings or conducted to other parts of the body.

The heat necessary to raise the temperature of the spot, assumed to be a cube with sides equal to 0.1 mm, is

$$Q_H = mcV \, \Delta T \qquad (10.2\text{-}11)$$

where Q_H = necessary heat, cal
   m = density of spot, kg/m^3
   c = specific heat, cal/(°C)(kg)
   V = volume, m^3
   ΔT = change in temperature, °C

Combining (10.2-10) and (10.2-11) and assuming a 10 percent efficiency, we get

$$\frac{0.1Pt_0}{4,184} = mcV \Delta T \qquad (10.2\text{-}12)$$

Thus

$$P = \frac{41,840mcV \Delta T}{t_0} \qquad (10.2\text{-}13)$$

Using the data given and assuming a body temperature of 40°C, we get

$$P = \frac{(41,840)(1,000)(10^{-12})(80 - 40)}{10^{-3}} \approx 1.67 \, \text{W}$$

This input power is easily achieved with a semiconductor pulsed laser.
////////

Other applications utilizing the concentrated power of the laser involve welding hard to reach spots, fine cutting of metals, etc.

An alarm system using lasers A semiconductor diode laser has an area of about 1 mm^2 and can be made to lase in infrared at about 3×10^{14} Hz so that its radiation is not visible to the eye. Using this type of laser, an arrangement as shown in Fig. 10.2-8 could be used as an alarm system. Assume a room 10×30 m. On one of the 10-m sides, at a height of about 1 m, we install two diode lasers; at room temperature they are usually pulsed lasers. As shown in Fig. 10.2-8b, with an input consisting of 50-A 1,000-Hz pulses, the output will be a series of laser pulses of power $P = 20$ W and width $\Delta T = 0.2 \, \mu$s. The beam spread is about 0.2 rad, thus covering a large part of the room. Four detectors as shown in Fig. 10.2-8a are on the opposite wall. With no obstruction the visual or acoustic signal is zero. If we connect the detectors to an OR circuit, an obstruction in the path to any detector will result in a signal which trips the alarm. As an intruder goes about the room, he will be on and off the path to the detectors; thus he will either flicker a visual signal or open and close an acoustic alarm. This situation might also confuse him since he does not see anything; remember this is an *infrared* beam, i.e., not visible to the eye.

EXAMPLE 10.2-5 (*a*) For the alarm system shown in Fig. 10.2-8, calculate the power received at the detector, assuming a detector area A_d of 100 mm^2. (*b*) Assuming a man crosses the room parallel to the 10-m side at a speed of 1 m/s, find the number and duration of the alarm signals.

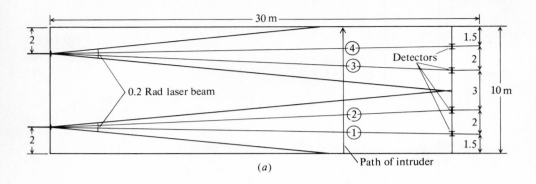

(a)

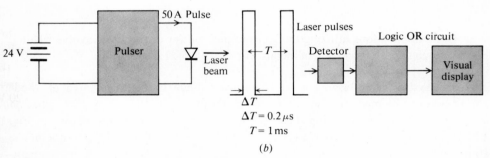

$\Delta T = 0.2\,\mu\text{s}$

$T = 1\,\text{ms}$

(b)

FIGURE 10.2-8
(a) Alarm system. (b) Elements of the devices used in the alarm system.

SOLUTION   (a) Assuming that all the power of the lasers goes to the opposite wall, we note, using Fig. 10.2-8, that the power per unit area on the opposite wall is, approximately,

$$P_A = \frac{P}{A} = \frac{20}{\pi(2.5)^2} = 1.02 \text{ W/m}^2$$

The detector power is then

$$P_d = P_A A_d = 1.02 \times 10^{-4} \text{ W} = 0.102 \text{ mW}$$

(b) Assume the intruder traverses the room at about 21 m from the detector (Fig. 10.2-8a). He will enter the first beam after 1.5 s. Assuming a lateral extent of 1 m (his bulk, hands, and leg movement, etc.), he will sound the alarm for 1 s, then immediately enter the path of the second detector, sounding the alarm for another second. Finally, 3 s later, the alarm will sound for another 2 s due to his entering the path of detectors 3 and 4.

////////

The above are only a few of the many applications of the laser. With the availability of lasers which can deliver hundreds of kilowatts in nanosecond width pulses, proposals have been made to use lasers for welding and cutting metals and other applications where high power for a short time and over a small area is required. Other applications, in which use could be made of the high carrier frequency, are communications, where, for example, 100 television programs can be transmitted using one laser beam; three-dimensional photography without a lens (holography); etc.

10.3 CONCLUSION

In the preceding pages we have described some of the devices used in power conversion. We have barely touched on the vast amount of power-conversion devices in use today. We did not discuss electroacoustic power conversion, electrothermal power conversion, electrochemical power conversion, and many others. In all our discussions we kept one guiding principle foremost: all energy is associated with bodily motion. The different types of energy are nothing more than different states of motion of different bodies. Thermal energy is nothing else but a random motion of molecules; acoustic energy is a harmonic motion of molecules; electric energy is a motion of charged particles; electromagnetic energy is a motion of photons; chemical energy is a certain relation and exchange in the state of motion of ions and electrons; etc. Energy conversion thus becomes a change in the state of motion of certain bodies due to collision with other bodies; this exchange is governed by the two laws, conservation of energy and conservation of momentum, which are related to the two characteristics of any velocity, magnitude and direction. All other concepts of different types of energy are auxiliary concepts which help us classify different types of motion, and thus help us create a more systematic and rational understanding of the world around us.

The fields of study open to any student in this area are tremendous. Creation of more efficient power-conversion devices using the great resources provided by new types of energy such as atomic energy and high-frequency coherent sources will change the world around us. Many devices and applications wait to be invented, and a serious student will find ample reward in following this path.

PROBLEMS

10.1-1   Derive Eq. (10.1-5) starting with (10.1-4).

10.1-2   Derive the power relations in a generator by multiplying Eq. (10.1-5a) by v_x and (10.1-5b) by I. Let $P_m = F_x v_x$, $KE = \frac{1}{2} M v_x^2$, $P_d = I^2 R$, and $P_e = IV$. Show that

$$P_m = \frac{d}{dt} KE + P_d + P_e$$

10.1-3   In Example 10.1-1, the output voltage is applied across a load resistance. What is the value of this resistance?

10.1-4   It is known that 1 cal $= 4,184$ J. How many calories per second are dissipated in the resistance?

10.1-5   The magnetic flux in Example 10.1-1 is changed to $B_0 = 0.5$ Wb/m². If the external force F_x is kept the same, find the new values of the current I and of the constant velocity v_x.

10.1-6   Derive the motoring laws in terms of per-unit-volume forces, current densities, and electric fields. [HINT: Use (10.1-4) as a guide.]

10.1-7   Derive Eq. (10.1-12).

10.1-8   Assume that the current in Example 10.1-3 is supplied by a voltage source. Find the required magnitude and output resistance of such a source. Assume that the maximum variation of the current is 1 percent during the time it takes the carriage to gain the velocity v_1. Neglect resistance of carriage and rails. Assume $M = 20$ kg.

10.1-9   Assume that the carriage in Example 10.1-3 starts descending the ramp with zero velocity.
   (*a*)   Find its velocity at the bottom of the ramp.
   (*b*)   Find the required value of current supply so as to stop the carriage at point *A*.

10.1-10   A generator delivers 1,000 kW. If its angular velocity is 1,800 rpm and its efficiency is 95 percent, find the torque on the driving shaft.

10.1-11   The mechanical power for the generator in Prob. 10.1-10 is supplied by a steam turbine. The steam drives a wheel 3 m in diameter, and the area of the paddle is 0.05 m². Find the steam pressure in pounds per square inch.

10.1-12   Repeat Example 10.1-4 for the case when the magnetic flux is doubled in value and the angular velocity is reduced by 20 percent.

10.1-13   The generator of Prob. 10.1-12 supplies a variable load. Plot the change in output voltage as the load varies from zero to a load of 5×10^4 A. What is the regulation of the generator?

10.2-1   Verify Eq. (10.2-2b).

10.2-2   The wavelength of a CO_2 laser is 10.6×10^{-6} m. If it radiates 1 W, what is its brightness?

10.2-3   The directivity of the laser in Prob. 10.2-2 is 1.5 minutes of arc. The directivity is given approximately by the ratio λ/D, where D is the diameter of the radiating surface. Find D.

10.2-4   Using the relation $f\lambda = v_p$, show that the wavelength of the laser beam in Eq. (10.2-5) is given by

$$\lambda = \frac{2L}{N}$$

10.2-5   Using the result of Prob. 10.2-4, show that the phase shift of the radiation in a Fabry-Perot interferometer is $2\pi N$ for one round trip (from one reflector to the other and back to the first reflector). This phenomenon is called *resonance*.

10.2-6   Show, using Eq. (10.2-5), that the distance between two axial modes is given by (10.2-8).

10.3-1   A simple example of electrothermal power conversion is a hot plate. Find the temperature of a 500-W hot plate. Assume that the area of the plate is 0.01 m² and use Stefan's law.

10.3-2   The hot plate of Prob. 10.3-1 has a thickness of 0.01 m and is made of iron [$m = 7.5 \times 10^3$ kg/m³, $c = 0.1$ cal/(°C) (kg)]. Find the time it takes for the plate to reach the steady-state temperature found in Prob. 10.3-1.

10.3-3   Solar batteries are devices which transform the solar radiation energy into electric energy. If the solar flux is 1,400 W/m² and the area of a solar battery is 2 m², what is the power supplied to the battery?

10.3-4   The battery of Prob. 10.3-3 is energized for 10 h, and it is used for 4 h. How much average power does it deliver if its efficiency is 25 percent?

10.3-5   A piezoelectric crystal is a device which transforms electric energy into acoustic energy, and vice versa. Figure P10.3-5 shows an acoustic delay line with two piezoelectric crystals used as *transducers*. The first, at the transmitting end, transforms electric energy into acoustic energy, whereas the second, at the receiving end, transforms acoustic energy into electric energy.

(a)   If $V = 100$ V and $I = 2$ μA, find the input power.

(b)   If the efficiency of the transducer is 80 percent, find the input acoustic power to the delay line.

(c)   If the velocity of the acoustic wave is 1,500 m/s, what is the time delay of the line? (HINT: $\lambda f = C_q$.)

(d)   If the attenuation of the line is 2 dB/m, what is the power at the receiving end of the line?

(e)   If the load $R_L = 2$ MΩ, what is the voltage across the load?

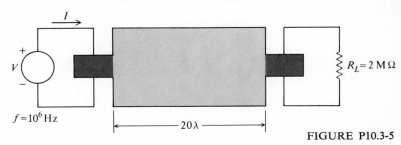

FIGURE P10.3-5

10.3-6   Nuclear plants use atomic energy to generate electric power. By this method atomic energy is used to heat water under pressure. The heated water circulates and heats, in a heat exchanger, other water which becomes steam. The steam is used to drive a steam turbine. The steam turbine in turn delivers mechanical power at the shaft of an electric generator. Using your imagination, draw the block diagram of a nuclear plant.

10.3-7   Assume the nuclear plant in Prob. 10.3-6 delivers 100,000 kW of power. If the efficiency is 1 percent, what is the power released by the atomic energy?

10.3-8   Atomic energy is released by splitting uranium atoms. Assume that the energy released by an atom when it splits is 5×10^{-10} J. How many atoms must be split in a year in the nuclear plant of Prob. 10.3-7?

10.3-9   If 0.235 kg of uranium contains 6×10^{23} atoms, how much uranium is used by the plant in Prob. 10.3-8 in a year?

REFERENCES

FITZGERALD, A. E., and D. E. HIGGINBOTHAM: "Basic Electrical Engineering," McGraw-Hill Book Company, New York, 1957.

LEVI, E., and M. PANZER: "Electromechanical Power Conversion," McGraw-Hill Book Company, New York, 1966.

SIEGMAN, A. E.: "An Introduction to Lasers and Masers," McGraw-Hill Book Company, New York, 1971.

SMITH, W. V., and P. P. SOROKIN: "The Laser," McGraw-Hill Book Company, New York, 1966.